DURRUTI

DURRUTI

THE PEOPLE ARMED

by Abel Paz

Translated from the French
by Nancy Macdonald

BLACK ROSE BOOKS   Montréal

BLACK ROSE BOOKS NO. F.28

Hardcover — ISBN: 0-919618-73-1
Paperback — ISBN: 0-919618-74-X

Canadian Cataloguing in Publication Data

Paz, Abel
    Durruti

    Translation of Durruti: le peuple en armes
    ISBN 0-919618-73-1 bd.
    ISBN 0-919618-74-X pa.

1. Durruti, Buenaventura, 1896-1936.
2. Spain—History—Civil War, 1936-1939.
3. Anarchism and anarchists—Spain—Biography.
I. Title.

DP264.D87P39   946.081'092'4   C77-000122-X

Cover Design: Michael Carter

BLACK ROSE BOOKS LTD.
3934 rue St. Urbain,
Montréal H2W 1V2,
Québec

Printed and bound in Québec, Canada

CONTENTS

Part I

The Rebel (1896-1931)

Part II

The Militant (1931-1936)

Part III

The Revolutionary (1936)

BLACK ROSE BOOKS

Wishes to acknowledge the contribution of our friend and comrade Art Bartell towards the publication of this book. This solidarity with our work has also permitted the selling price of the book at a reasonable level.

DURRUTI
The People Armed

Part 1
The Rebel (1896-1931)

1

UNION CARD NUMBER 12

ON THE AFTERNOON OF JUNE 4, 1923, in a place called "el Terminillo" on the outskirts of Saragossa, two strangers opened fire on an automobile which was slowing down to enter the grounds of St. Paul's school. One of the occupants, the Cardinal-Archbishop, Don Juan Soldevila Romero was killed on the spot. The chief steward, nephew of the prelate was wounded in the arm. The chauffeur was also slightly wounded.

The attack was sudden and no witness was capable of supplying the slightest clue about the attackers. The nuns of the school and their personnel asserted that there were two men of an uncertain age who had dissappeared across the fields. The police could only confirm the impact of fourteen bullets in the body of the car, one of them in the gas tank. The local press, lacking other information, could only report the event as an "unusual and abominable attack" and published a photo of the victim.

The authorities were bewildered. Around eight in the evening two telegrams arrived: condolences from the king, Alfonso XIII and an order from the Minister of the Interior to investigate this affair thoroughly. At the same time the Confederación Nacional del Trabajo (CNT) issued a manifesto threatening to launch a general strike if the authorities tried to accuse and imprison workers who were innocent of the assassination. Syndicalists and Government people both passed a sleepless night. The Government people couldn't decide what repressive steps to take and the Syndicalists feared that they would be victims of a repression.

The next day, June 5th, the national press reported the event: "El Heraldo de Madrid" portrayed the anarchists as authors of the crime. "La Accion", paper of the extreme right, accused the notorious band of terrorists led by the dangerous anarchist Durruti. And after a terrifying biography of this "redoubtable" character, the paper demanded that the Government take suitable steps to put an end to the activities of this "scourge of God".

Buenaventura Durruti [1], born on the 14th of July, 1896, was the second son of Santiago Durruti Malgor and Anastasia Dumange Soler. The Durrutis were French Basques and the Dumanges were Catalans [2], but both families lived in Leon. Leon subsisted, as did most Castillian cities, on agriculture, breeding, and the rudimentary industries of leather dressing and weaving of wool. Intellectual life was dominated by the clergy. Political power was in the hands of the clerics and the military and they controlled both municipal life and representation in the Cortes.

It was a time when Spain was passing through a serious crisis which affected the economy and also the political and cultural institutions. The remaining colonial possessions had risen up against the mother country. The Cubans, led by Jose Marti, had started a revolution and the first minister of the Crown, Canovas del Castillo, sent General Weyler to put it down. The Philippines were also in ferment and in revolt against the Government representatives and the Dominican monks, who were administrators of the islands. Cuba became a concentration camp, while the Philippines were submitted to a severe repression, in which its eminent poet, Jose Rizal, was shot.[3]

In the peninsula itself the unrest was general. The peasants, especially in Andalusia, crushed by "caciquisme" and by the landowners, threw themselves into uprisings which assumed the form of a real social war[4]. This same violent climate also existed in the mining areas in Andalusia and Asturias. The workers' demonstrations and strikes followed each other practically without interruption in the industrial areas of the Basque country and Catalonia. The Government repression proceeded without pity; the prisons were full of militants and executions were frequent. The culmination of unrest and the economic crisis came in 1898, the year when the last colonies were lost (Cuba, the Philippines, Puerto Rico)[5].

In 1900, Buenaventura Durruti entered a school in Misericordia street in Leon and stayed there for four years. We have only a few documents from this period, such as his teacher's report: "undisciplined student but with generous feelings and very affectionate". Later, Durruti would write his sister, Rosa: "From the time I was very young, the first thing I noticed around me was suffering, not only that of my family but also of our neighbors. Intuitively I was already a rebel. I think that is when my future was decided"[6]. This confession probably refers to special events which touched him deeply: his father's arrest and imprisonment for his active part in the leather dressers' strike in 1803, when Durruti was seven years old. This strike was the first important social conflict in Leon and lasted nine months. The firmness of the workers in the face of their growing hunger and the severity of the repression marked the first triumph of the working class and was the beginning of proletarian organization in the region.

The workers of Leon owed their awakening to Ignacio Durruti, Buenaventura's uncle, who founded the first workers' organization[7]. Until 1900 the most progressive milieu in Leon had been made up of a group of Republican intellectuals whose moderate and conciliatory ideology was incapable of frightening the local authorities and clergy. But from the first years of the century the situation changed. Thanks to the construction of a railroad between Valladolid and Leon, the first Socialist and anarchist publications started to turn up in the area and in the mining region of Asturias[8]. The leather workers, comrades of Ignacio Durruti, became aware through his reading, that social agitation was breaking out all over Spain, especially in Bilbao and Barcelona.

At that time, the eight hour day was the principle demand and it had been won by the tailors in Madrid. The leather workers of Leon demanded a wage increase and a reduction of work hours. It was reasonable since the bosses had improved the methods of production and extended their markets. Until then the wages for the three categories of workers went from 1 peseta 25 to 1 peseta 75 for a full day's work from sunrise to sunset. The members of the committee presented their demands to the bosses: 50 centimes more a day and a 10 hour day. The delegates were Ignacio Durruti, Santiago Durruti (Buenaventura's father), Antonio Quintin and Melchor Anton. Their demands were considered excessive and were rejected. The workers replied by calling a strike. Leather working was the only local industry and the work stoppage slowly paralyzed the whole region.

The authorities imprisoned all those they considered responsible for the revolt. The people could not bear to see honest workers arrested and imprisoned like scoundrels, and they showed their solidarity. The tradesmen gave credit to the strikers. Lorenzo Durruti, the owner of a lunch room, put it at the service of the workers on strike. Ignacio Durruti sold his shop and gave the proceeds to the strikers. Their solidarity impressed the authorities; "it seems that the bishop (whom public rumor considered the instigator of the repression) intervened to free those who had been arrested. This did not wipe out the 15 days they had spent in prison"[9]. But as the strike dragged on for nine months, hunger was felt deeply in the worker's homes and with hunger the spirit of the rebellion was subdued. Little by little the strikers gave up and, to the great satisfaction of the bourgeoisie, the strike had to end. Still there were workers like Durruti's father who preferred to change their trade rather than capitulate. He became a carpenter in the shops of the Northern Railroad Company.

Later, recalling these events for his sister Rosa, Durruti reminded himself of the consequences to his family of this conflict. Until then, despite his father, Santiago's, slim income, the Durruti family had enjoyed a high standard of living in comparison with other workers because the men of the family, Lorenzo, Pedro and Ignacio, had trades. From then on, life changed for all of them. Lorenzo had to close his lunch room. Ignacio disappeared without explaining to anyone the reason for his leaving; it is believed he emigrated to America. Pedro Dumange, Santiago's father-in-law, saw his textile trade go to seed little by little because of a systematic boycott by the local "caciques". The family was forced to live on the wages of Santiago. He earned only two pesetas a day as a carpenter.

It was necessary to give up the ambitious projects they had made for Buenaventura's future. His grandfather, Pedro, wanted to send him to college to study seriously so that later he could take over the management of his textile trade. But that was too expensive. Buenaventura was sent to Ricardo Fanjul's school which was better suited to the modest means of the family. He was a mediocre student, but when he had finished his studies, Fanjul found him "gifted in literature"[10].

14

Durruti (standing) in primary school with his brother Santiago (seated).

When he was 14, old Pedro insisted on paying for his studies in Valladolid but he refused. Buenaventura wanted to become a worker like his father, and he decided to become a machinist. In 1914 he entered the shop of Master Melchor Martinez as an apprentice. Martinez had a reputation as a wild revolutionary because he read "El Socialista" openly in the bars. Actually the socialism of Martinez was not well defined and his coherence left much to be desired. He had been a militant worker in Bilbao and, now already old, full of admiration for Pablo Iglesias[11], he had retired to Leon. He set up a machine shop and smithy and there a number of workers used to get together to talk with the old man about the progress and the projects of the Socialist Party. At that time. Leon had two workers' associations which belonged to the "Unión General de Trabajadores (UGT)": the "Unión Ferroviaria" and the "Union Metalúrgica".

The young people were starting to break away from the influence of the Church. From the age of 12 Buenaventura had shown that he no longer wanted to take the catechism lessons which the priest of the parish of Ste. Anne held every Thursday. He no longer went to Church, and the following year he refused to take Easter communion, which created a great scandal. In this way he was making a reputation for himself as a non-conformist[12].

Melchor Martinez approved of the child and stood up for him. He told Santiago: "I will make a good machinist of your son, but also a Socialist". Leading the boy to the forge, he took the pliers, seized the red iron which he started to beat on the anvil and said "There is your work, to beat the iron while it is red hot, until you give it the required form". After watching Buenaventura for an entire day he concluded: "You will be a good smithy because you know how to strike hard. But don't forget this, the blows must be aimed with precision. Strength is not enough, intelligence is needed to know where to give the blows". Melchor took an interest in the intellectual development of his apprentice and advised him to enroll in night school at the center called "Los amigos del Paiz". After two years he said to Buenaventura: "I can't teach you anything more, either in mechanics or in socialism". The young man moved to another shop.

After a year in the shop of Antonio Miaja he was accepted as a "second class lathe worker", and in April 1912 he entered the "Metallurgists Union" with the card Number 12[13]. It was the beginning of his life as a militant and trade unionist. He was seen at the meetings of the Metallurgists, but he came as an observer and rarely took part in the discussions. At this time the Socialist theoretician in Leon was Iglesias Muniz, who three years later founded the first Socialist magazine in the city, "El Socialista Leones". He was a militant and an educator and all the workers, like Buenaventura, listened to him as if he were an oracle. In the course of one of his talks, Iglesias commented on the progress of Socialism in Spain and about the Party's electoral successes, despite the opposition of the workers of the C.N.T. (Confederación Nacional del Trabajo). He didn't give a very precise explanation for this antagonism and Durruti wanted to know more. The answers to his questions were ambiguous and they didn't convince him. He soon began to free himself from this influence and to think out problems on his own.

From then on, Durruti started to take part in the discussions and he provoked interesting reactions among the members of the leadership. They criticized his revolutionary impatience and preached moderation. He answered, "Socialism is active or it doesn't exist". He claimed that the emancipation of the working class could not occur without a fierce struggle against the bourgeoisie, without revolutionary action which could only stop when the destruction of the capitalist system was complete. When the leaders opposed him and gave their reasons for political expediency, he continued to believe that the actions of the working class cannot be subject to the expediencies of bourgeois politics. The clashes between Durruti and the leaders were continual. But his words found echo among the young people in the Union, who were as impatient as he was to undertake a revolutionary action and rebelled with him against the "eternal advice of moderation" by those who felt that "things were not yet ripe"[14].

These discussions went their way until 1914 when, with the first World War, the economic conditions of Spain changed. The belligerents were eager to get indispensable products and materiel from neutral Spain. The bourgeoisie was able to carry on profitable trade with the Germans and the Allies at the same time. Industry, commerce and marine transport began to grow at a faster tempo. Metallurgical and mining industries were specially favored. Old businesses were revived and mines were worked intensively. This new rhythm of production increased the number of workers in the factories and mines and brought about the migration of people to the industrialized zones. The influence of the proletariat increased. In Barcelona, which had absorbed a massive migration, trade unionism developed rapidly. In Leon and its mining basin, the phenomenon of the revival of production was the same as in the rest of the country. The mines functioned to full capacity and the machine shops of Antonio Miaja tripled their production.

But even so it was not possible to fill all the orders. To relieve this situation, work gangs were sent to the mining centers of Matallana del Torio, Ponferrada and La Robla, to install mechanical "washers". Durruti was responsible for a gang sent to Matallana. This was when he and his comrades met the celebrated miners of Asturias.

The first days passed quickly because of the absorbing work. But soon the mine workers launched a strike to protest the attitude of one of the engineers towards them. They demanded his dismissal and the management refused. The rest of the miners made common cause with the strikers and the work stoppage was general throughout the basin. Buenaventura understood that if he continued with the installation of the mechanical "washers", the strike would do no harm to the mining company. It would even be advantageous to it since this would economize on salaries until the modernization was put into operation. So Durruti explained to his gang: "By stopping our work we will force the Company to satisfy the demands of the strikers or else refuse the orders of the clients".

The Management demanded that the machinists fulfill their contract. Buenaventura answered that the machinists would start working at the same time as the miners. The Management tried various kinds of pressure, but faced by the firm decision of the machinists, it ended by giving in and the engineer was fired[15]. The attitude of the young people of Leon, in particular that of "grandote" as Durruti was called, impressed the miners. A mood of confidence was established between the two groups of workers. The miners even began to call Durruti by his first name. Buenacasa could write that "Durruti became a popular battle-cry in Asturias"[16].

Once the installation of the machines was completed, Durruti returned to Leon. A surprise awaited him. Miaja called him to his office to speak to him about his behavior in the mining basin. He warned Durruti that the Guardia Civil was interested in him and advised him to rein his enthusiasm because "Leon is not Barcelona". The same lack of understanding and the same warnings came from the

Leon 1915 in Metallurgical workshop of Antonio Miaja, Durruti is standing in the middle surrounded by his fellow workers.

management at the Metallurgical Union. The young people, who envied the part he took in the miners' strike, gave him an enthusiastic welcome. But his former teacher, Melchor Martinez, also preached prudence, even advising him to leave Leon because the Lieutenant General of the Guardia Civil, José González Regueral, who was Governor of the Province, and Major Arlegui didn't tolerate extremists.

At home Buenaventura found his father in bed, very ill and happy to tell his son that he had found him a job as a machinist in the mobile workshops of the Northern Railroad Company. This upset his plans, but the family situation left him no choice and he accepted. It was in this way that he took part in the famous strike of August 1917.

Footnotes

1. The name DURRUTI comes from the Basque. URRUTI. meaning far. It seems that Basques who lived in isolated houses were given this name. It probably came originally from the French Basque province of Labourd (Lapurdi).
2. For information about the Durruti family we follow the recollections of Anastasia Dumange. Durruti's mother. in letters which she kindly loaned us. She writes that her father-in-law, Lorenzo. came to live in Leon and spoke Spanish very poorly. As to her father. Pedro Dumange. Anastasia says that he had to leave Catalonia for obscure reasons and came to live in Leon. where he opened a textile shop and married Rosa Soler. Anastasia was born in 1875 and she married Ignacio Durruti when she was 16.
3. José Rizal. doctor. poet. Philippine writer. born in Manila. was shot the 30th of December 1896. He left two novels which denounced Spanish colonialism in the Philippines: *Noli me tangere* (1887) and the *Filibustiers* (1891) Georges Fisher has written a documented study of José Rizal published by Editions Maspero. 1970.
4. For information on the social climate. we refer the reader to the following books: Juan Diaz del Moral. *Historia de las agitaciones campesinas andaluzas.* Ed. Alianza. Madrid. 1967 and Renée Lamberet, *Mouvements ouvriers et socialistes en Espagne (1750-1936).* Ed. Ouvrières. Paris. 1953.
5. Tuñon de Lara. *España en el siglo XX.* Ed. Libreria Espanola. Paris. 1966.
6. Letter sent by Durruti from a Paris prison on March 10. 1927.
7. We know very little about this association. It had headquarters in Calle del Badillo. in the Sainte-Anne district. Its orientation was mutualist. Its members met once a month to discuss their professional problems. This information is supplied by Francisco Monroi. childhood friend of Durruti and later his comrade in the struggle.
8. The publications of the mining region of Asturias were. according to Monroi: *Fraternidad* and *La Defensa del Obrero.* Anarchist publications both edited in Gijon in 1900 and *El Cosmopolita.* also Anarchist. edited in Valladolid. *The Socialist publications were El Bien del Obrero.* edited in El Ferrol and *Solidaridad* in Vigo (Galicia).
9. Francisco Monroi.
10. Anastasia's correspondence.
11. A typography worker. who was a member of the original group which belonged to the International in Spain (1869). At the time of the split in the International. he followed the reformist tendency. headed by Karl Marx's son-in-law, Paul Lafargue. He founded the Spanish Workers' Socialist Party in 1888.
12. Francisco Monroi. in letters which he sent us. sums up his recollections about the period when he was already a fellow worker of Durruti.
13. A document from private archives. There are 20 letters written by Durruti at various times in his life. unedited photographs. personal documents. documents about the Durruti Column and other items which we have been allowed to use.
14. Francisco Monroi. Valentin Roi (Orobon Fernandez) also refers to these facts in his *Durruti-Ascaso-Jover* published by Antorcha. Buenos Aires. 1927 (32 pages).
15. Anastasia refers to this in her souvenirs. but the facts of the story were given to us by Monroi.
16. Manuel Buenacasa. from unedited notebooks sent to the author.

2

AUGUST 1917

THE PROLETARIAT HAD INCREASED and become strong
because of industrial expansion in Spain and now it was entering a
really revolutionary phase. A climax was reached in May and June
when Spain found itself on the verge of revolution.

From the beginning of the century, the industrial bourgeoisie of
Catalonia and the Basque regions had understood clearly that the
principal obstacle to its expansion came from the economic structures
and politics of the country. As long as political power was monopolized by the conservative and traditionalist bloc (clergy, aristocracy,
military), Spain could not leave the quagmire it was in.

These sectors of the bourgeoisie launched an offensive aimed at
removing from power the parties which alternately held it. Their
strategy had a solid psychological base. This was the profound feeling
for autonomy of the Catalans and the Basques who were rapidly becoming nationalists and separatists. Those feelings skillfully man-
oeuvered by the leader of the Catalan bourgeoisie, Francisco Cambo,
soon became a real challenge to the central power in Madrid.

During the first World War the bourgeoisie accumulated wealth
without worrying about modernizing its industries. And it took no
remedial steps with which to face the inevitable crisis which would
occur as soon as the doors of foreign commerce were closed again. At
the same time the State saw that its situation was desperate. It was
not only carrying a deficit of more than a thousand million pesetas
but there were also new expenses to be met in order to be able to continue the disastrous military compaign in Morocco[1]. Nevertheless
the monopolistic bourgeoisie was getting rich.

To try to collect part of the profits cleared by the Basque and
Catalan industrialists for the State treasury, the Minister of Finance,
Santiago Alba, outlined a program for fiscal reform creating a direct
tax on the extraordinary profits of companies and individuals. But
this tax didn't affect the landowners and thus showed once again the
influence that the feudal landlords had over State decisions. Francisco Cambó, spokesman of the industrial bourgeoisie, exploiting this
fact, attacked the project in such a way before the Cortes, that he not
only thwarted it but brought about the downfall of the Conde de
Romanones.

This same bourgeoisie in turn passed through a crisis when foreign purchases decreased at the end of the war. It showed itself incapable of drawing the necessary conclusions imposed by the international situation and ideologically found itself in the same position as the conservatives.

Confronted by the high cost of living since 1916, the working class organized an important national protest, well fitted to worry the ruling class. The CNT and the UGT were united for the first time by an agreement which spoke explicitly about social revolution[2]. The Catalan bourgeoisie in particular showed its reactionary and intransigent character before the workers' demands. From then on the struggle was to assume the dimensions of a real social war. To this already complex situation, two events of extreme importance were now added.

The first was the Russian Revolution where the working class and the peasant class had shown for the first time that they were capable of choosing their own destiny. In Spain the news had the effect of an explosion, and enthusiasm extended beyond the towns to reach the rural areas where sporadic uprisings burst forth to the cry of "Long live the Soviets." The objective conditions for a revolutionary explosion were taking shape. In May 1917, they appeared to be concentrated and ripe.

Secondly it was learned that a part of the army, the infantry, had mutinied for reasons which were not strictly political. There had been a reaction against the monarchy which favored the "African" military clique, who wanted to carry on the Moroccan war to the end[3]. The pre-revolutionary situation forced the leaders of the central unions to plan a common action, faithful to the pact for unified action agreed on in 1916.

For the CNT it was urgent to take advantage of the contradictions which were revealed at the core of the bourgeois parties and to exploit the dissensions between the Army and the State thoroughly, in order to destroy the monarchy and proclaim a Republic favoring social progress. The UGT led by the Socialist Party didn't see the real social dimensions of the situation. The important thing for the UGT was to form an opposition bloc which would impose a liberal government without overthrowing the monarchy.

These two ways of looking at the situation produced confusion in the discussions between the two working class organizations and soon put an end to their period of agreement. The Socialist Party, through the UGT, reined the popular enthusiasm and put off the moment of mass action, pleading before the representatives of the CNT that the UGT wasn't ready for a general strike and that it was premature to rush into the streets.

Then two events occurred which weakened the position of the partisans of revolution. First, Eduardo Dato entered the Government and in June he hastened to give satisfaction to the military heads of the Infantry. It was in this way that he was able to reestablish discipline in the Army. Then the complete failure of the Parliamentary Assembly occurred. It was meeting in Barcelona in order to name a provisional government and when it learned that the workers in Barcelona had erected barricades and raised the red flag, these members of Parliament became frightened, broke up their meeting and abandoned the demonstrators to the repression (July 19, 1917).

The Assembly dissolved and, the political dream of the Socialist Party destroyed, the UGT remained without directives in face of the continually increasing social agitation. Its leaders and those of the Socialist Party arrived at a solution: to disarm the working class. Pablo Iglesias advised that they be satisfied with a peaceful demonstration or a general strike to calm the masses. From then on, the UGT acted in this way toward the CNT, claiming for itself the exclusive responsibility of leading the movement. It named a national strike committee, which fell into the hands of the police a few hours after the general strike was proclaimed.

This caused a witness to comment: "The movement started without deciding on a precise duration and lasted one week. The workers of Asturias, remarkably heroic, prolonged it for eight more days. In Biscay there were many victims. The movement was so complete throughout Spain that nothing like it had been seen before in the world. There were hundreds of victims among the workers throughout the peninsula." Another witness, G. Brenan, wrote: "The troops were called out and used their machine guns against the strikers and were thought to have behaved barbarously. It had been necessary to demonstrate that only the Army could defend the State, and that they should develop a strong reputation on the national political scene from their actions. From now on it was, with the King, the only real power in the country".[4]

A few months later when the Right was criticizing his Party, Indalecio Prieto, the Socialist leader declared before the Cortes: "It is true that we gave arms to the people and that we could have won the struggle, but we didn't give them ammunition. What are you complaining about?"[5]

Such were the broad outlines of the social and political movement in Spain in August 1917. What was going on in Leon? There was a general strike there too as in the rest of Spain and it stimulated the most rebellious young people, among them Buenaventura Durruti. This handful of young people, after having taken an active part in the movement, once the strike was over joined the struggle of the Asturian miners and blocked the train traffic in that area. Many workers following their example collaborated with them in acts of sabotage, setting fire to locomotives and machine depots and taking the rivets out of the railway tracks.

The Socialist leaders, seeing the character of the strike and because worker action was getting out of its control, hastened to order a return to work. And they publicly condemned the sabotage as they considered these actions unfitting to the working class. For this reason, the people who had carried out these violent acts were disowned and isolated when they faced police repression. During this active period there were numerous confrontations with the Guardia Civil. More than once the police forces were greeted with stones by the striking pickets at the gates of the railroad shops, because they lacked other weapons. The young people were not the only ones who were moved to act. A good many of the workers didn't agree either

22

Durruti pouring wine, in the company of French anarchist comrades during his first exile in France (1917-1920).

with the order to return to work, since they knew that strikers were being machine-gunned in the streets of Asturias.

But little by little these activities lost their strength. The shops started to function but the sabotage on the tracks continued and things didn't become completely normal until it was learned that the Asturian resistance had ended. Then the repression started. The "Compania Ferroviaria" announced that it was firing all the workers collectively and that each one of them should ask individually to be rehired. This meant a loss of former rights. Also in this way the company could pick its personnel. The most rebellious were dismissed and among them was Buenaventura Durruti.

The "Unión Ferroviaria" completed the repression by expelling from its organization the group of young people who had been the backbone of the resistance. Durruti was at the head of the list. The statement of expulsion ordered by the Board of Directors, read: " This was a peaceful strike in which a disciplined working class showed its strength to the bourgeoisie. The actions taken by this group of young people are contrary to the tactics of the Union. These young people are expelled from the ranks of the Union for lack of discipline."

The group of young people who had been expelled couldn't defend themselves against such measures. The Union itself pointed them out as the authors of the assaults and it made the job of the police easy. In such conditions they had no choice between falling into the hands of the forces of repression or leaving the city and waiting for better days [6].

Footnotes

1. In January 1906 an international conference was convened by the German Reich and it met at Algeciras to decide the fate of the Moroccan empire. The final act of the conference, while guaranteeing the integrity of Morocco and the authority of the Sultan, entrusted France and Spain, the two powers who had the most direct interests there, with keeping order. Germany, which could not swallow this diplomatic defeat, fomented the rebellion. Morocco became the focus of a war declared against France and Spain with Abd el-Krim heading the rebels, whose battle cry was "The Rif to the Rifians". Spain's interference in this war was unpopular and the people of Barcelona revolted in 1909, making common cause with the mutinous soldiers, who had refused to go to Morocco.

2. The CNT-UGT treaty. On March 12th the 12th congress of the UGT met in Madrid. The delegation of Asturian workers decided to organize a national protest against the high cost of living and proposed signing an agreement with the CNT to make the protest more effective. The Congress approved and in July 1916 a detailed agreement was signed by the two workers' organizations (Largo Caballero and Julian Besteiro for the UGT, Angel Pestaña and Salvador Seguí for the CNT). On December 18 a twenty four hour general strike was called which was a complete success. But in spite of this massive protest, the Government carried on its old policies as before and the two organizations were obliged to remain faithful to the agreement that had united them.

3. The men in the infantry, seeing themselves downgraded by the Government, decided to organize themselves secretly in Military Defense Juntas, coordinated nationally by a Central Junta, presided over by Colonel Márquez. Their demands were for economic improvements and measures aimed at reforming and purging the organization of the Army. At the end of May 1917, the Government ordered the imprisonment and trial of the members of the Central Junta. To protest this measure the Military Juntas published a manifesto on the 1st of June which was an ultimatum, demanding that the prisoners be released and a reply given to their demands within 24 hours. The Government resigned. It was the conservative Eduardo Dato who formed the new Government.

4. Manuel Buenacasa: *Historia del Movimiento Obrero Espanol* published in Paris in 1966. Gerald Brenan: *The Spanish Labyrinth*, Ed. Ruedo Iberico, p. 53.

5. Manuel Buenacasa: oc.

6. As for these activities of Durruti, we follow the testimony of Monrol, Orobon Fernandez, oc., and Manuel Buenacasa: unpublished notes.

3

FROM EXILE TO ANARCHISM

AT THE BEGINNING OF SEPTEMBER 1917 DURRUTI, with this friend "El Toto", sought refuge in Gijon. It is likely that he had renewed his ties with the Asturian miners after the events at Matallana. He stayed only briefly in this province. In December his family received a letter postmarked Vals-les-Bains in the Ardèche in France, in which he tried to reassure them that he was "fine thanks to the help of a Spanish family named Martinez."[1]

"El Toto" was being searched for because of the sabotage he had carried out during the strikes. And Durruti was a deserter, because a few days before the strike broke out, he had been called up to serve in the artillery in the San Sebastian regiment. He was to have been enrolled at the end of August. In a letter written later to his sister, he told her: "My wish to serve the country was small, but even that little wish was taken away by a sergeant who commanded the recruits as if they were already in the barracks. Leaving the recruiting station, I said to myself that Alfonso XIII could count on one soldier less and one more revolutionary"[2]. It is probable that when the Asturian miners learned of his desertion, they decided to hide him and make it easy for him to cross into France.

Buenacasa, who was also fleeing from the repression, must have met Durruti during this period. He reports about this first contact: "We were not sympathetic. I was more studious, he more rebellious."[3] Buenacasa was without news of Durruti until the spring of 1920. When they saw each other again at San Sebastian, Buenacasa was impressed by Durruti's progress "on the theoretical level". He says also that when they visited the Unions of the Confederation of San Sebastian, he saw Durruti produce a card of the CNT. This affiliation and his "theoretical progress" were the fruits of his years in exile in France from December 1917 to March 1919.

His correspondance with his family shows that he changed his residence frequently. He was to be seen in Marseille, Beziers, Toulouse, Bordeaux, Biarritz, etc. When he arrived in France, there was already an important nucleus of Catalan militant Anarchist exiles in the Midi and especially in Marseille. They had organized themselves in the classic way, in affinity groups. In Marseille there was a Commission for Anarchist Relations. This city was also a very important center for communications with Barcelona as the port workers were profoundly influenced by the revolutionary syndicalism of the first CGT.

One of the principal activities of these militants was the collection of funds among the Spanish emigres. The funds were used to finance the propaganda sent to Spain, or publications (such as *Prisma* edited in Beziers) designed to guide ideologically the groups of Spaniards scattered throughout France. It was also necessary, and much more difficult, to find arms and send them to Barcelona.

All this meant frequent moves. At first Durruti probably went to and fro between Marseille and Bordeaux, another suitable port where a conspiratorial center for the Basques and Asturians could be set up. Nevertheless Durruti was able to maintain contact with his friends in Leon. "El Toto", who lived among the Asturians until 1919, received news from him throughout his exile. [4]

As to the ideological evolution of Durruti which Buenacasa calls "theoretical progress", Kaminski says that "he burned the way stations. It took him less time than Bakunin to declare himself an anarchist." [5] Kaminski wrote this in July 1936, impressed by the personality of Durruti. In fact, with Durruti, there is no transition between Socialism and anarchism: he was always a latent anarchist.

Spanish Marxism, from the time of the arrival of Paul Lafargue in 1872, was opportunist and soon became reformist. Except for the very orthodox notion of party, all was forgotten by the Socialist Party. If one of the leaders spoke very belatedly about the seizure of power by the working class, it was without faith or conviction. Apart from the contributions of the group of Andres Nin[6], the traditional ideological level among the Spanish Marxists was that of German or French Social Democracy of the 1930s. On the other hand, anarchism was developing on fresh and fertile ground. In a country where everything was moving towards decentralization, where the working class looked on parliamentary manoeuvers with disapproval the rejection of the State was grasped perfectly. [7] When Durruti understood anarchism, first in practice, then in theory, he identified it with revolutionary socialism as he had already defined it in Leon. One can therefore speak about his "theoretical progress", as Buenacasa did, rather than "transition", as Kaminski wrote.

In March 1919, Durruti was in the military hospital at Burgos. He wrote in a letter to his family: "I was getting ready to visit you, when I found myself enrolled in my regiment. I was brought before the War Council and I was assigned to Morocco. But as they discovered I had a hernia, during the medical examination, I am in the hospital, but only for a short while. I don't want to leave for Morocco before seeing my friends once again, the ones you know. It is urgent that they come and visit me." As usual he disguised the truth. His arrest was connected with a mission he was carrying out in Spain together with his friends in Bordeaux[8].

On the first of January 1919 he had crossed the frontier in order to tell the organization in Gijón about his plan for activities in France. His mission ended, he decided to remain for a while in Spain, seeing the possibilities for action offered by the situation in Asturias. "El Toto" brought him up to date on progress in Leon. The group of young people, who had been expelled (Tejerina was among them),

Exiled in Vals-les-Bains, France

had founded an Anarchist association and a union of different trades (Sindicato de Oficios Varios) of the CNT which consisted of a large number of affiliates. In the rest of Spain, the expansion of the CNT continued, especially in Barcelona where syndicalism, given life by Salvador Seguí and Angel Pestaña, was terrorizing the bourgeoisie. One out of two workers belonged to the Confederation, which had 370,000 members.

Durruti got a job as a machinist at Mieres, center of activity for metal workers where anarcho-syndicalism was very influential. He got his first CNT card there. His stay was short although important. He returned quickly to the mining basin of Leon, because a bitter conflict had just broken out in the area of la Robla. "El Toto", who until then had been in charge of the contacts with Leon, had been in Valladolid for three months. As it was necessary to carry out sabotage in the mines quickly, Durruti was considered as he was unknown in the region. They gave him two militant delegates from Coruña as assistants. As foreseen, after the sabotage was carried out, the management of the mine signed a pact with the workers.

Durruti wanted to go as far as Leon in order to see his old friends again. A meeting place was arranged at Santiago de Compostela. But during the trip he was arrested as a suspect by the Guardia Civil and sent to La Coruña. Recognized as a deserter, he was taken to San Sebastian, where after passing before the Council of War, he complained of his hernia to gain time and to be able to escape. He succeeded with the help of his friends from Leon, who had been alerted by a letter sent to his sister, Rosa. He hid himself for several days in the mountains, and in June went into exile again in France.

27

This time he went as far as Paris where he worked for some time in the Renault workshops. There are very few letters dating from this period. Only a few post cards with deliberately neutral and harmless messages in which he says that he is "living alone, cut off from everybody and working as a machinist". The photographs of this period disprove these words as he is seen surrounded by friends. We don't know what his activities were. We know only that he kept up a regular correspondance with Tejerina, the secretary of the anarchist group in Leon.

Alexander Gilabert, in his account of the life of Durruti, writes that "the comrades kept him regularly informed on the political and social situation in Spain." The principal aim of this correspondance was to keep him informed on "the progress that the anarchist groups were making in the country" as well as the "agreements which the anarchist groups had undertaken in a National Conference, in order to be able to join the National Confederation of Work, thanks to their active militancy"[9]. He adds that "this decision of the groups was taken so as to be able to confront the pistoleros whom the police and the Government were organizing to assassinate the militant workers".

Gilabert goes on to say that Durruti also learned about the "big Congress which had been convened in Madrid by the CNT in December 1919; a congress where representatives of almost a million workers took part. This Congress decided to join the Third International and Angel Pestaña was named as delegate to the Second Congress of the Communist International in Moscow in 1920." Gilabert inferred that Durruti was carried away by this news and this influenced him to return to Spain in the spring of 1920.

Many young people like Durruti were fascinated by the Russian Revolution, to such an extent that they were marked in their ways by a certain Bolshevik style. However they kept their distance from the methods used there, feeling that the Spanish revolution should be carried out in its own original way, because of the different historical conditions. This was reaffirmed later, when the bureaucratic and authoritarian character of the Bolshevik dictatorship was unmasked. But at the time, ideas and feelings were still confused. Actually nothing was known exactly about what was going on in Russia. But one could smell the calumnies which the bourgeoisie spread in all the press about the revolutionaries. For this reason, their brothers in every country defended them. The only way to help the Russian Revolution was to start revolutions in other countires. It was this determination which settled Durruti's return to Spain.

Footnotes

1. Letter from Durruti, December 1917.

2. Letter of March 25, 1927.

3. Manuel Buenacasa, editor of libertarian publications, member of the National Committee of the CNT in 1918, methodical organizer. Among other works he has left an excellent *History of the Workers' Movement from 1888 to 1927*. He died in exile in France in 1964. He collaborated in producing this biography of Durruti, by turning over parts of his memoirs to us and when we quote him, we are referring to these memoirs.

4. Testimony of Tejerina (the son). He talked to us about the correspondence which his father had with Durruti at that time. This voluminous correspondence was hidden by Tejerina in 1936 when the Fascists took over Leon. Tejerina (the father) remained hidden for a number of years in Spain. He died in this refuge which he had chosen, somewhere in the province of Leon.

5. Kaminski, *Ceux de Barcelone*, pg. 58, Denoel, Paris 1938.

6. Andres Nin, born in Vendrell (Tarragona), in 1892, assassinated by the GPU in June 1937. He worked as a journalist for *La Publicidad* in Spain. In 1917 he belonged to the Socialist Party. The following year he became a member of the CNT, in the Professional Workers Union of Barcelona. He represented this Union at the 2nd Congress of the CNT in 1919.

In 1921 he made a trip to Russia and during his stay was in complete agreement with the Bolshevik theses. Later he joined the Russian workers' Opposition. He finished by rallying to Trotsky's position. Expelled from Russia, he returned to Spain in 1931. From then on in Spain, through the publications of the Fourth International (left Communist) and of *La Batalla* (paper edited by Maurin of the group, Obrero y Camperol), he started to come out publicly for revolutionary Marxism, in opposition to the Spanish Communist Party and the Spanish Socialist Workers Party. Both in his beliefs and his actions Andres Nin can be considered as the most eminent Spanish Marxist.

7. Franz Borkenau: *El renidero espanol*, Ed. Ruedo Iberico, Paris 1971.

8. In Anastasia's memoirs, already quoted, we read: "Sent by the CNT in 1919 to Asturias and Leon (La Robla)". Additional information is found in a letter sent from the military hospital of Burgos, March 1919.

9. The National Conference held in November 1918 is referred to. Until then many Anarchists didn't belong to the CNT and acted exclusively as autonomous groups. After that, they joined the CNT but operated in general from the union base, without taking representational responsibilities. Items about this conference can be found in M. Buenacasa's work already quoted, and in Alejandro Gilabert's *Durruti*, Barcelona 1937.

4

"LOS JUSTICIEROS"

WHEN DURRUTI ARRIVED IN SAN SEBASTIAN, the CNT was starting to infiltrate an area until then dominated by the Socialist Party and its union the UGT. Until the second Congress of the CNT, anarchism had limited itself to propaganda through publications put out by small groups in the Basque region. But after the strike in August 1917 and the strong growth of anarcho-syndicalism throughout Spain, the anarchist groups of San Sebastian and Bilbao started using direct action and organized themselves more solidly.

During this same period the construction of a Casino, the Grand Kursaal, had been started at the mouth of the Urumea and for this work manpower came from Aragón and Logroño. The anarchist group in San Sebastian, inspired by Moises Ruiz, started to unionize this group of emigrant workers but Moises Ruiz, an old militant anarchist, was quick to understand that certain tactics would be opposed by the people of the region, who were used to mild socialist methods. To fight against socialism on the ideological plane, Ruiz appealed to his friend Buenacasa and had him come from Barcelona. The latter's qualities as organizer and theoretician were soon felt, not only in the development of the militants but also in the creation of the first Construction Union. The ideas he presented at conferences and the arguments brought against the Socialists in the course of public debates, served effectively as propaganda.

The militants of the Socialist party understood the danger rapidly and called in more experienced comrades from other regions. And it was in this way that a fierce struggle began in the Basque region between Socialists and anarchists. The Basque bourgeoisie saw this as an opportunity to break up the strength of the working class and started to encourage parliamentary socialism, hoping to divide and conquer[1].

"One day", Buenacasa wrote, "a big, strong young man with a joyous look presented himself at the Union. He greeted us warmly as though he had always known us. He told us without preamble, showing us his CNT card, that he had just arrived in the city and that he was looking for work. As in all such cases, we took care of him and found work for him in the machine shop at Rentería. From then on, he used to come every evening after work to the Union. He sat down in a corner, picked up a magazine from the pile on a table and read. He took very little part in the discussions and when night came he went back to the house where we had found him lodging."

This man made an impression on Buenacasa. After some thought he remembered their earlier meeting. It was that very antagonistic young man, whom he had known three years before at Gijón. "Then", Buenacasa goes on to say, "I was curious to know him better and I sought his friendship. From the first conversations I had with him, the only thing I found out for sure, was that he had lived for several years in France. But he didn't tell me the reasons for his stay across the Pyrenees and he also made no mention of our encounter in Gijón. I was sure that he had recognized me and I was intrigued by his silence about this meeting. Was it because we both had a disagreeable memory of it? The fact is that neither he nor I ever made a direct reference to it."

Buenacasa, who always considered himself "a good judge of people", his favorite expression, continues: "He enjoyed talking, not disputing. In conversation, he always avoided digressions and kept to the subject. He was neither stubborn, nor fanatical, but open, and willing to admit the possibility of his being in error. He had the rare quality of knowing how to listen, considering the argument of the opponent and accepting it in so far as it seemed reasonable. His union work was quiet but efficient. With the other metallurgical workers enrolled in our union "de Oficios Varios" and also in the "Unión Metalurgica" his voice began to be heard, and more than once a Socialist leader began to worry when Durruti asked for the floor. His comments at the Union as well as later in meetings were short and incisive. He expressed his thoughts simply and when he called bread, bread, he did it with such power that there was no way to refute him."

He was proposed for responsible positions in the metallurgists' committee. But he never wanted to accept. To his comrades "he answered that the position was not important, the important thing was vigilance at the base which would compel those at the top to carry out their obligations, and not permit bureaucratization."

"Months passed. We were bound by friendship and he told me about his life. On my side I tried to have him meet the best militants in San Sebastian, but doing this in such a way that he couldn't suspect that I had intervened. Very soon they were drawn to this silent young man from Leon." [2] These militants were Gregorio Suberviela, foreman of the mines; Marcelino del Campo, bricklayer and son of a teacher; Ruiz, son of a stationmaster; and Albadetrecu, who belonged to a bourgeois family from Bilbao, with whom he had broken because of his sympathies with anarchism. Besides, being attracted to each other, they created an anarchist group called "Los Justicieros" which operated simultaneously in Saragossa and San Sebastián.

At the same time that this group was being formed, there was intense ferment in the mines and metallurgy in the North. Strikes followed each other like an epidemic and the rank and file outdid their leaders. The Madrid Government, faced with increasing agi-

31

tation, installed military men in the provincial governments, and named Lieutenant Colonel Jose Regueral as the Governor of Biscay. He was no different from General Martínez Anido or Lieutenant Colonel Arlegui of the Guardia Civil. His first act during a press conference was to declare that he would force the unions to toe the line. And to back up his assertion with intimidation, he personally grilled "the prisoners and installed Detención Gubernativa." [3]

In Barcelona the situation was worse. The systematic repression ended by transforming the union struggle into a class war. The militant workers were literally hunted in the streets by bands of "pistoleros" in the pay of the bourgeoisie. The police made a common practice of the "ley de fuga" [4]. The best trained militants of the Catalan proletariat were sent to prison. Only the young could bear up under this harsh struggle because they were not yet known to the police and the "pistoleros".

The National Committee of the CNT which was carrying on underground work, was unable to deal with this situation and asked the militants throughout Spain for help of all sorts against the offensive of the bourgeoisie and the police in Barcelona. An authoritarian persecution, hot-tempered and stubborn, followed the police assassinations on the streets. "The best of militants", Buenacasa wrote, "had to face the dilemma: kill, escape or go to prison. The violent ones defended themselves and killed; the stoics died as well as the brave, who were shot in the back; the cowards and the prudent hid; the imprudent went to prison" [5].

This offensive by the Government and the employers was one of the most extreme weapons used by the ruling class against the growth of trade unionism in Barcelona and the maturity attained by the proletariat. The bourgeoisie which locked out 200,000 workers at the end of 1919 and which as a result had been weakened, had actually no other recourse than this shameless agression.

"Los Justicieros" were not indifferent to the appeals which came from Barcelona and they thought that "the best way to help their comrades was to transform Spain into one immense Barcelona". But "this meant making a strategic plan, which, for the moment, it was impossible to carry out, because they were thinking constantly of having to go to Barcelona to occupy the positions that the struggle had left empty" [6]. Buenacasa intervened more than once "to rein their youthful elan with all his moral influence, advising them to stay in San Sebastian where the social struggle was as important as in Barcelona, though less spectacular" [7].

One thing that happened in Valencia made a big impression on "Los Justicieros". This was an assault on August 4, 1920 organized by an anarchist group against the ex-Governor, Jose Maestre de Laborda, Count of Salvatierra, who, while he was Governor of Barcelona, had allowed the "ley de fuga" to be used against thirty-three unionists.

For the "Justicieros", this assault was exemplary. Soon they began to plan one against the Governor of Bilbao, Regueral. While they were preparing it, they learned that Alfonso XIII would take part in the inauguration of the Grand Kursaal. "They thought that an attempt to kill the King would do more for the cause of the proletariat"[8]. The most practical way to succeed would be to make a tunnel which would go under the center of the hall where the guests would be received. With Suberviela in charge, they started to dig the underground passage from a neighboring house. Durruti's job was to find the explosives and hide them. The work was difficult and tiring. Once the foundations of the building were reached, they advanced very slowly. The area under which they were digging the tunnel had been disguised as a coal depot. But the police must have suspected something because of the great number of bags of earth which came out. The work in progress was discovered and the group which was at work had to flee under fire.[9]

When this occurred Durruti was in Gijon but nevertheless he was considered responsible for the attempt, along with Suberviela and Marcelino del Campo. "Under such conditions", Buenacasa told them, "you can't stay in San Sebastian. I have prepared everything for you to leave for Barcelona". Their retreat from San Sebastian wasn't easy. The police had been mobilized to try and catch "the three dangerous anarchists denounced by the local press". Some railroad workers, close to Buenacasa, helped the three men to escape via Saragossa, in a freight train and so elude the police[10].

Footnotes

1. Clemente Mangado, member of the group, gave us an unpublished memoir with his personal recollections. These helped us to reconstruct these events. C. Mangado died of tuberculosis in exile in France in 1968. We will refer to these documents with the acronym: T.C.M.
2. Unpublished notebooks of Manuel Buenacasa.
3. "Detención Gubernativa" means the following (and still does): a provincial Governor (Prefect) has the right to send to prison for three months, any individual whose activities he suspects. At that time, thanks to this procedure, militant workers were kept in prison for many years. Later, during the Franco repression this same measure was used. For example Alejandro Zotter, Austrian Consul in Madrid in 1935, was arrested in 1939 by Franco's troops and detained through this legal procedure until 1950. He was then freed thanks to the intervention of the American Ambassador.
4. "Ley de fuga". This meant that prisoners were assassinated during their transfer from the police station to the prison under the pretense that "they had tried to escape".
5. Buenacasa, op. cit.
6. T.C.M.
7. Buenacasa, Cahiers inédits.
8. T.C.M.
9. Orobon Fernandez, op. cit.
10. Buenacasa, Cahiers inédits.

CONFRONTING
GOVERNMENT TERRORISM

MARCELINO DEL CAMPO and Gregorio Suberviela were known in Saragossa. But Buenaventura Durruti was coming into the Aragonese area for the first time. They had been given the address of Inocencio Pina, one of the "Justicieros" of Saragossa but it was still early and they went directly to the Union local in Agustin Street.

It was very different from the little office which Durruti had known in San Sebastian. This Center for Social Studies, similar to the one in Gijon run by Quintanilla [1] which Durruti had never chanced to visit, was large, modern and adapted to all the union activities, material as well as intellectual. There was an office for "Food", a sector for "Metallurgy", another for "Electricity", etc.. There was also a well furnished library; a newspaper, El Communista, mouthpiece for the workers unions of the area and defender of the International Proletariat; and the paper of the CNT unions of the region, Cultura y Accion.

When the young people arrived at the Center, only the president, Santolaria, manager of El Communista, Zenon Canudo and the janitor were there [2]. Gregorio Suberviela knew the first two and introduced them to his comrades. They spoke about Ascaso, whom Durruti didn't know yet. The young man had been locked up since December 1920 in the prison of the Predicadores and was expecting a death sentence. He had been accused of the murder of the editor-in-chief of El Heraldo de Aragon [3]. The newcomers then asked how the struggle was going in Saragossa. In the midst of all this, Jose Chueca, the editor of El Comunista burst into the room to give them extraordinary news. He had just learned about the discovery of an attempt on the life of Alfonso XIII, whose presumed authors were...., and he gave the names of the young people who were in front of him, causing much laughter.

Santaloria, before leaving his three friends, advised them "not to visit the local, which was or could be under observation" [4]. When night fell, they met Inocencio Pina in his home on the outskirts and had a conversation with Torres Escartin [5]. They learned that Manuel Sancho, Clemente Mangado and Albadetrecu were in prison, accused of an attempt on the life of Hilario Bernal, director of the Quimica S.A., virtual leader of the bourgeoisie in Saragossa [6]. All four were members of the group "Los Justicieros".

"To avoid their being given death sentences or prison terms", Pina said, "we must mobilize the working class and confront the bourgeoisie and the authorities. The group can only count on the two of us, Escartín and me, to do this. It's very little. Don't you think it would be better if you stayed here instead of continuing your trip?" "In reality", Mangado wrote, "Durruti and his comrades had already made a decision, for it was not our custom to abandon friends. From that moment the young Asturian" as Durruti was called when he first came to Saragossa, and his comrades became an integral part of the revolutionary movement of the Aragonese capital."[7]

At this time the bourgeoisie was avenging itself with a disguised lock-out for the concessions it had had to make after the light and gas strike, as well as the strike of waiters and Trolley Car workers the year before[8]. Using the economic crisis as a pretext, it cut down on hiring and practiced a systematic repression urged on by the Comte de Coello y Portugal, Governor of the Province, and by Cardinal Soldevila. This was why the three fugitives had difficulty in finding work. Durruti got a job quite easily in the shops of the machinist Excoriza, thanks to his professional competence. But the others had to be satisfied helping Pina in his small fruit and vegetable business.

Saragossa, despite everything, was enjoying a breathing spell while both sides, the bourgeoisie and the workers were profiting by it and strengthening themselves. The strength of the workers had even increased in spite of the repression in 1920 and workers were becoming unionized in greater numbers. The workers' press, persecuted, distorted by censorship, nevertheless managed to appear. Life, despite increasing unemployment, seemed peaceful.

This apparent and superficial calm in Saragossa contrasted with the open struggle taking place in Barcelona where Martínez Anido, the Civil Governor, was carrying out a systematic business of assassinations. The unions were forced to go underground, the militants were imprisoned, and among them was Angel Pestaña, who had recently returned from the U.S.S.R.. The young people organized themselves into anarchist groups to oppose the police. The purges had brought about a premature promotion of certain militants who lacked experience. When the National Committee of the CNT was arrested in March 1921, it was necessary to improvise a new one of untried members and militants who had only recently become members, like Andres Nin, who had been affiliated to the CNT less than two years[9].

Evelio Boal, general secretary of the CNT was also arrested. He had just been handed a document which Angel Pestaña had sent him from prison. This was Pestaña's report of his work and impressions during the IInd Congress of the IC in Moscow in August 1920. He pointed out that "for various reasons and specially because of the twenty-one clauses adopted, it was necessary for the CNT to revise its agreement to join the III International, an agreement concluded with enthusiasm in 1919"[10]. Boal didn't have time to pass on this message to the unions. The new steering committee, presided over by Nin, had been left in charge of this document. The committee put off its distribution, keeping to the literal interpretation of the Confederation's statutes. They decided the unions didn't have the power to correct the decisions of a congress and as long as there was no new congress, the agreement of 1919 would continue to be in force. The new leadership and its pro-Bolshevik interpretations, as well as the intrigues related to this problem and the difficulties caused by the repression, all this slowed down the progress of the CNT.

About this time, the need to found an Anarchist Federation for the entire peninsula was felt in Saragossa. To discuss this question various anarchist groups "Via Libre", "El Comunista", "Los Justicieros", "Voluntad" and "Impulso", held a conference. They agreed to send a delegation to the south, the center and the east of the country to compare opinions and propose the project. Durruti was put in charge of this mission. It was the first time he had taken on such a responsibility and in February 1921 he left Saragossa accompanied by Juliana Lopez.

In Andalusia he was able to convince the militants to establish, on a trial basis, solidarity agreements between the different groups of each locality. A Committee for Anarchist Relations was to coordinate all the activities on the regional level. [11]

They arrived in Madrid the 9th of March 1921, the day after a spectacular assault. Some unknowns in a side-car in the middle of the Paseo de la Independencia, had opened fire on an automobile occupied by Eduardo Dato and had killed him. The police had immediately declared martial law in the capital, cordoning off entire sections to prevent the terrorists from leaving the city [12]. Under such conditions it was very dangerous to try and get in contact with the anarchists of Madrid. So Durruti and Juliana Lopez left againt immediately [13].

In Barcelona, they had a long interview with Domingo Ascaso in the restaurant where he usually took his meals and later in a house in the working class district of Pueblo Nuevo. They discussed the latest event at great length. Rumors were circulating that the central government, shaken by the death of Dato, had sent an emissary to ask Martinez Anido to stop the persecutions against the trade unionists. Would be allow himself to be intimidated by the central power? It was hardly probable [14].

Domingo Ascaso brought the two travellers up to date on the latest episodes in the repression: closing down of unions, imprisonment of the leading militants (Segui, Pestaña, Boal, Peiró) and of dozens and dozens of less well known militants. The "pistoleros" were functioning like an auxiliary police, recognizing each other by a blue identification card. They stood at the doors of the factories to intimidate the union delegates or to shoot them down if their bosses had given them the order. Stool pigeons had joined forces with the "pistoleros". Some had belonged to the Confederation, but cornered by the police in the dilemma, to betray or die, they ended by giving in. Faced with this danger outside and inside, the Anarchists had closed ranks, pushing out the suspects and carrying off spectacular actions like the attempt against Dato, true instigator of the tactics of Martinez Anido, and preparing new ones [15].

Under these conditions, Domingo Ascaso pointed out to Durruti that for the time being, his projects were not practical and that there were more pressing objectives. "You can report all this to the comrades in Saragossa and warn them that certain "pistoleros", too well known in Barcelona, will be taking refuge and will take up their activities there."[16]

Once back in Saragossa, Durruti gave a report about his trip. In certain areas, rivalry between individuals made things difficult. But in general most of the people were ready to establish durable agreements, the first steps toward an Anarchist Federation in the peninsula. The groups in Saragossa immediately set to work. The group "Via Libre" assumed the responsability for starting a forum in its newspaper, of the same name, to discuss the need for an anarchist organization on the national level. But "Los Justicieros" had an extra task, to get arms and money and send them to Barcelona to help the anarchist groups there. This difficult job was entrusted to Durruti and Suberviela, who knew the Basque militants rather well. They left for the North and at the first contact with the comrades they were told: "Since the arrival of Reguera in Bilbao, the CNT hasn't left the underground. The treasuries of the unions are empty because money has been needed to help the families of the prisoners or to pay for trials. So impossible to count on us for financial help." Nevertheless they made some appeals to their comrades for money or arms. The result was almost zero. They received very little money and only a few weapons of low calibre and this, thanks to the sacrifice of certain comrades of Bilbao "who gave up their pistols at a moment when a weapon was the best identity card".

Then Gregorio decided impetuously that "for big troubles one needed big remedies". They should try to rob some banks since the State was emptying the treasuries of the workers' organizations. Torres Escartin and Durruti approved but said they lacked experience. True they had had armed encounters with the police and with the "pistoleros", they had succeeded in assaults with dynamite, but they had never used arms to attack a bank. However they shared the responsibility and started to make plans for an attack on the Bank of Bilbao. This attempt failed.

Zabarain, liaison agent between them and the North, proposed that they be content with "any theft". He suggested robbing the paymaster of one of the metallurgical centers of Eibar, who, in all probability would be carrying important sums of money from the bank of Bilbao to the factory, accompanied by only one chauffeur. On the day set, Durruti and his comrades feigned an accident and blocked the road from Bilbao to Eibar just before the car of the paymaster passed. After disarming the two men, they left them gagged on the floor of the car and fled with the money.

The next day, the local press reported the bold theft of 300,000 pesetas. The police suspected a band of Catalan "atracadores" (highwaymen). "Los Justicieros" hid in a house in the district of "Los Siete Calles". During this time Zabarain went to look for and buy 100 Star type pistols in Eibar, a model called at this time "the pistol of the trade unionists". The money that remained was divided in two parts, one for Bilbao and the other taken to Saragossa by

Juliana López. A few days later the three friends left for Logroño, to return to Saragossa later on[17].

Footnotes

1. Eleuterio Quintanilla was one of the founders of the CNT. He was a teacher and founder of the Social Studies Center of Gijon, and editor of the weekly *Acción Social*. At the Congress of the CNT in 1919, he was already denouncing the authoritarian character of the Russian Revolution. He joined the group within the congress which opposed the CNT's joining the Third International. He died at the age of 80 in Bordeaux in 1965.

2. The CNT, in accordance with its statutes, did not employ functionaries or paid workers. In the CNT locals there was usually a caretaker. These regulations were aimed at combatting union bureaucracy.

3. This attempt was carried out by Domingo Ascaso. His brother, Francisco, had nothing to do with it. The principal reason for the assassination was the victim's collaboration with the police. He had denounced the soldiers who had taken part in the uprising of the del Carmen barracks, on the night of the 8th to 9th of January 1920 (See *El Comunista*, February 1920).

4. The text between the quotation marks and the interview in general we owe to a witness, C.B., who now lives in Spain.

5. Born in Huesca, son of a well-to-do family, a student, he learned about Anarchism through professor Ramon Acin (shot in 1936 by the Fascists). He was active in the Food workers Union in 1919. He was shot by the Franco forces in 1939 in Barcelona.

6. Mangado writes about this: "Any worker in Saragossa could have made this attack on Bernal, because he acted like a tyrant in the Quimica, S.A. and denounced the workers who belonged to the CNT (...) we had nothing to do with the attempt. Actually we were preparing one against the Civil Governor, Conde de Coello. He and Cardinal Soldevila had introduced to Saragossa "pistolerismo" and the methods which Martinez Anido had used in Barcelona."

7. T.C.M.

8. The Lighting Workers Union forced the company to recognize its union organisation and to grant a wage increase of 60% and the gift of a raincoat for each worker in the rainy season. In the Tramway Company a wage increase was given to all categories of employees. The union organization was also recognized. See "*El Comunista*, no. 14-20.

9. See note 6, Chapter 3.

10. Pestana published two articles on this subject: "Information about my activity at the 2nd Congress of the I C" and "Opinions about the Third International". These articles were published in Madrid, in 1922 by the publishing house *Nueva Senda*. In 1969 the publishing house ZYX published them again (Madrid).

11. T.C.M. and C.B.

12. This assault was the work of an anarchist group in Barcelona, "Metalurgico". Three of its members went to Madrid to carry it out: Pedro Mateu, Luis Nicolau and Ramon Casanellas. Mateu was detained in Madrid but the others managed to escape. But Nicolau was turned over to the Spanish authorities by the Germans and Casanellas went into exile in the U.S.S.R., where he was converted to Bolshevism.

Mateu and Nicolau were condemned to death and pardoned, freed in 1931. At that time, Casanellas, recently returned from Russia, died in a motor accident. Pedro Mateu is an exile in France.

13. During Durruti's short visit in Madrid he was held as a suspect. But he was able to convince the authorities that he was the "son of a good family, that he was in Madrid with a woman friend, and that if this was known it would have terrible consequences for the honor of the family". "The commissioner was convinced by his good manners, this elegance, his foreign bearing and his natural attractiveness. He let the rich heir and his mistress leave freely." Buenacasa, *Cahiers Inédits*.

14. Allende Salazar replaced Eduardo Dato and ordered his Minister of the Interior, Bagallal, to take the necessary steps to put an end to terrorism in Barcelona. The latter sent an emissary to convince Martinez Anido, the Governor of Barcelona, who replied: "Things being as they are, it is impossible to change the pace." He added: "as the Government is just as much compromised as I am, each must take their responsibilities."

On this subject one can consult among other sources, José Peirats: *Los anarquistas y la crisis política española* and Alberto Barcells, *El sindicalismo en Barcelona*.

15. Domingo Ascaso alludes to an attempted attack on the headquarters of the "pistoleros" organized by eight groups of anarchists in Barcelona.

16. For this interview, T.C.M.

17. Testimony of T.C.M.

6/

SARAGOSSA, 1922

A NEW POLITICAL CRISIS WAS DEVELOPING in Spain at this time. The unpopular Moroccan war had turned out to be a disaster. The troops of General Silvestre had been crushed by the army of Abd el-Krim at the battle of Annual where 14,000 Spanish soldiers died.

When the final defeat was announced on August 11, 1921, the Spanish people were full of indignation and demanded not only an end to the war but also that those responsible for the massacre and the politicians who had favored the operation in Africa be brought to trial. In certain areas social agitation took the form of riots and in all the industrial regions big strikes broke out. The guns of the Guardia Civil couldn't stifle the protests and the Premier, Allende Salazar, stunned, went to the Royal Palace to hand in his resignation to the King. Alfonso XIII, with his usual contempt for "the rabble", was getting ready to spend the summer in his palace at Deauville.

He called in Maura, asking him to form a strong government, capable of imposing silence on all those who were demanding an accounting about the Moroccan campaign. And he asked him to appoint a Minister of War capable of winning the war, not in Morocco against the Moors but in Spain against the Spanish workers Maura, a skillful and experienced man, understood that Alfonso XIII was asking him "to make Spain toe the line"[1]. He formed a government and appointed the ex-governor of Saragossa, the Count de Coello y Portugal as Minister of Interior. His political program was to repress the working class and make things pleasant for the bourgeoisie, specially the Catalan bourgeoisie which was showing a profound contempt for the central power in Madrid.

Maura achieved "pacification" of the nation by increasing street assassinations, extending the interminable lines of prisoners, flowing along the roads of Spain [2] and filling the prisons with workers. But the attempt to conquer the Catalan bourgeoisie failed completely. The latter wanted to take over the Ministry of Finance for themselves and as they had not been successful they provoked a new government crisis and the resignation of Maura in March 1922.

Alfonso XIII thought of the precedent set by Mussolini and Victor-Emmanuel. The man for the job should be a general with fascist tendencies, who would control the country and permit him to rule in peace. And so he gave his instructions to Sanchez Guerra. But the latter felt that he would only last a short time in the government and limited himself to establishing a class truce, restoring the constitutional guarantees of April 22, 1922.

It was at this time that Saragossa was living through the tragedy of "pistolerismo," imported from Barcelona by the Count de Coello and Archbishop Soldevila. When they learned about the failure of Maura and the nomination of Sanchez Guerra to replace him, these local authorities decided to take the offensive. First they encouraged the courts of justice to liquidate the cases which remained in suspense and to sentence those believed to be guilty of the attempt on Bernal and those involved in the affair of the journalist Gutierrez, and to carry out the heaviest sentences possible, as quickly as they could.

Immediately, "Los Justicieros" put themselves on a war footing, supported by lawyers who came from Barcelona and Madrid. Eduardo Barriobero, principal lawyer for the defence and legal counsel of the CNT, presented his point of view to the committee to aid the prisoners: "With Sanchez Guerra in the government, politics will change and with the restoration of constitutional guarantees, the CNT as well as the rest of the opposition will leave the underground. But if the trial is completed before this liberalization and if the prisoners are condemned, there will be no review of the trial in spite of the political "truce" and those condemned will go to prison for many years. For us to win out in this situation and to free the prisoners from their prison, the best possible defense is for the people of Saragossa to proclaim their innocence in the streets. Only this popular pressure can turn things in our favor".

The delegate of the anarchist groups also gave his opinion to the same committee. He said that the best defense was a general strike and violent manifestations in the street. The delegate of the CNT had reservations: "As the unions had been closed down, the declaration of a general strike would not be followed by the workers". To avoid this the anarchist groups decided to assume the responsibility themselves as well as the consequences, if the CNT would not take the responsibility for declaring a general strike.

Durruti took part in a delegation which was chosen to look into the problem. The local committee of the CNT called together the representatives of the unions to study, in plenary session, the attitude to adopt at Saragossa. Either the working class would answer the call to strike and this would be a victory for the CNT and the prisoners. Or else the strike would not be general, the CNT would find itself weakened and the authorities would have a free hand to strengthen the repression.

Durruti proposed that the call for a strike should be issued to the workers by the anarchist groups. In case of failure the CNT could accuse these groups of "adventurism", while if the strike was successful, the CNT would be the sole beneficiary and its influence with the masses would be strengthend. The proposal was accepted. It was necessary to act quickly because the trial of those accused of the plot against Bernal had been announced for the 20th.

The 19th of April leaflets were distributed describing the nature of the trial and its development, and calling for a general strike and massive demonstrations at the door of the prison and of the law court. The next day the Guardia Civil had occupied the most important positions in the city, as well as the environs of the jail and the court and dispersed the mob with a thick volley of shots. Mangado reports: "The prisoners were awakened by the shots and deafening noises. The fusillades continued for two hours, until the time when the prisoners were to be taken to the Court. When they came out in the street, a big crowd greeted them with cries of: "Hurrah for the innocent prisoners, long live the CNT". The courage of the workers hadn't been broken by the intimidating shots of the police and the demonstrators escorted the prisoners as far as the courtroom which was filled up quickly."

Once the judge had declared the session open, the audience rose and cheered the prisoners. The same cheers mounted from the street, cut short by the police firing in the air still trying to break up the mob. Immediately everyone understood, and specially the defense lawyers, that it was in the interest of the court to finish quickly, perhaps under pressure from the Governor. They foresaw victory! Eduardo Barriobero began his plea with these simple words: "The proofs of the innocence of my clients? It is not I who will furnish them. When the entire population proclaims it in the streets, innocence is proven!" The cries of the crowd orchestrated this declaration. And soon afterwards, Bernal, the victim of the attack, confessed that he didn't recognize any of the accused as authors of the deed. An hour later, the judges announced that the accused were innocent. When the latter went out to be taken back to prison, the police were outflanked by the crowd. Cries of victory rang on all sides[3].

On April 22, 1922, Sanchez Guerra restored constitutional guarantees. The people of Saragossa, without waiting for the official opening of the union locals, immediately started to revive union activity. The restoration of guarantees, specially in Barcelona, produced the feeling of a real class holiday. The offices of the unions opened and the "detenidos gubernativos" (political prisoners) regained their liberty, the people could express themselves once more and the workers' press could start publishing again.

In Barcelona each union held a general assembly in the movie houses or the theaters rented for the occasion. One of the most important ones was held by the Woodworkers' Union at the Victoria Theater and a list was read of the 107 members of the Confederation killed by the "pistoleros". Liberto Calleja (Marco Floro) read out the names of Evelio Boal, Antonio Feliu, Ramon Arch, etc. [4]

In the other Catalan unions these same assemblies were held in increasing numbers. Responsible unionists were elected and the undemocratic procedures which had been inevitable during the underground period were ended. The CNT speedily found its old members again and even strengthened its ranks. But soon it had to face a difficult problem, its relations with the Third International[5]. To clear up the confusion, the new National Committee and Juan Peiro, the new secretary, decided to convene a new congress. But how would it be possible to convoke a Congress when, despite the legality of union work, as a national organization it was illegal? To solve this difficulty, the new National Committee used a dodge. It asked the Governor of Saragossa to allow them to organize a national reunion of workers on June 11, 1922, to discuss social problems in Spain. Victoriano Gracía opened the meeting in the name of the Aragonese workers. Then Juan Peiro spoke, directing his greetings to the Spanish working class. The Government delegate understood very soon the nature of the congress and taking advantage of an incident, tried to end the meeting. Gracía told him that "the working class of Saragossa was not ready to tolerate such high handedness" and threatened to call a general strike. The Government delegate had to yield and the assembly continued. It ended with a meeting in the Plaza de Toros.

During this conference the question of the Third International was studied at great length. Hilario Arlandis[6] maintained that his delegation named by the Plenum of Lerida had been the authentic delegates. Gaston Leval and Pestaña gave full reports on their stay in Moscow. Then "the Conference decided that the delegation of Nin, Maurin, Arlandis, had abused the confidence of the CNT, profiting by the fact that the CNT had been forced underground." It ratified the agreements of the Conference of Logroño and approved Angel Pestaña's report. Andrès Nin was repudiated as representative of the CNT to the Red International Union (ISR). After examining the famous "21 clauses," the Conference decided that it was impossible to go on taking part in this International. On the other hand it was proposed that it join the International Association of Workers (AIT) recently reorganized in Berlin. The Conference was unable to make a decision on this question and sent it back to the unions to take a vote, which was needed before it could join the IC[7].

Conference discussions and conclusions were made known at a meeting in the Plaza de Toros of Saragossa. Salvador Seguí, chosen as secretary general, denounced the governmental repression in a fiery speech. "I accuse the Government of being responsible for the terrorism during the years 1920-1922". Then Victoriano Gracía spoke, demanding the liberation of Francisco Ascaso, victim of the intrigues of Pedro Aparicio, chief of police. The Press reported the important political scope of the meeting. *Solidaridad Obrera* of Barcelona captioned its editorial: "The dead you have killed are alive and well."

Footnotes

1. "Meter a España en cintura", expression used by a number of historians, among them Alberto Barcells in the o.c.
2. Those condemned to prison were escorted by the Guardia Civil. tied to each other and on foot. derivation of the term "string of prisoners".
3. On this point we follow the testimony of Clemente Mangado. As a member of "Los Justicieros" and as a prisoner accused of the assault against José Bernal. his contribution is valuable.
4. Valentin Roi. o.c.
5. Evelio Boal. General Secretary of the CNT was arrested along with part of the National Committee. Andrès Nin and Joaquin Maurin. both enthusiastic supporters of the Russian Revolution joined the National Committee. Some time later they received invitations to take part in the Congress of the Red International Union. which was to take place in June 1921. A group of militants met in April in Barcelona (the Plenum of Lerida as it was erroneously called) and without considering Pestaña's report. they named a delegation composed of five members. among them Andrès Nin. Joaquin Maurin and Hilario Arlandis. The Anarchist groups added an observer to the delegation. Gaston Leval. a young Frenchman who was active in the Catalan Anarchist groups.

A national conference of the CNT meeting at Logroño in August 1921. rejected this plenum as out of order. The contradictory agreements. the secrecy now a necessity in Spain. the enthusiasm of the pro-Bolsheviks. and the great interest that Lenin and Trotsky had to conquer the organization of the CNT. all this created an enormous confusion in the ranks of the CNT.
6. Andrès Nin and Joaquin Maurin remained in Russia. The former held the position of International Secretary of the ISR. Ruiz. Hilario Arlandis and Gaston Leval returned.
7. For Gaston Leval's report one can read *Ni Dieu, ni Maitre* by Daniel Guérin. Editions de Delphes. Paris 1964. page 57. For Pestaña one can consult the articles already mentioned and in general the works of Jose Peirats and Manuel Buenacasa. They deal with this problem and the Congress of 1919 at great length.

43

7

"LOS SOLIDARIOS"

FRANCISCO ASCASO LEFT PRISON soon, thanks to worker agitation. Soon after being freed, he spoke at a meeting to denounce the police manoeuvers of Aparicio and his clique. The bourgeoisie took revenge by boycotting Ascaso. The workers called this "the hunger truce". With his usual energy, Ascaso fought this declaration of war. At the first meeting of the "Justicieros" since his liberation, he met Durruti and Torres Escartin. The problems to be discussed were important. One of them would test the ideological unity of the group. Durruti and Inocencio Pina held two different points of view. The latter believed in a Bolshevik revolutionary vanguard. He had also proposed to his comrades that they organize themselves as "professional revolutionaries" [1]. Durruti had completely opposite ideas, not only about the role of the avant-garde but also about "professional revolutionaries". For him, the proletariat were the real leaders of the revolution and if the anarchist groups had a lot of influence, this was only because of their radicalism. "The important theoreticians" Durriti said, "had taken their ideas from the life of the proletariat, because the latter are in revolt by instinct and necessity. Their condition as the exploited class imposes the need to struggle for their own emancipation".

This struggle for freedom should be based on an organization whose principal incentive is solidarity. For Durruti the social history of Spain showed that, before the theoreticians had presented solutions or directives to the proletariat, the latter had found the tool for its own liberation through the federation of workshop and factory groups. And the interference of the "professional revolutionary" could only bring one result, it would alter the political maturing process of the proletariat. Therefore the aim of the anarchist was to understand this natural process. From then on, to separate oneself from the working class under the pretext of serving it better, meant treason and the prelude to bureaucratization, that is to say a new form of domination [2].

Ascaso was fascinated by the thought and the person of Durruti. He had stated his own views in an article published in *Voluntad*, "Paty or worker's organization" [3]. His ideas coincided with those of Durruti. Together they provided a rein to bolshevisation" and to other falsifications arising from a false idea of the Russian Revolution.

After the meeting, where for reasons of security they left two by two, Durruti and Ascaso left together. This was the beginning of a strong friendship which a set of circumstances was later to strengthen. The differences in their characters only brought out better the resemblances between the two men. Ascaso, small, thin, nervous; Durruti, athletic and calm. Ascaso with his strained and suspicious glance, seemed unlikeable at first sight; Durruti, on the contrary, radiated sympathy. Icy calculation, rationality and mistrust in one; passion and optimism behind an apparently calm exterior in the other. If from the first moment Durruti gave himself totally to friendship with Ascaso, the latter showed himself more reserved, waiting to know Durruti better. But once a complete climate of confidence had been established, great projects were born from the dialogue between the two revolutionaries.

One day they received a letter from Francisco Ascaso's brother, Domingo, who described the situation in Barcelona: "The calm is false and omens of tragedy can be seen. The pistolerismo of the employer has now found a new form, with the creation of a yellow unionism whose members enjoy the same privileges as did the pistoleros established by Bravo Portillo not so long ago. If the leaders of the CNT believe in this calm, the anarchist groups, to my way of thinking, are not fooled as they prepare for a new offensive which will be launched any day now against trade unionism... The new struggle will be decisive and many of our comrades will fall, but the struggle cannot be avoided". He advised Francisco to remain in Saragossa until a complete change had taken place in Barcelona[4]. But Barcelona enticed Durruti and Ascaso like a lover and they told the group their decision to go there. Torres Escartin, Gregorio Suberviela and Marcelino del Campo decided to join them. With a new name, "Crisol", the five friends started a new life in August 1922.

When they arrived in Barcelona they learned that the "pistoleros" had attacked the celebrated anarchist. Angel Pestaña a few hours earlier; an event which made the atmosphere of Barcelona even more stifling in those hot days of August 1922[5]. As a counter thrust, the workers had decided on a general strike in Catalonia. A group of Catalan intellectuals published a formal condemnation of the leaders of the bourgeoisie and their actions. In the Cortes, the Socialist deputy, Indalecio Prieto, also denounced them, demanding the dismissal of Martinez Anido by the Government. The President, Sanchez Guerra, pressured by the Cortes and by the wave of popular indignation, was forced to intervene. From then on "the star of Martinez Anido began to pale"[6]. Nevertheless, "pistolerismo" continued to exist and to operate through the "free unions", organizations created and manipulated by the bosses, and also protected by the Church which was trying to introduce Catholic unionism. Ramon Sales, who was the organizer, wanted to make them the rivals of the CNT. Formerly the leader of the "pistoleros", he imposed on these unions his own way of behaving. The employers demanded that their employees become members of the new unions and laid off the CNTers. The "pistoleros" supported his methods with terror in the streets and at the doors of the factories. In this way the bourgeoisie hoped to crush anarcho-syndicalism. As for Martinez Anido, he continued to persecute the

45

Confederal unions, despite the politics of truce adopted by the central government. All this created a state of war without mercy.

The majority of the Catalan intelligentsia, led by Francisco Macia[7], was opposed to this state of affairs and once again began to advocate "autonomy". This position was helpful to the CNT, which had been tracked down and forced to survive through violence. Its most active milieu was the Woodworkers' Union in San Pablo Street, where the most radical militants, anarcho-syndicalists, met. It was in this union that Durruti and his comrades established friendship with the Catalam militants. Later in October 1922, they formed with the latter the celebrated group, the "Solidarios"[8].

These militants joined together for three reasons: "to oppose 'pistolerismo', to maintain the syndical forms of the CNT and to found an anarchist federation which would bring together all the groups which were close to each other ideologically but were scattered through the peninsula"[9]. In their eyes the problem of organization came first and was an indispensable condition for the triumph of the revolution. Even the struggle against the bourgeoisie and terrorism came second. They founded a weekly, *Crisol*, and from the beginning, Barthe, a French exile, Felipe Alaiz, Liberto Calleja, Torres Tribo and Francisco Ascaso, manager of the review, wrote for it.

The group decided to attack Marfinez Anido and Arlegui who were responsible for anti-worker politics. They were already making plans when they learned that these two military men had organized a fake attack against themselves, to try and justify their politics of terror in the eyes of Madrid. A journalist of the Catalan press had foiled their plot by telephoning to the President of the Council that "Martinez Anido had prepared a fake assault in order to make it the pretext for a Saint-Bartholomew of the militant unionists". Sanchez Guerra, worried by the turn that events were taking in Barcelona, telephoned to Marfinez Anido the morning of October 24th to tell him that "according to certain reliable information which had reached Madrid, Colonel Arlegui, after what had happened, could not continue in office". He commanded Anido to transfer the police command to the colonel of the Guardia Civil. Marfinez having answered that "he couldn't submit to the orders from Madrid" was told to consider himself fired and to hand over the government of the province to the Chief Justice[10]. This change of the men in control forced Sanchez Guerra to make constitutional guarantees in Catalonia effective and thus brought about the normalization of political and trade union life in this region.

"Los Solidarios" profited by this situation to hold an anarchist congress of the Catalan-Balearic region. It was well attended and it was clear that the regional groups were not indifferent to the organizational plans that "Los Solidarios" advocated in *Crisol*. A regional Commission for Anarchist Relations was set up, the embryo of what would become, a few years later, the Iberian Anarchist Federation (Federacion Anarquista Iberica, FAI). The groups studied the new political situation and came to the conclusion that "considering the interests which were at stake in the political evolution which existed in Spain, specially in Catalonia, this period of calm couldn't last long. The repression in Catalonia was not a caprice of Marfinez Anido, but

Barcelona, March. 10, 1923. Salvador Seguí, secretary of the National Committee of the CNT, assassinated by the police of Alfonso XIII. The site of the crime is pictured in the upper half.

the natural result of class antogonism. Marfinez Anido was only an instrument of the bourgeoisie, and the fact that this individual had disappeared from the political scene didn't mean that the bourgeoisie had renounced its repressive methods. They would change in form, but the bourgeoisie, considering its reactionary nature, would continue to use terrorist tactics''[11].

The groups who met, understood that Sanchez Guerra's policy of "class truce" was unwillingly accepted by the right wing cliques. The Army, backed by the landowners and by the clergy would take

47

advantage of a favorable event to seize State power and impose a military dictatorship. The monarchy couldn't curb this tendency, because its fate was irrevocably bound to the Army, which, since 1917, had shown its intention to come forward until it placed itself at the head of the nation.

Facing an imminent military coup, the groups found no other solution than to speed up the revolutionary process through a campaign of agitation in the industrial and rural areas. The Commission for Anarchist Relations would coordinate plans and activities on the peninsula. The organs of libertarian propaganda in Catalonia, *Crisol, Fragua Social*, and *Tierra y Libertad*, participated.

The congress revised its antimilitarist tactic which had been in operation until then. This tactic had resulted in a considerable decrease in the number of militants. Many had been obliged to go into exile because they refused to do military service. It was decided that it would be more realistic for the young people to go into the army and form cells of revolutionary action in the barracks: the "antimilitarist" committees which were to be in touch with local anarchist groups. To spread revolutionary ideas among the soldiers, a special bulletin was created *Hijos del Pueblo* (Sons of the People).

In the Commission for Anarchist Relations there were three "Solidarios": Francisco Ascaso, Aurelio Fernandez and Buenaventura Durruti. The first was secretary general, the second was in charge of antimilitarist committees, and the third was in charge of assembling an arsenal of arms and explosives. With another metallurgical worker, Durruti set up an underground shop where grenades were made and they started a foundry for that purpose. Other arms deposits were established in other districts. They managed to accumulate a stock of six thousand grenades in a very short time. Aurelio Fernandez worked his way into the ranks of the army, winning over several corporals to the revolutionary cause, followed by some sergeants and even some officers. Antimilitary Committees began to proliferate in the regiments situated outside Catalonia. Francisco Ascaso extended their ties with the rest of Spain. He established contacts with other autonomous regional commissions of anarchists which had been created since Durruti's trip the year before.

After the first initiatives, results showed that conditions were ripe for undertakings of a wider scope. In this climate of intense and fruitful activity on March 10, 1923, the news burst forth that Salvador Seguí, one of the best brains of Spanish Anarchism had been assassinated. Mercenaries in the pay of Felix Graupera, President of the Employers Federation, had coldly shot him and his comrade and friend, Paronas, in Cadena Street, in broad daylight and in full view of the entire neighborhood, terrorized by the arms of the "pistoleros".

Furious indignation took hold of the popular masses. The prestige of the victim was considerable among the workers and intellectuals of Barcelona. The CNT quickly called a meeting of Catalan militants. It was decided to prevent the revival of the old repression by every means and to put an end once and for all to "pistolerismo" and its leaders. It was also necessary to find funds to reprovision the treasuries of the unions, continually emptied by the authorities (12).

The "Solidarios" decided to eliminate various counter-revolutionary personalities: Marfinez Anido, Colonel Arlegui, the ex-ministers Bagallal and Conde de Coello, José Regueral, Governor of Bilbao and the Cardinal Archbishop of Saragossa, Soldevila; who were directly responsible for the politics of terrorism.

On their part, various anarchist groups in Barcelona joined together to attack the Hunters' Circle, refuge of the "pistoleros" and meeting place of the most reactionary employers. This attack had the most overwhelming psychological effects: such audacity seemed unbelievable, fifteen people bursting into drawing rooms and shooting point-blank. The capitalists asked for police protection in their homes and many "pistoleros" fled from Barcelona.

The disorder created by this event was considerable. A relentless war had begun. Durruti and his friends lived through the most dramatic chapters of their lives at that time. A witness during this period reports that "this has no other precedent than the period which the Russian revolutionaries lived through between 1906 and 1913. These young people who, brushing aside the advice of cautious adults, appointed themselves judges and avengers in the four cardinal points of Spain, often pursued by the repressive forces of the State, had no other moral support than their own conviction and their revolutionary faith" [13].

Foonotes

1. Evidently, Pina was not a special case. A number of anarchists started to imitate Bolshevik methods.
2. In his letters. Mangado analyzes the discussion: "Durruti not only objected to the professional revolutionary, but he also attacked trade union red tape, germ of a new bureaucratization.". Mangado adds "that later, Durruti always maintained this position".
3. "The daily struggle is no more than the revolutionary preparation of the working class and it is through this preparation that the workers acquire the experience which will make them able to show that economic and political emancipation must be their own job." *Voluntad*, no. 3 (1918-1919).
4. TCM.
5. This happened on the 25th of August at Manrésa. The spectacular element in this attack was that the "pistoleros" of the free Union left him wounded and couldn't complete their crime, because the passers-by interfered. But they had the audacity to enter the hospital with the idea of finishing off the wounded man. The personnel of the hospital drove them away.
6. José Peirats: *Los anarquistas en la crisis política española*, Edit. Alfa, Montevideo 1963, p. 35.
7. Francisco Macia was born in Lérida in 1858. He broke with the army when he was a colonel in the infantry. In 1905 he started his struggle for the autonomy of Catalonia. He represented the romantic spirit of Catalanism. At 68 he organized a guerilla band with the idea of freeing Catalonia from the dictatorship of Primo de Rivera (1926). On this question one can read Henri Torres' *Accusés hors série*, Ed. Gallimard, Paris 1957, p. 34. He died in Barcelona in 1932 while he was president of the "Generalitat de Catalunya".
8. The consolidation of "Crisol" with the Catalans group became "Los Solidarios". This group was composed of Francisco Ascaso, waiter; Durruti, machinist; Manuel Torres Escartin, pastry cook; Juan García Oliver, waiter; Aurelio Fernandez, machinist; Ricardo Sanz, textile worker; Alfonso Miguel, cabinet maker; Gregorio Suberviela, machinist; Eusebio Brau, foundry worker; Marcelino Manuel Campo (Tomas Arrate), carpenter; Miguel García Vivancos, chauffeur; Antonio del Toto, day laborer.
9. Testimony of Aurelio Fernandez.
10. José Peirats, *op. cit.*
11. Testimony of Aurelio Fernandez.
12. Idem.
13. Robert Lefranc, article in the *Libertaire*, November 1937.

8

REGUERAL AND ARCHBISHOP SOLDEVILA

DURRUTI HAD OPPOSED HIS FRIEND PINA, who believed in the need for "professional revolutionaries". And now the rhythm of events forced him as well as his comrades to lead an existence similar to the one advocated by Pina. For the "Solidarios", this required a radical change in their life styles. It should be noted in passing that Durruti and his comrades were never salaried revolutionaries, which distinguished them from the bureaucrats and the "permanents" of the Socialist, Communist and Syndicalist organizations.

One of the first difficulties they had to face was the financial problem: all available funds had been used to buy arms and explosives. It was now necessary for them to take care of all their own needs in order to throw themselves into their new activities. They therefore decided to make an attack on the employees of the city hall in Barcelona when a transfer of funds was being made. Taking big risks, they caught these employees with their police escort, unprepared at the crossing of Fernando Street and the Ramblas, two steps away from the Bank. They managed to disarm the police and to lay hold of the spoils which the press appraised at 100,000 pesetas[1].

Durruti left immediately afterwards for Madrid where he was to take part in April 1923 in the Anarchist Congress convened by the group "Via Libre"[2]. The trial of Pedro Mateu and Luis Nicolau, both accused of an assault against Eduardo Dato, President of the Council of Ministers, was taking place and Durruti brought a financial contribution for the expenses.

At the same time in Barcelona events were accelerating. "Los Solidarios" had discovered the hiding place of one of the most celebrated of the "pistoleros", Languia, right arm of Sales, the leader of the free unions. They suspected him of having taken a hand in the assassination of Salvador Seguí. Ascaso and García Oliver reached his retreat in Manresa. They found out that Languia never moved without being escorted by three "pistoleros" and that he passed the best part of his time playing cards with them in the back of a bar. Without wasting time, they decided to catch him by surprise, burst into the room, sent a short volley of shots in the direction of the players, and profiting by the effect of surprise, left quickly and took the road to Barcelona. The evening papers already spoke about the assault which had cost his life to "el ciudadano de orden, señor Languia" (the "honorable citizen" Languia).

The death of this famous "pistolero" caused a sensation in the underworld of "pistolerismo" of Barcelona. Sales commanded his killers to shoot down all those who were suspected. The names of García Oliver, Ascaso, Durruti were cited again, as always, on the day following an attack. Thus virtually condemned and pursued, "Los Solidarios", from then on, had to lead a clandestine life, constantly depending on their sixth sense to escape from pitfalls and searches by the "pistoleros". However they were still determined to pursue their plan to exterminate the principal people responsible for the repression.

So as soon as they knew precisely where Martinez Anido and José Regueral were hiding, they moved into action. Ascaso, Torrès Escartin and Aurelio Fernandez, started off towards the hiding place of the first, while Gregorio Suberviela and Antonio "El Toto" went to Leon where Regueral had sought refuge. Martínez Anido was at Ondarreta, the upper class neighborhood of San Sebastian, living in a chalet with two policemen who went with him wherever he went. But every day he went through the tunnel that separates Miracoucha from Ondarreta and he took a long walk on the road which follows the beach of la Concha and ended the evening in the military casino or at the big Kursaal.

Wanting to verify this information, the three anarchists posted themselves in a cafe which overlooked the route. After a while they noticed a shadow which was trying from the outside to identify the customers. Intrigued, Torrès Escartin went out and... found himself face to face with General Anido. Powerless, he permitted Anido to leave, furious that he had left his arms in the hotel. The three went to get their weapons, deciding to kill Anido no matter where they met him, but their search was vain. They were told that the General, perhaps informed of their presence in San Sebastian, had suddenly left the city for La Coruña.

They decided to go there separately. Once there, Ascaso had to find out about the shypment of arms from Galicia to Barcelona. He therefore went toward the port with Aurelio, while Torrès Escartin was making contact with the CNT. They were to meet at noon in a cafe in the center of town. Now while they were wandering around the harbor, Ascaso and Aurelio were stopped and questioned by the police and taken to the police station of the port. They were accused of traficking in drugs. During a severe interrogation they were able to convince the police that their presence around the boats could be explained by their wish to emigrate to America. They were released and they hastened to leave the city.

It was Martínez Anido who had set up this drug trap in order to implicate his persecutors. What was his fury on reaching the police station to interrogate the suspects, to learn that they had been released after their identity had been verified! He informed the commissioner that they were actually two dangerous anarchists who were following him step by step to kill him. And he swore that, because of this unfortunate initiative, the commissioner could consider his career as a policeman finished [3]. The police tried to find them again, searching the

51

hotels, arresting suspects. But they had left La Coruña abondoning their project.

Disappointed, they arrived in Barcelona to find that Durruti had been arrested in Madrid. As we know, he was to have taken part in an anarchist congress. When he arrived in the capital, he found that it had been postponed by eight days. To wait patiently until that date? It was not to be thought of. He went to see Buenacasa to help him with the financing of the trial of two comrades. Buenacasa didn't recognize him: "He was dressed in English style, changing his appearance with thick set glasses". He wanted to visit the prisoners and Buenacasa tried to convince him by every possible means of the folly of this rash expedition. Durruti maintained that his visit would raise the morale of the prisoners. Finally Buenacasa told himself that with Durruti's disguise as a foreigner, the guards would take him for an eccentric tourist [4]. He therefore led his friend to the prison. There, Durruti could only see one of the prisoners, the journalist Mauro Bajatierra [5], in the visiting room. And Durruti was unable to communicate with him because of his deafness. When he left, he decided to take a walk alone in the city. Going along Alcala Street he was seized by a policeman, immediately surrounded and disarmed by others. They took him by car to the central police station. Identified, he was charged with three offences, armed theft from the business man, Mendizabal, in San Sebastian, an attempt on the life of Alfonso XIII and desertion when he had escaped from the military hospital in Burgos. He was imprisoned in San Sebastian where his crimes had been committed.

This arrest was profusely commented on in the Madrid and Barcelona press. The newsmen portrayed Durruti as one of the principal terrorists of Spain, an exceptional individual, consummate "atracador", train robber, born bandit, mentally unbalanced, briefly, a type such as the one described by the criminologist Lombroso in his preposterous study on the anarchists [6].

The imprisonment of Durruti shook the morale of his friends, "Los Solidarios", specially when they learned that Arlegui was on the Security Board of Madrid. They felt that their comrade was lost, the "ley de fuga" could be applied to him anywhere in Spain. But Ascaso didn't permit himself to be flustered. With the lawyer, Rusiñol, he examined closely the legal problems which were posed by the charges. Of the three accusations, the worst was that of armed robbery. There was actually no proof of the plot against the King. As to desertion this could be used to his advantage. It was therefore only necessary to convince Mendizabal that he would commit a "grave error" in recognizing Durruti as one of his attackers.

Francisco Ascaso, Torrès Escartin and the lawyer, went to San Sebastian, taking along the meager resources belonging to the group. They asked for an interview with the financier. The latter informed them that he had made no complaint against a man named Durruti and that he was ready to swear this before the judge. "Declared innocent by Mendizabal, his participation in the attempt on the King put in doubt, and with a good sum of money, the lawyer asked for freedom for his client. The judge granted it. But there was the third offence" [7].

Mug shot of Durruti when he was detained in Madrid in March 1923.

At the end of the visit from his lawyer, who had come to bring him up to date on the steps he had taken, Durruti wrote to his sister, Rosa: "It is already two days since I was to have been freed, but it seems as though someone has become fascinated by the man named Durruti and is holding me for I know not what reason... I am writing at night by the light of a candle, because with the noise made by the ocean waves breaking against the walls of the prison, there is no way to sleep.... I am confident in your good sense to keep our mother from making another trip to San Sebastian, a very tiring trip for her and a hard trial for me to see her through bars. She must have returned worn out. Persuade her that I am in good health and that my release is a matter of days, perhaps hours"[8].

While Durruti was waiting to be let out of prison, in his birthplace at Leon, everyone in their own way was celebrating the Fiesta Mayor, festival of the Patron Saint. The rich were making an even greater display of their power than usual. The poor were spending their savings with substantial meals and various purchases. Once a year, it was an occasion for them to eat well. There had been fireworks in the worker's districts. The wealthiest were to be found in the center of the city for the annual dance at the Casino or for a show at the theater. That year, a drama group had come to Madrid to play "El Rey que rabio" (The King who caught rabies). The first presentation of this work took place on May 17, 1923 before all the notables of the city. Ex-governor Regueral, escorted by the police was present.

For an unknown reason, the latter wanted to leave the theater before the end of the play. This made it an easy job for Gregorio Suberviela and "El Toto" who were on the look-out for him, hidden in the crowd on the square. They saw Regueral appear on the steps,

53

standing for a few moments at the top of the stairs, preceding the two policemen who were with him. No one in the festive square noticed this personage except the two "Solidarios". He started to come down the stairway when two shots rang out which mingled with the fireworks and fire-crackers. Regueral, mortally wounded, rolled to the bottom of the stairs. His bodyguards rushed forward and, incapable of discovering where the shots had come from, stood dazed before the lifeless body of the man who had been so relentless in his hatred of the working class. Profiting by the panic that followed, Suberviela and "El Toto" disappeared in the warm and starry night.

The following day the press reported the facts fully, but in a fantastic way, because nobody really knew what had happened. They incriminated a group of anarchists of Leon, whose main leader, Durruti, was in prison.... Others asserted that the authors of the assassination were already in the hands of the Leon police. In fact, the police, incapable of clearing up the situation, struck out blindly, arresting suspects haphazardly. Among those arrested was Durruti's brother, Santiago. They even wanted to imprison the father of these young people. He was sick in bed and his wife and the neighbors protested effectively. All the friends of Durruti were jailed and among them Vicente Tejerina, secretary of the local committee of the CNT. But after twenty four hours, no proof having been furnished against any of them, they were all released. And the inquest was closed; the crime went unpunished.

Its authors were hidden in a house close to the cathedral. A week later, "like the good peasants of Leon, they left for the fields one morning to find a new refuge in Valladolid"[9]. This affair had spurred the authorities to look more closely into the case of Durruti, and put off his liberation. Escartin and Ascaso who were still waiting in San Sebastian for their friend to come out of prison, decided it was wiser not to prolong their stay in that city, and in agreement with the lawyer, decided that they would all meet again in Saragossa.

However it was not a better refuge for them as the press had published their names as "bandoleros" (bandits). A Catalan Anarchist, Dalmau, offered them his home on the outskirts as a hiding place. They found there the old propagandist, Teresa Claramunt, who was having a rest after a tiring tour in Andalusia. She only knew them by name and received them grudgingly because she disapproved of the violence committed in Saragossa. She told them straight out that she considered them responsible for the "recent death of a strikebreaker and of a security guard, both of them men with families". These actions, she felt, only did harm to the ideals of the working class, who condemned them. If violence must be used, it should be used knowingly against those who practiced it: heads of State, ministers, bishops, but not against unfortunate people like this "blackleg"[10].

The two men listened, stunned, while she uttered her reproaches. When she had calmed down, they assured her that their idea of the use of violence coincided with hers, and little by little a human dialogue was established between them. They questioned her about the situation in Saragossa. It was very similar to the one in Barcelona.

The "pistoleros" who had fled from Barcelona had found refuge here, and under the orders of one of their leaders, Pallas, they were committing violent acts, thefts and even assassinations. The local bourgeois press was ascribing all these misdeeds to the unionists, influencing public opinion, even among informed people like Teresa Claramunt. It was evident, however, that in such an aroused atmosphere the syndicalists were also committing unfortunate mistakes. It was necessary to interfere before the situation deteriorated even more.

With the militants of Saragossa they agreed on the only solution possible. Only a psychological act, would be capable of not only shaking the local set up, but also even the foundations of the State, and could stop this wave of violence which threatened to rot even the sanest and best balanced minds. Now in the city there was one person who exactly symbolized the Machiavellism of the whole situation: the Archbishop-Cardinal Soldevila. It was he who had brought in the "pistoleros" and was protecting them. Everyone spoke about his weekly orgies in a certain religious convent[11]. His execution would be the cleansing social act par excellence. Ascaso and Escartin decided to be responsible for it.

The 4th of June 1923 around 3 P.M., a black car left the Archepiscopal Palace of Saragossa. In the back of the vehicle, separated by a lattice, two clerics, one of forty and the other of eighty, were talking about the health of their relative, the mother of the first and the sister of the second. She was showing signs of mental derangement. Having gone through the center of the capital, the car was moving towards the outskirts and the las Delicias district, towards "el Terminillo" where an estate is located "white, cheerful, surrounded by abundant vegetation, the School-Asylum of San Pablo".

The car slowed down as it reached the doorway. "At this moment, three or four meters away, two men fired their pistols at the occupants of the automobile. It seems there were thirteen bullets. One of them passed through the heart of the Archbishop who died immediately. The aggressors disappeared as if by enchantment and no one was able to furnish an exact description of them or details of the occurrence". The news was broadcast very quickly. By five o'clock in the evening, the King, who thought highly of Cardinal Soldevila, sent a telegram of condolence and sent one of his secretaries to the location of the tragic event to clear up the affair as fast up possible.

The entire press reported the event fully. *El Heraldo de Aragon* headlined "Unusual and abominable assault yesterday: The Cardinal Archbishop of Saragossa, Don Juan Soldevila Romero Assassinated", with a photograph of the victim and long commentaries on his personality. Three pages followed on the facts and the police investigations: "The chief of police has followed the route, supposedly taken by the fleeing assassins. He found a pistol of the type 'Alkar' and the trademark 'Alkarto' of an arms factory in Guernica. Caliber 9. No bullet in the cartridge. The investigators followed their trail across fields to the working class district of Las Delicias. On the way no one could give the slightest information on the route of the assassins". *Acción* of Madrid commented: "This crime reflects clearly the state in which Spain finds itself". And *El Heraldo de Madrid* went into details: "The crime has not been the work of trade unionists but of Anarchists"[12].

All the investigations of the police on the night of the 4th and 5th of June were in vain. However, urged on by the Minister "de Governacion" (Interior), Señor de la Cierva, who was also leader of the conservative party, the Civil Governor of Saragossa, Señor Fernandez Cobos, ordered the chief of police, Señor Fernandez, to increase the investigations. The police directed its search towards the anarchist and Syndicalist milieux, fully determined to imprison suspects and start a case against them. But Victoriano Gracia, then secretary General of the local Federation of Unions of the CNT of Saragossa, warned the Civil Governor that "if a single worker was arrested who was not fully responsible for the coup, it would be the authorities and they alone who would be responsible for what might happen in Saragossa"[13].

Because of the public outcries of the CNT, the Governor was intimidated and subdued by the audacity of the coup. And he gave an order that no arrest should be made without proof and only to draw up a list of suspects. One by one, the prisoners were released: first Santiago Alonso Garcia and José Martínez Magorda, young people of 18 and 17 years of age, arrested en route to Madrid, where they were going to look for work, and after them Silvino Acitores and Daniel Mendoza.

On the 14th of June a notice in *La Vanguardia* of Barcelona stated that the Civil Governor of Saragossa had told the Minister of the Interior that he was preparing a case against an individual who appeared to have been mixed up in the assassination of Soldevila. But the same publication on the 23rd of June, declared that the tribunal which was studying the case of the assassination of Cardinal Soldevila with great care, had come to no conclusion.

It was only from the 28th of June on that the authorities in Madrid decided to find a victim, whether he was the author of the crime or not, and it ordered a general round up. Pestaña and other anarcho-syndicalist leaders were arrested on suspicion of terrorism. The charge rested on a clandestine leaflet circulating in the barracks, which informed the soldiers about the manoeuvers being carried out by their leaders to install a dictatorial regime. They were invited to make common cause with the people.

During the raid on June 28th, the Saragossa police arrested Francisco Ascaso. He was able to prove that at the moment of the attack on the Cardinal, he was in the Predicadores prison visiting some political prisoners, and he even produced witnesses. Nevertheless he was accused of the crime. The national press immediately fastened on the news. The assassin of Soldevila had been arrested and he belonged to the celebrated band of terrorists headed by the famous Durruti.

Together with this news one could read the declarations of the conservative politicians: "In Barcelona daily assaults, 'atracos', are made which remain unpunished and the perpetrators are not found; like the armed robbery at the Tax Collection Bureau or the coup prepared in Bilbao against the lawyer for the blast-furnaces. We must ask the government, as representatives of our country, if they have the means of putting an end to these acts of terrorism"[14].

The pressure of the Church increased against the government authorities as it had in Saragossa and it was decided to round out the dossier by arresting two unknown anarchists, Esteban Salamero Bernard and Juliana López Maimar. The former was not at home when the police came to arrest him. They took away his seventy year old mother as hostage until her son should give himself up. The second, suffering from tuberculosis, was pulled out of her bed where she was lying. Twelve hours later, Esteban Salamero gave himself up to the police in Saragossa announcing that he would rely on justice "from which he had nothing to fear" and demanding the liberation of his mother. Before freeing the latter, they tortured her and then beat her in front of him. He couldn't bear the sight and admitted his complicity in the assassination. The day of the trial, he disclosed publicly how the police had forced his confession. But justice held the assassins Ascaso and Escartin and two accomplices, Salamero and Juliana López[15].

Footnotes

1. Ricardo Sanz, *El sindicalismo y la política*, Toulouse 1967, edited by the author.
2. See the collection of *Cultura y Acción*, Saragossa, 1922-1923.
3. Testimony of Aurelio Fernandez.
4. Notebooks sent to the author by Manuel Buenacasa.
5. The author of a number of novels and plays on class subjects, collaborator in the Anarchist press and magazines, chronicler of the war on the Madrid front (1936-1939) for *Solidaridad Obrera* and *CNT*.. At the end of the war (April 1939), he resisted the police who came to arrest him in his home and died during this struggle at the age of 84.
6. When the Press reported that Durruti had been arrested, the following anecdote was circulated in Madrid. In the suburbs of Madrid a Count and his little girl, who were out driving, were attacked by "bandits". According to the press, one of them was Durruti. The little girl who was four of five years old started crying. Durruti tried to comfort her: "We won't do you any harm, only your father has a lot of money and we have none. We are making a distribution. And tenderly he tried to dry her tears." Told to the author by García Tella, a painter living in exile in Paris.
7. Ricardo Sanz, *op. cit.*
8. Letter from private archives.
9. We don't give the name of this witness as he is in Spain.
10. Facts given the author by a number of militants of the CNT of Saragossa.
11. In *Tiempos Nuevos*, Paris, April 2, 1925. No. 10, a publication of anarchists in exile, there is a biography of Cardinal Soldevila. Later in 1971, an employee of the Municipal Library of Saragossa, who at the time of the assault was employed at the "Registro de la Propriedad" disclosed the following: "After the death of the Cardinal and when his will was read, it was disclosed that he had left a large fortune (estates) to a nun, who, later, left the order. This fact offended many people in the Catholic milieux of Saragossa".
12. *Heraldo de Aragón*, 1923, June 5th and the following days.
13. Manuel Buenacasa, *Cahiers cités*.
14. *La Vanguardia*, Barcelona, same date.
15. *Tiempos Nuevos*, Paris, April 2, 1925.

9

TOWARDS THE DICTATORSHIP OF PRIMO DE RIVERA

IN SARAGOSSA all sorts of pressures were used in order to hand over the possible assassins of Cardinal Soldevila to the bourgeoisie. Meanwhile the man whom everyone pointed out as the central actor in the affair, "the terrible bandit Durruti", was freed from the prison of San Sebastian. Inconsistency of the judicial machinery!

Durruti planned to spend a few days in Leon with his family. But learning about the arrest of Ascaso and his friends, he gave up his plan and headed immediately for Barcelona. The situation was confused there on the social as well as the political level. In the CNT three tendencies opposed each other. Militants were in favor of revolutionary violence, others like Pestaña and Peiro, publicly challenged the responsibility of the CNT in these actions and finally, trained Bolsheviks (Nin, Maurin) had formed revolutionary syndicalist committees working within the CNT unions to divide them.

In politics, even greater confusion. The parties were going through a profound crisis while the influence of the Army was increasing, now openly backed by the Church since the assassination of Soldevila. In the Government, the weak and fainthearted García Prieto was in possession of an explosive dossier on the Moroccan war. It showed clearly with material proofs to back it up, that certain important people and the King himself were responsible for the massacre of Annual, Frightened by the scandal which was brewing, Garcia Prieto hoped for some important event which would force his resignation, his servility hindering him from openly attacking the King.

Actually, Alfonso XIII was intriguing to overthrow the Government in office in order to replace it with a dictatorship of the Mussolini variety. He had called on General Primo de Rivera and they were working together to establish this kind of regime, alleging that urgent measures were needed to fight against "workers' banditry".

Their manoeuvers were made easy by serious dissension in the Cabinet. The Minister of the Navy, Silvela, was trying to put an end to the war in Morocco. He had sent General Castro Gerona to negotiate with Dris Ben Saïd, delegate of Abd El-Krim. Now, the Minister of War, Alcala Zamora, backed by groups who profited by the continuation of conflict, didn't want an armistice. A violent struggle brought the two men in opposition, and when Zamora learned about the steps taken by Silvela and General Castro Gerona, he demanded the resignation of the former. His successor sent General Martínez Anido to Melilla, who cut short the "pacifist" manoeuvers of his predecessor through the assassination of Dris Ben Saïd. The way was clear for Alfonso XIII and Primo de Rivera.

All these problems were discussed during the meeting organized by "Los Solidarios" when Durruti arrived in Barcelona. Captain Sancho, who served as liaison with the Barcelona barracks, was present. Sancho informed them that in the officers' meeting rooms, a military coup d'état led by General Primo de Rivera was being talked about openly. And not much resistance could be expected among the military since most of the soldiers had had no political education. The antimilitarist committees had just been established in the army and several had already been discovered because surveillance had increased in the barracks. There was still some hope that there would be some kind of protest by the mass of workers, forcing a confrontation with the troops in the streets. They could discount any fraternization of soldiers with the people, such as had occured when a few companies had made common cause with the rebels.

So there was nothing left to do but to prepare a revolutionary strike. To carry this out the workers' organizations had to be rebuilt by agreement between the anarchist groups and the organizations of the CNT, as they had been disorganized by the various waves of terror launched by the bourgeoisie and the Government. But once again financial means and arms were lacking to undertake such a large scale action. All the groups had exhausted their reserves[1]. So it was decided to attack a bank in Gijón, and Torrès Escartin and Buenaventura Durruti were assigned to make preparations for this action.

Under a ferocious sun, favorable to fires in the wheat fields, a train was moving across the Aragonese plain, carrying Durruti and Torres Escartin towards Saragossa, where they were to stop off before Gijón. Through the window, Durruti was looking at the parched Aragonese countryside, white with dust. A few years later, on this same earth, he would march through village after village, at the head of a powerful revolutionary army, as conqueror of the bourgeoisie and the reaction.

He was thinking of Ascaso still in prison in Saragossa. He was thinking about the struggle they had carried on together. He recalled many ups and downs, such as the day in Barcelona when death lay in wait for them at every corner of the street. They had come out of the little underground print shop where *Crisol* was published in the old district of Santa-Catalina, when they saw that a number of "pistoleros" were following them, they themselves were not armed.... Mastering their fear, they had tried to surprise their pursuers by an abrupt about face. The manoeuver was successful, the "pistoleros" slipped away throwing themselves into the hallways of neighboring houses, while they took advantage of this, taking to their heels to save themselves. And Ascaso had spoken about "the shock that we gave them and the fear that we felt..."[2].

Durruti and Escartin stayed in Saragossa only long enough to reassure themselves about the fate of Ascaso and his comrades in prison. The Secretary General of the CNT was optimistic and told them: "The bourgeoisie will not have the pleasure of seeing Ascaso hung"[3]. So they resumed their trip towards the North. In Bilbao they bought long arms (rifles). As soon as they arrived in Gijón, they started methodically studying their plan of attack on the branch office of the Bank of Spain, undisturbed since no one knew them.

Meanwhile, Alfonso XIII's plans for a dictatorship were taking shape in an alarming way while the so-called political opposition didn't appear to be worried. The only organization that was stiring was the CNT. Garcia Oliver, in the name of the anarchist groups, had discussed the possibility of launching a general strike with the National Committee of the CNT. But the prospects of succeeding were problematical. The militant cadres of the CNT had been decimated and some of the unions had only a symbolic existence. Years of repression had resulted in the disorganization of the workers' movement. Pestaña remarked to García Oliver: "The Revolution is an activity which requires an organization. Only a very small amount of spontaneity is involved. To succeed, ninety percent must be organization and we are far from having fifty percent." They also talked about the confusion caused by Bolshevism, which in certain areas, such as in Sabadell, had managed to disorient the militants completely. A great deal of energy which should have been used to fight for the working class had been wasted in bitter polemics among comrades.

On the other hand, the UGT appeared to show no interest in testing the strength of the proletariat confronting a military coup. Pestaña had questioned members of this organization and had accepted the evidence: the CNT would find itself completely alone facing the dictatorship. "Nevertheless", Pestaña concluded, "since the military revolution is directed against the authentic revolutionary forces of the country and since these are sheltered under the acronym of the CNT, anarcho-syndicalism will be a credit to the revolutionary tradition now, as it always has been"[4]. The anarchist groups, and specially "Los Solidarios" understood that the decisive hour had come and redoubled their activities during the last days of August 1923.

From Gijón, Durruti and Torrès Escartin asked that all available men come to lend them a hand. It was important that the attack on the bank be successful. A group of anarchists had signed a contract with a Mr. Zulueta, who served as intermediary between them and Garate y Anitua, makers of arms at Eibar. An important supply of arms was waiting for them for cash.

At noon on the first of September, a number of men burst into the bank, pistols in hand, and ordered all the assistants to throw themselves on the floor. While the employees and the public were kept in check, they had the safe opened and the contents handed over to them, about 650,000 pesetas. Two of them quickly dove into a car taking the money along with them. The others stayed a moment to cover their retreat. But just as they planned to leave, they ran into the Guardia Civil, which had been alerted by a neighbor. They faced the Guardia trying to protect the flight of those who had taken the booty. They broke up into two groups and exchanged fire with the police.

Suddenly someone called out, "the big one, the big one, it's Durruti!" These cries paralyzed the fighters for a moment, then the shooting started again harder than ever, the Guardia Civil concentrating its shots on Durruti. This permitted the others to escape. Some found shelter in corners and from there shot at the police to try and rescue Durruti from his awkward position. He was able to make his way to the upper floors of the building while the Guardia Civil, under fire from the attackers began to retreat. The crowd started to cry out that a man was escaping on the rooftops. Durruti took advantage of the diversion to jump into a neighboring house, to leave the city and get lost in the mountains. After a thousand difficulties, he was able to reach Barcelona and find Gregorio Suberviela, who had also been able to escape. Torrès Escartin and Eusebio Brau were unable to elude their pursuers and had to confront them the following day near Oviedo[5].

The Guardia Civil had lost several men during this action. And spurred on by the loss of the large sum which had been stolen, it mobilized itself throughout the region. Once the traces of Escartin and Brau were discovered, they were encircled. They resisted for several hours. Finally, short of ammunition, they tried to seize the weapons of the police who had been shot down nearby. But Brau was killed and Torres Escartin was knocked down by the butts of guns. He remained in the hands of the Guardia Civil for several hours, which was enough to destroy him physically. They took him to the prison at Oviedo, in a pitiable state with no more medical help than the care improvised by his comrades in prison.

The Press picked up this story, and since Durruti was also spoken about, they linked him with the assassination of Cardinal Soldevila. The law in Saragossa did the same. In a few days it prepared the case of Torrès Escartin, attributing the crime and the hold up to him. The transfer of the prisoner to the city was being prepared when some of his prison comrades asked him to join them in a plan to escape. He hadn't recovered enough for such an adventure, but since a certain death awaited him, he was roused and decided to take a chance. He turned his ankle while jumping from a wall and was unable to move as he had not yet recovered from the police tortures. He convinced his comrades to abandon him to his fate. He tried to go on, leaning against the walls. His strength left him just at the foot of the stairs of a church where he collapsed. A priest coming out found the suspect and alerted the police. Taken back to prison, he remained there after the scandalous trial of March 1925 until the 14th of April 1931, the date when he had to be committed to an insane asylum [6].

The attack on the bank had been exploited by the bourgeois press. It went on at great length about "Durruti's celebrated gang". The papers in Leon featured the photo of Durruti (familiarly called Pepe), with a long list of his misdeeds. They went so far as to say that he was able to escape thanks to a priestly disguise and that for this he had attacked a priest in a church, obliging him to hand over his cassock by menacing him with his revolver [7].

It was the main subject of conversation in the Santa Ana district. Anastasia, Durruti's old mother, became the most famous woman in

Leon. More than once she had to argue against the accusations brought against her son. To those who said that her Pepe stole and was a bandit, she answered: "I don't know if my son handles millions. The only thing I am sure of is that each time he comes to Leon, I have had to clothe him from head to foot and pay for his return trip" [8].

All of Spain was heedlessly commenting on these events while it was moving rapidly towards a show of force between the people and their executioners. Time was not working in favor of the "Solidarios" who hoped to have the arms they had bought in hand before the coup d'état. Thanks to the baseness of the politicians, the plans of Alfonso XIII were developing without any hitches and even with such ease that the King thought of proclaiming himself dictator. Maura dissuaded him. He therefore put the last touches to the plans for a coup d'état during an interview with Primo de Rivera on September 7, 1923. They set the 15th of September as the date for the putsch. But various reasons forced them to advance the coup d'état by one day. On the one hand, General Sanjurjo, military Governor of Saragossa, asked that the execution of the plans be speeded up. On the other hand, the commission named by the Cortes to draw up a dossier about the responsibilities in the Moroccan War, was to publish its findings on the 19th of September and it was necessary to avoid damaging the prestige of the King.

The 13th of September at two in the morning, Primo de Rivera published a "Manifesto to the Country" announcing that a military directory was taking the situation in hand. This was a movement of *men* (machos males). Whoever was not sure of his virility should refrain from taking part so as not to interfere with the proper course of events under the guidance of the new leaders. The plan was justified for reasons of safety; it was no longer possible to watch with arms crossed the assassination of prelates, ex-governors, chiefs of police, etc. For a better administration of the country, political parties were not necessary. In conclusion, it was time for the bourgeoisie to react and organize itself into militias, auxiliary to the Army.

Learning about this proclamation, the working class was inflamed but its indignation was not transformed into violent acts opposing the fascist move. The coup d'état took place entirely at the palace level; nothing was visible in the streets.

Before leaving for his summer holiday in San Sebastian, Alfonso XIII had left orders with one of his trusted men that, as soon as the coup d'état was proclaimed, the Chamber of Deputies should be taken over and he should seize the dossier "on responsibilities". In Madrid the Government convened a Council of Ministers, allowing the rebel generals to occupy the active nerve centers, while discussing how to paralyze the uprising. Convened in a permanent Council, the Government published an announcement promising to carry out its duty and to remain at its post. It would only abandon this duty if faced with force and if the architects of sedition decided to assume all the consequences of their acts. It announced that His Majesty the King was to return to Madrid that same day.

And in fact the King came. At the station, the Government in full force, came to receive him. The Prime Minister, García Prieto, proposed that the King dismiss Primo de Rivera. In reply the King told him to consider himself dismissed. Having arrived at the Palace, Alfonso XIII sent a telegram to the future dictator, telling him that, anxious to avoid bloodshed he was handing over the power to him in person.

On September 14th, the CNT called for a general strike and in its turn published a manifesto: "In this hour when cowardice is the rule and when civil power without a struggle has turned over power to the military, it is up to the working class to make its presence felt. And it must not allow itself to be trampled on by men who, infringing all forms of the Law, wish to reduce to zero all the rights won by the working class after long and difficult struggles".

But the national committee of the CNT had no illusions about the effectiveness of this antifascist counter-thrust. It knew that the CNT was too isolated and disorganized to offer real resistance. And what should have been a unanimous counter-thrust of the working class was reduced to a few sporadic actions which, though really heroic, did not manage to rouse the masses.

The UGT and the Socialist Party, which formed part of the Government in office, published a discouraging statement favoring the Government and signed by the head of the party and Pablo Iglesias, its secretary. Ignoring the CNT manifesto, it simply recommended not to "support the uprising". And the following day another notice simply stated that they accepted the dictatorship and alerted the people "against the sterile movements which could justify repression". It repudiated "any committee which took initiatives on its own" [9].

The strike failed. The CNT and the Anarchist groups had no other choice but to go underground. "Los Solidarios" began by hiding in a safe place the arms bought in Eibar and which they had not yet picked up. Durruti was commissioned to organize a Committee for Revolutionary Coordination in France.

While the CNT and the anarchist groups were setting up their clandestine organization, the military leadership was forming its government. Primo de Rivera limited himself to changing the names of the ministries and placing all his own men in these positions. General Martínez Anido became Under Secretary of the Interior (Gobernacion) and he promoted Lieutenant Colonel Arlegui to General and named him Director-General of Security. But these window dressing changes didn't satisfy him. He wanted the backing of the working class. Following Mussolini's example, he created a single party, the Patriotic Union, formed of groups, the "Somaten", faithful copies of the "Black Squadrons" (Escuadras Negras). But all the dictator's efforts to win over the people ran into apathy.

The dictatorship appeared clearly like a colossus with feet of clay. By suppressing the liberal constitution, by shutting down the Cortes, by declaring political parties and workers' organizations illegal, it thought it could wipe out the revolutionary tradition of the Spanish proletariat.

After the last semi-legal meetings of December 30, 1923 and of May 24, 1924, the CNT dismantled itself and went into hiding [10]. The UGT agreed to submit to the humiliating conditions under the dictator and actually collaborated with him. But this political behavior was fatal to it. Its most active members went into hiding and joined in the work of the anarchist groups. Groups of young Catalonians also joined them. The dictatorship had succeeded in "filing down the roughness and even what may be called neighborly antagonisms between Catalanism and syndicalism". The diverse revolutionary groups were brought together by common objectives to form a united front. A climate of confidence and solidarity was created among all these elements. To coordinate the struggle, a Revolutionary Committee was formed where all tendencies were represented. "Los Solidarios" played an important role in the formation of this committee, explaining to everyone that a climate of mutual confidence is the essential condition for revolutionary organization. Not content with being the creative spirits of the committee, they offered it the revolutionary machinery of their group[11].

"Los Solidarios" were also making a plan for Francisco Ascaso and Torrès Escartin to escape. García Vivancos was preparing Escartin's flight from his prison in Oviedo by gaining the confidence of the soldiers who were guarding the prisoners. He had succeeded in rallying them to the cause and was assured of their help with the plans for escape when the soldiers changed garrison. He tried to take up his psychological warfare again with the new guards but he was suspected and imprisoned. He was able to prove that he had a job as a commercial agent for an important Catalan textile establishment but decided it was wiser not to prolong his stay in Oviedo. When he returned to Barcelona, he gave a report about his unsuccessful mission although he had shown himself to be talented in organization. He was told that Francisco Ascaso had been able to escape [12].

In Barcelona the situation of the "Solidarios" had gotten worse. Martiínez Anido had a personal account to settle with "Durruti's gang" and he sent a special police team to locate Durruti and Ascaso. The group was quickly informed and they decided to send the two anarchists into exile, instructing them to organize a revolutionary sub-committee in France which would help the group in Barcelona with its subversive activities. It was also to found a publishing house in France. To carry out these activities an important sum of money was entrusted to them, the remains of the booty from Gijón.

Footnotes

1. Ricardo Sanz: *El Sindicalismo y la Politica.*
2. Anecdote reported by Rudolf Rocker, *op. cit.*
3. Buenacasa, *Cahiers cités.*
4. Aurelio Fernandez, testimony already quoted.
5. Ricardo Sanz, *op. cit.* And other witnesses questioned by the author.
6. When the troops of General Franco occupied Barcelona, January 26, 1939, Torrès Escartin was taken out of the asylum where he was and shot.
7. It was also said that he had hidden himself in the house of the Commander of the Guardia Civil of Léon, where one of his aunts who was working as a cook, had hidden him... And in Burgos, he had bought the clothes of a juggler with his monkeys. Disguised in this way he had been able to escape from the police.
8. Anecdote related by Liberto Calleja. It is also to be found in an article in *Solidaridad Obrera* of Paris, No. 4, 1944.
9. M. Buenacasa, *op. cit.* (See also, Tuñón de Lara in *La España en el Siglo XX*).
10. Buenacasa in the work quoted gives excellent information about these plenums of the CNT.
11. Testimony of Aurelio Fernandez and Ricardo Sanz, *op. cit.*
12. Ascaso's flight was organized by Manuel Buenacasa, who was secretary of the CNT in Aragón at that time.

EXILE IN PARIS AND GUERRILLA IN THE PYRENEES

IN DECEMBER 1923 the central headquarters of French anarchism were located in Paris at number 14 rue Petit in the 19th arrondissement (not far from the metro Laumière and the rue Crimée). In a small shop window publications were displayed, among them *Le Libertaire,* organ of the French Anarchist Union. The interior looked like a simple bookstore where, however, a number of individuals were to be found talking excitedly. The shop in the rear sheltered not only the administration and the editorial staff of the weekly, but was also a center for connections with the various groups of the Union and with the federations of other countries.

It was here that Ascaso and Durruti went to establish necessary connections with the French militants and to create with them the International Anarchist Publication. They were received sceptically and all their projects were opposed because money was lacking. Durruti told them then that the Spanish anarchists came to cooperate with a contribution of a half million, which he placed on the table. Immediately everybody agreed to name an International Commission for management, administration and publication[1].

Durruti and Ascaso then began to study how anarchism appeared in exile. The Spanish element predominated, followed by the Italian. The Spaniards were mostly scattered in the south of France. Some of them were resigned and were waiting passively for better days. Others, impatient, wanted to throw themselves into the struggle. The latter enlivened the weekly *Liberion* and the leaders were young people like Liberto Calleja, who was also in exile. Durruti and Ascaso got in touch with them to form a Committee of Coordination. Their comrades, still in Barcelona, reminded them, in a letter received when they arrived in Paris, that there was an urgent need for the Committee[2]. But it moved slowly and the funds reserved for its use were rapidly exhausted. So Durruti and Ascaso started to look for a way to earn their living. The former became a machinist in the Renault workshops, the latter, a laborer in a lead factory. They took a room on rue Belleville. At this time Paris was a center of disorganized political activity: various tendencies of the workers' movement were thrown together, each one struggling fiercely to monopolize the leadership of the working class, guided mainly by the CGT.

The leadership of reformist Socialism (Social Democrat), despite the disrepute of the Socialist Party and its men, was still very influential in the CGT. But soon a violent polemic broke out with the leadership of the new Communist Party, whose leading officials (former Socialists and anarcho-syndicalists) advised the workers to strike against paying union dues in order to cut the supplies of the Socialist-Syndicalist bureaucratic apparatus.

Militant anarchism had been subdued by the blows received from the Russian revolution. It had drawn back on itself, keeping on the defensive while at the same time denouncing the bureaucratic character of the Bolshevik dictatorship. Its theoretical analysis, although conveying profound truths, didn't manage to penetrate to the masses. Nor could it disarm the anarcho-syndicalists who had been won over by Bolshevism and conquered by the prestige of the Russian Revolution and the brilliant personalities of Lenin and Trotsky.

For Durruti and Ascaso the Russian experience was full of lessons. In their opinion every conscientious revolutionary owed it to himself to analyze the problem of the revolution in the light of this experience: its economic organization, its political direction, the Bolshevik solutions adopted by it in various areas. This critical examination always ended in an impasse: was revolution always fated to die in the hands of Bonapartism and bureaucracy?

Some anarchists ended by advising that their action be limited to educational work for a continuing critical opposition. Durruti and Ascaso, more men of action than theoreticians, full of enthusiasm and overflowing with energy, didn't share this point of view. They didn't believe in the inevitable death of the revolution. And they thought that the historical failure of the Russian Revolution was due, not to a lack of revolutionary practice by the masses, but to the monopoly of power that the Bolsheviks had imposed on the proletariat. This corruption, they believed, was avoidable in a revolution which was active at all levels, which would awaken a sense of responsibility in the working class.

The job of the revolutionary for Durruti was not only to set in motion a violent revolt, arms in hand, but specially to nurture the revolution constantly. Thanks to the practice of direct participation, the working class would develop from within, its own theory of the revolution. And when the moment for collective action came, this conscience developed and completely unbridled, would start to reconstruct society free of preconceived schemes. He thought of this new society as a hive where each individual would be an active cell and where a contagious enthusiasm would push endlessly forward[3].

Meanwhile, if the organizational work in Paris was barely moving, in Spain things were going from bad to worse. Martinez Anido had vowed to break up the "Solidarios" group. A network of spies kept him very well informed about the politico-social situation in Barcelona. His first success was the seizure of arms belonging to the group, in a cache in the Pueblo Seco district of Barcelona. Suspecting the presence of an informer among their neighbors, the "Solidarios" hastened to move. But the net tightened around them again and on March 24, 1924, the police surrounded the houses of Gregorio Suberviela, Marcelino del Campo, Aurelio Fernandez, Gre-

66

gorio Jover and Domingo Ascaso. The first tried to escape and managed to get as far as the street, but there he fell under the bullets of the police, lying in ambush at every corner. In the home of Marcelino del Campo, the police, in disguise, had presented themselves as "comrades" who were being pursued. He pretended to believe them and offered to lead them to "a safe place", hoping to get rid of them en route. But once outside he too was surrounded. He tried to break away, mortally wounding several of the policemen escorting him, but outnumbered, he succumbed, and was also killed. At Aurelio Fernandez's place, the surprise was so effective that neither he, nor his brother Ceferino, nor Adolfo Ballano, had time to use their weapons; they were led off to prison. The same scenario for Gregorio Jover, but the latter, taking advantage of a moment of carelessness by the guards, jumped through a window and escaped. As for Domingo Ascaso, he began by holding back the police, who had come to catch him by surprise and then was able to escape by sliding down a rope from the fourth floor where he lived.

The next day in the papers, the police congratulated itself on having, at last, thanks to its own efforts, annihilated Durruti's terrible band "and thus the public will be persuaded that crime is always punished and the authorities always end up by restoring order".

Martínez Anido knew however that his success wasn't complete. Actually a number of the "Solidarios" had escaped from the raid, and without being intimidated, they began to reconstitute the Revolutionary Committee, with Ricardo Sanz and Alfonso Miguel, and to place militants in the positions which had been left empty.

Domingo Ascaso had found refuge with friends, but not wanting to compromise anyone, he had to change his hiding place often. He ended by finding refuge in the cemetery of Pueblo Nuevo, as he knew the night watchman, an old Aragonese. After several days he was able to make contact with García Oliver. It was decided that it would be better for him to go to France to help Durruti and his brother, Francisco, to create the revolutionary organization.

At about the same time, the Catalan politician, Francisco Macia, was trying to organize a guerrilla operation from the Catalan Pyrenees for a revolutionary uprising in Catalonia. He was supported in Barcelona by a group founded in 1922 called "Estat Catala" (Catalan State), formed by young active elements, who wanted to make contact with the anarchist groups. As the dictatorship stiffened, the bonds between these two groups became closer and closer, to such a point that the Catalan separatist group entered the revolutionary committee founded by the anarchists. It was the first time that the Catalanists and anarchists had decided to take action together.

The plan for a revolutionary uprising in Catalonia was discussed by the anarchist groups and by the local CNT. It was decided to send Buenacasa to France in order to study directly with Colonel Francisco Macia the plans for an uprising. The interview took place at Font-Romeu, without positive results[4]. So the CNT and the anarchists decided to carry on by themselves their own plans for guerrilla organization with two centers for invasion, one situated in the Pyrenees Orientales and the other in the Basque region.

Arriving in France, Domingo Ascaso brought instructions from

Barcelona to coordinate this action, either with or without Macia. He discussed everything with his brother and Durruti. This revolutionary plan revived the enthusiasm of the two exiles. Again they started intense organizational activities among the groups of Spanish emigres.

In Barcelona the revolutionary plan also received a favorable response. Steps were taken to get hold of the weapons bought at Eibar, which were still waiting for someone to transfer them. Zulueta received the order to ship them as if they were going to Mexico which he did. But once on the high seas, a small merchant ship paid for by the Revolutionary Committee, took them on board and headed for Barcelona, where they remained in storage. At this time, Macia was secretly in the city. The Committee asked him where his plans for revolution stood. His answer was still evasive and he suggested that the arms be kept in the port, waiting for the conspiracy to come to a head (5). But in the meantime the legal time for the deposit of goods having elapsed, the cargo was sent back to the sender (6). And this was why the uprising which broke out several months later, lost its principal trump card.

During this time the public life of the CNT came to an end with the National Congress of May 4, 1924. The National Committee took part in full force; 237 delegates came directly from the Catalan unions and numerous delegations from other regions. The most important subject of discussion was still the question of the Third International. Several militants already won over to Bolshevism — like Maurin — clung to the idea of keeping the question open, despite the conclusion of the Congress of Saragossa and the referendum in which the majority of the unions considered it settled. The discussion came to the same conclusions as before that the CNT had as its objective the introduction of libertarian communism via armed insurrection. The agreement was ratified by 236 votes against one. The dissenter was the delegate from the unions of Sabadell, Moix, who wanted a neutral syndicalism. The Congress ended dramatically as the police had surrounded the meeting hall. Fortunately most of the participants were able to escape but García Oliver was arrested, condemned to prison, incarcerated at Burgos, where he remained until the amnesty of April 14, 1931.

From then on, the CNT went underground. The dictatorial government, alleging that this organization had not submmitted to the new social legislation, in contrast to the UGT, tracked down all the confederal committees and forbade the publication of the syndicalist press. And so the CNT and the anarchist movement were forced to adopt a change of tactics and this, for six long years. First a secret Congress was convened which voted for the implementation of a subversive plan. The anarchist groups, leaning on the anti-militarist committees, were to attack the barracks, while simultaneously an attack would take place from two distant points on the Pyrenees front. The Congress instructed Gregorio Jover to go to France to inform the Revolutionary Committee in France about their decisions in order to have all activities well coordinated.

When Gregorio Jover arrived in Paris at the end of July 1924, he met the militant exiles at a small meeting. He told them about the situation in Spain and the decisions of the Congress of Barcelona. All those who took part agreed unanimously to join the armed insurrection. Durruti and Ascaso started preparing actively for what they took to be the beginning of a general uprising. For weapons, everyone joining a patrol, agreed to pay for his own arms and ammunition. To defray other expenses the group "Germen" (Seed), which published *Iberion* (which had taken over from *Liberion* suspended by the French police) made an appeal and the proceeds largely helped cover their needs. A Belgian arms dealer was found who sold them a collection of guns for thirty francs apiece with a supply of 100 cartridges per weapon[7].

Towards the end of September, a general plan of attack from two points on the frontier had been agreed on: one important one in the Catalan Pyrennes, the other simply as a point of diversion of the enemy at Vera de Bidasoa, in the Basque Navarese Pyrenees. But during this time, things were becoming complicated in Barcelona. The soldiers who had agreed to cooperate in the uprising, were starting to hesitate. Also it hadn't been possible to take possession of the arms stored in the Barcelona port. Finally, they were not at all sure of massive support from the working class. The militants were actually only counting on their own revolutionary enthusiasm. They believed that in spite of all the difficulties, they could carry through the original plan. Gregorio Jover crossed the frontier to advise the exiled groups and to act as liaison between the two countries. The day and the hour of the attack was to be announced from Barcelona through two telegrams. The first was to alert them and the second to indicate the beginning of operations.

In Paris the atmosphere was not very animated. Durruti tried to inspire the rebels with enthusiasm in a speech glowing with revolutionary faith: "The revolution is a continuing activity with ups and downs. It contains unforeseen factors, which actually decide its fate and these unknowns must be taken into account in a strategic plan. While the conditions required for a revolution lie hidden, an audacious act suffices to spread and set fire to collective action. How is it possible to know ahead of time when man has reached the limits of his patience? What wise man is capable of fixing the propitious hour and day for the revolution? There is no rule to go by. A serious study of the situation must be made and then a good dose of subjectivity is needed to interpret it. Actually the revolutionary beginning is almost always an adventurous and audacious way of trying out the masses. It is possible that we may be mistaken, that we may be beaten in this battle. This defeat will not be definitive, it will be one more chapter in the history of the proletariat. As conscientious revolutionaries, our mission is to act as fuses, once, twice, twenty times if necessary, until the collective explosion, the only one which can make the revolution a continuing activity, prolonged to its only real end, a total change in the way men live". This speech was decisive and more or less eagerly, everyone headed for the strategic positions[8].

A few days later, the morale of this group was rekindled by a wave of revolt among the intellectuals. Miguel de Unamuno and Rodrigo Soriano arrived in Paris after a fabulous escape from the island of Fuenteventura (Canaries) where they had been confined by the dictatorship. The independent intelligentsia of France received the escapees with enthusiasm and the editor of the paper *Le Quotidien* offered them the columns of his publication to state their case against the dictatorship. They also received the support of Eduardo Ortega y Gasset. Finally, the novelist, Blasco Ibañez, came out of his seclusion to write a brochure, *España, Nación Secuestrada,* which caused a great stir not only because of the personality of the author but also because of the facts it revealed. The Spanish authorities hastened to send a protest to the French Government, through the Ambassador Quiñones de León, "for its toleration of propaganda injurious to the good name of a friendly nation"[9]. Since Spain had thus been placed in the limelight of international politics, the beginning of guerrilla warfare would seem to be more like a virile answer to the dictatorship of Primo de Rivera and Alfonso XIII.

At last the telegram, which had been awaited for such a long time, arrived. But it was not the text agreed on. Actually it was not the first telegram which was only to have been a warning, but the second one giving the order to attack. First mix-up. The Revolutionary Committee in Paris quickly telegraphed to the different groups so that they should go to the operational sites. The Ascasos left for Perpignan and Durruti for Vera de Bidasoa. As soon as they arrived, they put into action the guerrilla techniques which had been agreed on. But they didn't realize that, not only had the attempt failed in Barcelona, but also that the Government alerted, had mobilized troops to guard the frontier[10]. So as soon as the groups at Vera de Bidasoa had crossed the frontier, they ran into strong resistance from the Guardia Civil. The guerrilleros managed to kill two policemen and to rout the rest, which encouraged them to carry forward their gains to a place easier to transform into a stronghold for resistance. When they reached this place, they were greeted with an intensive volley of shots. Two guerrilleros fell, dead. The others, surprised, separated into two groups. Those who were ahead, tried by attacking quickly to break through the circle which had trapped them. They managed to make a breach and to escape into the mountains where they were better able to defend themselves. But the second group, which was larger, could no longer advance and the attacking circle closed back on it, cutting off all retreat towards France. Durruti was in this group. Seeing that the situation was desperate, he understood that it was necessary to risk everything and he attempted on his side a strenuous breakthrough. The manoeuver succeeded and the second group was now able to escape and even managed to recross the frontier. But the guerrilleros of the first group, encircled again while retreating, succumbed outnumbered after two days of resistance. All of them were killed or made prisoners.

Things turned out less tragically for the Ascaso brothers and their groups, but the defeat was more depressing. While they were still on French soil, they ran into an increasingly suspicious local police which had been alerted. Many of the guerrilleros were arrested leaving the train at Perpignan. Only about fifty of them including the Ascasos, were able to elude the police and reach the place where they had planned to enter Spain. They were all discouraged by the news brought by the guide Marti. The attempt in Barcelona had failed, the Catalan frontier was guarded by the Army which occupied all the bordering villages, and as a measure of precaution, many workers had been arrested. Under these conditions the guerrilla project was suicidal. One of the participants was to comment: "Weeping with rage and impotence for having been beaten without fighting, we had to go back to our starting place. However one thought sustained us, we had been pushed back but not vanquished. This was perhaps not our last defeat but in the end we would conquer"[11].

However these apparent defeats in the field had very important political repercussions, as they aroused the higher ups in Madrid. The dictatorship approached the French Government to bring about the destruction of the exiled groups in France. Moreover at the suggestion of Martínez Anido, a group of agents were sent to France and instructed to poison the emigre milieu by spreading rumors casting doubt on the revolutionary integrity of the most celebrated militants. But this manoeuver had little success, the agents were quickly exposed.

Primo de Rivera's requests to the French Government were more dangerous, as actually at that time, the latter had an unresolved problem about Morocco vis-a-vis the Spanish Government. The plans of Primo de Rivera and Marshall Petain coincided for the settlement of the conflict. And to prove their good will, the French responded eagerly to the Spanish advances. The Spanish Ambassador, Quiñones de Leon, paid a huge price for a campaign of denunciation against the Spanish emigres, especially Ascaso and Durruti, both accused of having assassinated the prelate of Saragossa. The bourgeois and reactionary press conducted this campaign, adopting the arguments supplied by the Ambassador. The police began to use a heavy hand and many exiles were arrested and deported. The majority left for Brussels to join the International Committee of Anarchist Solidarity, whose leaders were the Belgians. Hem Day and Leo Campion. This organization either arranged to settle them in Belgium or to send them to South America with the port workers of Antwerp acting as go-betweens.

For Ascaso and Durruti, Belgium did not offer strong enough guarantees and they couldn't think of emigrating to America without knowing about the new plans for action being decided on in Barcelona. While waiting, they stayed hidden in St. Denis, a suburb of Paris, in a small house, placed at their disposal by some French Anarchists. After waiting a month, an emissary, Ricardo Sanz, who had replaced Gregorio Suberviela, came to bring them news from Spain. He reported that the repression continued worse than ever and the prisons were full of militants, while money was getting scarce. However the struggle was going on and new groups were joining the movement, attracted by the revolutionary dynamism of the Anarchists. One of these groups came from the Catalan movement and the young people who led it had decided to organize an attempt against the life of Alfonso XIII. The revolutionary committee had given them money, arms and explosives [12].

Ricardo Sanz also brought them suggestions from the Committee in Barcelona for getting financial support. They could start a propaganda and agitation campaign among the Spaniards living in South America. They started then to get ready for the *American excursion*. First they would go to Cuba, then to Mexico where they would form a group with the youngest of the Ascasos, Alejandro, and Gregorio Jover, who would be brought over from Spain. Domingo Ascaso would settle in Antwerp to ensure contact with them thanks to a network of sailors organized from this port to Montevideo. Towards the end of December 1924, provided with false passports, Ascaso and Durruti embarked at Le Havre on a Dutch cargo boat for the Antilles[13].

Footnotes

1. *Le Reveil* of Geneva, June 18, 1924, reports the creation of this International Anarchist Edition.
2. Testimony of Liberto Calleja.
3. Idem.
4. Manuel Buenacasa, *op. cit.*
5. Ricardo Sanz, *op. cit.*
6. When the IInd Republic was proclaimed, Durruti and Ascaso returned to Spain. The latter tried to retrieve these arms, but in the meantime, Miguel Maura had turned them over to the "Delegación de Orden Público" of the new autonomous government of Catalonia. It was with these arms that Dencás, Counsellor of Public Order in Catalonia, armed the members of "Estat Catala" in October 1934. But the revolt failed; the arms were abandoned in the streets and the workers of the CNT picked them up. The 19th of July 1936, they were used to fight the military insurgents. And Aurelio Fernandez concluded: "In this way, at last, they were used for the purpose for which they had been bought".
7. Information supplied by García Vivancos.
8. Testimony of Liberto Calleja.
9. V. Orobon Fernández, *op. cit.*
10. Idem.
11. Idem.
12. This attack took place on June 3, 1925. The police discovered a bomb weighing some 176 pounds on the railroad track near Costas de Garra (Barcelona). This was supposed to explode on Alfonso XIII's return trip from Barcelona. The attack was attributed to the young Catalanists, Miguel Badía and Jaime Compte.
13. Ricardo Sanz and Orobon Fernandez, *op. cit.*

GUERRILLEROS IN SOUTH AMERICA

DURRUTI AND ASCASO were only going to make a short stopover in Cuba on their way to Argentina, where the anarchist movement was going through a hard struggle against Capital and the State. But the workers who took them in, gave them such a picture of the social situation in the island that they decided to stay for a while. Gerardo Machado, who was dictator at the time, had established a fictitious pacification program which depended strictly on the domination of American big business and the landowners. A superficial and misleading opulence in Havana hid the harsh reality of misery and corruption. The police were unrestrained and high handed, and violently checked the frequent tensions among the exploited working classes. Popular revolt rumbled secretly.

Nevertheless the Cuban anarchists advocated a strategy of long and patient uninterrupted work without upsets, the only way, in their view, towards the social revolution. They reproached Ascaso and Durruti for "their activist impatience". and told them "Your undertaking is condemned to failure. The Spanish workers, even if they lack food will give you some pesos but the exploiters will denounce you to the police".

Durruti and Ascaso got themselves jobs as stevedores in the port. At work, in the canteen, they didn't stop telling the workers of the port the need for organization, for sticking together, for solidarity, warning them about the dangers of bureaucratization in the unions. "Don't ever put your fate and the solution of your problems in the hands of political professionals and don't allow leaders to appear among you. Both will betray you and you won't escape from your situation as slaves. You will start to be free when you are capable of conducting your struggle yourselves". Soon the port workers organized themselves in a powerful union and federated with others which existed in Havana: the Restaurant Workers' Union and the Tobacco Workers, both of them with marked Anarchist influence [1].

It was an important period for Durruti for he showed himself to be an excellent orator during his daily harangues to the workers. His simple speeches, so full of expansive warmth, soon made his name known and valued. His fame also came quickly to the ears of the police, who set out to look for him and arrest him. He and Ascaso then prudently left the capital and a young Cuban steered them to Santa Clara. They found work cutting sugar cane there in a hacienda situated between Cruces and Palmira. A few days after they were hired, the cane workers tried to start a strike. Their wages had been cut under the pretext that the price of sugar had dropped and they refused to work. The foremen, menacing the workers, forced them to assemble on an esplanade near the house of the boss. The latter appeared and harangued the rebels with violent reproaches, and pointing out three among them at random, accused them of having led the revolt. The foremen seized them and escorted them under arms to the nearest center of the "guardias rurales". An hour later a group of the guards brought back to the scene of the strike the motionless bodies of the three men, who, though still alive, had undergone horrible tortures. They were thrown to the ground while the boss announced: "This is what will happen to you if you don't start working again immediately. Furthermore, you will receive less wages because of the hours you have lost". The intimidation was successful and the work started again.

Durruti and Ascaso discussed the affair with their Cuban friend. They decided that they must execute the boss. Summary justice and rapid vengenace would be a serious warning to the other landlords and would open up a little the blocked horizon of the workers. The next day the body of the boss was found in his office with this warning: "La Justicia de los Errantes" (Justice of the Wanderers). The police threw themselves in pursuit of the three men but they had already reached the Province of Camaguey. The news of this execution became known everywhere from Palmira to Cruces, then to Santa Clara and as far as Havana. Legend began to exaggerate the story: a band of Spanish criminals "Los Errantes" had assassinated half a dozen hacienda landlords. All the soldiers, rural guards and foremen were mobilized to capture the fugitives, bullying the peasants who were suspected of having hidden them, torturing them to learn more. To complicate their search, it was learned that a foreman in the district of Jolquin had also been killed and the murder signed like the first one. The ubiquity of this formidable gang bewildered the authorities and frightened the landlords, who had their homes fortified.

Durruti and Ascaso had arrived in Havana and were trying to go to Mexico. They rented a pleasure boat which was visiting the bay and in the middle of their trip had themselves taken to an anchored fishing boat. They boarded and forced the skipper to start the boat. He took them as far as Yucatan, happy, once he was au courant, to take part in their dangerous mission. But when they landed, they were questioned by treasury agents who thought they were smugglers and wanted to take them to the port of Progreso to hand them over to the authorities. "On the road, Durruti offered them money for their freedom. The customs men accepted and showed them the way to enter Merida. They stayed for a week before embarking at the port of Progreso for Vera Cruz"[2].

Alejandro Ascaso and Gregorio Jover had been waiting for them for a week. They met them at the headquarters of the CGT, at number 3 Plaza de la Vizcaina. It was the old "Casa del Obrero

Mundial" (Workers' International House) but all its former dynamism was ossified. The Mexican revolution had become something "official" without any effective reality. Flores Magon, who had died a few years before in a Yankee prison, had said to Madero: "The law is a rein, and with a rein one cannot be free. The law castrates and with castrated people one cannot aspire to be men. Expropriation takes place by trampling on the law, not by carrying it on one's shoulders". He also said: "The law preserves, the Revolution renews. For this reason, if it's a question of renewal, one must start by breaking the law. The real revolutionary is preeminently outside the law"[3]. The anarchists, inheritors of these instructions were being hounded. The others were allowing themselves to be led towards state reformism.

Once in Mexico, Durruti and Ascaso inquired about the situation in Spain. It was still very distressing. Nevertheless the travels they had just made strengthened their belief that revolution has no country. They therefore decided to help the libertarian movement in Latin America as much as they could. They arrived right in the middle of a sharp discussion among responsible members of the CGT on the financial difficulties of the anarchist movement and its publication. They offered their money in answer to a subscription appeal. A few weeks later, Durruti came to the office of the periodical, *Regeneración*. They told him about the general progress of the Confederation as well as of the publication. The latter was sold in the streets but was kept alive with difficulty because the readers were not accustomed to paying the price asked. Durruti was surprised. He placed a large bundle of bank notes on the table saying: "Here is enough to allow you to breathe a little but you must insist that the workers pay for workers' publications". The members of the Committee looked at the money suspiciously. He reassured them by taking a letter from Sebastien Faure out of his pocket. The French anarchist was thanking him for an important donation of money for the benefit of *Editorial Internacional*. Durruti explained that "Los Errantes", worked silently and were ready to risk their lives at the service of their ideas. "You work struggling against the State legally, we fight illegally and defy it. But your ends and ours are identical". In fact, it was evident that they were the authors of various recent attacks on banks.

"Los Errantes" had chosen to live and work illegally, not for temperamental reasons but because they had learned that the anarchist groups of the old and new continents needed money as their publications absorbed a good deal of it. Above all it was necessary to help the unions which wanted to set up rationalist schools on the order of those founded by Francisco Ferrer in Spain in 1906. The Oil Workers Union had already opened one of these schools with more than two hundred students. The Restaurant Workers also wanted to open one. Its president received a letter from Durruti asking him to lunch. He reported later that he had been told to dress elegantly "because we are going to eat in a restaurant frequented by 'well bred people'. I refused, not because of scruples but because I was opposed to all this decorum which was against my life style and my ideas, as a militant. Durruti insisted in a letter, saying that I must

75

come, that he had to talk to me and he couldn't invite me to a simple restaurant because in Tampico he was posing as a rich man. I went, mastering my aversion, thinking that he had important things to tell me. He said: 'What would you think of the idea of opening about a hundred schools like the one opened by the Oil Workers Union?' I answered: 'It's a beautiful dream...' Miguel, the name used by Durruti in Mexico, answered: 'It's not a dream but a reality. In a little while you will have one hundred thousand pesos for this work.'"

And during the four months that Durruti was in Mexico, the attacks on banks increased. And the police organized harsher round-ups each time. But the searches were usually made in disreputable areas, while Durruti and Ascaso lived in one of the most luxurious hotels of Mexico, calling themselves Mendoza and pretending to be rich mine owners from Peru. "One day, without any luggage and only a few pesos in their pockets, they left the hotel and the bill for "Mendoza" to pay and they left the capital to make their way to the South of the continent"(4). They were hounded from all sides and all the American police had been alerted against "Los Errantes" or "banda mexicana" (Mexican gang) as they were called. They had to use all their courage and wits to escape.

Argentina was traditionally the country most hospitable to Italian emigration, especially at the time when Mussolini seized power. A few days before the arrival of "Los Errantes", one of these exiles, Severino di Giovanni, an enthusiastic and sensitive young anti-fascist teacher in revolt, who had adopted Anarchist ideas, became famous for a brilliant coup. On June 6th, 1925, the Italian Ambassador, Luigi Aldrovando Marescotti, had organized a splendid fete to commemorate the twenty-fifth anniversary of the crowning of Victor Emmanuel II. All the members of the Italian colony were invited. Among the attractions there was to be a party at the Colon Theater which the President of the Argentine Republic, D. Marcelo T. de Alvear and his wife, Regina Paccini, were to honor with their presence. Order was guaranteed by the paramilitary fascist groups of the Ambassador, who also controlled the entrances. The attendance consisted mostly of rich Italians, big Argentine potentates and diverse representatives of the ruling class of the country. When the Italian royal march was heard after the national anthem, everyone was surprised to hear cries bursting out from the balcony: "Assassins! Thieves! Long live Matteoti!" Di Giovanni was quickly silenced by the Black Shirts of the Ambassador. But he succeeded in freeing himself and started to deliver a diatribe against the Italian dictator. He couldn't say much as he was seized with the comrades who surrounded him and violently mauled. The police led them to a police van, but before entering, di Giovanni spat in the face of a soldier, shouting "Long live Anarchy!" (5)

When Durruti and Ascaso arrived in Argentina a few days later, Donato Antonio Rizzo, manager of the periodical *La Antorcha* didn't fail to tell them about this exploit and the personality of its author. They felt a great deal of sympathy for this young man. It is probable that they met since di Giovanni's publication *Culmine* was edited in the same building as *La Antorcha,* whose editors they often visited. But perhaps they were unable to have regular meetings with him, since they were always followed, and couldn't get too much involved in the anarchist milieu. One should really say the anarchist milieux because there were many kinds, perpetually polemicizing with each other. However they were able to make contact with a small troup of Spanish exiles from Barcelona and were specially drawn to two of them: Pedro Boada Rivas and Teodoro Peña, who had been militants since 1923[6]. Together they decided to try and ease the differences which were tearing the libertarian movement apart. They concentrated on two principal groups. The first used to meet around the magazine *La Protesta* and with its editors Diego Abad de Santillan and Emilio Lopez Arango who were fierce partisans of an evolutionary line in action. The other group, centered around the Argentinians, Rodolfo Gonzales Pacheco and Teodore Antilli, who published *La Antorcha*. They criticized what they called the reformist practice of the other group and advocated armed struggle and insurrection.

La Protesta influenced the FORA (Federacion Obrera Regional de Argentina) and through it the largest number of people in the movement. While *La Antorcha* (as well as another radical publication, *El Libertario*) was most influential in a number of independent unions with anarcho-syndicalist tendencies. They had created a union platform, the Union Alliance of Argentina. A few marginal groups led by strong personalities, through their violent actions, provoked polemics between the two principal groups. Di Giovanni was the leading spirit in one of these and was the cause of one of the most serious confrontations between the two factions, before disappearing tragically [7]'.

Durruti tried to use all his influence to stop these quarrels, but only succeeded in attracting the attention of the police and the surveillance and repression fell heavily on them. Durruti and Ascaso decided to stop all their illegal activities for the time being, in spite of the pressing requests for money sent to them from Antwerp by Domingo Ascaso. Durruti got himself a job in the port under the name of Ramon Carcana Caballero and Ascaso became Teodoro Pichardo, a very competent well-digger while Gregorio Jover found a job as cabinet maker. The police redoubled their efforts against the workers. Many were arrested, on one pretext or another, and were locked up in the all too famous prison of La Terre de Feu, Ushuaia [8]. The anarchists protested in vain against the arbitrary and violent behavior of the Argentine police, which even started openly to protect the Italian Fascist groups. Among the latter, the "Liga Patriotica", openly and with impunity devoted itself to making all sorts of demands on the peasants and the trade unionists [9].

The workers answered all the provocations with vengeance or self-defense when it was possible. A "Committee for Prisoners and Deportees" had been formed to help their families pay for lawyers and finance escapes. Money was needed, and the man who was responsible for this organization, Miguel Angel Roscigna, was obliged to use "illegal means which circumstances made necessary" [10].

The lives of Durruti, Ascaso and Jover developed on a different plane as their struggle was ideological. Since they didn't have to enter the underground world where repression was keeping many excellent militants, they had nothing to fear from the repression. But this didn't last long. One day in the Palerme district, the employees of the tramway station of Las Heras saw three men, one of them masked, burst into their midst, forcing them to turn over available receipts. The loot was trifling. Those present told the police that the assailants must have been Spaniards because of their accent and the few words they had spoken. One month later, the same scenario, the 17th of November 1925, in the underground station Primera Junta at Caballito. This time and for an equally ridiculous haul, a policeman was killed.

The police put together these facts with information given them by the police of Mexico and Chile. According to these facts "a certain band of "atracadores" had sought refuge in Argentina". They were "Spaniards or Mexicans or Cubans, who on the 16th of July of this year had made off with 46,923 Chilian pesos from the Bank of Chile, Mataderos branch". The Chilian police had their photos and went into details: "This gang is composed of five individuals, one of them had embarked at Valparaiso for France. The boarding house where they had lived in Santiago, Chile, has been discovered. Their landlord stated that they were five well bred men, who talked continually about social struggles and described themselves as Spanish revolutionaries on a tour of America to collect funds to be used to overthrow the Spanish Monarchy. They were named: Ramón Carcana Caballero, Mexican; Jose Manuel Labrada, Cuban; Manuel Serrano García from Valencia; and finally Teodoro Pichardo Ramos, also a Mexican[11].

And so the police of Buenos Aires threw themselves onto this trail. They showed the photos to the tramway employees, who thought they recognized their assailants. As they couldn't be found anywhere, their faces were posted in the subway. La Prensa, publication of the capital City gave descriptive details. "They are individuals of good appearance, correctly dressed with nothing in their looks to render them suspect. Much more, their bearing is attractive, according to the people who saw these gangsters yesterday". Pointed out and described in this way, the small group of Anarchists had to hide and disappear from the capital. They effaced themselves so well that until the 18th of January 1926, one loses track of them completely. On that day the Bank of San Martin, branch of the Bank of La Provincia, was attacked: "While the inhabitants of the quiet town of San Martin were lunching at home, safe from the sun and heat, a group of bandits, armed with rifles, placed themselves at the entry to the branch of the Bank of la Provincia, facing the Plaza Principal. These seven unknowns, four of them masked, had gotten out of a car at the corner of Buenos Aires and Belgrano Streets, two blocks away from the police station. Four of them went inside, leaving the others as sentries in the street, menacing with their weapons the pedestrians who tried to move. During this time the others were busy gathering up 64.085 pesos, a strident voice having called out to the employees: 'If someone moves, four bullets will stop him! The thieves then fled with their loot in a car. There was a rush in pursuit of them but their flight was covered by shooting without sparing gunpowder". The police had no doubts that the author

78

of the hold-up was Durruti. But this time there were seven to carry out the coup, without counting the chauffeur. Many suspects were arrested but their questioning brought no results. The Spanish police alerted, leveled all their suspicions on Durruti, Ascaso, Jover, specifying: "This concerns a formidable gang of anarchists who operated for a long time in Barcelona and committed numerous offences, attacks, robberies, assassinations". And they named Ascaso as responsible for the death of Cardinal Soldevila.

The Argentine police reported the history of this "gang" to *La Prensa* and the sequal which it knew: "From Gijón they went to Mexico, where they robbed a bank in Caroline. Then in Cuba they attacked another bank with success. In Havana they embarked on the boat "Oriana" which took them to Valparaiso, Chile, where they arrived the 9th of June 1925. They worked there until the 11th of July and this time they attacked the Bank of Chile in Santiago. They resumed their work as laborers until the beginning of August, when they went by train to Buenos Aires". From now on the police focused its search on the Anarchist circles but always in vain[12].

A few months later the news came from France about the arrest of Durruti and Ascaso, at the moment when they were preparing an attempt against Alfonso XIII, the King of Spain. They had arrived in France on the 30th of April 1926, landing at Cherbroug, Durruti, under the name of Roberto Cotelo; Ascaso as Salvador Arevalo and Jover as Luis Victorio Rejetto. These names were those of three famous Argentinian anarchists and the police started to search for them diligently. It was only able to put its hands on the first, who declared that he had lost his Uruguayan passport a few hours after having gotten it. He firmly maintained this ingenious alibi in spite of the repressive power of the police, and the judge had to let him go. Nevertheless, Argentina asked France to extradite the group of Spanish anarchists.

Footnotes

1. Facts supplied by an old militant anarchist who knew Durruti in Cuba. He prefers to remain anonymous. He is in Cuba (1970).
2. "Durruti en tierras de Americas" An article in *El amigo del Pueblo*, organ of "Los Amigos de Durruti". Number II November 20, 1937.
3. An article in *Regeneración*, organ of the Mexican Anarchist Federation, by Flores Magon, April 1970.
4. *El amigo del Pueblo*, the issue already quoted. *Ruta* (Caracas, Venezuela), number 38, article by Victor García telling about Durruti's trip to Mexico.
5. Osvaldo Bayer, *Severino di Giovanni, el idealista de la violencia*, Ed. Galerna Buenos Aires, 1969.
6. Pedro Boada, Teodoro Peña and Agustín García Capdevila, had to go into exile in France. Then after the defeat of the guerrilla attack at the Bidasoa, they left for America. In Spain they had been especially active during their military service, in the antimilitarist committees. Condemned by Court Martial, they fled from the military prison. The authors of many important dynamite attacks. When they left Spain they were condemned to death in absentia.
7. This polemic worsened because of the unfortunate interference of di Giovanni. This young man was non-violent by nature. But the development of the trial against Sacco and Vanzetti in America obliged him to change his tactics. He thought that a direct attack on the financial interests of the United States would bring about a change of heart in America towards the two Italian Anarchists who had been condemned to death. Di Giovanni placed several deadly weapons in American banks and attacked the Italian Consulate in Buenos Aires with dynamite. But the bomb exploding at the wrong time, missed its destined victims and created innocent ones. The Argentine police took advantage of this to attack the Anarchist movement. It deported and imprisoned numerous militants. *La Protesta* publicly condemned this tactic and disassociated itself from the di Giovanni group, showing that the latter was a stranger to the Anarchist movement. *La Antorcha* and the colony of Italian exiles defended di Giovanni. Divided into two camps and engaged in polemics, the anarchists reached the point of personal confrontations. Osvaldo Bayer's book illustrates this period well.
8. The repression reached its peak in 1909. An army colonel, Falcon, distinguished himself by massacring hundreds of peasants in order to put an end to their revolts and strikes. From then on the repression grew, ending with the tragic week of Buenos Aires (January 1919). Everything had started with a strike of the metallurgists, which the governor had tried to break by protecting the non-strikers with the police and the army.
   In the first onslaught there were deaths among the workers. But at their funeral the bloodiest deeds occured. There were some 1,500 deaths, more than 5,000 wounded and 50,000 arrests (*Panorama* of January 5, 1971 gives a long report about these occurrences). The government was not successful in subduing the workers revolt through these repressions. Conflict remained the characteristic means of communication between workers and bosses. This struggle was going on when Durruti and his friends arrived in Buenos Aires.
9. The "Liga Patriotica" was heir to the "Guardia Civica", an organization created by the bourgeoisie with the idea of using its affiliates to break strikes. The "Liga Patriotica" turned out to be a Fascist organization and sons of the richest families of the country, as well as Navy and Army officers, became members. Dr. Manuel Carles was its founder and guide (see, among other sources, *Los nacionalistas argentinos*, Oscar Troncoso, Ed. Saga, Buenos Aires, 1957).
10. Expropriation and armed robbery were rare in Argentina. It is not even sure that this was the work of the anarchists. The real author seems to have been German Boris Wladimirovich, born in 1876. A Russian aristocrat, he broke with his milieu by marrying a revolutionary worker at 20. From then on he had devoted himself to the class struggle in Russia, spending his personal fortune. For a while he taught biology in Zurich, Switzerland. He was active in the Social Democratic Party and took part, as a Russian delegate, in the International Socialist Congress at Geneva in 1904, where he clashed with Lenin. Since then he had been active in the ranks of anarchism. For reasons of health, he went to Buenos Aires around 1918. He lived through the "tragic week" and the manoeuvers of the "Liga Patriotica" against the Russian colony. The partisans of Carles, in response to the Russian Revolution, devoted themselves to hunting down Russians living in Argentina.
   German Boris and his Russian friends thought of publishing a paper to enlighten Argentine opinion on the meaning of the Russian Revolution and to try, at the same time, to restrain the savage attacks of the "Liga Patriotica". To obtain money, they decided to attack a jewelry store (1920). It was the first act that initiated the practise of "expropriation" for revolutionary ends. Angel Roscigna member of the "Comite Pro-presos", also had to use these methods to provide for the prisoners, who had become more and more numerous.
11. *Todo es historia*, a Buenos Aires magazine. In an article "Los anarquistas expropiadores", Osvaldo Bayer supplies questionable information about Durruti's trip to the Argentine (numbers 33 and 34).
12. Our account agrees with the remarks quoted from Osvaldo Bayer. However it is necessary to be explicit. None of the members of the group "Los Solidarios", who helped with this biography hid the facts about Gijon and Mexico. But they repeatedly denied they were the authors of the deeds attributed to them in Buenos Aires and Cuba, except for those we report about in the sugar cane strike. For ourselves, we think that the activity of Durruti and his comrades in Argentina was limited to "Spanish matters". They only took part in "prisoners' escapes". They organized a collective escape from the prison of Montevideo through a tunnel. It was in this city that they lived in hiding while the police were searching for them in Argentina. The testimony which we have from Roberto Cotelo, who was involved in this affair, can be vouched for unconditionally (Cotelo died in Uruguay in 1971).

12

UNSUCCESSFUL ATTEMPT AGAINST ALFONSO XIII AND CAPITULATION OF POINCARÉ

AFTER THE ATTACK ON THE BANK of San Martin, the police kept an eye on all the frontiers and especially the port of Buenos Aires. However the "three dangerous anarchists" were able to embark for Montevideo. They hid there until they left for France. They left on a boat which wouldn't stop at a Spanish port. However, during the trip, an order came from the navigation company to anchor at the Canary Islands (Santa Cruz de Tenerife). This change in the itinerary worried the three men who thought they had been discovered and were about to be turned over to the Spanish Governor. But they learned from an anarchist sailor, a member of the crew, that it was only a technical stopover for an emergency repair of the engines. Reassured, they gave up the plan which they were preparing, to take over the boat. At Santa Cruz the passengers were put up in a hotel while waiting the arrival of another boat belonging to the company, which was to take them to Le Havre. All these mishaps worried them a great deal so they decided to leave on an English boat, and from England they went to Cherbourg and then to Paris.

They settled themselves in the rue Legendre, near the Avenue de Clichy. They soon realized that the situation had changed: most of the exiled Spanish anarchists had gone to Brussels where Russians and Italians had joined them. So they planned to go there too. But then they learned that the King of Spain, Alfonso XIII and his Prime Minister, Primo de Rivera, invited by the French, were to arrive at any moment on an official visit. It was the occasion they had dreamed about for a spectacular action to threaten the dictatorship — to remove Alfonso XIII and Primo de Rivera.

The coup was difficult to prepare for they lacked time, means and comrades, since the best anarchists were now in Brussels. However everything was ready when suddenly the police came to arrest Durruti and Ascaso and then Gregorio Jover. They never knew how the police had gotten wind of their project. Imprisoned the morning of June 25th, 1926, it was only on the 2nd of July that the press was authorized to publish the news: "The French police were on the track of a plot to make an attempt on the life of Alfonso

XIII, invited by the French Government for the festivities of the 14th of July." They also announced that the "exiled Spaniards had been arrested", without giving their names.

In the meantime the diplomatic services had gotten into motion. Spain was pressing for the extradition of the prisoners, accusing them of robberies and assassinations. Argentina asked for their extradition, basing its demand on the fact that the suspects were carrying Argentine bank bills and attributing to them the hold-up of the bank of San Martin.

French justice turned a deaf ear and held to the normal procedures related to offences of rebellion, false passports, carrying weapons and breaking the law by foreigners. On the 17th of October they appeared before the court of petty sessions. They proudly defended the right to work unceasingly to overthrow the Spanish dictatorship and admitted that they wanted to seize the King, Alfonso XIII, and make an end to the monarchy. Henry Torres, their defense lawyer, was able to bring the question back on to French ground and made them promise to submit to French law. So provisionally he was able to protect them from the Spanish and Argentine claims [1].

Durruti could then write to his family: "The influence of the Spanish police has no effect in France and I hope to regain my liberty soon, as fair amends for the injustice which has been done me" [2].

They were condemned to six months of prison without appeal. However the Spanish and Argentine Ambassadors continued their manoeuvers to get hold of the prisoners and joined forces to be more effective. Their representatives Quiñones de Leon for the one and Alvarez de Toledo for the other, supported by the French bourgeois press, tried to mobilize opinion so that these dangerous bandits would be judged in their respective countries.

In Buenos Aires the affair brought about increased social action and the police profited by this to mount a spectacular trial of the anarchists of the country. Immediately the FORA and the Alianza Sindical Libertaria united to protest against the repression, making common cause with Durruti and Ascaso, whom they claimed were innocent.

Bourgeois diplomacy, making common cause across the frontiers, then began to study the case of the three men, who for six months felt relatively safe in French prisons. They looked for legal tricks so as to be able to hand over the prisoners with the least inconvenience possible for the government of Poincaré. The Minister of Justice, Louis Barthou, again took up the study of Argentina's request for their extradition [3].

Henri Torres wrote that "From then on the case became serious because two requests for extradition had been made against each one of the men. The French Government rejected the one from Spain but followed up on the one from the Argentine. For according to a recent law, the Spaniards who had been sentenced must appear before a new tribunal. This second trial could have disastrous effects" [4].

The Anarchist Union which, until then, had limited itself to assuring the defense of the prisoners, intervened directly in the affair, entrusting Louis Lecoin with the job of mobilizing French public opinion[5]. The latter had scarcely enough time to study the dossier when the trial started. On that day the Palais de Justice and its surroundings were heavily guarded but this demonstration of force left the three Spanish revolutionaries unmoved. One of the lawyers, Berthou[6], in charge of defending these "three fierce pistoleros", addressed the court with these words: "I have the honor with my colleagues of ensuring the defense of men who represent the most advanced position of the Spanish liberal opposition".

But all the efforts of the defense were useless and the court decided for extradition to Argentina. The lawyers didn't consider themselves beaten and presented another petition to gain time. But the ruling of the judges was received with enthusiasm in the interested countries. In Spain the press commented in *El Diario de Leon:* "The Argentine Ambassador in Paris, Senor Alvarez de Toledo, met with M. Aristide Briand and there is no doubt that this interview settles the final details of the extradition to Buenos Aires of the terrorists Durruti, Ascaso and Jover." In Argentina there was rejoicing when three of the best policemen, who specialized in hunting down anarchists, had been sent to Paris as advisors to the Ambassador. At their request Argentina sent a warship, the "Bahia Blanca", to extradite the three anarchists. It was only a matter of days and Durruti would be shot in Buenos Aires.

The news brought consternation to the Argentine anarchists. Far from intimidating them, it made them fiercely determined to organize a formidable agitation throughout the country. The Government of Teodoro Alvear, spurred on by the police of Buenos Aires, prohibited meetings and all public demonstrations organized to broadcast the innocence of the three Spaniards. This didn't weaken the resolve of the anarchists who reassembled their forces around *La Antorcha* and the Committee Pro-Presos, whose publication and organization relied on the independent unions of bakers, painters, chauffeurs, carpenters, etc.

Lightning meetings were organized. "They use really unusual methods. For instance they announce a demonstration in Once Square. Mounted police surround this Square and disperse an insignificant crowd. Then an anarchist appears from nowhere and leans on a railing while two others quickly attach him to it with chains. The anarchist, immobilized, starts talking loudly, his voice well trained by hundreds of public meetings, where no amplifier or electric system was used to reach the public. 'Come here and listen to me. We are anarchists who are here to tell you the truth about Durruti, Ascaso and Jover!'".

The police rushed in to face an incredible spectacle, a crucified man, talking like a machine gun. First they tried to shut him up by hitting him. But the people were revolted by the spectacle of a defenseless man being hit. And the anarchist continued to talk, talk, bringing together hundreds of people. This scene lasted almost always for more than an hour until a blacksmith came to break the chains. All this time the orator had spoken, not only about the case of the Spaniards, but also about American justice in the Sacco

Vanzetti affair, the case of Radowitzki, etc., and the repressive politics of Alvear's government [7].

In France the trial and its outcome had upset all the liberal intelligentsia, and they with the left wing press considered the delivery of Durruti and his comrades to the Argentine Government illegal and demanded their immediate release. In the middle of all this agitation, the indefatigable Louis Lecoin was organizing protests with the support of the Ligue des Droits de l'Homme (League for the Rights of Man). The latter had at first been intimidated by the Minister of Justice, who had informed its president, Victor Basch, that it was useless to intervene in this affair "as the three Spaniards were guilty". But Lecoin was able to overcome his qualms thanks to Mmes. Severine and Mesnard-Dorian, who convinced Victor Basch that Durruti and Ascaso were anarchists who had nothing in common with those who professed this ideology only to be able to "live their life". The protest reached the Chamber of Deputies where various Socialist Deputies proposed bills for reforming the extradition law. The French Government began to realize that the ground was becoming slippery and that they couldn't carry out the extradition without fulfilling certain legal conditions.

For Lecoin and the other supporters this meant an opportune respite, which they put to good use, mobilizing public opinion and workers' support, for the fight must now be won in the street. The left wing press organized an intense campaign which lasted until April 1927. The Aid Committee organized demonstrations and meetings. But everything still remained in suspense. A letter written by Durruti to his family at this time expressed his keen anxiety. It was in the middle of this excitement that the French Government decided in April to uphold their decision to hand over the three anarchists to the Argentine Government [8].

It was an unexpected blow to Lecoin and his friends. In Buenos Aires *La Antorcha* echoed their discouragement: "France gives meat to the wild animals, France, rotten, traffics in human lives". And farther on: "A barbarous, uncivilized country without individual or collective guarantees, wide open so that every abuse and violence coming from above, finds a foothold immediately. That is Argentina... Here, only a disgraceful fear governs and, even more, a base fear obeys. The only safeguard is the ambiance of cowardice, the ambiance of lies and the ambiance of filth".

The Spanish Ambassador in Paris, Quiñones de Leon, once again urged the Argentinian Ambassador to intervene with the French Government to make the extradition effective. A paragraph in the bourgeois press announced that an Argentinian warship would arrive soon in Le Havre, the second sent to take away "the precious merchandise". The French and Argentinian anarchist press answered, violently attacking both the Ambassadors. *La Antorcha* went so far as to publicly denounce "certain irregularities in public administration" and wrote that President Alvear had obtained this favor from the French "thanks to the shipment of an oriental courtesan in exchange for the three anarchists". Finally, they reached the point of threatening to launch a mass movement, uniting the defense of

Paris, July 14, 1927. Ascaso, Durruti and Jover posing in the editorial office of "Le Libertaire" upon their release from prison.

Durruti to that of Sacco and Vanzetti. This threat had the desired effect. Alvear began to teeter between his wish to please the Spanish monarchy and his fear of seeing the situation deteriorate in Argentina [9].

While the Argentine President tried to find a smart way out, Spanish diplomacy as determined as ever, was needling the French Government. Now in France the protest movements were becoming generalized. Lecoin attacked to the limit, although without hope: "Tyranny was triumphing, scorning public opinion, which was demanding manfully freedom for the prisoners". He asked himself however "if this challenge would not be costly for the French Government". Then he decided to make a public scandal: "To slap the Minister of Justice, Louis Barthou, while he was among his colleagues". To carry out this act he found his way into the Elysee Palace, sliding in among the journalists, when the Government was in session. A policeman recognized him and asked for his papers. He showed his card as editor of *Libertaire* but the policeman decided that "this wasn't real journalism" and kicked him out. "This reverse stimulated me", Lecoin wrote, "not being able to slap Barthou in the flesh, I would destroy him politically". And he threw himself into a campaign of agitation, meetings and revolt [10].

During a meeting at Bullier a motion was passed unanimously addressed to citizens Painlevé and Herriot asking them "in a leap of real republicanism that they speak out with a solemn 'no' to Spain, via the Argentine". As was expected, Painlevé did nothing because "he was a broken reed". On the other hand, Herriot asked for the dossier so as to place it before the next Council of Ministers. Lecoin recognized the importance of Herriot's action. If the latter involved the Chamber of Deputies in this affair, it could put the Government in a difficult spot. He dared raise a real parliamentary question: Poincaré was defying public opinion and public opinion took up the challenge. Another parliamentarian, Renaudel, agreed to add his name to the parliamentary question and together with Lecoin, he wrote a statement which they gave to the press. The principal left wing journals printed it in full. They were even surprised to see that *Humanité,* the organ of the French Communist Party (which until then had barely noticed the case of the three Spanairds) also published the statement in full, not signed by Renaudel but by Vaillant-Couturier [11].

Lecoin, whom everyone realized was behind this questioning, established his headquarters in the hall of the Pas Perdus, in the midst of the Chamber of Deputies. He won the confidence of the Radical-Socialists Durafour and René Richard, who promised to speak out in the name of their party. The Independent Socialist, Moro-Giafferri, agreed to join them. Lecoin had managed to get the signatures of 250 deputies, but that wasn't enough, as his aim was not only freedom for the prisoners but also the fall of Poincaré. He lacked only fifty names and he was even seeking them in the Prime Minister's party.

As for the prisoners, they had begun a hunger strike and every day the press reported their physical condition to an exacerbated public opinion. The authorities tried every means possible to make the strikers change their minds, but they continued resolutely. The Keeper of the Seals authorized Lecoin to visit the prisoners in the infirmary of the prison of Fresnes to convince them to eat. They answered that they wouldn't end the strike until they were freed.

All this had raised tension to the maximum before the parliamentary questioning set for the 13th of July 1927 at 2 P.M. On the morning of that day, Poincaré discussed the case of Louis Lecoin with his Minister of Justice. They decided to send an emissary, Malvy, to him. He was a personal friend of the Prime Minister and President of the Treasury Commission. "What do you want Lecoin? Does the fall of Poincaré interest you so much?" — "Not at all! We only want one thing and with all our strength, the liberation of Ascaso, Durruti and Jover!" Malvy promised Lecoin to speak to the President of the Council of Ministers and to set an hour to let him know the result of his petition. It was the hour in which the parliamentary question was to be raised. The answer came before this: Poincaré and Barthou capitulated. The three Spanish outlaws would be freed the next day[12].

In the evening papers enormous headlines announced their release. The following day the press commented on the event. Maurice Delépine wrote in *Le Populaire*: "The opening of the prison gates for these three innocent people is a victory for the working class". In *Le Quotidien,* Huguette Godin told in a very sentimental way about her interview with the discharged prisoners: "And now...?" Durruti looked at me smiling: "Now? Starting the struggle again... but in Spain." And the journalist closed: "It is true that they have come out of prison, but they must leave France in not more than fifteen days, deported perhaps to another country where they will be persecuted in the same way"[13].

Footnotes

1. Henri Torres, *op. cit.*
2. Letter from Durruti, September 17, 1926. Private archives.
3. The Spanish monarchy added to this manoeuver "the discovery in Madrid of a vast anarchist plot of international character. These anarchists had prepared attempts on Primo de Rivera, Poincaré and Mussolini. The attack on Primo de Rivera was to take place at the funeral of the President of the Supreme Court of Justice, Señor Tornos, *La Vanguardia*, December 2, 1926.

The Spanish Government thought that through this trick it could frighten Poincaré and force him to hand over the prisoners. To increase the reality of "this discovery", García Oliver was accused of being the organizer of the plot. He was transferred from the Burgos prison to the one at Pamplona, where he was to be tried.
4. Henri Torrés, *op. cit.*
5. Louis Lecoin, *Le cours d'une vie*, Ed. Liberté, Paris, 1966. Lecoin, who died in 1971 in Paris at the age of 83, was a well known French anarcho-Pacifist, who devoted his life, in and out of prison, fighting for peace.
6. Not to be confused with the Minister of Justice, Barthou.
7. Osvaldo Bayer, rev. cit. No. 34, February 1970.
8. Louis Lecoin, *op. cit.*
9. Quoted by Osvaldo Bayer, op. cit.
10. Louis Lecoin, op. cit. The dailies most concerned with this affair were, *Le Populaire, Le Quotidien,* and *l'Oeuvre.*
11. Louis Lecoin, *op. cit.*
12. Idem.
13. *Le Populaire* and *Le Quotidien,* July 15, 1927.

HIDING IN EUROPE

THE "COMITÉ D'ASIL" FACED insurmountable difficulties trying to get visas for the Spanish anarchists, Durruti and Ascaso No country wanted to have them. They even made contact with the U.S.S.R., but the Ambassador in Paris had to consult Moscow and they heard nothing further [1]. However the two men were not discouraged and hoped to return to South America, or better, to Spain. Anarchism had gained a new prestige there since the founding of the Iberian Anarchist Federation (FAI) in July 1927 [2].

During the fifteen days Durruti and Ascaso stayed in Paris after their liberation, two things happened which gave a new turn to their lives. They met two young Frenchwomen in the International Library who belonged to the Syndicalist Youth Movement, Emilienne Morin and Berthe Favert. A great friendship was established between them which resulted in two solid unions, Emilienne with Durruti and Berthe with Ascaso.

Also during this same period they had a meeting with the Ukrainian guerillero, Nestor Makhno who was profoundly depressed at that time because of a bitter polemic with his exiled Russian comrades [3]. As a rule he received no one, but knowing about the adventurous life of the two Spaniards, Makhno agreed to meet them in the modest hotel room where he lived. "We come to salute you, the symbol of all those revolutionaries who struggled for the realization of Anarchist ideas in Russia. We also come to pay our respects to the rich experience of the Ukraine." Durruti's words produced a profound effect on the despondent militant. Then Ascaso reported: "This very short, thick set man, seemed to come to life again. The look in his slanting eyes became penetrating and forceful, clearly expressing the intense vitality hidden in his sick body".

He answered them: "In Spain, conditions for a revolution with a strong anarchist content are better than in Russia. There is a proletariat and a peasantry with a revolutionary tradition whose political maturity is shown in its reactions. May your revolution come in time so that I can have the satisfaction of seeing anarchism alive and warned by the Russian experience. In Spain you have a sense of organization which we lacked in Russia. It is organization which assures the success in depth of all revolutions. That is why I not only admire the anarchist movement of the Peninsula, but I also believe that right now, it is the only one that can carry out a sounder revolution than the Bolshevik one, and without the bureaucratic peril which menaced the latter from the beginning. Fight to maintain this feeling for organization and do not allow it to be destroyed by those who think that anarchism is a doctrine which has nothing to do with real life. Anarchism is the opposite of sectorianism and dogma. It perfects itself in action. It has no defined doctrine. It is a natural occurrence which appears historically in all collective human situations. It even represents the progress of history and it is the power which pushes history forward."

Makhno was making a great effort to express himself in French but he had to turn continually to his friend Dowisky to translate certain expressions. And while the interpreter talked to the Spaniards, Makhno watched carefully to see the effect that his words were making on these young men, interrupting sometimes brusquely to speak passionately himself for fear that his throughts were being falsified. For several hours, Durruti and Ascaso listened to the account of events in revolutionary Ukraine, of the life of the anarcho-communist group of Gulyai-Polye, and the revolution of the Free Soviets in the zone where they operated.

"Our agrarian commune was at once the economic and political vital center of our social system. These communities were not based on individual egoism but rested on principles of communal, local and regional solidarity. In the same way that the members of a community felt solidarity among themselves, the communities were federated with each other. Our practice in the Ukraine showed clearly that the peasant problem had very different solutions from those imposed by Bolshevism. If our experience had spread to the rest of Russia, a pernicious division between the country and city would not have been created. Years of famine would have been avoided and useless struggles between peasants and workers. And what is more important, the revolution would have grown and developed along very different lines. It has been said against our system in the Ukraine, that it was able to last because it was based only on peasant foundations. It isn't true. Our communities were mixed, agricultural-industrial, and, even, some of them were only industrial. We were all of us fighters and workers. The popular assembly made the decisions. In military life it was the War Committee composed of delegates of all the guerilla detachments which acted. To sum up, everyone took part in the collective work, to prevent the birth of a managing class which would monopolize power. And we were successful. Because we had succeeded and gave the lie to Bolshevik bureaucratic practices, Trotsky, betraying the treaty between the Ukraine and the Bolshevik authorities, sent the Red Army to fight us. Bolshevism triumphed militarily over the Ukraine and at Kronstadt, but revolutionary history will acclaim us one day and condemn the victors as counter-revolutionary grave-diggers of the Russian revolution."

During the conversation Makhno gave frequent signs of weariness, specially while recalling painful memories. Once he sighed, saying: "I hope that when the time comes, you will do better than we did." When they were leaving, he said to the two Spaniards, with an optimistic smile: "Makhno has never refused to fight. If I am alive when you start your struggle, I will be with you"[4].

The days when France would allow Durruti and Ascaso on its soil were limited, and these men found themselves in a Europe which had closed its doors to them. Six days after being freed, Durruti wrote his family that they would soon have to start new travels and forced wanderings. On July 29, 1927, the French police took them to the Belgian border. Tragi-comic episode: the French police expelled them and the Belgians didn't allow them to enter. So the French police managed to send them in secretly to their neighbor's land! Thanks to the hospitality of the Belgian anarchist, Hem Day, they were able to spend the month of August in Brussels. But by chance they were arrested by the Belgian police and were taken back to the frontier and sent back into France by the same means employed by the French police!

Once they were in Paris, the police were quickly on their heels. All the homes willing to take them in were watched. They tried to find a refuge in the Yonne Department, with a militant pacifist. But there too they barely had time to sneak off while their host was trying to convince a police captain, who had come to investigate, that he didn't even know them[5]. The most active militant libertarians (and specially Emilienne and Berthe) were also closely watched. This made life impossible for the two fugitives.

The Revolutionary Alliance Committee[6], which had recently been revived, had been joined by "Los Solidarios" to take part in a new plan for revolution in Europe. The Alliance advised them to go to Lyon, a quieter city, where it would be easier for them to hide and take part in the revolutionary plans which were being formulated. They therefore falsified papers for themselves and quickly found work in Lyon. But they were soon discovered, arrested and accused of violating the alien laws. Again the French anarchists started a campaign to alert public opinion to the possible manoeuvers of the French police. To make things less complicated, they were condemned hastily to six months in prison. After that they were once again forced to cross the Belgian frontier secretly. A year had passed since their last odyssey, but the Ambassadors remained adamant. No one would give asylum to men capable of assassinating prelates and attacking banks.

After a thousand vacillations the U.S.S.R. declared that they were ready to receive Durruti and Ascaso. In spite of all the warnings given by the Russian anarchists, they decided to chance it. In a letter to his friends, Durruti wrote: "When this letter reaches you, the distance which separates us will be enormous. You cannot imagine with how much sorrow I am moving away from Spain. We have received a favorable response from the Russian government, and I have my suitcase ready for the big adventure"[7]. Durruti had decided to make the trip. But this decision was short lived. The Consulate of the Soviet Union in Brussels told them that since their application had been made in Paris, their passports had to be issued there too. They argued that they had been fordidden to stay in France, but the Soviet officials remained adamant. So the two Spaniards were forced to go to Paris again illegally.

At the Consulate they were sent to the Ambassador. There they were subjected to a tough questioning about what they intended to do during their stay in Russia. They were asked to fill out forms in which they had to promise to defend the Soviet State, to do it no harm, to recognize it as the genuine expression of the popular will... They considered these conditions intolerable and decided to give up the trip[8].

Whether they turned towards France, Belgium, Switzerland, Germany, Luxemburg, these two men always received the same negative answers: undesirable everywhere. These men who systematically rejected all laws and political blocs, could only live somewhere illegally.

They decided to go to Germany and in October 1928 arrived in Berlin where they were received by Agustín Souchy. He consulted with Rudolf Rocker, an important German anarchist, on how to solve their problem. First, it was decided to keep secret the presence of the two Spaniards in Germany. They were settled in an unobtrusive house in a working class neighborhood of Berlin. Then Rocker got in touch with the libertarian poet, Erich Mühsam [9] and both of them went to ask help from an old comrade in the struggle, who had subsequently joined the Social Democratic party. This man named Kampfmeyer, was an important connection as he had an administrative job. He had been helpful in previous interventions for Emma Goldman and Nestor Makhno. He decided to intercede for Durruti and Ascaso.

They had to wait for fifteen days for the results of his intervention. Those who knew the danger that these two Spaniards were exposed to, suffered from terrible anxiety during this period. Durruti and Ascaso however remained movingly serene. They studied German and tried to talk with the children of the household where they were living. In the evening they received visits from Rocker or Souchy, while Mühsam hardly ever left them. They reminisced about their personal experiences. The Germans recalled the revolution and the workers' councils of Bavaria, while the Spaniards reported on the international anarchist movement. And in this way they established strong and lasting bonds of friendship.

Finally Kampfmeyer told Rocker that he could do nothing further for the Spaniards. If they had assassinated the King of Spain, their affair could have been arranged. But they had killed one of the prelates of the Catholic Church. That was something the centrist Catholic party couldn't pardon and it was with this party that the Social Democrats had formed a coalition. The situation was serious. If the Spaniards were arrested, they would certainly be turned over to the Spanish police. The Social Democratic party, because of its political alliances, would do nothing to prevent it. The alternatives open to them were equally dangerous: to live in hiding in no matter what country, go to Spain or return to South America.

They decided to cross the ocean. But this time they had an important financial problem. Rocker, secretary of the German Anarchist unions (FSA) could not use the solidarity funds without giving an accounting to the other comrades. Besides it was important to avoid indiscretions. Mühsam decided to collect the necessary money from friends, among others, the altruistic and generous German movie star. Alexander Granach. The latter, when he was told about the problem, handed over all the money be had, about 400 marks. Other gifts supplemented this amount and Durruti and Ascaso were able to leave for Antwerp, where they planned to embark for Mexico[10].

By early 1929 Belgium had fortunately changed its policy of political intolerance towards aliens. Hem Day was able to try once again to help the two Spaniards and the police authorized them to remain in Belgium, with the proviso that they assume new identities. This was a great surprise to these men who were fundamentally against all laws. Here was legality playing at illegality! And Ascaso commented: "This is the strangest thing that has happened to me in all my life"[11].

They wrote to Rocker immediately to bring him up to date on the change in their plans and to send back the money collected for them, keeping only enough for an eventual trip to Spain. And once again they tried to stabilize their lives as far as possible. Durruti took a job as a machinist in a factory. Ascaso changed his job as a painter a number of times. Because of his irritable character, he couldn't tolerate vexations. Emilienne and Berthe soon joined them. Trained by their previous periods of exile, the four kept away as much as possible from milieux composed solely of exiles, where common resentments and personal disputes, fueled by their illusions and dreams, were aggravated. Ascaso began to study in various fields and Durruti used his free time to work with the International Anarchist Committee which, with the Edition Internationale de Paris, published a wide range of propaganda[12].

Meanwhile in Spain the Anarchist revolutionary movement was entering a period of fruitful activity and new life was given to the trade union cadres of the CNT. The National Committee sent a number of messages to the groups in exile. It was said that the year 1929 would be a vital one for the development of the workers' movement. Reading these reports from Spain, Durruti and Ascaso learned that the foundations of the monarchy were shaking. The King, Alfonso XIII, didn't hesitate to admit this in his own circles. Politicians were moving away from the monarch who had been discredited, and in the barracks, once again, there was open conspiracy. Niceto Alcalá Zamora and Miguel Maura had even broken off relations with the King [13] and there was a rapprochement between the intellectuals and the working class. It was probable that 1930 would be the year when the exiles could return. The National Committee guaranteed it.

In January 1930 the King dismissed the old dictator, Primo de Rivera, and replaced him with General Damaso Berenguer, who restored constitutional guarantees on January 20th 1930. Amnesty granted on February 16th didn't affect the workers but only the professional politicians who had conspired against the King (like Sanchez Guerra, architect of the military conspiracy of June 1929 in Valencia). Nevertheless many exiles acted as if the amnesty was for them and returned to Spain. The National Committee of the CNT believing "that the iron must be struck while hot", came out of hiding and demanded that the Civil Governors legalize the unions. In the big cities like Barcelona, the workers didn't even wait for this authorization to open their locals. The CNT of Catalonia immediately organized a Congress publicly and named a Regional Committee. Among those elected were Mayo Ferran (metallurgical union), Manuel Hernandez (wood), Luzbel Ruiz (health), Juan Guillen (food), Juan Chiva (textile), Emilio Bassous (glass works). This Congress ended with a big meeting in the Teatro Nuevo del Paralelo in Barcelona. The crowd swarmed into the theater and the streets around it. The speakers, Angel Pestaña, Juan Peiro and Sebastian Clara, brought the monarchy to trial publicly, arousing the protests of the government spokesman. But nobody listened to his protests and, frightened, he didn't dare to stop the meeting.

By August the principal unions were functioning regularly. The regional committees and the local federations were already in action in all of Catalonia. Another regional Congress decided to resume publication of *Solidaridad Obrera*. The first number appeared on August 31st. Juan Peiró was the publisher and its editors were Eusebio Carbo, Sebastian Clara, Pedro Foix, Ramón Megre, etc. Little by little the Confederation gave proof of its vitality. A meeting was organized by the Committee Pro-Presos in the Palais des Beaux Arts in Barcelona. The speakers, Angel Samblancat, Luis Companys, Rovira i Virgili and José Alberola, demanded a general amnesty. Another meeting was held at Reus, where the Cuban anarchist, Domingo Germinal spoke. He had escaped recently from the prisons of the dictator Machado[14]. One emotion followed another, right up to the explosion in December. The Revolutionary Committee formed after the treaty of San Sebastian [15] had settled on a general uprising for the 13th of December. At the last minute there was a counter-order. But two captains, Fermin Galán and García Hernández, revolted with their regiments and proclaimed the Second Republic. This putsch was put down quickly as there was no support for it throughout the Peninsula. A court martial condemned the mutineering officers to death. They were shot the next day. December 14th, the date which marked the first dastardly act of the future Republican rulers[16].

The CNT had been faithful to the agreement for an uprising. But the Regional Committee was arrested just as it was trying to take over the airport of Prat de Llobregat in Barcelona and the general strike was not carried through. The prisons were full of revolutionary workers again, but it was the last time that the monarchy could resort to these repressive measures. Abandoned, Alfonso XIII instructed Admiral Aznar to form a government and to prepare general elections for the 12th of April 1931. The vote overthrew the monarchy. The Republic was proclaimed on the 13th of April 1931 in Eibar (Province of Guipuzcoa). The following day, the declaration was official for all of Spain. The King left Spain from Cartagena and had the nerve to declare that he was leaving to avoid bloodshed. In Marseille he had the reception he deserved. One of his "subjects", the dock worker, Escudero, slapped him publicly, expressing everyone's contempt. All the partisans of the King fled to France, frightened by the popular anger which had finally been unleashed. On the way they passed the trains with those who were coming back to

Spain after their long wait. Durruti and Ascaso were among the enthusiastic returning exiles.

Footnotes

1. See further on, the letter from Durruti to his family.
2. *El Productor*, Anarchist weekly, issued in Blanes in 1926, began the publication of articles on this subject, "Anarchist organization?" That same year the Spanish Anarchist groups in France, held a Congress, where they decided to regroup all the Anarchist cells scattered in France, in one *Anarchist Federation of Spanish Exiles*.

These are the antecedents of the National Congress of Anarchist groups which met in Valencia (El Cabañal) in July 1927. Representatives came from almost all the Spanish groups, a representative from the exiled groups, and two delegates from the Portuguese anarchists.

They agreed to integrate Spanish anarchism in one Federation. For structure they adopted the early form of the *affinity group*, with local Federation of Anarchist groups. The various local federations would form the regional federation, coordinated by a Peninsular commission, which took the name of Peninsular Committee.

The records of this meeting were destroyed by one of the members of the Commission just before being arrested in Seville. The first document published by the FAI was the manifesto recorded by José Peirats, in the first volume of his work already quoted: document dated the 19th of December 1929.

According to José Peirats, the FAI was "to inspire the revolution, to watch over the true spirit of the Spanish Libertarian Movement, and to avoid the danger of deviationism. This danger was already noticeable in certain leaders of the CNT in these later years of the dictatorship".

3. This was a polemic on organization. The Anarchist group in which Makhno and Archinoff were active, published a blue print for anarchist organization which they called *Organizational Platform*, (1927). They felt that the international anarchist movement, and in particular the Russian one, should learn from the lessons provided by the Russian revolution. The group in which Voline was active was opposed to controls or organization and polemicized publicly. The polemic went beyond theory and culminated in personal criticisms.

4. For this interview, we rely:

1. On *Solidaridad Obrera* of July 31, 1934, an unsigned article, but written by Francisco Ascaso, commenting on the death of Nestor Makhno.

2. On *Solidaridad Obrera* of November 22, 1936, which outlines the biography of Durruti.

3. On the reports made to us by Aurelio Fernández and Liberto Calleja.

4. On Makhno's movement one can consult: *La Revolution Inconnue*, published by Belfond, Paris 1970. *La Révolution Russe en Ukraine (1918-1921)*, memoir of Nestor Makhno, published by Belfond, Paris 1970. *Histoire du Mouvement Makhnoviste* by P. Archinoff, ed. Bélibaste, Paris 1970.

5. On Rudolf Rocker, who in the *op. cit.* writes that "the Spaniards had formed a plan for a revolutionary uprising and Makhno had agreed to take part in this insurrection."

5. Testimony of Emile Bouget, French pacifist, who took them in. As the reader can see, since Durruti came out of prison, we are no longer concerned with Gregorio Jover. The latter, armed with false papers, was able to settle in Beziers, France, and didn't live with Durruti and Ascaso during this period.

6. This Revolutionary Alliance Committee was a continuation of the old Revolutionary Committee formed in 1924, which had organized the attempted guerrilla action at Vera de Bidasoa and Perpignan.

César M. Lorenzo, in his book *Les Anarchistes Espagnols et le Pouvoir*, page 58, speaking of this Revolutionary Alliance Committee, wrote that "the members of the Alliance were the first libertarians to advocate participation in the government". Actually Lorenzo confuses this Committee with the revisionist faction which had already appeared in Spain under the name of "Possibilist Syndicalists". "Los Solidarios" had nothing in common with them and actually considered them as their main enemy.

On the other hand, Lorenzo speaks of a secret gathering in Paris towards the end of 1926, where there was only one speaker, García Oliver, who developed the theory of a Bolshevik Anarchism and advocated the "seizure of power". Lorenzo doesn't mention his sources. According to our information, García Oliver had been in prison in Burgos since 1924. In 1926, while he was a prisoner, he was implicated in an attempt on the life of Alfonso XIII. For this reason he was transferred to the Fort of St. Christophe in Pamplona for his trial. García Oliver was freed after the proclamation of the Second Republic, the 14th of April 1931. And so García Oliver could not have been in Paris in 1926. At that time, Ascaso and Durruti were also in prison, the rest of the group were in Barcelona and only García Vivancos was living secretly in Paris.

7. Letter from Durruti, dated Brussels, October 1928.

8. Information given by Liberto Calleja. Martin Gudell, in *Campo*, November 20, 1937, published an article "Durruti in Russia" where he gives the same facts.

9. Erich Mühsam (1878-1934), revolutionary poet and German anarchist, author of *Marseillaise des Conseils Ouvriers*, took part in the Bavarian "Council" movement (April 7, 1919), with the anarchist, Gustav Landauer (1870-1919), author of various works, among them *Incitación al Socialismo*. Landauer was brutally assassinated by Noske's army. Mühsam was court martialed and condemned to 15 years in prison. He was amnestied in 1924. On February 28, 1933, he was arrested by the Nazis and assassinated by the S.S. the night of the 9th to the 10th of July 1934 (Roland Lewin, Erich Mühsam, supplement to *Le Monde Libertaire*, June 1968.)

10. For Germany, we followed the text quoted by Rudolf Rocker.

11. Anecdote told by Liberto Calleja, who was also an exile in Brussels at that time.

12. For the Brussels period the facts came from Ida Mett, Emilienne Morin, Berthe Favert, Juan Manuel Molina (Juanel), Dolores Iturbe and the brochure of Léo Campion, *Ascaso-Durruti*, Edit. Emancipateur, Brussels, 1930.

13. See *Así Cayó Alfonso XIII*, Miguel Maura, Edit. Ariel, Barcelona, 1968.

14. Bernardo Pou and J. R. Magrina, both members at that time of the Regional Committee of the Catalan CNT wrote about their activities in a book called *Un año de conspiracion* edited in Barcelona in 1931. We follow this text in describing the reorganization of the CNT during that period.

15. "The Treaty of San Sebastian" is the name given to decisions taken by the leaders of various political blocs, who met in San Sebastian during the summer of 1930. The parties and men who took part in these meetings decided to work towards founding a Republic, through a military conspiracy and a popular uprising. To organize these actions, a Revolutionary Committee was formed with headquarters in Madrid. Its members were Alcalá Zamora, Miguel Maura, Indalecio Prieto, Manuel Azaña, Marcelino Domingo, Alvaro de Albornoz and Fernando de los Rios.

16. Fermín Galán Rodriguez (October 4, 1899 — December 14, 1930). He was the author of a book on Anarchism, *Nueva Creación*, which was written during his imprisonment in Montjuich (Barcelona), Ed. Cervantes, 1930. A second edition was published by Ed. Nueva Era in 1937. José Arderius wrote a biography about him, *Vida de Fermín Galán*, published in Barcelona, 1931. Part of his correspondence is collected in an article, "Lo que se ignoraba de Fermín Galán", written by Antonio Leal and Juan Antonio Rodríguez, Barcelona, 1931.

DURRUTI
The People Armed

CASA PACHO
COMIDAS Y BEBIDAS
ESPECIALIDAD EN SIDRA ASTURIANA
TELEFONO 241

Part II
The Militant (1931-1936)

1

APRIL 14, 1931

IN 1931 IT WAS CLEAR that the country was moving towards the dissolution of the monarchist regime. After the abortive rising of Jaca (followed by the execution of captains Fermín Galán and García Hernández) and the general strike which broke out two days later, the provisional government actually became a second power recognized by the King and the Church.

Sanchez Guerra, Gregorio Marañon, and the Count de Romanones, calling on Niceto Alcalá Zamora in the name of the King were preparing the way for the Republic. While the Church seeking to be assured of the attitude of the new government towards religion, sent the Nuncio himself, Monsignor Tedeschini, to visit the future President of the provisional government, who was in prison. The assurances, which Alcalá Zamora and Miguel Maura gave to the emissaries of the king and the clergy, facilitated the transfer of power and the King, accepting the results of the national plebiscite, abdicated and left the country.

The results of the election of April 12 were surprising. In twenty-four hours history changed its direction. But the treaty of the Union of San Sebastian was accepted although it was only a political poultice and not a real remedy for the ills of the country. The Republic was proclaimed and not real remedy for the ills of the country. The Republic was proclaimed and greeted with enthusiastic manifestations in the streets. The changeover took place without resistance, so that the people thought it was possible to impose a new historical order without having recourse to violence, an attitude which threw a note of discord into the revolutionary tradition of the working class.

With the proclamation of the second Republic a new stage in the life of Durruti began, an important and decisive one. His revolutionary activity, limited until then to sabotage, was extended from then on to mass action. At the same time it was necessary to face the difficult problems created by a pre-revolutionary situation which little by little was gaining in intensity, as the combativeness of the working class increased.

When Durruti arrived in Barcelona on April 15, 1931, the enthusiasm of the 14th was still strong. The popular masses, passionately devoted to the new regime, showed a confidence which contrasted with the attitude of the working class during the preceding year, a year shaken by numerous strikes, partial or general, and by the abortive uprising of Jaca.

Actually, the Republic, as a solution to the political problems of Spain, had been born in an impasse. The Spanish problem was not a royal one, but a social one, and it required a radical solution. Nevertheless a way was chosen, which rested on a fragile political pact. a union between heterogeneous and antagonistic forces which didn't represent the working class and was not inspired by a plan for historical reform. A solution wouldn't be found by giving the country legal and constitutional foundations. Under these conditions it was inevitable that as soon as the enthusiasm of the people had subsided, the Republic would find itself facing the same social problems as the preceding regime.

The peasantry, made up of millions of lower and middle class laborers and farm workers, subjected to economic as well as political bondage, formed the foundation of the nation. But although feudal structures constituted the principal wealth of Spain, they hindered the economic and industrial development of the country. An immediate reform was needed as the situation was deplorable. The peasants without land were literally dying of hunger, working a third of the year for wages which ranged from one and a half to three pesetas, and this for a day of 12 to 14 hours (from "sunrise to sunset"). As to the others, owners of wretched bits of land, they too were starving in misery.

The Spanish nobility, masters of more than 53% of the arable land, held sway over vast properties. Among them, ten owned estates whose dimensions varied between 37,000 acres (like those of the Count de Romanones) and more than 195,000 acres (belonging to the Duc de Medinacelli). The social domination of the big proprietors was such that, like a spider's web, it enveloped all the rural life. They were the sole arbiters of conditions. The social relations between them and the dispossessed country masses illustrated perfectly the most schematic and the most flagrant dialectic between the master and the slave. This ruling class which found an ideal base in the monarchy, enjoyed economic and political power. The progress and the backwardness of the country depended on it. In fact, the national political life served no other interests than those of the aristocratic rural class. All attempts at change automatically came up against this economic-political group. Planning and nationalization of the land, to succeed, first had to bring about the destruction of caciquisme. Every other solution to this problem came to a dead end and provided no way out for the country. This economic stagnation created an explosive social situation, brought about by the plight of the small owners of tiny parcels of land, often less than 25 acres, and by the peasants without land. The latter, numbering about three million, worked at best 180 days a year, and less during periods of crisis which were frequent in agriculture. At that time in the village squares, specially in Andalusia, one saw crowds of people looking for jobs.

The worker's situation was less dramatic. But Spanish capitalism, born late and evolving very slowly, continued to be marked by its alliance with the most reactionary forces, the latifundists, the clergy and the army. This increased the antagonism between the

100

Barcelona, May 1931. From left to right: Garcia Vivancos, Juan García Oliver, Louis Lecoin, Odeon, Francisco Ascaso, Durruti.

social classes and the slightest occurrence was enough to bring about violence in the world of work.

The unequal industrial development created the same kind of concentration of workers, specially in the northern regions of Spain (Biscay and Asturias) and in Catalonia, the region which had become more and more the center for vast social struggles. In 1930 the Spanish proletariat numbered two million workers, distributed as follows: 35,000 in metallurgy, 222,000 in textiles, 119,000 in the manufacture of clithing, 24,300 in the manufacture of metals, 373,351 in the building industry, 378,000 in other jobs and lastly industry and transport employed half a million workers.

It was expected that the Republic would rationalize exploitation and would make it competitive, that it would develop the circulation of products within the country and also in export. The social truce that Republicans and Socialists had asked from the country depended on the solutions which would be adopted. The working class and the peasantry were looking for practical and immediate solutions from the Republic. Despite the late development of the economy, the social and political education of the Spanish proletariat had been rapid, to such a degree that in 1931 this working class, because of its class consciousness and its organization, appeared to be one of the most advanced in Europe.

Besides the aristocracy they were faced with two backward forces, the Army and the Church. These three had been the main support of the Monarchy. In return the latter had assured the Church of a privileged position. The royal constitution declared the State, Catholic. The Clergy and the religious orders were exempt from all control. They monopolized teaching, information, and possessed a stifling ideological power coupled with the economic administration of considerable fortunes. The Army and the Clergy were as one. The Army, inclined to intervene more in political than in its own affairs, seemed like a political group, which not only absorbed the most important part of the national treasure, but, in addition, imposed its rule with the menace of the "pronunciamento".

The Republic, always at the mercy of these two forces, had to get rid of them. Already in the previous century the young intellectuals, eager for new values, had risen up against the monopoly that the Church held in the field of teaching. After 1914, men had appeared among the intellectuals, who had social ideas which were still timid but also progressive. Ortega y Gasset, Americo Castro, Fernando de los Rios, Manual Azaña and a handful more stood out. Active within the Leaguè of Spanish Political Education, they tried to promote the formation of a minority which would undertake the political education of the masses. Nevertheless these intellectuals who were to become, after 1931, the political leaders of the country, made the same mistake that the "generation of '98" committed, they failed to adjust their approaches to the social evolution of the worker's movement, which was much more advanced in theory than the philosophy and science of the bourgeoisie.

We know that the working class, which was going to play the principal role in this period, was divided into two factions, one with a Social-Democratic tendency within the Socialist Party and the General Union of Workers (UGT) and the other, with an Anarchist orientation in the Iberian Anarchist Federation (FAI) and the National Confederation of Work (CNT).

In 1931 the first tendency was itself divided into two factions: Julian Besteiro, Andres Saborit and Trifón Gomez were in the opposition and were against collaboration with the provisional government, which was bourgeois in character and headed by Alcalá Zamora. The other faction, the majority, headed by Largo Caballero. Indalecio Prieto and Fernando de los Rios was in favor of participating and took part in the provisional government.

The National Confederation of Work (CNT) was also divided into two tendencies, but its plight was worse than that of the Socialist Party. The latter and the UGT had not lived through the underground period or the repression that the CNT had born during the seven years of the dictatorship of Primo de Rivera.

Only a National Congress could try to resolve the crisis in the CNT. This was a handicap which kept it from playing the role which it should have played as the most important faction of the working class. Nevertheless the CNT, in a manifesto, stated its position in relation to the Republic: "We are not enthusiastic about a bourgeois Republic, but we will not accept a new dictatorship. If the Republic is to strengthen itself, it must count on the organization of the Confederation. If it does not, it will not be able to survive."[1]

There were other groups of lesser importance, which were affiliated with the Communist International, and inspired by the Bolsheviks. One of these was the Communist Party founded in April 1921.

Since then it had made little progress, prey to a serious crisis, reflecting the crisis which Russia was living through under Stalinism. In 1931 it had barely a thousand members, scattered throughout Spain. Its position towards the Republican Government was clear: "In no case was the Republican Government to be defended or supported." [2]

Another group, originally inspired by the Bolsheviks, was led by Joaquin Maurin and its center of activity was in Lerida (Catalonia). This was the Workers and Peasants Bloc (Bloc Obrer i Camperol), which in time would become the POUM.

Finally, as to the political forces within the provisional government one must return to the Pact of San Sebastian (April 1930), a real political crucible where the signers had no other aim than to keep the masses away from the political game. For them, actually, it was a matter of going from one situation to another without upsetting public order or changing social structures. Their plan was successful thanks to the enthusiasm of the people for the idea of a Republic with federalist characteristics. And in fact the municipal elections of April 12, 1931 aroused a big response.

But from August 1930 to the elections of April 1931, the Revolutionary Committee, which was to become the provisional Government succeeded in only one thing: *to unite*. But it was a heterogeneous unity without a political program, in which the Socialists needed the Republicans, who, in turn, relied on the Constitution. [3] Both needed a relative calm in order to exploit the electoral success and establish their political parties, non-existant until then. Also the Pact of San Sebastian had only one goal; to safeguard public order and to guarantee to the monarchy and the classes that backed it, that there would be no revolution. The change in the regime was the work of cold, bureaucratic parliamentarians, lacking any popular base and with no other historical importance than their ability to deaden the fall [4] of the monarchy.

The bases for the Radical Socialist Party of Marcelino Domingo and the liberal Republican Party (representing the reaction) of Alcalá Zamora and Miguel Maura had also been laid at San Sebastian. In addition there were the Radicals of Lerroux and Republican Action of Azaña and Martinez Barrio; the Organizacion Regional Gallega Autonoma and the Esquerra Catalana. These different groups and parties and the Socialist Party formed the Provisional Government on April 14, 1931.

Exiles and prisoners, almost always freed by the people taking the prisons by assault since they didn't trust the Republic, found themselves facing a contradictory situation: on the one side, a Republican current, born from the enthusiasm for the elections, and on the other the positions of the CNT clashing with the general euphoria. Since April 15, 1931 *Solidaridad Obrera* had demanded that the prisoners be freed and asked the Provisional Government to tackle the peasant problem immediately: "We do not know the intentions of the Provisional Government concerning this agonizing problem but we are sure that if the Republic plans to use the methods of the monarchy, the problem will remain the same and this will not be tolerated by our peasant comrades." [5] Little by little the incessant appeals of *Solidaridad Obrera* were alerting public opinion which was in a state of confusion. While in Barcelona many workers in the local unions were forecasting the treachery of the new government.

The CNT and its most important militants were concentrating on the Socialists who had entered the government and whose cabinet politics were no more devoted to combatting the anarcho-syndicalist forces than to seeking a solution to the internal problems of the country. In Barcelona the meetings of the militants followed one after the other, commissions were organized and sent throughout Catalonia to reorganize the unions. In the rest of Spain they were also hastening to give greater cohesion to union strength and to settle clearly the political positions of the working class.

Sunday the 18th of April, the regional committee of the CNT brought together the best known militants to organize propaganda in Barcelona and in the provinces. At the same time dozens of meetings were called for the next day. The themes were invariably the same: the liberation of the prisoners (waiting for an amnesty which was endlessly delayed); the needs of the working class and the peasantry; the dissolution of the Guardia Civil and the purging of the army and public administration; the problem of education and the separation of Church and State — these were the most important. On Sunday April 19th, from nine o'clock in the morning all the meeting places were full. The people from the workers' districts of Sans met at the "Teatro de Proyecciones", the workers from Gracia came to the Romea Theater and the textile workers went to the Cinema "Meridina", the district of Clot and the "Triunfo" Theater of Pueblo Nuevo.

Durruti's strident voice rang out for the first time in Barcelona. "If we were Republicans, we would maintain that the provisional government is incapable of making a success of the victory given to it by the people. But we are authentic workers and in their name we say that, following this path, we will not be surprised if the country finds itself on the edge of a civil war tomorrow. We are not at all interested in the Republic, but we accept it as the point of departure for a social democratization. But only provided that this Republic guarantees that liberty and social justice are not empty words. If the Republic fails to take the aspirations of the working class seriously, then the small interest that the workers have in it will be reduced to nothing, because this institution will not correspond to the hopes that our class put in it on the 14th of April."[6]

It was the same thing at other meetings. Everywhere the discussion showed that if the government thought it could weaken the popular will by delays, it was being deceived. The working class, tired of waiting, was ready to find a solution to its own problems. "As anarchists we declare that our activities have never been and never will be at the service of any political party or any State. The anarchists and the syndicalists of the CNT, united with all the revolutionaries and backed by pressure from the street, have as their goal to force the man in the government to carry out their mandate."[7]

Contact with the people was valuable for the "Solidarios". Ascaso was shown to be sure of himself and a good lecturer. García Oliver, a fine orator, showed promise of becoming a speaker of stature. As for Durruti, here is the portrait given by a witness: "He improvised in short sentences ringing out like blows. From the beginning a contact was established between him and the public which lasted throughout his speech. The orator and the listeners formed one single body. His energetic voice and his imposing presence helped give his criticism a powerful, incisive and clear character. To these qualities was added the modesty of his person. He mounted the speaker's platform only when he was to speak and got down immediately afterwards to mix with the people, where he continued the discussion with the workers as if he had always known them."[8]

This week of agitation was succeeded by another week, no less important, in which the demonstration for the lst of May in Barcelona was to be organized. The CNT hoped it would have a special significance. In these fifteen days, three important events took place. First of all, Francisco Macia, without waiting for the decision of the central government, had proclaimed "l'Estat Catala". Secondly. Azaña, then Minister of War proposed that the army be reformed and modernized while requiring the commanders and officers to take an oath of loyalty to the Republic. Any officer who refused to sign was to be excluded from the army but was to receive full pay corresponding to his rank. And thirdly, more than 10,000 officers and senior non-commissioned officers, notorious anti-Republicans, refused to sign and formed the political group "Accion Nacional", a refuge for the worst Spanish reaction. It was presided over by Angel Herrera, director of the daily, *El Debate*. Financiers, landed proprietors, aristocrats, retired military men, found a legal cover-up for their activities in this group. A campaign of calumnies, flight of capital, fallow lands abandoned, exemplified their tactics. "Accion Nacional" made legal by the Minister of the Interior, Miguel Maura, was encouraged to organize an anti-Republican offensive in Madrid to the cries of "Long live Christ the King", which brought about clashes with the worker population. In the provinces where the Guardia Civil, thoroughly monarchist, shot at the people and produced the first victims, the situation was no less alarming.

It was in this tense climate that the proletariat's holiday, the first of May, was ushered in. In Barcelona, where passions were smouldering, the anarchist groups hastily assembled, were taking measures to protect their demonstration. The "Solidarios", notably Durruti and Ascaso, already busy reorganizing the union, had to face up to a new job. The regional committee of the CNT had put them in charge of receiving the delegates of the international anarchist movement who were coming to Barcelona to take part in the May lst demonstration and to study the political intentions of the new regime. The German Anarchist Federation sent Agustín Souchy; the Russian anarchists, Voline and Ida Mett; the Italians, Camilo Berneri; the Swedish anarcho-syndicalists, Rüdiger; the French Anarchist Union, Louis Lecoin and Odéon. During the week, Ascaso and Durruti devoted a good part of their time to the delegates, especially to the French delegation, for whom they felt a special attachment.

On Friday May 1, 1931, at nine in the morning, the Palace of the Beaux Arts was full. On the esplanade between the Park of the Citadelle and the Promenade of Victory, a dense crowd was going up toward the Arc de Triomphe and was spreading out in all the neighboring streets. On the posters one could read: "Down with the Guardia Civil", "The factory to the workers", "Land to the peasants", "Long live the CNT", "Federación Anarquista Ibérica"....

In all the short speeches which denounced the Republic, the people were offered only one solution to their problems "to occupy the factories and run them and to seize the land. The working class is capable of doing that; all that is lacking is the revolutionary courage." After a dozen of these short speeches, the regional Committee of the CNT, acknowledging publicly the problem of the "Cortes Constituyentes" (Constituent Assembly), defined the position of the organization: "Our job does not stop here, we must march, march, vigorously to the conquest of the future, whose only meaning for the working class can be the total destruction of capitalism and the State. Only after this can a "classless" society be established."[9]

But essentially the character of the demonstration was peaceful. After a march through the capital, it ended in front of the Palace of the Generalitat, where a delegation was to give the authorities the motion voted by the people. Three trucks were at the head of the procession. Behind them the Commission marched, which in the name of the unions presided over the manifestation and consisted of Santiago Bilbao, Francisco Ascaso, Buenaventura Durruti and Juan García Oliver. Immediately after them, without any special order, a throng moved along tightly packed together, which the bourgeois press appraised at more than one hundred thousand people.

The demonstrators marched through the main arteries of the capital, reached the Plaza de Cataluña and going by way of the Ramblas came to the top of Fivaller Street where only one truck entered, preceded by the members of the Commission. It was one o'clock when the vanguard of the demonstration came face to face with the police which forbade its entry to the Square. An officer of the Guardia Civil stepped forward and, revolver in hand, went towards the members of the Commission, ordering them to leave. The Guardia Civil were standing behind him, their mausers pointed towards the demonstrators.

Francisco Ascaso moved forward to confer with the officer, but the latter wouldn't listen to anything and demanded that the demonstration be broken up immediately. Ascaso disarmed him with a blow. The officer seeing himself disarmed, retreated, and the troops fell back. Then Durruti, brandishing a red and black flag, called out in shrill voice: "Make way for the FAI." Immediately, through the open streets the crowd began to advance and in a moment occupied Constitution Square.

The members of the Commission advanced slowly towards the Palace to deliver the resolutions passed by the meeting. But they had barely passed the entrance when the doors were closed again brusquely. A shot came from the building, followed by another and soon a regular volley of shots was aimed against the demonstrators. Most of them threw themselves on the ground, while many women tried to leave the throng and started screaming. Confusion grew with the shooting and already there were some casualties.

However there were groups of armed workers in the crowd and if they were to answer the government forces by using their pistols, a massacre was to be feared. The members of the Commission understood at once that this clash, which could only be harmful to the workers, must be avoided. Durruti's quick reactions averted the catastrophe. Perching on a lamp-post, despite the bullets, he spoke to the armed groups and recommended calm and self-control. The spectacle was admirable in view of the dramatic atmosphere. A bullet had scratched his chest and his shirt was bloody, but he went on imperturbably. At one point, the end seemed to have been attained, shooting stopped and the place started to empty.

Now, Durruti, still perched on his lamp-post, addressed his remarks to the authorities, whom he blamed for the situation. Near him, Ascaso, who was wounded in the arm, refused to have it cared for by Ida Mett. An open space had cleared around Ascaso, Durruti, Oliver and Santiago Bilbao and they became a sure target as shooting started up again. After that the armed groups no longer held their fire but answered the attack of the government forces.

The Caribineros who were billeted in Regomir Street, came out and soon a company of infantry appeared in Fivaller Street commanded by Captain Miranda, which took the side of the demonstrators. Durruti climbed up again on his lamp-post and harangued the troops even though The Guardia Civil and the Carabineros continued to shoot. Faced with the spectacle of Durruti perched on top of the lamp-post, the troops hesitated, but Captain Miranda ordered them to shoot at the Guardia Civil and the Carabineros. A tremendous "Hurrah" echoed in the square and in an instant the Guardia Civil and the Carabineros disappeared, leaving the soldiers and demonstrators masters of the situation. But the balance sheet of the demonstration was heavy: fifteen wounded and one dead on the side of the demonstrators two dead and a number of wounded on the side of the Guardia Civil. [10]

When night fell the anarchist groups published a report about the event: "Just when the Workers' Commission was about to deliver the resolutions of the meeting, three legionaires started to shout: "Long live the Clergy", firing their revolvers in the direction of the delegates. As if this had been part of a prearranged plan, the Carabineros of Regomir Street also started to shoot. Was this a provocation by the Carabineros who, as everyone knows, didn't wish to swear allegiance to the Republic, or a provocation by the Guardia Civil? Such an attitude calls for an explanation on the part of the authorities in charge of keeping public order.....

"(...) When bourgeois order is incapable of putting order in its disorder, it is up to the revolutionary to do it.

"(...) In the name of the people, we demand the dissolution of the bands of assassins who conspire against peace and against liberty." [11]

Footnotes

1. *Solidaridad Obrera*, April 15 and 18, 1931.
2. José Bullejos; *España en la Segunda Republica*, p. 53.
3. For the Pact of San Sebastian one can consult the book of César Falcon, *Critique de la Révolution Espagnole*.
4. This word, certainly correct, was used by Miguel Maura speaking about the role played by the provisional government. *op. cit.*
5. *Solidaridad Obrera*, April 21, 1931.
6. Idem.
7. Idem.
8. Alejandro Gilabert. *Durruti*. This same theme is discussed by Gonzalez Inestal in an article which appeared in the magazine *Umbral*. November 19, 1938, recalling various anecdotes in the life of the orator, Durruti.
9. *Solidaridad Obrera*, May 2, 1931.
10. The confederal militants. Tomás Perez and Juan Molina, who were eyewitnesses, told us about this manifestation.

Dolores Iturbe, referring to the impression she preserved of Durruti climbing on the street lamp wrote: "At that moment, his action impressed us all. Big, with uncombed hair, defying the bullets, recommending calm to the crowd." And in a letter which she sent us, Ida Mett recalled Ascaso: "More than a third of a century has gone by but I still see him before my eyes. His supple and agile body, his eyes full of malice and intelligence, his smile a little ironic and knowing, ready to throw himself into the fight because his idea of courage forced him not to give in."
11. Report copied from *Libertaire*, May 18, 1931, Paris.

2

THE "NOSOTROS" GROUP CONFRONTS THE REPUBLIC AND THE CNT

AFTER THE MAY 1ST demonstration the tendencies coexisting in the CNT confronted each other with greater bitterness. The Reformists felt the need to adapt themselves to the new situation created by the Republic and to restructure vigorously the unions of the CNT without turning to violent solutions.

For the faction which we can call extremist, the FAI, such an attitude of compromise meant to abandon the struggle, and even the idea of anarcho-syndicalism. Actually in order to submit to Republican legality, it was necessary to accept the law of April 8th decreed by the Minister of Labor. The result for the CNT would be that all its preparations would come to nothing. This law provided for the creation of mixed juries presided over by the Minister of Labor (settlements between employers and workers), advance notice of a strike (legalization of the strike), and collective agreements (regularization of disputes between employers and workers). In a word, it aimed at the integration of unionism within the State, just what Social-Democracy had already brought about in Germany and France.

It was necessary to act quickly, so that the CNT could find its dynamism again and its internal cohesion. The "Nosotros" group [1] believed that the preparation for a IIIrd Congress which the CNT was to convene in June 1931, was the period when this work of renovation should occur. In the workers' assemblies it was necessary to criticize the line proposed by the moderates, for accepting it would mean the death of trade unionism.

At a time when union life in Barcelona was at its most intense, where meetings and assemblies followed each other daily, Rudolf Rocker arrived, invited by the National Committee of the CNT to represent the AIT at the Congress. In his *Memoirs* he recalls a conversation he had during his stay with Ascaso and Durruti: "We talked about the perspectives of the anarchist movement in Spain. Both of them appeared to have great hopes while being conscious of the difficulties to be overcome before a new social movement could be victorious. This attitude was even more comprehensible if one takes into account the state of chaos in which the monarchy had left the country. Durruti felt that the situation could be mastered by constructive

109

and persistant work, and by creating solid new bases for the social structure. As for Ascaso, he was certain that the harrowing situation which had preceded the birth of the Republic had been worse than the birth itself. Under these conditions the decisive changes in the economic and social field, the solution of the agrarian problem, for example, which was particularly crucial in Spain, could not be found until after a long period of revolutionary preparation and this job could not be entrusted to any government. Ascaso thought that the legislative elections in June would clarify the situation and would permit the CNT to play an important role.

"After this conversation", Rocker wrote, "we separated and arranged to meet Sunday morning at the gathering which the Regional Committee had organized in one of the Palaces of the Exposition to greet the foreign delegations." [2] This meeting was a surprise to Rocker because in Germany he was not accustomed to such enormous mass demonstrations. According to the bourgeois press, more than 15,000 people, jammed into the theater and the environs, had come to hear the speakers. When Durruti had finished his speech, he went to sit near Rocker to talk with him for a while before leaving. "One of the things that surprised me most", Rocker remarks, "was the attentiveness with which the public listened to the speakers, as if they identified with them. But contrary to what happened in other countries, there was no applause to express enthusiasm. Durruti himself, who spoke with harsh words, calling things by their names without euphemisms, received no ovation, but it was obvious that the crowd was moved. Afterwards I was able to exchange a few words with Durruti and I asked him why the public hadn't applauded. He started to laugh and said: "But, friend Rudolf, you know perfectly well that we anarchists don't give homage to a personality. Applause and ovations which go to orators, that is the cheap music which arouses the worm of vanity, and finally creates the leader. It is right to recognize the competence of a comrade, but to think him superior is to practise the cult of the leader, and this is not the custom among anarchists!" [3]

The IIIrd Congress opened its meetings Tuesday afternoon in the big hall of the Conservatory of Madrid. 700 delegates, representing 800,000 Spanish workers, were present. One of the most important delegations numerically was the one from Andalusia, which came to the Congress in work clothes, because the workers had no others. The economic situation of the working class in that area was so miserable that the National Committee had agreed to exempt the members from paying dues. This Congress took place in a climate of crisis, both in agriculture and industry.

Very soon the different tendencies were clashing. The Pestaña-Peiro tendency, which wanted the CNT to adapt itself to republican legality, was face to face with those who held the "tough line". The struggle between these two opposing positions was at the heart of the debates. The problem of the modification of the structure of the unions into industrial Federations was taken up. Some defended the industrial Federation, arguing that there was more efficiency and coherence in the struggle. The rest, on the contrary, saw a danger of union bureaucratization and a break in worker's solidarity. Actually the latter felt that the unions had to transcend the idea of localized "guild" action in order to generalize the struggle against capitalism, which was to be waged by a coordinated front of all revolutionary workers. The most intransigeant delegation on this point came from the Woodworkers Union of Barcelona, represented, among others, by García Oliver, who was working during this period as a varnisher.

Another point to be discussed concerned the attitude which the CNT had to adopt and the demands it had to present regarding the Constituent Cortes. The majority of the National Committee considered this business of the day to be an abuse, since the aim of the CNT was the establishment of libertarian communism through armed struggle. To some of the members of the Congress, it was not up to anarcho-syndicalism to help reformist syndicalism which was fooling the workers and making them believe that the only aim of their struggle was to improve their standard of living. To reduce their struggle to this one aspect, was not only to prolong the life of capitalism, but also to fortify it and dig the grave of the working class. For the CNT the revolution alone could destroy capitalism.

At the end of the Congress nothing had been decided and everyone was convinced that sooner or later these opposing tendencies would bring about an internal crisis, a crisis which would also be aggravated by the systematic repression inspired by Miguel Maura.

The members of the Congress had barely had time to return home when the telephone employees strike broke out. The demands of the telephone and communications union had to do with work conditions. They also demanded the return of the employees fired under the dictatorship, the right of female employees to marry and to receive a wage allowance during the weeks prior to childbirth, a revision of wages and the recognition of the union organization of the CNT. [4] The Minister of Interior declared that the strike was illegal and sent the Guardia Civil against the workers. The repression was particularly severe and more than 2,000 strikers were imprisoned. In solidarity with the telephone workers, other strikes broke out immediately, accompanied by sabotage. There were a number of areas of unrest: in Andalusia, among the fishermen of Pasagès (San Sebastian) and the metallurgists of Mieres (Asturias), etc.

The general strike which started in Seville in July was the high point of the whole movement. Miguel Maura, who was not inclined to give in, ordered these disorders stopped by every means possible. The Guardia Civil took over the local Federation of the CNT in Seville, named "Casa de Cornelio", by force. During the take over, twenty workers were killed. When the Constituent Cortes met, the Socialists were in the majority with 116 deputies and it was with the approval of the PSOE that Miguel Maura made this declaration: "My duty is to say to the CNT and the FAI, seeing that they don't accept the laws which govern work, that they ignore the round table committees, the mixed juries and specially the authority of the government, that for them there will be no law of association of meeting, nor guarantee which will protect them. Let them submit to the social legislation and respect the law which regulates relations between workers, employers and government, and they will have the right to live normally in relation to the government."[5]

A general strike in Saragossa, Granada and Santander was the answer to this politics of repression. In Barcelona 20,000 metallurgists went on strike, out of solidarity with the political prisoners, who again filled the prisons. The governor of Barcelona, Anguera de Sojo, ordered the Assault Guards to declare martial law against the Construction Workers Unions and to attack their headquarters with the pretext that a secret meeting of the FAI was taking place inside. The encirclement lasted several hours and shots were exchanged. In the end, the troops commanded by Captain Medrano who was in sympathy with the unionists, intervened. The workers gave themselves up to the soldiers but the latter turned them over to the police, and a number of them were assassinated at the very door of Police Headquarters. The other prisoners, after being savagely beaten in the cellars, were taken, as there was not enough room in the Model prison, to a boat which was not being used called the ''Manual Lopez''. Among them was a young man of 21, who was making his debut in anarchosyndicalist activity, Mariano Rodriguez Vasquez, who was soon to become famous under the nickname of ''Marianet''.

Meanwhile, in Andalusia and La Mancha, and specially in Cordoba and Toledo, the situation of the peasants was becoming unbearable. The landowners flouted the law with the consent of Miguel Maura, letting the fields lie fallow. The peasants answered by seizing the lands, and between August and September these acts of collective expropriation became generalized. General Sanjurjo, a declared monarchist and head of the Guardia Civil, ordered the latter to oust the peasants from the fields.

The CNT and the anarchists supported the strikes and the occupation of the lands, while the Socialists controlling the UGT made themselves the instrument of government policies. Opposition was reflected within the CNT, where the moderate faction in a manifesto of the so-called ''Thirty''[6] denounced the ''dictatorship'' of the FAI, as responsible for the ''radicalism'' of the CNT. This manifesto justified the policies of class collaboration advocated by the Minister of Labor, the Socialist Largo Caballero, and the repression carried out against ''the uncontrolled elements''. The bourgeois press, specially Catalan, published the manifesto in full, bringing out its constructive character and took the occasion to treat García Oliver, Durruti and Ascaso as thieves and scoundrels.

In a courageous article, Federica Montseny denounced the political campaign and explained the libertarian position of the CNT, not as the work of the FAI but as the historical expression of its anarchist principals.[7] The FAI suddenly became a subject which preoccupied politicians as well as workers and housewives. Little by little a legend was being built up around this organization. Meanwhile, certain people, formerly allied with the FAI were now busy discrediting it, such as the Catalan politicians like Macia, Companys and Miguel Badia. The latter, who in 1925 was still an adolescent and had offered to make an attempt on the life of Alphonso XIII now in 1932 uttered a sentence which became famous: ''Those people are bandits with a CNT card''.

While this campaign of denunciation was going full blast, Rosa, the sister of Durruti, paid him a visit. This is what she reports: ''The conditions in which my brother was living, filled me with horror. Since his installation in de Freser Street, in the Clot district, the house was empty. One or two pieces of furniture, a bed without a mattress with a blanket on the springs, these were the only conforts owned by my brother and my sister-in-law Mimi, who was pregnant with Colette. I scolded him for not having asked us for money. He shrugged his shoulders and got out of it with a joke: "You know Emilienne eats a lot. You will see what a magnificent child I am going to have.' He had an incurable optimism.''[8]

In reply to the internal crisis and the repression which became harsher daily around the CNT, specially in Catalonia, the unions decided to hold a regional congress. The result was a condemnation of the minority which had broken the solidarity agreement, to a point of turning to the bourgeois press to attack the organization in which it was active. The Congress asked the signers of the manifesto for a public retraction. And Juan Peiro was replaced by Felipe Alaiz, as editor of *Solidaridad Obrera*. [9] For the second time, those in the minority who had been attacked, broke the solidarity agreement and engaged publicly in a struggle against those whom they called the "FAIistas".

The Esquerra Catalana (left-wing Catalan) which was following the ins and outs of this break attentively, hastened to create a worker's organization, the Catalan Worker's Federation (FOC) in order to welcome into it the dissidents of the CNT. But the latter turned their backs on the FOC and organized themselves as an unaffiliated opposition union. It was a schism since the CNT fought it and wasted a good deal of energy on it. [10]

Footnotes

1. In the first meeting of the anarchist groups of Barcelona the "Solidarios" were confronted by another group, which had taken the same name during the period of the dictatorship. To avoid confusion the older "Solidarios" took the name. "Nosotros".
2. Rudolf Rocker. *op. cit.*, Volum II. p. 162.
3. Idem.
4. Canovas Cervantes. *Apuntes historicos*. See also Vol. II of Peirats' work already mentioned.
5. Miguel Maura. *op. cit.* p. 289.
6. The complete text of this manifesto can be found in Volume I of Peirats' book. already mentioned.
7. *El Luchador*. September 18. 1931.
8. Letter from Rosa Durruti to the author.
9. Felipe Alaiz wrote an article on Francisco Ascaso in the November 1938 issue of the magazine *Umbral*: "Francisco came with García Oliver and they told me. 'You should become the editor of *Solidaridad Obrera*. since you had more votes than Macia. The Catalan Confederation of the CNT elected you by 400,000 votes.'
   N.B. — This refers to a plebiscite organized in Catalonia where the Constitution was voted in by 300,000 electors.
10. The Unions of the opposition took root in only one area of Catalonia. in Sabadell. Already a few years before this area. where Moix was a militant. had wanted to create a neutral union. The pro-Bolshevik campaign was carried on in the years 1922-24 relying on him. These Unions also had a certain strength in Valencia and in Huelva (Andalusia). The most outstanding people in them were Juan Lopez. Juan Peiro. Angel Pestaña. Ricardo Fornells. etc. But Angel Pestaña with Fornells and others soon founded the Syndicalist Party and Pestaña became a deputy in the elections of February 16th.

3/

THE "BUENOS AIRES", A FLOATING PRISON

THROUGHOUT THIS PERIOD DURRUTI, like all his comrades, was overwhelmingly busy; conferences, assemblies and meetings followed each other almost daily. It was a time for clarifying the positions of the CNT and anarchism, and for making public denunciations of the activities of the government against the working class.

Durruti was in the forefront of this struggle, and the politicians and bourgeoisie from their side came to consider him, with Francisco Ascaso, the country's enemy number one. All sorts of calumnies were resorted to against them. The bourgeoisie pictured them as people who used violence because of their delight in disorder. To the Republicans and Socialists in power, they had sold out to the reaction and were the grave-diggers of Republican order. The new Catalan politicians, formerly allies in the struggle against the dictatorship, now appealed to the regionalist sentiments of the population by presenting Durruti and Ascaso as "Murcians" and "Castillians" and therefore enemies of the new Catalonia. All of them were trying to arouse the working class against these men, but this kind of politics was shown to be ineffectual. When *Solidaridad Obrera* denounced the arbitrary detention of Ascaso and the violent beating he received in the cellars of the Central Police Station, the reaction of the population was unanimous. To point up their solidarity with Ascaso, his comrades at work declared a strike and demanded his immediate release. To sustain this protest movement, the Regional Committee of the CNT undertook an information campaign and organized meetings throughout Catalonia.

Durruti took part in a number of these public manifestations, each time denouncing the repressive politics of the government: "The politicans in power have shown their weakness once again. They promised the people profound social reforms and this is why the people elected them in June. Because they haven't kept their word, they have betrayed their mandate. We are living as we did in the time of the monarchy! Nothing has changed. The reactionary elements continue to occupy the bureaucratic posts and plot openly against the people. At the head of the army and the police one finds the same generals as before and with the same results: massacre of the starving peasants and the striking workers by the Guardia Civil and the Assault Guards.... Facing this situation something must be done. The people must look for its salvation outside party politics, outside the bourgeois Parliament, and develop its own action in the street. For the working class there is no other effective politics but the revolutionary struggle."[1]

After one of these meetings Durruti was arrested by order of the government which pretended he had "insulted the authorities". His detention was brief, but this didn't stop the press from speaking about the imprisonment of the agitator, Durruti. In a letter to his family Durruti commented: "I think you will have learned from *La Tierra* of Madrid about my detention, which must have worried our mother a lot. I don't know who wrote about this but the fact is that no one has bothered me. My life is going on as usual. I have not missed a single day at work and I visit the union daily. Ascaso is the one who is in prison, but he will come out one of these days.... *Solidaridad Obrera* is carrying on a strong campaign for his liberation..."[2]

A few days later Durruti wrote: "Today I didn't go to work because all the comrades left prison, and among them Ascaso. These days I have been very busy trying to get them released. I created a big scandal throughout Barcelona. I think that I won't be able to avoid passing a few days in prison."[3]

His fears were confirmed at the time of a meeting organized in Gerona by the local unions. Durruti was to speak but when he got off the train, the police arrested him and took him to the police station, accusing him of having organized a plot against Alfonso XIII in Paris. The workers immediately organized a demonstration and marched towards the City Hall to demand the immediate release of Durruti. The Mayor understood that the people would not accept the farce of a plot against the King, who had been deposed several months before, and he gave the order to free the prisoner.

Returning to Barcelona, Durruti wrote to his sister, Rosa: "You see, Rosita, my instinct didn't fool me. The Republican authorities wanted to arrest me for plotting against the monarchy. Greater foolishness cannot be imagined... but let's move on to more serious matters. To compensate me for my arbitrary dismissal of which I was victim during the railroad strike in 1917, I have been given 2,600 pesetas which have been a great help to us. Mimi went out with friends yesterday for the first time since the birth of Colette, and she bought things which we lacked at home and necessities for the little one." And a few days later: "Colette is very pretty and she is already beginning to smile. She is the delight of all our friends and they say she is very beautiful and I reply with the smile of a tender father. Her mother has a good supply of milk and eats with relish, so that the little one is in good health too. We have bought a lot of things: wardrobe, mattress, blankets, cradle, shoes... Come, Rosita, decide before they put me in prison. If you come, we will fix up a bed for you now that we have a mattress."[4]

In these letters the personality of Durruti is reflected clearly: one sees his great sensibility, a characteristic little known even by his comrades in the struggle. The few letters that have been preserved from this period give a faithful image of the daily problems of the revolutionaries at that time.

In that same month of December 1931 — and for the first time since 1921 — Durruti went to Leon and was able to embrace his mother. Actually he made this trip because of the health of his father, who died, however, before he arrived. The burial became the occasion for a demonstration as the proletariat of the city wanted to take part in the burial of a good man, but also to show their solidarity and sympathy for his son, who had been maligned by all the bourgeoisie.

When the ceremony was over, the local unions of the CNT asked Durruti to prolong his stay for a few days in order to take part, the next Sunday, in a meeting they were organizing in the Plaza de Toros of Leon. The meeting was announced not only in Leon, but in all the mining region. The bourgeoisie and the Church put pressure on the commander of the Guardia Civil to bar the meeting. A pretext was quickly found: Durruti was arrested for his participation in the attack on the bank of Gijón. At the office of the commander of the Guardia Civil, when it was suggested that he take the train that very night for Barcelona, Durruti started to laugh. And after having told the commanding officer how the *pesetas* stolen from Gijón had been used, he asked: "Sir, don't you think it would be better for me to speak at the meeting tomorrow? Unless you would prefer a general strike in Leon?"

The next day the Plaza de Toros was full of people. During the meeting, presided over by Tejerina, the local secretary of the CNT, Durruti spoke at great length. In simple terms, supporting each assertion with a spirited gesture, he showed the reasons why the Republic was incapable of resolving the social and political problems of Spain. He concluded in this way: "I maintain that we are living in a pre-revolutionary period, that the revolution is incubating in the guts of the world of work. The day it breaks out, there will be no quarrel or political meeting but an authentic social revolution, which will bury the bourgeois world under its debris. And it will create another world, where the workers will give proof of their abilities, improving industry and agriculture so that there will be bread for everyone, liberty for all without privileges, without parasites. But so that this revolution can become a reality, it is necessary for all, absolutely all the workers who are aware, to work together, and orient all their activities towards one goal, the only one allowed a worker: to break his chains and find his dignity once again. Forward then for the social revolution." [5]

Durruti's enthusiasm at Leon wasn't new but a constant in his revolutionary attitude. When he appealed to the workers, it was not as a demagogue but as a sincere militant. Nevertheless his faith in the revolution didn't blind him to the contradictions to be found in the working class. This is shown clearly in the testimony of Pablo Portas when he reports a conversation with Durruti, held at a particularly critical moment for the CNT. Durruti stated that it was necessary to conceive the revolution as an extended dynamic process, with its ups and downs, and that the militant should not permit himself to be defeated by those moments of general depression. On the contrary, it was necessary to bypass these occasions to go to the heart of the situation. This is what Durruti was forcing himself to do at that very moment, according to Portas, when the anarchist movement was undergoing "the worst phase of the repression".

"The workers, on the other hand, were spending their time on sports and amusements, forgetting completely that the anarchists and the anarcho-syndicalists were being tracked down like wild beasts." Faced with this depressing attitude, Durruti persisted in repeating: "You will see, little by little as the situation deteriorates, the working class will know how to react accordingly. In the meantime it is necessary to hold the fort.... There is no doubt that during this period, it will be the most active and the toughest who will fall. But this struggle is not sterile, it is a forfeit for the harvest of the future. There are no pre-revolutionary periods without many victims, but in the end the victory is assured." [6]

The miners of the pit at Cardona (Barcelona) organized a meeting with Vicente Perez Combina, Arturo Parera and Buenaventura Durruti as speakers, which drew hundreds of men coming from the pits of Figols, Suria, Sallent. In his speech, Durruti showed the need for a revolution, since bourgeois democracy had already risen in the world and the workers had nothing further to hope for from the reforms of the bourgeoisie, or from Social-Democracy, which was more discredited every day. [7]

A few days after this meeting, the region was the center of a bold revolutionary action. On January 19, 1932 an armed uprising led to the proclamation of libertarian communism, the abolition of private property and money. [8] Government reaction wasn't long in coming. The President of the Council of Ministers and the Minister of War, Manuel Azaña, gave formal orders to the captain general of the Catalan region that "in fifteen minutes" the revolt must be suppressed. Azaña's "fifteen minutes" had to be settled in five days of struggle, and there were arrests by the hundreds, the leaders being taken to a boat, the "Buenos Aires", anchored in the harbor of Barcelona. However the arrests were not limited to the area in revolt, they extended throughout the peninsula, specially to Barcelona, Valencia and Andalusia, which were the most troubled regions.

The round-up started the 20th of January. In Barcelona, at dawn, the police appeared at the homes of the leading militants of the CNT. One of the first to be arrested was Professor Tomas Cano Ruiz. He reports: "Arrested and locked up in a disciplinary cell at Police Headquarters, I was quickly able to realize that this was one of those raids so characteristic in the time of Martinez Anido. The cells of Police Headquarters were full of various "suspects" and anarchists, members of the unions and committees, shop and factory delegates, or plain union members, in a word, workers at the service of the cause which was dear to them."

On the morning of the 21st the Ascaso brothers and Durruti were arrested. On the afternoon of the 22nd all the prisoners were put aboard the "Buenos Aires", which the Transatlantic Company had put at the disposal of the government. The battleship "Canovas" pointed its cannons at this strange merchandise. Sailors with their fingers on the trigger, watched over the prisoners being led into the hold of the boat. They were there without mattresses or blankets, obliged to relieve themselves on the spot, and they were only allowed to get a little air through the lower port-holes. There was very little water, insufficient food. It was a cargo which reminded one of the slave trade — the Republic had become a slave-trader. Moreover the prisoners had no right to visits, nor to mail or packages. It was under such conditions that they lived until the morning of February 9th, the date on which the "Buenos Aires" lifted anchor for an unknown destination, without any civil or military authority having even questioned the prisoners. [10]

At the harbor about twenty women had waited patiently for the boat to sail. Among them the mother of the Ascasos, full of indignation, called out to her sons to have courage. The 10th of February 1932, Durruti's wife, in a letter to the Anarchist Union, reported the deportations. "At home we are in despair because this morning, at 4 o'clock, the "Buenos Aires" left the harbor in the direction of Spanish Guinea, probably for Bata. There are 110 prisoners in this boat and it is to stop at Valencia and Cadiz to pick up other prisoners. We were not allowed to go on board to take leave of them. Only the children, led onto the boat by sailors, were able to greet their fathers. Our little Colette, two and a half months old, was carried there and Durruti at least had the satisfaction of embracing her. Since his arrest, about three weeks ago, we have not been able to see him or speak to him except through the port-holes of the boat.

"While the boat was anchored in the harbor, a hunger strike took place, led by Durruti and Ascaso. After this, Durruti, Ascaso, Masana, Perez Féliu were separated from the rest of the comrades to be deported.

"The newspapers of the country, with the exception of *La Tierra*, approved the attitude of the Minister of Interior with servility, accepting the most absurd lies, the most vile calumnies, to justify this abominable deportation. *Solidaridad Obrera* was banned. Here indeed is the paradox of Spain: while 110 prisoners on the Buenos Aires' are deported without a trial (most of them have not taken part in the recent uprising in Catalonia), the monarchist conspirators walk around freely, the estate owners abandon their lands and the peasants die of hunger. The famous 'law for the defense of the Republic' is not used against the wrongdœrs but against the workers, whose sole offense is that they were faithful to their ideal.

"But if the socialists collaborated with Primo de Rivera, how can one expect that they will be interested in the rights of a people in misery. An eye for an eye, a tooth for a tooth, this must be our law. Despite the departure of our men and without knowing if we will see them again, we declare that we are not conquered, we do not bow our heads." [11]

The boat sailed to Cadiz to take on another load, while remaining far from the harbor for fear of an attack by the population of the city. Next stop: the Canaries. Behind them, waves of strikes were taking place in Spain in response to the government's action.

The 14th of February 1932 the anarchist groups of Tarrasa, an industrial city near Barcelona, held a meeting, where they decided to proclaim a revolutionary general strike to protest the deportations. During the night of the 15th to 16th these groups, armed with pistols and rifles, seized the principal strategic points of the city. Their first action was to lay siege to the barracks of the Guardia Civil, where 160 Guardias were gathered under the orders of a lieutenant. Another

118

January 1932 — Deportation to Canary Islands. Standing left to right: Juan Arcas, Durruti and Domingo Ascaso.

group took over the Town Hall and hoisted the red and black flag. By the 16th, from eight o'clock in the morning, police reinforcements from Sabadell began to arrive. Soon the struggle became general and the revolutionaries only yielded after the exhaustion of their forces. The same kind of actions took place in Andalusia, Saragossa and the Levant.

January 1932 — a group of exiled militants in Villa Cisneros (Africa). In the center of the picture is Francisco Ascaso.

January 1932 — Villa Cisneros. Group of exiled militants with children of the colony.

The government, which found itself in an impasse, mounted a large scale propaganda campaign, justifying to the Cortes the measures it had taken to restore order; measures of repression which the Parliament approved, including the socialist majority. But all these political stances, all these repressive measures, proved ineffective before the extensive popular revolt. Despite their defeat the two insurrections had attained their goal: to focus attention on the idea of libertarian communism, the goal of the proletariat. The Spanish "intelligentsia" started a polemic around this idea and Salvador de Madariaga emphasized the inability of the intellectuals to understand the true aspirations of the working class: "How is this idea of 'libertarian communism' to be taken? It is usually accompanied with a habitual refrain about Spanish illiteracy and that lack of education of the working classes, by those who distinguish themselves precisely by their *own* ignorance of the Spanish working class. But these libertarian Don Quijotes struggling for social emancipation, who tried like the knight of La Mancha to impose their dream on reality, were in no way illiterate. They were all just as capable of reading books as those who accused them of ignorance, but with the difference that, they had far greater creative faculties than those of their pen-pushing enemies. They preferred to create their own values and to live their own lives with a fidelity to their way of thinking which many scholars wrapped up in the comfortable refuge of their libraries would envy.''(12)

While the situation was becoming explosive in the peninsula, the ''Buenos Aires'' left the Canaries steering towards the Gulf of Guinea. At Dakar it took on a load of bananas, the only food given to the prisoners who were piled up in the bottom of the hold. But because of the deficient food and the lack of air, a number of cases of septicemia developed. It was in this state that the boat entered Sta. Isabel de Fernando Po, where all those whose condition required urgent care were hospitalized. Under these circumstances, the commander, cousin of General Franco, telegraphed to Madrid where the Minister of the Navy, Giral, ordered the shipment taken to Bata. Hastily, the sick people were put back on the boat and the ''Buenos Aires'', still accompanied by the gunboat ''Canovas'', made its way toward Rio Muni, where Bata is located. (13)

But a revolt started because of the contradictory orders, the bad conditions of the trip and the general exhaustion. The element of surprise played into their hands and the deportees took command of the bridge. Faced by such a situation and in order to reestablish order, the captain agreed to better the conditions of the prisoners. From then on the treatment aboard was more humane and the food better. They were given litters to sleep on and were allowed to go on deck.

Having at last left Fernando Po, the expedition arrived in Las Palmas where the sick people were landed. The rest of the boatload headed for Rio de Oro. But the commanding officer in this area, a certain Regueral, son of the ex-governor of Bilbao, killed in Leon in 1923, refused to admit Durruti in his area of command. Durruti was isolated with seven of his comrades and they were taken to Puerto Cabras de Fuerteventura. The others, once again, started off towards the African continent. After two months of comings and going on the Atlantic ocean they finally arrived at Villa Cisneros, their destination.

The government had ordered an official journalist to give a report of this strange expedition, in order to the show the country that there was no reason to get worried about the lives of the deportees. But the aviator, Ramon Franco, opposed to this official report, intervened and came to visit the deportees to propose a plan for escaping on a sailboat. (14) His idea was not accepted but when he returned to Spain, Ramon Franco wrote a series of articles on the life of the deportees in which he condemned the politics of the government.

Durruti has left us a vivid account of this dismal experience: ''My wanderings across these seas have ended and now that I am settled on this lost island, I can finally give news of myself. Yesterday I received the first letters since I left Barcelona, one from Mimi, one from Perico (a brother) and other friends. So until yesterday I lived with impatience, ignorant of the fate of Mimi, Colette and the rest of the family. The Republican Government, not content to deport us in the most criminal conditions, continues to hammer away against us, submitting us to the most rigorous isolation. These gentlemen are so barbarous that they think that because we are revolutionaries, we have no feelings and that our families are indifferent to our misfourtune.

"Through the press you have heard about part of our odyssey. I would need a lot of paper and much peace to be able to write about the tragedy of our deportation. We have suffered a lot, passing through dramatic moments, when we were on the point of being shot by drunken officers of the Republican Navy. The ignorant soldiers were ready to shoot us, faced with the orders and menaces of the officers.

"I had the opportunity to speak to a poor sailor. He was ashamed of his conduct on the "Buenos Aires': 'If we pointed our guns at you, it was because the officers had assured us that you wanted to kill us. I found myself on the battleship and I was told that the deportees wanted to kill my brothers, the sailors, and that we should not be cowards. To conquer our resistance they gave us lots of alcohol. It was in this state that my comrades and I had picked up our guns, ready to shoot.'"

Then Durruti speaks of Fuerteventura: "The island is miserable and completely abandoned. We live in a barrack and we are given 1.75 pesetas a day to feed ourselves. These gentlemen must think that we have private means like Unamuno, Soriano and other deportees. But we have no other wealth than our hands as workers. We have submitted a list of complaints and we are waiting for an answer from Madrid. The people in the neighborhood of the island are afraid because they were told before we came that 'we eat small children alive'. Luckily they were able to understand the lie as soon as they were able to make contact with us. Now there is a real bond of sympathy and the children come to play with us: up to now we have eaten none of them!

"I don't know how long they will keep me like this, since they have told me nothing, neither their motives, nor the length of this separation. They pretended when they arrested me in Barcelona, that it was because of the words that I spoke during an international meeting in which I had taken part a few days before.... and I am here, without being able to explain my action, nor being asked for explanations.

"When we return to the peninsula, these gentlemen the socialists — who have forgotten the meaning of socialism if they have evel known it — will have to answer to the working class for their vote on our deportation. And they will have to answer to me for my so-called collaboration with the monarchists and for this story about the millions which, according to them, I have received. [15]

"If this is the way they think to save the Republic without Republicans, they are fooling themselves, because, one day, we, the trouble-makers, who get up every morning to go to work and enter the factory like slaves, we will enter them like masters, because the sole owner of all the social riches is the working class." [16]

In the peninsula worker agitation continued, in agricultural as well as industrial areas and a day didn't pass without a strike breaking out. Meetings followed meetings and speakers pointed out to the government the danger of the country bogging down. The government, deaf to the appeal to free the prisoners and to bring about social reforms, was reaching a state of chaos.

It was under these conditions on August 12, 1932 that the first attempt to install Fascism in Spain occurred. General Sanjurjo, head of the conspiracy, launched the uprising. It failed in Madrid but gained strength in Seville. Facing this situation the anarchist groups of Seville were able to mobilize the working class by forming a Revolutionary Committee. They called the people out to fight and routed the insurgents quickly. And so the CNT saved the Republic, this Republic which, a few days before, had crushed the workers in the Parc de Maria-Luisa, at Arnedo, at Castiblanco, and in many other places. Nevertheless in Barcelona the CNT had to go underground. Its publications were banned, its cultural centers closed, its militants imprisoned by the hundreds.

The policy of the Minister of the Interior, Casares Quiroga, was identical with that of Maura and the policies of Azaña and Alcalá Zamora were similar. So the military rebels were treated indulgently by the government. Their deportation was reduced to a short and peaceful cruise to Villa Cisneros, which meant the transfer of the deported anarchists to Fuerteventura (Canaries).

Soon afterwards, in September, the freeing of the prisoners started to take place. The first to be released were the "terrible" miners of Llobregat, who had been rash enough to introduce libertarian communism for the first time in Spain. From Palmas as far as Barcelona, at all the ports of call, a big proletarian manifestation greeted the returning prisoners with shouts and hurrahs. Ascaso, Durruti and Cano-Ruiz were the last to leave Puerto-Cabra. But taught by the welcome given to the other deportees, the authorities wanted to avoid further demonstrations. So the boat which took them from Las Palmas, the "Villa Madrid", arrived in Barcelona without making stops. But in Barcelona it was impossible to prevent what had been avoided in Cadiz and Valencia and the exiles were greeted with an impressive demonstration. In one year the CNT had increased from 800,000 to 1,200,000 members.

Footnotes

1. Alejandro Gilabert, *op. cit.*
2. Letter from Durruti, October 31, 1931.
3. Letter from Durruti, December 14, 1931.
4. Letter from Durruti, December 16, 1931.
5. *Solidaridad Obrera*, December 23, 1931. A neighbor of Durruti's in Leon, who belonged to the CNT at that time and who is living in Madrid today, brought us this information.
6. *Sembrador*, a libertarian weekly, edited in Puigcerda, November 22, 1936. Article by Pablo Portas.
7. "He advised the miners of Figols to prepare for the final struggle and taught them how to make grenades with tin cans." Alejandro Gilabert, *op. cit.*, p. 11.
8. The destruction of the State and the abolition of classes are born from the same act: the abolition of money and property.
9. Tomas Cano Ruiz, one of the founders of the FAI in 1927. Testimony given to the author.
10. Idem.
11. Letter reproduced in *Libertaire*, February 14, 1932.
12. Salvador de Madariaga, *España*, p. 497.
13. Bata is in Spanish Guinea, in the region of Rio Muni. At that time the population numbered about one hundred. There was one building which housed the military Governor, and also a barrack, a storehouse, a hospital and the Catholic Missions center.
14. Testimony of Tomas Cano Ruiz. Ramon Franco, brother of the Spanish dictator. At the time Ramon was active on the left, putting his reputation and skill as an aviator at the service of the Republic. He died in a plane accident in 1936, after he had joined the insurgents and was preparing to bomb Barcelona. It is rumored that his brother, Francisco Franco, was not unaware of a plot to remove Ramon. The same was rumored about the accident which cost General Mola his life.
15. To justify their votes for deportation, the socialists invented various slanders: one of them reported that Durruti had sold out to the monarchists.
16. Letter from Durruti, Puerto de Cabra, April 18, 1932.

4

"OUR PEOPLE STAND FOR ACTION ON THE MARCH..."

WHEN THE EXILES ARRIVED in Barcelona they realized how much the social climate had deteriorated. The Republican Socialist Government seemed to be unaware of this. The new Minister of the Interior, Casares Quiroga was carrying on the work of Miguel Maura, who had resigned. [1] No change in the politics of the government had resulted from this resignation (and that of Alcalá Zamora), although it freed the Republican coalition of the Monarchist mortgage. Opposed by the workers as well as by the reactionaries, the government was no more than a boat adrift, which had foundered December 10, 1931. That day the Cortes with a Socialist majority, by a vote of 362, named as President of the Republic, Niceto Alcalá Zamora, truly representative of the reaction. For the Republicans and the Socialists this concession was to permit the continuation of the Republic, while the only safe course would have been to fight the right and to lean on the people.

To celebrate the promotion of Alcalá Zamora to the presidency, the Government had organized a ceremony with a military parade. At the same moment, the workers had started a general strike in Saragossa and in the Asturias (where the metallurgists had seized the factories at Mieres). And while the hurrahs in honor of the President were resounding in Madrid, the gunboat "Eduardo Dato" was attacking the coast of Gijón, driving the metal workers out of their factories. Following this bombardment which had caused casualties in the population, the breach between the people and the government grew even deeper.

The exiles were quick to sense the new character of the social struggles. But disagreements inside the anarchist movement blocked all initiatives. Three tendencies stood out in the CNT and in some groups of the FAI. The first, made up of a handful of "old" militants, rather close in theory to those who had broken with the organization, judged that the situation didn't present revolutionary guarantees. For them the important thing was to consolidate the union bases and, for this, they were ready to sign a sort of blank check peace with the government, agreeing to submit to its social regulations.

The second tendency, more important for its dynamism and its youth, consisted of the generation formed under the dictatorship.

A scene from daily life. The dispersal of a demonstration by the Assault Guards.

Its partisans held a thesis diametrically opposed to that held by the first group and wanted to carry the struggle to its ultimate consequences: to fight to the death with the Republican Government.

Finally the third tendency was composed of theoreticians. Despite brilliant political analyses, this group condemned itself to failure because of its doctrinal rigidity.

The "Nosotros" group (whose position was mistakenly classified as anarcho-bolshevik) was the most radical wing of the second tendency. This tendency succeeded in asserting itself and then began what was to be called the insurrectional clycle of anarchism. In the "Nosotros" group three personalities stood out, Garcia Oliver, Francisco Ascaso, Buenaventura Durruti. Although of opposing temperaments, these three men gave cohesion and balance to the group. All three had borrowed from Michael Bakunin two of their basic concepts: absolute confidence in the creative capacity of the working class and the necessity for a revolutionary organization.

Francisco Ascaso presented his theoretical theses in an article addressed particularly to the so-called "theoreticians": "Our movement is often criticized for its lack of ideological content and this objection is perhaps not free of all foundation. Nevertheless we are victims of a lack of comprehension and an unjust interpretation of things.

"If we compare our movement with those in other countries, I sincerely believe that its "theories" are not brilliant. But if the Spanish proletariat isn't educated at the European level, it has, to even things out, a richness of perception and a social intuition far superior. I have never supposed or accepted that the problem of intellectual improvement can be solved by accumulating mentally a large quantity of theoretical formulas or philosophical concepts, which will never be carried to a practical plane. The most beautiful theories only have value if they are rooted in practical life experiences and influence these experiences in an innovative way. This is how we operate and it is this which allows us to expect a lot from our movement.

"I don't pretend, far from it, that intellectual mediocrity is an advantage. On the contrary, I would like every proletarian, every comrade, to exhaust every source of learning. Since this isn't the case, we must then act, taking into account the real possibilities of each person.

"Anarchism has gone through various phases during its history. In its embryonic period, it was the ideal of an elite, accessible to only a few cultivated souls, who used it as a sharp criticism of the regime under which they lived. Our predecessors didn't do so badly since it is because of them that we are today where we are. But comrades, the time for criticism is past. We are in the process of building, and to build, muscular energy is also necessary, perhaps more than the mental agility needed for exercising judgement. I agree that one cannot build without knowing ahead of time what one wants to do. But I think that the Spanish proletariat has learned more through the practical experiences which the anarchists have caused them to live through, than via the publications that the latter have edited and which the former have not read.

"One must try to increase as much as possible the theoretical content of all our activities, but without the 'dry and shrivelled doctrinalism' which could destroy in part the great constructive action which our comrades are carrying forward in the relentless fight between the haves and the have nots. Our people stand for action on the march. It is while going forward that they overtake. Don't hold them back, even to teach them the 'most beautiful theories'." [2]

After the "Nosotros" group had taken this stand, the national committee of the CNT called a National Plenum to define the attitude to be adopted towards government repression. The regional delegates agreed unanimously: it was necessary to answer this violence by revolutionary violence. For this purpose it was decided to create a National Committee for Defense, whose job would be to coordinate on the national level, the actions of all the local Defense groups. Antonio Ortiz, member of the "Nosotros" group, was named secretary of the committee. The formation of such an organization meant clearly that they had gone beyond theory to practise, and to make a common front with the "Nosotros" group and its principals. But because of the differences we have spoken about earlier, certain militants launched a polemic aimed at discrediting the Defense Committee, pretending that because of its specific character, it opened the door to the danger of authoritarianism. This Committee even came to be considered as the military staff of a separate army.

At this point Durruti wanted to dispel the so-called misunderstandings, by clearly stating that the Defense Committee had no other role than to coordinate the activities appropriate to its duties.

In addition it was subject to the fundamental rules of the anarchist movement: federation at the bottom, initiative for everyone, places to meet, assemblies at all levels (local, departmental, regional or national). Thus the power to decide didn't belong to the body, but to the totality of the federated groups.

In spite of this internal polemic, the national coordination of the groups was a necessary elementary need. And considering the social conditions of the epoch, the passing from theory to practise necessarily had to open out into revolutionary actions on the national level.

Until then, criticism of power had been expressed in pamphlets, in the press and at meetings. But experience showed that acts were more effective. Thus the action of the miners when they established libertarian communism in Figols had moved the working class much more than the propaganda of the last sixty years. For the "Nosotros" group, the mission of the anarchists from now on was to make rapid progress by attacking the myths portrayed as the "sacred principles" of bourgeois morality and its repressive code. [3]

The militant activity carried on during the whole month of November permitted the anarchist groups to emerge from their isolation. An information campaign was organized to introduce the positions of the FAI to the people and to denounce the governmental repression. The meeting which opened the campaign was to be held on December 1, 1932, in Barcelona, at the Palace of Decorative Arts and the three speakers were to be Durruti, Ascaso and Tomas Cano Ruiz.

The entrance to the Exposition and the one to the Plaza de España were occupied by the police. The deployment of forces was impressive: the Guardia Civil was patrolling on horseback in the neighborhood of the park and in the Avenue, the Paralelo, the Assault Guards, in groups of four, were spread out all over the square, leaving access open to the adjoining streets. In front of the square Hotkins machine-guns were pointed towards the Exposition. Coming out of the subway, the workers hesitated at first to cross the occupied area, fearing that they would be surrounded. But they quickly understood that such a demonstration of force was only a manoeuver to intimidate them. Then in compact groups, the workers advanced through the ranks of the Guardia Civil, entering the gardens of the Exposition, whose alleys were also being guarded.

From nine o'clock in the morning, everything was full up and many groups had to stay outside. The meeting started with the song "Las Barricadas", and after the speakers had been introduced by Alejandro Gilabert in the name of the FAI, Cano Ruiz spoke and told in detail about his trip on the Atlantic.

Then it was Durruti's turn: "Your presence at this meeting and my presence on this platform show the bourgeoisie and the government clearly that the CNT and the FAI are forces which increase with repressions and become large in adversity. Despite all the blows received, they don't turn aside from their revolutionary objectives. This manifestation should be a warning to the bourgeoisie, to the government and to the socialist comrades. They can judge that the anarchists don't come out of prison and from exile subdued, but more courageous, angrier and stronger.

"The Republican-Socialist Government thought that by deporting a hundred or more workers, that the CNT would knuckle under. Acting as it did, it showed once again its ignorance of social reality and the reason for the existance of anarchism. The bourgois press has applauded the step the government took, the deportation, thinking that once the leaders were exiled the sheep would go back to the sheep-fold. In other words that 'the dog killed, the rabies would disappear'. The bourgeois scribblers were mistaken, just like the government itself. All these gentlemen haven't understood yet that the Spanish working class is not a herd of sheep offering their necks so that a yoke can be placed on them, but that it is composed of brave men and that they will die rather than allow themselves to be subdued.

"Such dreadful things have been said about me, as well as about my comrades in deportation, believing that I would be discredited, but the opposite effect was produced. A scoundrel Durruti is something that the workers can't conceive. They know themselves that scoundrels are not people who get up at six in the morning to earn their bread by the sweat of their brow. To fight us they have used the worst weapons. The theory of the 'leaders' of the CNT is identical to the 'scoundrels' of the FAI.

"Those whom the bourgeoisie call 'leaders' are workers whom all the world knows and their way of life is identical with that of every unfortunate worker. The way they differ is that they have the courage to choose the worst position in the struggle, to be in the front line to stop a bullet or to fill the prisons. The real bandits, the real scoundrels, are the politicians, who need to fool the workers and put them to sleep while promising them a month of Sundays so as to wrest their votes from them, which will bring them to the Cortes and will permit them to live as parasites on the sweat of the workers.

"When our comrades the Socialist deputies also merged their voices with this band of eunuchs, they showed their real faces. Because it is some years since they have ceased to be workers and therefore Socialists. They live only through their activities as deputies.

"(...) For the government, it was a political error to exile us, for they paid our trip to the Canaries so that we could make anarchist propaganda. For once the money that the State stole from the workers served the cause of the revolution.

"Another argument used against us is that we are in the pay of the Monarchists, that we play the game of reaction by fighting the Republic. The attitude of the CNT in Seville shows that this argument is also lame. It is the second time that the CNT has saved the life of the Republic. But the Republicans should not fool themselves. Sanjurjo said that "the anarchist will not succeed' and the anarchists did succeed, and Sanjurjo had to 'bite the dust'. Let the Republicans take notice: the CNT said no to Sanjurjo, but it says no also to the Republic.

"The Republican-Socialists should know that they should either resolve the social problem or else it will be the people who will do it. We think that the Republic cannot resolve it. Also we say this clearly to the working class that there is now only one dilemna: either to die like modern day slaves, or to live like admirable men, on the straight path of the social revolution.

"You then, workers who are listening to me, know now what to expect. The change in the course of your lives depends on you."[4]

Footnotes

1. The vote of 178 to 59 for the 26th article of the Constitution on October 13, 1931, created the first crisis for the Government and dealt with limiting Church power.

Miguel Maura resigned saying that this was a plot against the Spanish Catholic tradition. The 26th article made a clear separation between the Church and State. Subsidies to the Church and Clergy were abolished. Education was taken out of the hands of the Church and the Jesuit order was abolished. The crisis was brought to an end by making Azaña, President of the Council of Ministers and giving him the Ministry of Defense. Casares Quiroga took the Ministry of the Interior.

2. *Francisco Ascaso*, a pamphlet edited by the Peninsular Committee of the FAI, 1937. Article "Nuestro Anarquismo".

3. An echo of this polemic can be found in the press of the period: *Solidaridad Obrera. Tierra y Libertad* and in the magazines *Tiempos Nuevos* and *Revista Blanca*. For Durruti we follow the testimony of Liberto Calleja and Alejandro Gilabert, *op. cit.*

4. *Solidaridad Obrera*. December 3, 1932. A. Gilabert, *op. cit.*

5

REVOLUTIONARY CYCLE

THIS EXPERIENCE SHOWED THE CNT and the anarchist movement that although they were victims of a systematic repression, instead of driving the working class away from the struggle, on the contrary, its audacity increased, in spite of periods of comparative calm.

The situation created by government persecution was more and more intolerable: union shut outs, arbitrary imprisonment, endless fines for the confederal press. And unemployment increased because of the economic crisis, but also due to the deliberate action of the bourgeoisie, who wanted to drive the workers to despair.

For all these reasons the Regional Confederation of Work in Catalonia [1] was forced to study the situation and to search for the best answer. At first this study took place in secret union meetings and within the confederal groups, then in a regional plenary meeting which took place in December 1932. All the delegates present realized that the situation in which the CNT found itself was alarming, all the more since the government was trying to make its existence impossible, as Miguel Maura had announced in the Cortes.

Two solutions were possible. On the one hand it was thought that it would be preferable to continue to build the organization from its working class base, hoping for a popular reaction which would put an end to this state of things. On the other hand, in a more radical and perhaps impatient way, they were in favor of launching an armed insurrection, with all its consequences. The danger of a Fascist coup d'état was emphasized, so repressive that it would ruin all possibilities for revolt. To forestall this coup d'état, to carry the problem of the revolution to the people, to educate the working masses who were still following the socialist faction and oblige the leaders to break with reformist opportunism — these were the many reasons for launching an insurrection. [2]

A Revolutionary Committee was selected and Durruti, Garcia Oliver and Francisco Ascaso were among its members. No date was set — the insurrection would break out when favorable circumstances presented themselves. In a parallel direction, the FAI and the confederal groups held various meetings in order to better coordinate their activities. From the decisions of these groups and the unions a plan of action was evolved which was accepted by the regional organizations of Levant and Andalusia.

From the Revolutionary Committee, Durruti, who also represented the National Committee of the CNT, went to Andalusia at the beginning of January to take part in a congress, which was to be held at Jerez de la Frontera (Cadiz). The surveillance in Andalusia was extreme, the police having been given orders to arrest all the delegates taking part in this regional meeting. But the latter eluded the vigilance of the police. Delegations like those from Vejer, Medina and Casas Viejas, entered Cadiz on foot by skirting the city.

Vicente Ballester, Rafael Peña, the brothers Arcas from Seville, outlined an insurrectional plan along the lines recommended by the Plenum. As soon as the insurrection in Barcelona had taken over the radio transmitter and announced that street fighting had started, the reactionary forces in the Andalusian regions would be disarmed and a march on Jerez de la Frontera would be rapidly organized. Once this reactionary center was controlled, there would be a march on Cadiz and the better to hold this city, the electricity, water and food supplies would be cut off. [3]

All the insurrectional plans depended on the results in Barcelona. If the struggle became generalized there, Andalusia would immediately go into action, and would be followed by Aragon and by the North. But if Barcelona failed, there would be no national movement. [4] In the same way the region around Barcelona would also await the outcome of events in the city. Barcelona itself was divided into three sections: the group living in the first sector was to take over Tarrassa-Hospitalet, Sans, Distrito Quinto as well as the artillery barracks of Atarazanas where some soldiers and sergeants had been won over to the uprising. The delegate for this sector was García Oliver.

The second group was to attend to the districts of San Andres, Pueblo Nuevo, the lower part of San Martin and was to seize the military barracks of San Andres, the Park of la Citadela and Pueblo Nuevo. Francisco Ascaso was to coordinate all these forces.

The objective of the third group was Horta-Carmelo, Gracia and the upper part of San Martin, with the assignment of subduing the barracks of the Guardia Civil of the Travesera de Gracia and of Clot, as well as the barracks of the Cavalry of Lepanto. Durruti had taken the responsibility for this sector.

In the center of the city groups of guerillas were instructed to seize the central offices: telephone, post office, radio, and to paralyze all moves at the police station and Central Police Headquarters. Everything was meticulously organized in order to leave nothing to chance. But an event took place which forced the insurgents to throw themselves into the streets before the appointed hour. In the Clot district where the militants Hilario Esteban and Meler were responsible, there was an explosion in one of the storage workshops where grenades were made, which frightened the neighborhood and resulted in the discovery of the depot by the police. This discovery aroused the Senior Police Officer who ordered an examination of suspicious areas and the arrest of the best known militants.

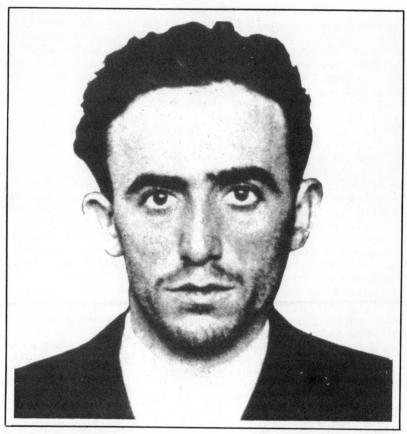

Barcelona 1933 — Francisco Ascaso photographed in a secret refuge following the abortive insurrection of January 8th.

What to do? To wait meant to run the risk of seeing the arms depots fall one after the other into the hands of the police. To launch an attack immediately was to risk a lot without much chance of success. Finally it was decided to profit by the effect of a surprise and the date of the insurrection was set for January 8th in the morning. The day of the 7th and the night were used to touch up the plan quickly and to transfer the arms and bombs to other sites.

The delegates of the Revolutionary Committee used the last hours to give final instructions, and among them was Ascaso. All of a sudden one of the participants interrupted him: "the plan is magnificent, but what if it fails?" Ascaso answered: "If it fails — which we don't wish — we will die like men." And he considered the incident closed. But the questioner returned to the charge: "I prefer to live like a dog than to die like a hero." Ascaso stepped up to him: "I was summoned to a meeting of revolutionaries was assured that it was a question of people convinced of the to carry this action to its limit. That is why I am here. My r is not to convince anybody of the need to risk his life, but to explain the plan for the uprising. It is logical that corrections to improve the plan be made, while protecting the points won in agreement with the other comrades. But to discuss if one should or should not carry out what has been decided on, that is absurd and mad, in this moment when there is no time. If the revolution was a matter of a song, of living, or of drinking a glass of beer, other militants would have made it long ago without waiting. But the revolution my friends, is not that. It's a long difficult march, a march towards the unknown, in which generally the best fall before reaching the goal. It is only at this price that the revolution is possible. If the price seems high to someone, let him continue to lick the feet of those who trample on him, but don't let him interrupt our progress." And going back to the blackboard he continued to explain the plan to be followed. [5]

A few hours later, in another section of Barcelona, near the walls of the Plaza de Toros de San Martin, Durruti was to be found, busy distributing revolvers and grenades to the delegates of the groups of the sector. A young boy, timid and sickly, with long hair, a large black scarf around his neck, approached: "I too want a weapon." He was a young teacher from a rationalist school which the anarchist groups of the de Gracia district had started and he was the son of a libertarian family well-known to Durruti.

The CNT was not rich in teachers and the struggle this day might not be decisive. Moreover the boy was non-violent by nature and if he had come, he had been stimulated by a need to die in a grandiose undertaking. Durruti told him: "This is not the hour to die, but to live. Our struggle is not only carried forward by shots. The rear guard is as valuable as the fighting avant-garde. Your place is not here but in the school." [6]

At 5 o'clock in the morning on January 8, 1933, an explosion rang out near the door of Central Police Headquarters on Layetana Avenue. The windowpanes and pavement were shattered. An enormous hole became visible while the bodies of the guards were embedded in the wall. The insurrection had just started. Explosions were heard in different parts of Barcelona. But what had been fore-seen as a surprise operation, failed. From all sides the Guardia Civil, on foot and on horseback, assisted by the Assault Guards, closed the way to the insurgent groups, stopped them from reaching the barracks where, fearing defeat, the troops remained passive.

In the districts of Pueblo Nuevo, San Martin and Clot Square, the clashes with the Guardia Civil on horseback were bloody and the struggle fierce. At 8 in the morning, the shooting was intense in the upper part of the capital, going from the Travesera de Gracia to-wards Le Guinardo and Horta. In the neighborhood of Sans, La Torrasa and Santa Eulalia, things were going better for the revo-lutionaries who had taken over the Town Hall on which the red and black flag was swaying. At the Center, shots were echoing, but none of the groups had reached their objectives. The officials at the center, well defended, were repelling the drive of the revolutionaries. As for the radio transmitter, light squads of the Guardia Civil prevent-ed every advance.

Towards noon, the insurrection had been crushed. Nothing was left for the insurgents but to hide or escape. The cellars of Police Headquarters were already full of prisoners who learned that one of the causes of their defeat had been the arrest of Juan García Oliver, who, at midnight, had been going to the Sans district in a taxi full of grenades.

In spite of the defeat of the insurrection in Barcelona, either for lack of liaison or because of the impatience of the militants, there was public unrest in Lerida. There the revolutionaries laid siege to the barracks of "La Panera", where the insurgents Burillo, Gou, Encina and Gesio died. In the province of Barcelona the revolutionaries triumphed and proclaimed libertarian communism in Tarrasa, Sardanola and Ripollet. In the Levant the uprising reached the rural areas of Bétera, Bugarra, Risaro, etc. But it was in the regions of Andalusia that it was the most intense: at Arcos de la Frontera, Utrera, Malaga. La Rinconada, Sanlucar de Barrameda, Cadiz, Alcala de los Gazules, Medinasidonia and in the regions of Casas Viejas. And there it was also savagely suppressed. In all of Spain there were men imprisoned and tortured.

The effects of the repression were specially tragic at Betera (Levant) and Casas Viejas (Cadiz), where some revolutionaries were sprinkled with gasoline and burned alive. These assassinations raised a popular wave of indignation and protests reached the Cortes. There, studying the case of Casas Viejas, it was possible to prove that the President of the Cabinet, Manuel Azaña, had asked Captain Rojas to raze the region. [7]

In Barcelona the repression followed the same course. The CNT unions were closed down and the prisons were filled with workers and militant syndicalists. Nevertheless some had been able to escape the repression, among them Durruti and Ascaso. And once again a price was put on their heads. From the refuge they had found in a villa in the Horta district, they cooperated effectively in the reorganization of the anarchist groups and the unions buried in the underground. They took part in secret meetings organized to deal with urgent problems: assistance for prisoners, aid to families, clandestine propaganda, limited at that time to a single publication, *La Voz Confederal (The Voice of the Federation)*. [8]

Perhaps the only article written by Durruti dates from this period, and it is in this underground organ of the CNT that it appeared. In it Durruti analyzes the January insurrection. Notably he writes: "It is certain that conditions were not ripe. If they had been we would not be in prison! But it is certain also that we are living in a pre-revolutionary period and that we cannot permit the bourgeoisie to dominate it by strengthening the power of the State. In the same manner, we must prevent the State from fortifying itself by taking over syndicalism, which is the political ambition of the socialists and of some of our former comrades.

"It is with this perspective that we must interpret the revolutionary attempt of January 8th. We never believed that the revolution consisted of the seizure of power by a minority which would impose a dictatorship on the people. Our revolutionary conscience is opposed to this tactic. We want a revolution by and for the people.

Casas Viejas (Cadiz) January 1933 — Assault Guards surpressing peasants revolt.

January 1933 — burnt corpses of the Casas Viejas peasants.

136

Without this idea no revolution is possible. It would be a Coup d'Etat, nothing more. And we, from the factories, the mines and the country, are seeking to develop an effective social revolution. There is nothing in this of Blanquism or Trotskyism, but the clear and precise idea that the revolution is something that one must work for every day. With this unknown quantity, one can never be certain when it will break out.''

Durruti, in this article, also alluded to the agonizing situation of the peasants and the phenomenon of the occupation of the lands, and he saw more despair than conviction in their actions. But according to him, such actions would give the peasant the consciousness of what he should destroy. "In this way", he said, "one attacked at its very heart the capitalist and statist system, wounded to the death since the uprising of the miners of Sallent.''

García Oliver had expressed the same ideas at a meeting in the Modelo prison of Barcelona and the stand that these two men took must have had widespread repercussions in the unions. (9) The latter, far from condemning the action in January, upheld it in face of the attacks coming from not only the bourgeoisie but also from the moderate tendency of the CNT, which was trying to create a break between the CNT and the FAI.

Ascaso, in an article called "Union independance?", maintained among other things that, under pretext of union independance, an attempt was being made to empty the CNT of all Communist libertarian content, in order to make it into a neutral and amorphous union body. With this in mind the fable of the dictatorship of the FAI in the CNT had been invented. But Ascaso wrote: "There is not a single militant who as a 'FAIistas' intervenes in union matters. I work, therefore I am an exploited person. I pay my dues to the workers' union and when I intervene at union meetings I do it as someone who is exploited, and with the right which is granted me by the card in my possession, as do the other militants, whether they belong to the FAI or not.'' (10)

In April 1933, while a polemic was going on, the two, who were in hiding in Horta, were surprised by the police at night as they were going to a meeting. The arrest caused an immense pleasure to the Catalan politicians who announced that the "two terrible FAIistas, the organizers of the January uprising" had fallen into the hands of the police.

The Chief of Police, Miguel Badia, and the Councillor of Public Order, Doctor Dencas, announced that the FAI was left "completely in shambles". Badia wanted to be the first to question them and to enjoy having them at his mercy. He knew both of them since the days of the dictatorship. He knew about their adventurous life in Europe and America, but facing them, even though he represented force, he found himself disarmed. Having buried his revolutionary ardor in his youth, in exchange for a social position, he was perfectly aware of the contempt which the two anarchists had for him. The interview ended rapidly with a total declaration of war. Durruti and Ascaso were then taken to the cells in the basement of the Central Police Station. They stayed there 24 hours and were then taken with a large escort to the Modelo Prison of Barcelona. It was the first time that Ascaso came out of the Central Police Station without having received one blow. He, who had always been the object of brutal treatment, was agreeably surprised.

Footnotes

1. In each region the CNT took the name of the Regional Confederation of....X, supporter of the CNT.
2. We received this report from one of the delegates, Francisco Isgleas, who was present at the plenum.
3. Federica Montseñy, *Maria Silva, la Libertaria,* brochure, Ed. CNT, Toulouse 1947.
4. In Montseñy's brochure she states that "only the committed parties were to throw themselves into the struggle if the insurrection had succeeded in Barcelona or the insurgents had been able to seize the official centers and the radio. However villages revolted when these conditions didn't exist. This happened because there was no electricity or means of communication. And they didn't have the patience to wait for the arrival of the delegates to tell them about the success or failure in Barcelona. That is what happened at Casas Viejas."
5. The CNT militant, Tomas Perez, who attended this meeting, sent us a report giving the details about this uprising of the federation.
6. Benjamin Cano Ruiz describes this incident in an article that he published in *Tierra y Libertad,* Mexico, November 1966.
7. There is an eye witness report by the journalist, Eduardo de Guzman, about Casas Viejas published in *Tierra,* January 1933. Peirats reprints this article in full in Volume I of his book.
   In the Cortes, Captain Rojas, who commanded the forces which destroyed this region, was asked for explanations. He said that he had obeyed the orders of the general Security Director. The latter, in turn, said he received orders from the Minister of the Interior, Casares Quiroga. The latter maintained that orders came directly from the head of the government, Manuel Azaña. The orders were: "No wounded, no prisoners; shoot to kill". Commenting on the conduct of Captain Rojas, Ascaso published an article in *Solidaridad Obrera* with the title "Even if they order you, captain".
8. In addition to this underground magazine, another one was issued called *FAI. La Voz confederal* managed to have a circulation of 50,000 copies.
9. This article was published anonymously and according to Liberto Calleja it served as an editorial. For the rest of the revolutionary cycle, see the report of the Revolutionary Committee of the Congress of Saragossa, 1936. The conference anticipated this report and García Oliver made this criticism not only in prison but also in later meetings with militants. *Actas Congreso de la CNT: Mayo 1936.* Ed. CNT, Toulouse 1956.
10. Francisco Ascaso in *Solidaridad Obrera,* March 19, 1933. After the events of January 1932, in the magazine *Estudios* of Valencia, articles began to appear and studies on the theory of libertarian communism, with the idea of formulating a program. Among these studies let us point out those by the engineers Higinio Noja Ruiz and Martinez Rizo, by the doctors Isaac Puente, Alcrudo and Remartinez, and those by the economists Gaston Leval, Diego Abad de Santillan and various theoretical works by Orobon Fernandez. Later a pamphlet by Isaac Puente appeared, *El Communismo Libertario,* which served as a base for discussion of the subject at the CNT Congress in Saragossa in May 1936.

6

"BANDITRY, NO; COLLECTIVE EXPROPRIATION, YES!"

WHEN DURRUTI AND ASCASO entered the Modelo Prison in Barcelona, they knew that the repression had been harsh. But there they realized it had been even more cruel than they imagined. Hundreds of workers held as "presos gubernativos" (prisoners of the government), had committed no crime except that they had a CNT card. For those in power, a repression as radical as this was supposed to discourage the lukewarm and to turn them away from the CNT, but they were wrong. The workers who had arrived in prison, often ignoring even the fundamentals of anarchism, left it with a solid theoretical education. The prisons became schools for revolutionaries, Ascaso and Durruti playing important roles in the discussions. Coexistance in the prisons developed class solidarity and in the cells a collectivist regime was established: money, food, everything was shared.

In July 1933 Durruti and Ascaso were transfered to the Fort of Santa Maria (Cadiz), as "presos gubernativos". Soon after they arrived a revolt broke out among the prisoners due to bad prison conditions. Durruti explains this rebellion in a letter to his wife: "There is a limit to human resistance, and the prisoners of Santa Maria fully demonstrated before revolting in August that they had come to the end of that resistance.

"Subjected to cell life, alone and deprived of elementary care, young Luna is dead. The revolt of the prisoners was justified and they became masters of the prison. Frightened, the director asked for help from the government. He was sent a company of Assault Guards, who invaded the interior of the prison using their weapons. The prisoners had only makeshift arms to defend themselves. The guards had guns. There was a savage hand to hand fight.

"In the end, brute force won over reason. Vanquished, the prisoners were isolated and bad treatment, insults, blows were increased. The prisoners answered with a fifteen day hunger strike. Finally the Directors of the prison gave in, but the victory had produced many victims." And Durruti concluded: "As long as such procedures are used in human relations, society can't call itself civilized. This system must be destroyed and replaced by a society where man is not a slave to man but his equal, and where it will be possible to develop all the capacities which man has within him. There will be no peace on earth as long as this kind of repression exists. Revolutionaries should not forget this for it is precisely they who are in charge of destroying it.''[1]

If the treatment of prisoners had become more human, bourgeois justice however was following its course. One day in September Durruti learned that he was to be judged as a "vagrant", a judicial formula invented by the Republic to justify the imprisonment of a citizen whom they were unable to charge with any specific crime. This law had been established for evil doers with no fixed address and no known means of livelihood. To apply this to workers was to inflict the worst of insults. For Durruti it was a slap in the face. "To apply the vagrant's law to me, who have exhausted myself with work! They can condemn me for firing against the police, for trying to transform, by every possible means, this society which I disapprove of and hate. But for vagrancy! No judge has the right to judge the worker Durruti, a vagrant! Tell this to your superiors." A few days later, faced with strikes and manifestations throughout the country demanding the freeing of prisoners, Durruti was released.

The government was outmatched and little by little had to free all the prisoners. At the beginning of October Francisco Ascaso was also freed. Passing through Madrid he violently denounced the savage attitude of the Republican authorities towards the prisoners of the Fort of Santa Maria. [2]

The situation was scarcely favorable for Durruti and Ascaso who were looking for work. There was unemployment and a systematic boycott by bosses of "public enemies". Emilienne Morin, Durruti's companion, had the same difficulties. Finally she found a job as cashier at a movie house.

Learning that a metallurgical workshop was looking for three workers as adjusters, Durruti, who was very fond of his craft, presented himself at the office with two comrades. As usual they didn't want him. The two comrades then insisted that the union delegate of the shop be informed. But Durruti explained to them that this would involve the risk of a strike by the workers in the shop. "The union must know nothing about this. Tomorrow you go to work. It is useless to strike the iron at this time: it is cold. Strikes are declared when the workers want them. If a strike broke out in the metal industry today, we would be playing the game of the bourgeoisie. I have never played the game of the opponent and today, out of amour-propre, I will not permit a strike to break out in which we have nothing to gain but a lot to lose." [3]

The year 1933 was marked by an economic crisis. It was the reflection of an international crisis and created an explosive situation, specially in Barcelona, where there was a heavy concentration of workers. Massive dismissals took place in almost all industrial sectors and unemployment touched practically every working class family. To deal with this situation, seeing that the unemployed received no indemnity from the State, and the CNT had no funds with which they could help, a kind of union for the unemployed was organized. The latter forced all the bosses, who needed overtime work done, to take charge of a few of their people. Groups of unemployed were also organized to go and eat en masse in the restaurants in town. Groups of women demanded credit in the grocery stores where they shopped. All these actions were crowned by a generalized rent strike, which to be effective required that committees be organized in each house, street and district, to create a common front against the police in case of eviction.

In addition there was the chronic strike of the Telephone and Tramway Companies of Barcelona, which forced the strikers, because of the bitterness of the struggle, to resort to acts of sabotage such as a bombing attack on the telephone exchanges or the burning of tramways.

And so it was not surprising that in such a climate of social tension, people pushed to despair, tried to find a solution, even going in for armed robbery. Certain militant anarchists were trapped in this net, but the FAI did everything in its power to stop the isolated actions of these comrades and to give priority to collective actions. There were many meetings where these problems were discussed. It was in the course of one of these, that Durruti had to confirm his position, when someone reproached him for also having practised this kind of action: "It is true that I attacked banks, not only in Spain but throughout the world, but... always for a general cause. The millions that were taken, went immediately into the funds of the organization. No one pocketed a cent. Often, a few hours after the expropriation, the militant involved found himself without anything to eat. That method was used then because the circumstances were different from those today.

"A million trade unionists, a people waiting for the favorable moment to carry out the great revolution requires other tactics, mass actions, expropriations of factories, of lands, of mines. When a factory closes, the workers must occupy it and we, the militants, must be the first to practise this revolutionary expropriation, heralding the way to total expropriation. Banditry, no; collective expropriation, yes! The March of History has gone beyond yesterday. And he who wants to relive it, shielding himself with the "right to live", is free to do so. But he must do so outside our ranks, renouncing his title of militant and accepting the responsibility of his act for himself only, without compromising the life of the movement nor its prestige before the working class." [4]

The decision was final: no more "banditry" in the ranks of the anarchists. And so the FAI could confront the bourgeois press campaign undisturbed, certain that none of its militants would be compromised in actions of this kind.

La Vanguardia of Barcelona, a well known right wing paper, had made itself particularly conspicuous in this campaign of running down anarchism and likening it to banditry. Ascaso and Durruti decided to put an end to this by paying a visit to the editor of this daily. Once in his presence, they revealed who they were: "We are the representatives of the FAI and we have chosen your paper to publish a statement for us and here is the text: 'The FAI proposes to organize collective expropriation in Spain by means of a social revolution and by establishing Libertarian Communism. The methods used will be mass action and revolutionary general strikes. Every other means, such as individual theft, that is to say banditry, is in opposition to the revolutionary practises of anarchism and consequently anarchism denounces this method as invalid.' This is what we ask. As editor of this publication, when you have learned, among other things, about armed thefts, limit yourself to reproducing the simple truth, without mentioning the names of the CNT or the FAI since these organizations have nothing to do with this kind of activity. We hope you pay careful attention to this matter and that you will censor the stories of your reporters who are too frivolous. Don't oblige us to revive the union practise of 'red censorship', which the Union of Graphic Arts is ready to use.''[5]

Footnotes

1. Letter from Durruti to his wife. The last paragraph describes the photograph of five militants (Ascaso, Durruti, Perez Combina, Paulino Diaz and Lorda), prisoners in Santa Maria, which had been enclosed and which was used for propaganda during the liberation campaign being carried on at that time. (Letter and photo in private archives)
2. *CNT*, November 3, 1933.
3. An article in the magazine *Umbral*, November 1938, by Gonzalez Inestal recalling the life of Durruti.
4. Juan Manuel Molina (Juanel), at that time editor of the anarchist weekly, *Tierra y Libertad*, was at that meeting and furnished these facts.
5. "Censura roja" was the method used by the typographical workers during the Barcelona general strike in December 1919. They censored all reports in periodicals of government activities which might be harmful to the strike movement. The Graphic Arts Union of Barcelona was even able to impose fines on the editors of publications which would not submit to the "red censorship". Anecdote reported by Liberto Calleja.

7

THE ELECTORAL STRIKE OF 1933

LERROUX'S TERM as President of the Council of Ministers ended on November 4, 1933. Alcalá Zamora turned to Martinez Barrio to form a government which would dissolve the Cortes and prepare new elections. The Socialist-Republican government had completed its term.

The electoral campaign was starting and the right formed a bloc and presented one candidate. Its electoral slogan was amnesty for the prisoners of the "sanjurjada", those who were involved in the anti-Republican uprising of August 10, 1932, organized by the monarchist General Sanjurjo. Two other topics were added: anti-Marxism and defense of the Church.

The left, divided between Republicans and Socialists, based their propaganda on the health of the Republic, which it was necessary to purge of the corruption of the Radicals (Lerroux) and to free from clerical domination (Gil Robles). The basic problems, general amnesty for "political" prisoners, unemployment, priority to agrarian reform, nationalization of the mines and monopoly in the hands of foreign capital, were entirely neglected.

Saving the Republic meant nothing to the working class. Save the Republic, why?

The CNT called a national plenum of the regional committees. The position adopted was published: "No one is to vote.... Politics only serve to fool the working class in its aspirations for complete emancipation... But we recommend that everyone prepare intensively so that we will be ready to oppose capitalism and the State, with some possibility of success." It was also decided that in case of a victory of the right, a general revolutionary strike would be started, to be pushed as far as armed revolution, and carrying along with it the workers controlled by the UGT.

The editorial in *CNT,* their national mouthpiece, was explicit: "The principal base of libertarian communism is the Commune. State centralism has not been able to destroy this popular manifestation in Spain. The historic aspiration of our people is rooted in it and it provides the essential base for a social and libertarian set up. To take over the Municipal Government and proclaim the free Commune is the first step of libertarian revolution. The Municipal Government having become the Commune, all its functions become collectivized in the hands of the people. The latter acts as administrator for maintaining equality, duties and rights, and the Popular Assembly becomes the executive power, sovereign and unequalled." [1]

The electoral campaign opened, marked by violence. *Acción Catolica* organized a veritable market for votes, putting into motion its machinery set up originally to collect alms, and protected by the "caciques" of each village. Gil Robles was the prospective leader of this reactionary and clerical bloc, the CEDA, made up of financiers, landlords, the big bourgeoisie and the military, who for centuries had impeded the forward march of the country.

In face of the CEDA, the poor had no other recourse than armed insurrection, since their so-called representatives, Socialists and Republicans, who had been in power for two years, had filled them with disgust for politics. Between the Fascist right and the left, represented by the liberal bourgeoisie, the CNT had only one course: to foster a revolutionary climate, orienting the working class towards the logical end to which the historic situation was inexorably leading.

A difference within the "Nosotros" group broke out for the first time at the regional plenum of Catalonia. With the exception of Durruti and Ascaso, everyone thought that an armed insurrection, because of current conditions, would bring defeat. There was no time to organize this movement. In addition, according to García Oliver, a paramilitary organization was indispensable. Finally, one should not forget the state of exhaustion in which the CNT found itself.

But for Durruti, a defeat was preferable to standing still or campaigning in favor of the left. He also thought that current conditions were better than those of January 8th, because at that time the movement had been inspired solely by anarcho-syndicalism, while the movement which was being organized now was more popular. It would be possible to attract the mass of workers who were still following the Socialists and Republicans. For the latter would undoubtedly suffer defeat on November 19, 1933. If the worst occurred "this revolutionary movement would serve as a warning to the government. In Spain it was not possible to govern against the CNT." In other words, Durruti meant that it was necessary to show those in power that the people were ready for anything. "There are circumstances", he concluded, "in which it is not permissible to doubt."

The situation offering no other solution than a revolutionary course, his position was adopted. It was one of the most reckless decisions which the CNT had ever taken. Actually the best of its militants were stagnating in prison. Andalusia had barely recovered from a bloody repression. In Catalonia, without a moment of peace, the people were moving from an underground existance to a legal one, at such a pace that no difference was made between the two.

The only confederal stronghold was in Aragon, with contagion spreading possibly to Asturias and Galicia. Aragon would thus become the principal focus of the insurrection. The uprising would be supported by general strikes in all the regional capitals and in the villages. A National Revolutionary Committee was chosen, composed of Durruti, Isaac Puente and Cipriano Mera. They would be helped by the militants of Saragossa, the city chosen as the seat of the Committee.

Because of the lack of militants, Durruti had to take on a second job: he was one of a group of speakers who were to take part in a propaganda campaign and he spoke before a number of gatherings. One of the most important was at the Plaza de Toros in Barcelona, which was attended by more than one hundred thousand people. The lawyer, Benito Pabon of Granada, the writer, Victoriano Orobon Fernandez, the cork factory worker, Francisco Isgleas and the metal worker, Buenaventura Durruti, followed each other on the platform. The last speaker proclaimed: "Faced with the defeat of democracy and the menace of Fascism, the CNT affirms its right to make the revolution. The Socialists and Communists say that abstaining from voting in the elections will help Fascism. But as we have always said that the State is the instrument of oppression at the service of a class, we remain faithful to ourselves. And as we think that the liberation movement must always oppose the State, that is why we advocate an active electoral abstention. That is to say, that while standing aloof from the stupidity of elections, we must remain actively on guard in the factories and in the streets.

"Consider the example of Germany, where the triumph of Fascism was preceded by all sorts of violence against the proletariat. There they advised people to vote right up to the moment when Fascism took power. The Socialists and Communists knew Hitler's intentions, which did not hinder them from favoring Fascism by voting. It was not the hour to vote but to pick up a gun. The dilemma was obvious: 'revolution or fascism'. There was no other issue.

"Today we are living in the same situation. Fascism says it will use 'the dialectic of fists and guns'. Workers, remember these words! Calloused hands must be lifted and the guns of the Fascists must be opposed by the guns of the proletariat. Spain represents an enormous hope for the world. If we raise a barrier against Fascism, it is very possible that we will set in motion a new turn in European and world history. History will not register the paltry actions or the internal struggles, it will only preserve the imposing work that we are able to create." [2]

On November 16, 1933, the electoral campaign ended with a big meeting organized by the FAI at the Palace of Decorative Arts, in which Vicente Perez Combina, Francisco Ascaso, Buenaventura Durruti and the French militant, Sebastien Faure, took part. Francisco Ascaso condensed his statement in a few sentences: "The revolution is not a barbaric act, but an historical necessity for the oppressed if the latter want to regain their dignity. By submission and reform, oppression and slavery are kept alive. Through tough and stubborn struggle, the slaves can break their chains and create a new world. It is up to you, working men, to choose! This job is yours, and the outcome is yours alone."

Durruti made the last speech: "Workers, the storms are approaching. To face all emergencies, the FAI advises the workers of the CNT, since it is they who control the factories and the production sites, not to abandon them. They should stay close to the machines.

Let us start to set up workers' councils and use the techniques which should be basic to the new social and libertarian economy. The anarchists, as always, will do their duty by being the first to throw themselves into the struggle. The occupation of the factories in Italy should be a lesson to us. The occupations should spread out towards the exterior, for like all insurrections, they must be on the offensive. To be on the defensive always means death to every uprising, so the seizure of factories without cooperation from outside means death through isolation. The workers have nothing more to lose than their chains. Long live the social Revolution."[3]

Footnotes

1. *CNT*, Madrid, November 3, 1933.
2. *Solidaridad Obrera*, November 7, 1933.
3. *Solidaridad Obrera*, November 17, 1933.

8

THE INSURRECTION
OF DECEMBER 1933

NO ONE WAS SURPRISED by the results of the general election of November 19, 1933. The victory of the right was assured because the left was divided, between a working class disappointed by the governmental policy of the Republicans and the Socialists, and the CNT which advocated an "electoral strike". [1]

The decisions of the federation had been followed, since abstentions of 32% were counted with a peak of 40% in Catalonia. The Socialists and Republicans were the big losers in these elections, which had the look of a real disaster for them. The big victor was Jose Maria Gil Robles, head of the "Confederación Española de las Derechas Autonomas" (CEDA, Spanish confederation of autonomous rights). This victory of the right meant the possibility of an effective revenge by the forces of reaction: increased repression and attacks against the timid social reforms introduced during the preceding period.

During the entire electoral campaign the CNT hadn't stopped denouncing elections, advocating armed insurrection as the only revolutionary way out for the working class. The Socialist leaders had turned a deaf ear to the appeals of the CNT. But no longer in power and taught a lesson by the fate of their German comrades, wouldn't they now join the anarcho-syndicalists to launch the revolution? This question was asked the CNT at the moment when they were making preparations for the insurrection.

Since the 23rd of November, the National Revolutionary Committee had been installed in Saragossa on the second floor of a building on the calle de Convertidos. There, the three militants chosen by the congress of the CNT, Durruti, Isaac Puente, Cipriano Mera, who had been joined by Joaquin Ascaso and representatives of the FAI and of the FIJL ("Iberian Federation of Libertarian Youth") were working out a plan for the uprising.

The map of Spain was divided into zones of different colors, each one determining the particular character that the insurrection would take in these regions. Thus, in the "red zone" (Aragon, Rioja and Navarre), the uprising was to be violent. In the "blue zone" (Catalonia) on the contrary, the general strike was to be the preferred weapon. Finally, the "green zone" (Center and North), where the Socialist influence was dominant, represented the areas where the anarcho-syndicalists hoped, under cover of the general strike, to win over the workers of the UGT. Two favored sectors were colored in both red and blue: Andalusia and the Levant.

The Revolutionary Committee also did not neglect propaganda material which was to be distributed in the areas in revolt. Leaflets called on the workers to occupy the factories, shops and mines and to take a hand in the control of production. The workers were invited to form themselves into councils, federated on the local level, while the villages, formed into communes, would be in charge of organizing distribution. Armed popular militia created in each commune, would assure the defense of the Revolution, etc., etc.. [2] These leaflets had been sent to all the Defense Committees of the CNT and to the anarchist groups in charge of coordinating the movement.

Everything seemed ready and nothing was left but to wait for the moment to act. But at the last minute the Aragonese had doubts: weren't the Catalans better located than they were to launch the insurrection and to take the leading part? Isaac Puente and Joaquin Ascaso having failed in their attempt to convince the Aragonese to keep to the original plan, Durruti, in turn, tried to persuade them. He presented himself at the meeting which the confederals in Saragossa had decided to organize, in order to find out if Aragon would take part or not, in the revolutionary movement. It was the third time this question had been discussed. During the two preceding assemblies, neither Puente nor Joaquin Ascaso had been able to influence the Aragonese. The latter maintained that the other more powerful regional federations should take over the beginning of the uprising. They stuck to their obligation, but they didn't want to be considered as the principal focus of the insurrection.

Durruti explained to these men, whose courage and worth he had known for a long time, that all the conditions were there to make Aragon the center of the proletarian revolution. He explained in detail the situation in Barcelona, where the militants had to suffer the serious consequences of the insurrection of January 8th. Andalusia was in no better condition. As to the Center and Madrid, its militants would bring an important aid as always, but facing the UGT they couldn't be decisive in a general strike.

And so it was only through Aragon and Saragossa that the CNT could keep its promise to the working class. If the Aragonese stuck to their position, the CNT would nevertheless launch the insurrection but it would go no further than a simple revolutionary general strike. On the other hand, if the latter agreed to change their decision and take part in the action, the insurrection could then extend to the rural areas. Durruti felt it was of great importance in the struggle to achieve this solidarity between the workers and the peasants, a union without which the revolution could never succeed.

Durruti presented his analysis coldly, forcing himself to curb the enthusiasm of his passionate nature. He added that "(...) the fact of losing a battle shouldn't alter the reason one might have for fighting for a cause, the weapon of the revolutionary being, exactly that faith which he had in the cause." And then returning to the question of *action,* that action which he considered the moving force of all social progress, Durruti at this point used the tone which was natural to him. A witness at this meeting reports that he "communicated his revolutionary fervor to all the militants of the Metal Workers Union of Saragossa who were present at the memorable meeting which was to settle the glorious revolutionary movement of the 8th of December in Aragon." [3] And he convinced the Aragonese that they should take part in the action.

At ten o'clock on December 8, 1933, the government warned by the provincial governors, declared a "State of Siege". The struggle had already started in half the peninsula. The strike was general in Saragossa, Barcelona, Huesca, Valencia, Seville, Cordova, Granada, Cadiz, Badajoz and Gijon. It was only partial in the zones controlled by the Socialists, in Asturias and Bilbao. In the other provincial capitals and in Madrid, great confusion reigned.

Throughout the country, the confrontation was generally in the form of a general strike punctuated by clashes with the police. The insurgents blew up several bridges and dynamited a number of official centers. In the sectors controlled by the revolutionaries, popular assemblies voted for the suppression of private property, the disbanding of the police and the army. It put an end to class domination and the defense of the revolution was turned over to the armed militia, posted at strategic points.

But this beautiful dream lasted only a few days, for most of these action centers remained isolated. Revolutionary contagion, which Durruti had hoped for, didn't occur. So it was not difficult, from that time on, for the forces of order to take over the rebel zones. Sometimes, as at Alfafar (province of Valencia), the army had to destroy union headquarters with cannons, burying the defenders under the ruins. Many people were imprisoned, such as at Beceite, a small village in Aragon, where 122 people were arrested. In the public squares of certain villages they went so far as to burn workers' libraries. [4]

December 15th the struggle ended even though the general strike continued in certain cities. The regions affected by the uprising were declared in a "State of Siege", and Saragossa took on the aspect of a besieged city.

The repression promised to be very harsh and since flight was impossible, the Revolutionary National Committee was preparing for the moment when it would fall into the hands of the police. Its members destroyed some documents and placed the most important part of their archives in a safe place. The police easily seized the members of the RNC, who had decided to assume all responsibility. The trials were public and the accused knew how to bring a case against the capitalist system and to demand the right of revolution for the working class.

During the first hours of imprisonment no one troubled to collect statements from the prisoners, and their friends feared the worst, for example the use of the famous "Ley de fuga" (Escape law). Martinez Barrio had telephoned from Madrid to the Civil Governor of the Province of Saragossa, Ordiales, and ordered him to be very careful of the lives of the prisoners. And as the Governor balked, the Minister threatened that he would hold him personally responsible for the lives of the principal leaders of the insurrection. The police, not able to assassinate them, put the prisoners through harsh questionings. Isaac Puente and Cipriano Mera had to be revived several times with cold water.[5]

The Government named a Special Court which was set up in the offices of the Commercial Court in Saragossa. All the evidence was gathered there in order to open the preliminary examination. Durruti, who had been arrested in Barcelona at the moment when he was giving his last instructions to the Defense Committee of Catalonia, was transferred to Saragossa to be judged there with the other members of the National Committee. Hundreds of workers had also been imprisoned and indicted, their only offense, belonging to the CNT. Statements had often been extracted from them under torture.

Mera, Puente and Durruti were talking about the situation while walking in the courtyard of the Predicadores prison, when Durruti suggested a plan, to make off with the documents for the preliminary examination. If the plan succeeded, it would be necessary then to reconstruct them, which would permit the accused to give a new version of the facts, more consonant with their interests. The three comrades decided to carry out this project and to bring about the attack on the Court of Justice from prison.

One week later, the papers reported the event in these words: "(...) a surprise attack has been organized with incredible audacity against the Court of Justice for Commerce in Saragossa, where the Special Court is sitting and preparing the dossiers on the recent revolutionary events. A group of individuals, seven in all, armed with pistols, entered the room where the judges were at work. Menaced with weapons, they were forced to keep still, while the group grabbed all the papers within reach, thus getting hold of the evidence for the preliminary examination about the December Movement."[6]

During the new examinations, only those mainly responsible and in particular the members of the RNC, admitted that they had taken part in the action. Hundreds of workers, thanks to this strategy, were able to leave prison. To speed up their release, the unions in Saragossa launched a general strike which lasted for four months. It only ended when the last of the prisoners was released. Faced with this new proof of strength, the Government, at the end of February 1934, transferred the group of leaders who had been indicted, to the prison of Burgos.

Footnotes

1. The defeat of the left at the elections and the victory of the right, inspired investigations to find out the causes of this defeat. To illustrate, we quote two opinions which seem significant to us:

Pierats: "People have wanted to put the blame for the defeat of the left on the women's vote, but the latter surely favored both blocs. On the other hand the influence of the absentees was appreciable. The election strike advocated by the CNT influenced proletarian ideas very strongly." (*La CNT en la revolución española*, Vol. 1, p. 64).

Gerald Brenan: "The principal cause of the defeat of the Left wing parties was thus the refusal of the Socialists to collaborate with the Left Republicans at the elections. They had been getting on badly ever since the scandal over the Casas Viejas affair. Their failure to put through any serious measure of agrarian reform and the knowledge that their continued participation in the Government was making them unpopular among their own followers had led to an increasing dissatisfaction among the party leaders." (*The Spanish Labyrinth*, Ed. Cambridge University Press, 1943, p. 265-6).

For Maurin and for Trotsky himself, the defeat of the left and of the Socialists in particular is explained by the fact that the CNT, which was the only really revolutionary movement, had decided on abstention.

As for the right wing coming into office, it is easily explained by the fear of revolution held by the middle class and the bourgeoisie. This was the reason for the drift towards the reactionary camp of the pro-Fascist Gil Robles.

2. Leaflet of December 8, 1933, edited by the Peninsular Committee of the FAI, Seville, 1935.

3. Manuel Salas attended this meeting and in the pamphlet, *November 20*, edited by the CNT in 1936, he refers to it. We have obtained further information by consulting various militants from Saragossa and another witness, Cipriano Mera, member of the National Revolutionary Committee. Thanks to all this testimony we have been able to reconstruct the event.

4. There were 87 deaths and numerous wounded, 700 condemned and some 6,000 detained.

5. Testimony of Cipriano Mera.

6. *La Voz de Aragon*, January 25, 1934.

9

"WORKERS' ALLIANCE
BUT BY THE RANK AND FILE"

POLITICAL PRISONERS had never been sent to the provincial prison of Burgos since it was built. Therefore the arrival of the small group of militants and leaders of the FAI created a lively curiosity in the city. The priests themselves devoted their Sunday sermons to the event, commenting fearfully about the "atrocities" committed by these heretics during the armed insurrection.

The calm which surrounded the prisoners contrasted strangely with the agitation they had known in the prison at Saragossa. Communications with the outside world were rare and difficult, but the papers permitted the prisoners to follow the political tides and the evolution of social life. This isolation, however, was beneficial to all of them, because it permitted these men, removed for the time being from the militant life, to think calmly about a number of problems. And so they studied in detail the political consequences of the insurrection of December 8th, and the question of the revolution.

Actually, anarchist agitation had started the day the Republic was proclaimed, and the events of December 1933 could not be understood except in the pre-revolutionary context that the CNT and the FAI had maintained since that date. If the insurrection of December took on a more radical character than the uprising of January, this movement could not, however, have occurred without the events which came before and which showed that new militants had joined the ranks of the revolution. The propaganda of direct action, used by the anarcho-syndicalists, was positive. The workers had understood that the political life of their country was narrowly conditioned by social agitation.

The tactic of abstaining from voting, recommended by the CNT had permitted the right wing to win. The latter, now in power, had lost its apparent cohesion, and the political line which it was following only intensified the class struggle and prepared new fighters for the revolution.

The right had succeeded in imposing a savagery which spared neither the Socialists nor Republicans. This is how a Socialist commented on the situation created by the victory of the right: "(...) From the first day, the government of Lerroux moved toward the counter revolution demanded by the parties on the right. Constitutional guarantees were repeatedly suspended. The counter-revolution showed itself more aggressive than ever. The government amnistied the enemies of the Republic, the monarchist generals were reinstated in their posts and the priests drew their salaries. Relations with the Vatican were reestablished and once again religious orders were allowed to teach. All the social laws of the Republic were revoked and the Socialist and Republican town councils were dismissed and municipal powers handed over to the enemies of the regime. The workers' organizations were pursued relentlessly; their papers banned their locals closed, while Fascist groups organized and armed themselves under the benevolent eyes of the authorities (...)!"[1]

The anarchists analyze this in detail:

"(...) Azaña's government, using monarchist laws, dealt severely with the workers, guilty of having betrayed the Republic. When the new Constitution took effect, the libertarians fell under the blows of the "Ley de defensa de la Republica" and the "Ley de Vagos y Maleantes'. These laws permitted the pursuit of the workers, strangling their press and closing their locals. When these same laws fell into the hands of the Radical-CEDA government, the Socialists, in turn, became aware of the implacable harshness of the laws which they themselves had helped pass. The famous law of 'Orden Publico', which justified special courts and allowed certain exceptional laws to become permanent, was now used against the Socialists who had been driven out of power by the caprices of politics."[2]

Finally, this victory of the right clarified the situation. An alliance between the CNT and the UGT, the two most important workers' organizations seemed more and more necessary, but the UGT remained very obedient to the political decisions of the Socialist Party. But now that the Socialists themselves were being persecuted, they were beginning to think of a revolutionary alliance with the anarcho-syndicalists of the CNT. The most optimistic among the prisoners in Burgos, such as Orobon Fernandez. thought that the Socialists had no other way out than to take sides after a long absence with "(...) the workers' organizations which had always remained in the avant-garde of the revolutionary struggle (...)." And this anarchist militant added: "(...) This alliance will be established on the revolutionary bases which have always been those of the CNT, a choice which the Socialists will make today after the crushing failure of their collaboration with bourgeois democracy."[3]

Durruti answered Orobon Fernandez' analysis saying that the electoral abstention advocated by the CNT, had actually permitted positions on the left and right to be clarified by driving the Socialists and Republicians from power. But he thought that this clarification was only beneficial to the working class, because the Socialist leaders had not abandoned power as a result of understanding the futility of their alliance with the bourgeois democrats but because the people drove them out. Today they were complaining that they had lost the power. And Durruti asked those who thought that the great alliance had already been achieved, if they sincerely believed that the verbal violence of the Socialists would develop into an authentic revolutionary fighting spirit. Durruti had a precise idea of what the alliance should be and he explained it in a letter to Liberto Calleja:

"(...) The alliance, to be revolutionary, must be genuinely working class. It must be the result of an agreement between the workers' organization, and those alone. No party, however socialist it may be, can belong to a workers' alliance, which should be built from its foundation, in the enterprises where the workers struggle. Its representative bodies must be the workers' committees chosen in the shops, the factories, the mines and the villages. We must reject any agreement on a national level, between National Committees, but rather favor an alliance carried out at the base by the workers themselves. Then and only then, can the revolutionary drive come to life, develop and take root." [4]

The CNT was not able to convene its national congress until February 1934 when its position on a workers' alliance was to be settled. In the meantime Largo Caballero, who had suddenly become a scathing orator, defended this thesis of a workers' alliance with the help of the Communist Party, which still had legal status under the Lerroux government. The Fascist menace was taking shape and the young people of Catholic Action had chosen Gil Robles as their supreme leader.

As soon as the Plenum of the CNT took up the problem of the alliance, various currents were revealed. The Catalan delegation immediately clashed with the representatives from Madrid and Asturias, who favored the alliance. The Catalan workers were not opposed but they wanted a workers' agreement at the rank and file level and flatly rejected any compromise resting on a pact with the Socialist Party aimed directly, or through the "Esquerra Republicana de Cataluna" (Left Republicans of Catalonia) against the CNT of Catalonia.

After lengthy debates, the Plenum unanimously adopted the following resolution: "The National Confederation of Work demands that the UGT express its revolutionary objectives clearly and publicly. We declare that for us the revolution cannot be a simple change of government as it was on April 14, 1931. We want the total abolition of capitalism and the State." [5] The UGT didn't answer the CNT declaration. Already the CNT partisans of an alliance at any price were accusing the Plenum of having blocked the workers' negotiations, by requiring the UGT to renounce its statist ideas completely.

But actually the UGT had been totally conditioned by the tactics of the Socialist Party. In January 1934, the Party had outlined a program of revolutionary action, having as its goal to remove the Radicals and to seize Power. This plan, which was not revealed until much later, was in no way revolutionary. It was, on the contrary, reformist from beginning to end. Working class unity advocated by Largo Caballero was only a lure. The Socialist program stated for example: "(...) After having taken power if the revolution triumphs, the Socialist Party and the General Union of Workers will allow those elements who worked directly for the revolution to participate in the new government." [6] So either the Socialist Party was convinced that it needed no one to make the revolution which would bring it to power, or else, not wishing this revolution, it thought that the best way to avoid it would be to break up any real workers' alliance. The rank and file militants of the CNT, unaware of the tactics of the

154

"Puerto Santa Maria" prison, Cadiz, 1933. From left to right: Paulino Diaz, Francisco Ascaso, Vicente Perez Combina, Durruti and Bartolome Lorda.

Socialists, were struggling to create a real workers' alliance. They were carefully avoiding all contacts with the local organizations set up by the Socialist Party. These were above all vigilance committees, created to watch over the workers of the UGT so that the latter would not be influenced by the revolutionary propaganda of the CNT.

In May, under pressure from the working masses, the government had to give the order to free the last of the political prisoners arrested at the time of the December events. Durruti and his comrades left the provincial prison of Burgos. Durruti arrived in Barcelona. The discussion which took place immediately brought to ganized to debate the question of the alliance. He took part in this meeting, representing the local Federation of the Unions of Barcelona. The discussion which took place, immediately brought to light the difficulties of an alliance with the UGT. But passions this time were less intense than in February, because now the militants had guessed the tactics of the Socialist Party whose revolutionary declarations were a poor cover-up for their real wishes to win elections. And the silence of the UGT didn't help bring about a reconciliation which had been hoped for. The general assembly reaffirmed its first position: the need for a rank and file alliance with the UGT.

Following the discussions Eusebio C. Carbo and Durruti were chosen as delegates to the National Plenum of the CNT. This important assembly took place on June 23, 1934 in Madrid. When the Plenum affirmed that the UGT had remained silent and the debate was going to begin, the delegation from Asturias announced that it had already signed an alliance agreement with the UGT and the Asturian Socialist Federation on March 28, 1934. [7]

Because the Asturian regional federation had taken such a step, the CNT was faced with an accomplished fact. The Plenum accused

155

February 1934 in Preachers' Prison, Saragossa. From left to right: Durruti, Ejarque, Ramon Alvarez, Dr. Alcrudo (members of the Revolutionary Committee of December. 8, 1933)

the Asturians, who had signed the appeal to the UGT in February, of breaking the solidarity agreement and party discipline in the name of revolutionary realism. The Asturian delegation did its best to justify its position, insisting on the revolutionary character of Asturian socialism and showing that the alliance had been achieved without the intervention of the Socialist Party leadership, and only through the pressure of the rank and file militants.

If the statements of the Asturians were legitimate, neverthelsss it was true that in the rest of Spain the Socialist Party was fundamentally reformist and an enemy of the revolution. Hadn't Gil Robles declared in the Cortes, addressing Indalecio Prieto: "You will never make the revolution, because you fear it as much as we do."[8]

Despite the attitude of the Plenum, the Asturian delegation, faithful to its agreement, assumed responsibility for the pact it had signed with the UGT. It was in this way that the first attempt to create a workers' alliance between the CNT and the UGT ended.

Footnotes

1. Rodolfo Llopis, *Octubre 34*, Madrid, 1935, p. 33.
2. José Peirats, *op. cit.*, Vol. I, p. 69.
3. Orobon Fernandez, article published in *La Tierra*, February 4, 1934. See the complete text in José Peirats, *op. cit.* Vol. I.
4. Remarks made to the author; testimony of Liberto Calleja.
5. Resolution passed at the Plenum of February 1934.
6. This program was published in *El Liberal*, January 11, 1936. The complete text can be found in Peirats' book.
7. See the text of the agreement in Peirats' book.
8. G. Munis, *Jalones de derrota: promesa de victoria (España 1930-1939)*. Lucha Obrera, Mexico, 1948.

10

OCTOBER 6TH IN CATALONIA AND THE ASTURIAN COMMUNE

JOSE MARIA GIL ROBLES had decided that three stages had to occur before he could come to power: first the government of Lerroux; then a transitional government based on a coalition of the Radical Party and the CEDA; and finally the appearance of a specifically reactionary government, whose motto this time would be: all power to the leader. The first stage lasted until October 4, 1934, the date when three ministers of the CEDA entered the Lerroux government. This beginning of the second part of Gil Robles' plan was to provoke the revolution of October 6th.

From the 2nd of October changes occured rapidly. On that day, Gil Robles attacked the government presided over by the radical, Samper, who immediately resigned. But nobody was fooled by Gil Robles' manoeuvers; everyone understood that in reality it was a question of the entry of the CEDA into the government. The CEDA was not a Republican party; it defined itself as Monarchist. The Republican parties protested energetically and the Socialist Party reaffirmed that if the CEDA entered the government, it would choose insurrection in order to block it from gaining power. The Communist Party, allied with the Socialists since the month of September, declared:

"The Socialists believed that their threat would lead Alcalá Zamora to think things over and to refuse to take part in the same government with the CEDA. Actually the Socialist leaders gave the reactionaries the chance to decide on the date of the future insurrection at their convenience (...). The Socialist Party (...) thought of the revolutionary movement as depending on it alone, the objective of their movement being the seizure of power. It is for these reasons that this party had never tried to unite with the CNT nor to coordinate its actions with the Generalitat of Catalonia, nor to mobilize the peasants (...). Even though the Socialist leaders had obtained some weapons, they totally neglected any technical preparation and the organization of the insurrection (...)." [1]

On the 4th of October a government was formed. Three ministers of the CEDA were included. By order of the Socialist Party, a general strike was declared October 5th. Armed confrontations took place in Madrid, in Catalonia and in the provinces of Biscay,

Leon and Palencia. The revolutionary insurrection triumphed in Asturias.

In Madrid, immediately after daybreak, the Socialist and Communist groups failed in their attempt to capture the barracks of the 6th regiment by storm. The strike was to go on until October 13th in the capital. But as the movement had not succeeded in attaining its main objectives, the revolutionary elan was shattered. In other cities the struggle was confined to a few clashes, often bloody, between strikers and the police. It became evident that the movement was without clear guidance and lacked organization. The disagreement between the UGT and the CNT only aggravated these deficiencies. The confederal organization, while backing the strike, refused to send its militants into the streets as long as the Socialists and Communists had not demonstrated that they would commit themselves to the revolutionary path.

The insurrection developed principally in three areas: the Basque region, Catalonia and Asturias. In the Euzkadi, the "Nationalist Basque Party" (PNB) advocated abstention, and its central union "Solidaridad de los Trabajadores Vascos" (STV) adopted a passive attitude. And so the initiative remained in the hands of the Socialist Party and the UGT, who monopolized the leadership of the workers' movement. The strike was general. Nothing of importance occurred in the center of Bilbao; in contrast, fierce confrontations between the armed workers and the police forces took place in the outlying districts of the capital of Biscay. At Portugalete, Hernani, Eibar... committees of the alliance managed, for a while, to play the role assigned them, but no revolutionary contagion backed them up or prolonged the action. In San Sebastian and its environs the militants of the CNT tried to contact the UGT, but the local leaders of the Socialist union held to their basic position, which was to hinder, at any price, the intervention of the CNT in the movement.

In Catalonia, a general strike was declared by the Workers' Alliance on October 5th. The night before the police had arrested a number of confederal militants, among them Durruti. *Solidaridad Obrera* appeared on October 6th several hours late, due to the cuts required by the censor. Faced with this situation, the CNT's Regional Committee decided to use underground leaflets for its directives and to keep the Catalan workers informed. [2] It was not an easy thing to enforce this decision because José Dencás, the counsellor of public order for the Generalitat of Catalonia was also one of those responsible for the Catalan uprising and he had given a strict order: "Keep an eye on the FAI." [3] For the rank and file Catalan worker, the majority of them controlled by the CNT, everything was thus clear: the insurgents, pretending to follow the politics of the central government, were actually orienting their action in order to destroy the CNT. After that, how could they collaborate with the reactionary movement which was directing its blows against the working class? Here was the paradox of the Catalan uprising of October 6, 1934.

On October 5th at nightfall, the president of the Generalitat, Luis Companys, proclaimed "The Catalan State within the Federal Republic of Spain". Groups of peasants, armed with Winchester rifles, the Assault Guard and a big crowd assembled in front of the

Palace of the Generalitat and enthusiastically welcomed Companys' proclamation.

An hour later, the military leader of the area, General Batet, answered Companys' challenge by declaring a state of war. The army began to patrol the streets, while on the ramblas the first volleys were fired between the troops and the armed groups of the "Catalan Proletarian State", a nationalist extremist faction, led by young Jaime Compte, who was to die defending his party's headquarters. The Palace of the Generalitat was bombarded by artillery. The morale of the insurgents, whose ranks were beginning to thin out, was at its lowest. Most of them fled without fighting, abandoning arms and uniforms. At daybreak, Companys, abandoned by everyone, broadcast a pathetic appeal "to all citizens without ideological distinction." Evidently he was also speaking to the militants of the CNT, whom his lieutenant, José Dencás, was holding prisoner in the cellars of Police Headquarters.

Groups of peasants, who tried to enter the suburbs of Barcelona, were disarmed by the soldiers who controlled the approaches to the Catalan capital. At the first canon shots, Companys and his government gave themselves up, except for the counsellor of public order, Dencás, who had escaped through the sewers.[4]

The same disarray occurred in all the cities and the large towns of the region. The Alliance no longer existed, but the weapons, abandoned in the streets, were picked up and hidden in safe places by the workers of the CNT. In a few small towns of Catalonia, such as Granollers, the CNT took over the leadership of the movement, marking it with a definitely revolutionary character. The government authorities profited by these actions to organize a systematic repression against the CNT and the FAI. The unions were closed and *Solidaridad Obrera* banned for five months.[5]

By October 6th Lerroux's "order" reigned in Barcelona again, while in the western part of the peninsula the Asturian miners were starting their heroic struggle. During the night of October 5th to 6th in the mining basin of Asturias, twenty-three barracks of the Guardia Civil fell into the hands of the workers. Hour after hour the workers recorded new victories: Mieres, Robellada, Santallana, Sama... Workers' militias were organized everywhere. The committees created were efficient forerunners of a new social system.

The CNT was well established in Gijon and the workers immediately set up barricades. The struggle promised to be specially tough in this region. Because of its strategic position, it was chosen by the Staff Officer of the Ministry of War, General Franco, as the place to land the Moroccan troops, whose job it was to stamp out the revolt.

At Aviles, the workers occupied the gas factory and the central power station. At La Felguera, the machine shops remained in the hands of the CNT which immediately organized the manufacture of arms. A Socialist Republic was established in the entire valley of Turon and the radio transmitter of the central power station of the coalmines of Turon broadcast the first revolutionary proclamations.

In Oviedo the workers were fighting in the streets. And the miners of the region came to the rescue of the insurgents and took over the key positions of the city. The government forces fell back on the Pelayo barracks and found refuge in the cathedral. The arms factory fell into the hands of the workers, who salvaged 21,000 guns, 300 Bren-guns and many machine guns. The metal working centers worked night and day to make weapons. La Felguera produced as many as 30,000 gun cartridges a day. This tremendous effort, however, was not enough to equip the proletarian army of 40,000 men, entrusted with the defense of the Asturian Commune, which had already been surrounded by the troops from Morocco.

During these struggles life was being organized just the same. Workers chosen by the Committees carried on the struggle, which was coordinated by the Provincial Revolutionary Committee installed in Oviedo. Men and women enrolled and hastily trained were drafted into the popular militias. Almost everywhere the doctors supported the revolution, but medical supplies were lacking to take care of the many wounded.

At the Ministry of War, General Franco lead the struggle against the workers' unprising. On October 5th he ordered General Bosch to march against Asturias, at the head of the 56th Infantry Regiment. At Vega del Rio a batallion and a company of machine gunners coming from Palencia, joined this first contingent. However General Bosch was immobilized at Vega del Rio by the revolutionary columns.

In Galicia Lopez Ochoa also received the order to win over Asturias by a forced march. But the insurgents barred the way at the mountain pass of Penaflor. Then General Franco ordered the Navy to attack Gijon, a vulnerable spot in the Asturian defense: "(...) At Gijon the situation was desperate. Fighting went on throughout the city. The workers who defended the suburbs faced the sea. Weapons were scarce and the Socialists didn't keep their promise to bring supplies to the insurgents. The Revolutionary Committee of La Felguera came in great haste to help the inhabitants of Gijon, bringing men, supplies and munitions (...)."[6] The Madrid government told the journalists: "(...) In Asturias the combined efforts of the land army and the navy are about to obtain their objective (...) the complete submission of the rebels is only a question of hours."

On October 7th the cruiser "Libertad" started to bombard Gijon and succeeded in landing a batallion of naval infantry, which was, however, immobilized at Serin. At nightfall gunfire started again and the population continued to resist. The 10th, planes flew over Oviedo and threw down leaflets which called on the insurgents to yield. Two warships, the "Jaime I" and the "Miguel Cervantes" joined the cruiser "Libertad". Covered by an intense artillery fire, a "bandera de Tercio" (Foreign Legion) and the 8th Batallion of African troops succeeded in landing. The command gave them "carte blanche" and a fierce struggle took place. The revolutionaries lacked ammunition and left dozens of dead on the field. But the aviation continued to throw down leaflets where one could read: "Asturias have been abandoned by everyone, the deadly circle is closing in."

The 12th, Yague, leader of the Moroccan troops, attacked Oviedo with a "bandera" of the Foreign Legion, a "Tabor de Regulares", a batallion of African Chasseurs and an artillery battery.

The action was prepared and backed up by planes. At 5 P.M. after a furious struggle, the Moors and the legionaires managed to take over the arms factory. The insurgents fell back but the fight continued, street by street, house by house, and it went on until October 17th. All the population, including women and children, resisted at the side of the revolutionaries.

The 18th the situation was desperate; all resistance became useless. During the night the Revolutionary Committees met to put an end to the struggle. The Provincial Committee of Asturias issued a proclamation to the workers:

"(...) The glorious insurrection of the proletariat against the bourgeoisie broke out on October 5th. After having shown the revolutionary capacity of the working masses, we consider that the struggle must end and arms be laid down in order to avoid the worst. An agreement has been reached among all the revolutionary committees. It asks you to start working again in an orderly, calm and sober fashion. Comrades! We consider this decision is honorable and inevitable... For we have only our enthusiasm to pit against the powerful war machine of the government. But this is only a postponement because one can flay the proletariat but one cannot conquer it." (7)

On October 19th the troops of General Aranda occupied the mining zone. The members of the Revolutionary Committee were the last to abandon the field, but not before organizing the evacuation of those militants who had been most involved. Many miners in guerilla groups carried on the struggle in the mountains before surrendering.

The reaction was ruthless. The Revolutionary Committee had made only one condition for the surrender of the mining area, that the population should not be handed over to the repression of the Moorish troops and the legionaires. General Aranda had accepted this provision, but he was incapable of seeing that the terms of the agreement were respected. The Moroccans and the legionaires were the first to enter the rebel zones. A savage repression swept down on the entire region; summary executions, lootings, rapes, followed. The special brigades of the Guardia Civil, commanded by Commander Doval, "cleaned up" the area. And a special judge, named by the government in Madrid, legalized these arbitrary actions, declaring that the measures taken against the rebels were clearly humanitarian. During this period, scenes of violence multiplied throughout the region. In its issue for October 24th, the Parisian daily, *Le Temps,* reported that "(...) a hundred miners had been buried alive in a mine shaft." Officially there were 1,335 dead and 2,951 wounded. The government, satisfied, declared that "order and peace" reigned again in Asturias. However, the right wing leader, Calvo Sotelo, pointed out before the Cortes that, "(...) the Asturian Commune was only the first act of the revolution", which could still sweep them all away, and he demanded that the repression be intensified.

While the Right called for heads, the Left was making up the balance sheet. It did not seem to have understood the meaning of the events which had just shaken Asturias. As for the Socialist Party, it resumed the course which was to lead it to the Popular

Front. The CNT however, drew certain conclusions from this heroic battle, and its historian, José Petrats, wrote: "One of the main weaknesses of the movement of October 6th was the absence of a serious plan and of coordination on the national level. Except in Asturias, the Socialist leaders of the movement side-stepped all contact with the confederal organization (CNT). The motion of the General Assembly of the Regional Committees of the CNT of February 13, 1934, had not been answered by the UGT." [8]

"If the Socialists had really wanted to start a revolutionary movement in Spain — which remains to be proved — the support of the CNT was indispensable, at least in Catalonia, in Aragon, in the Levant and in Andalusia where the offensive capacity of the National Confederation of Labor was evident. The attitude which denied this reality puts a strange light on the problem: either the Socialists were following no other end than to launch a conflict that would provoke the resignation of the government; or else wanting to maintain the leadership of the movement, they considered themselves strong enough to win a victory through their own forces alone, supported, when the occasion arose, by republican elements and the popular masses."

"In the first hypothesis, the Socialists deceived themselves about the reactions of the government, the police and the army. In the second hypothesis, the risks involved in the revolutionary undertaking were excessive. In both cases they gave too great an importance to the projects and fighting value of the troops of the 'Estat Catala' and the 'Esquerra Republicana' of Catalonia."

"Socialists and Catalan Nationalists had collaborated in the repression against the CNT in Catalonia. The 'Esquerra' and the Socialist Party were involved in the crushing of the insurrectional movements of January and December 1933. The alliance of the Socialists and Catalan Nationalists could therefore only tend to accentuate the separation of all movements of a political character from the CNT."

And Peirats goes on: "The CNT counted on 22,000 organized workers in Asturias. The principal confederal centers were Gijón (13,000 members) and La Felguera (4,000 members). On the eve of the insurrection a congress of the Confederation was convened in Gijón. The militants of this city and of La Felguera were divided on the problem of the alliance with the left. La Felguera, which doubted the revolutionary sincerity of the Socialists, came out against any alliance with them. But even before these discussions, the Socialists had brought in by sea a shipment of arms, whose arrival proved obviously, their intention of being the only builders of the movement. Actually, and contrary to the terms of the alliance agreement signed by the CNT, it was the Socialists who gave the order for the uprising. The Revolutionary Committee, specifically Socialist, had secret headquarters in Oviedo.

"Nevertheless from the first hours of the insurrection the CNT intervened on its own and it fought until the end. In Gijón, the confederal forces, (CNT) lacking arms, had to establish their positions in the outlying areas of the city. The anarcho-syndicalists made many and perilous excursions to Oviedo, in order to obtain arms and to get into contact with the Revolutionary Committee. Lacking munitions, Gijon fell the 10th of October, despite the arrival of reinforcements coming from La Felguera. The 11th, the Revolutionary Committee, considering that the uprising had failed, gave the order to retreat. This decision caused strong discontent among the combattants. It is from this date that the Socialists agreed to collaborate with the forces of the Confederation. José Maria Martinez (CNT), one of the main activists in the Asturian Alliance, was killed on October 12th at Sotiello, while he was carrying out a mission for the Revolutionary Committee.

Even though the Socialists had tried fiercely to keep the leadership of the movement, it took diverse paths, depending on the predominant influences in each rebel area. As far as the political and economic results of the Asturian revolution, an authoritarian tendency was evident in the areas where the Socialists and Communists were strongest. On the other hand, the anarchists, following the example of La Felguera, proclaimed libertarian communism everywhere, as well as the suppression of private property and the abolition of the principal of authority."(9)

Footnotes

1. P.C.E. (Spanish Communist Party): *Guerra y revolución en España.*
2. Peirats, in the *op. cit.*, reproduced this manifesto in full.
3. On the October movement in Barcelona, in addition to the books of Gerald Brenan and Peirats, one can consult the monograph of Manuel Cruells, *El 6 de octubre a Cataluñya.*
4. Idem.
5. Manuel Villar, *El anarquismo en la insurrección de Asturias.*
6. Peirats, *op. cit.*
7. Peirats, *op. cit.*
8. This manifesto was a public declaration of the CNT following the decisions made at its national Plenum. After considering the seriousness of the current situation, it decided that "The National Confederation of Work should ask the UGT to demonstrate clearly and publicly the nature of its revolutionary aspirations. But it must be acknowledged that when speaking of revolution, it is not simply a matter of changing who has the power as on April 14th, but it means the total supression of capitalism and the State." Peirats, *op. cit.*, Vol. I, p. 79.
9. Peirats, *op. cit.* Beside the works mentioned, one can also consult: *España*, by Salvador de Madariaga. *Historia de España* by Ramos Oliveira, a Socialist writer; *Historia de la Segunda Republica* by Victor Alba; *La Revolución de Octubre* by Solano Palacio, an anarchist and activist in this revolution; *Actas del Congreso de la CNT de Zaragosa*, May 1936; *Octubre 34* by Rodolfo Llopis, a Socialist. In Llopis' book, the program of the Socialist Party is published. It was prepared in case of victory and it was published by *El Liberal* of Bilbao, on January 11th, 1936.

11/

TOWARD THE POPULAR FRONT[1]

THE ASTURIAN COMMUNE set an example for the Spanish peasant and worker: revolution was no longer a utopia, but something attainable, something which only required a previous agreement among the workers. But while the working class and the peasantry thus understood the revolutionary process, the political and union directors of the central reformist UGT Union believed the contrary. Workers' united action was subordinated to political agreements. The contradiction became flagrantly clear between the leaders and the led. And the revolution couldn't move forward as long as the working class was saddled with these leaders. Could it free itself while following the reformist policies of its leaders? In numerous sporadic negotiations with the workers of the CNT, those of the UGT showed their tendencies clearly.

The reformist leaders understood the seriousness of the situation and to keep it from getting worse, they used all their influence with the working class, employing such sentimental themes as the freeing of 30,000 prisoners to divert it from its real objectives. The most important reason for this strategy can be defined as follows: either to force the CNT to modify its tactic of anti-parliamentary struggle, by concluding a pact with the UGT, a pact which would leave the initiative to the political parties; or to isolate the CNT and form a political coalition opposing it, so that the working class would keep its parliamentary illusions. This strategy wasn't new in the social and political history of the country. The parties led by the Socialist Party had already used it in August 1917. The same occurrences recurred in similar circumstances and these pushed the working class into "radicalizing" its struggle. It had this revolutionary opportunity and the so-called Pact of San-Sebastian (1930) had diverted it from its objective.

After the Asturian revolt had shown that the working class wasn't crushed but, on the contrary, foresaw the path that the struggle should take, the same parties, led by the Socialist Party, began to plot again to ruin the revolutionary possibilities which were in the process of being born. Alas! certain factors played into their hands. And the CNT couldn't fight against them without playing the game of the reaction, which was openly conspiring in order to install its dictatorship. The politicians of the right, headed by Gil Robles, hoped that the CNT would act in Spain as the Communist Party had done in Germany. If the CNT put into practise a similar tactic towards the Socialist Party and the UGT, this would produce conditions in Spain similar to those which had helped Hitler seize power.

The CNT could not risk commiting such an error, and yet it was indispensable to break the balance of opposing forces (between Socialists and anarchists), because the whole future of the Revolution depended on this break. Actually, if the Socialist masses continued to follow their leaders, the latter would remain in neutral gear.

To this already complicated situation, confusion about international politics was added, since the country which called itself the "Fatherland of the Proletariat" was only interested in its own problems. Before going on with our story, we must stop briefly to speak about the creation of the Popular Front in Spain.

What was the tactical facade of the new foreign policy of the Soviet Union? Once Hitler had made clear his aggressive intentions towards the U.S.S.R. and his pact of January 26, 1934 with Poland had completely modified the nature of the strategic relations between the European states, Stalin laid the foundations for a new foreign policy, seeking alliances with the democratic-capitalist states, specially France and England. His principle trump card, with an eye to a political victory, was the Communist International (IC) and his propaganda theme "the fight against Fascism", a euphemism which hid the tactical turn which had recently been taken.

This policy harmonized with the wishes of France, which felt menaced by the warlike spirit of Hitler. The geographical imperatives appeared again. As to political imperatives, they overlooked the change of leaders on the international scene; Stalin or the Tsar, it didn't matter. The French and Russian governments were fully conscious of this subjection to geography. Both lacked a common policy, which would defend their mutual interests. The new policy was to be called the "Popular Front". The idea was launched by the Workers' Socialist International (IOS), made up of parties which, for a long time, had renounced the Revolution. Reformists to the marrow, they persuaded themselves that through reform they could transform capitalism into socialism. The seizure of power by the working class didn't enter into their projects at all. For them it was a matter of governing, while sharing the responsibilities by common agreement with the bourgeois parties. The line of conduct was clear: class collaboration. This line implied a political ideology fed on bourgeois culture and values: Family, Country, etc.

After the triumph of Hitlerism and the disappearance of German Social-Democracy, no stronger party was left in Europe than the French Socialist Party, heir to the Sacred Union of 1914. Faced with the German peril, it had to renew its ties with the liberal bourgeoisie and French patriots. This weighed heavily in the IOS settlement of February 1933. To have success with the anti-fascist policy, it was necessary to end the polemic with the IC. The manifesto of the IOS addressed to all the workers of the world was significant: it was ready to open discussions with the IC in order to undertake a common action against fascism. In return, it asked for an end to recriminations between the two internationals. The IC didn't answer and later we will understand the reasons for this silence. The IOS launched a new appeal in August 1933 after a conference where the two participants, the SFIO and PSOE (the Spanish Socialist Workers Party) settled on a new line, a common front against fascist attacks. The only choice left to the working class was the struggle for power. It was evident that the struggle for power didn't mean an armed struggle to the IOS but a parliamentary one.

In all of this one senses the fear of the Socialists facing fascism in Germany, with its evident intentions. It must be made clear that during this conference, two different points of view were in collision as a result of the respective social conditions of the two countries. It was Largo Caballero versus Leon Blum. Caballero's position brought out the difference between their respective bases. As we saw in Asturias, a weak revolutionary spirit still animated the rank and file Spanish Socialist militant; while among the French reformists, not even the smallest spark of revolutionary spirit existed. One can assume that the last position taken by the IOS was the result of the presence of Caballero at the conference. His declaration for the continuation of the policy of the IOS was to be: "The seizure of power by the working class which it means to accomplish by parliamentary means".

The principal obstacle for the French Socialist Party (SFIO) was the anti-militarist position of the French Communist Party, which adopted the attitude of the German PC towards Social-Democracy: Social Democracy equals social Fascism". The only way the Socialist leader Blum could secure power was to make a pact with the Communist Party by "making it accept its responsibilities" in the administration of the government. This was all the more urgent for Blum because among the rank and file of the workers of the CGT a strong current for working class unity was appearing, a current which the Communist Party was beginning to channel through the Committees for *Unity*. This situation could not be settled as long as the IC didn't change its political tactic. The first announcement of this revision took place on May 31st 1934. On that day *Humanité,* organ of the French Communist Party, reproduced an article from *Pravda.* "It was perfectly acceptable to propose unified action to the French Socialists". From that day the PCF changed its tactics rapidly and in July of the same year, an agreement was signed between the two parties.

The orders were not only followed by the French but also by the Spanish entering the Workers' Alliance organized by the Socialist Party. In other words, the order was general for all the parties obedient to the IC. How could one explain this sudden turn in Muscovite policy? It was logical to think that the source of inspiration for the article was Stalin himself, since the IC hadn't held a congress or a conference. From January '33 until January '34 Stalin had been very reserved in his public declarations about the Soviet Union's foreign policy in relation to Germany. Why this silence? The facts give a clear answer: "since Hitler came to power, the Soviet government is actively seeking an alliance with the democratic capitalist states". But there is a certain phase just between the victory of Hitler and the beginning of 1934 during which this search is associated with the successful effort to safeguard the spirit of Rapallo. [2]

Three months after Hitler became Chancellor, the extension of the German-Soviet pact of 1926 was signed. This pact was the prolongation and the true copy of the Rapallo agreement. Meanwhile Molotov declared, "that the Soviet government had no reason to change its policy towards Germany". But on January 26, 1934 two significant things occurred: one was the meeting of the Congress of the Russian Communist Party and the other, the signing of the German-Polish treaty. For the first time Stalin made declarations about the international political situation. He recognized that the danger of war was imminent, but at the same time he pointed out to the bourgeoisie that: "if the war broke out, it would create revolutionary cells in all the countries affected by the conflict and that these cells, concentrating their efforts would unleash the revolution". He added, that if war was declared against the country of the proletariat, the numerous friends of the Soviet working class would rise up in arms against the aggressors, attacking them from the rear. Then talking about the Nazis, he added: "as long as Germany doesn't break away from its old policies determined in the treaties between it and the Soviet Union, there would be no reason for things to deteriorate." Naturally, Stalin went on "we are far from being enthusiastic about the German regime. But it is not a question here of fascism, for the simple reason that fascism in Italy has not hindered the U.S.S.R. from establishing relations with that country." And Stalin concluded: "The Soviet Union is for peace; it doesn't want war, but it doesn't fear this threat and is ready to give blow for blow to the warmongers. Whoever wants peace and intends to establish economic relations with us, can always count on our aid." [3]

In addition to the impact in Moscow, the German-Polish pact had an effect on France, where the government considered its own policy of alliances had been destroyed. French diplomacy started moving and on May 25, 1934. Barthou declared in the Chamber of Deputies that the entry of Russia in the SDN would be a considerable contribution towards a European peace. Five days later, *Pravda* published the article we quoted above, recommending that the PCF should come to an agreement with the SFIO. This agreement involved a radical change in the policy of the PCF, which now adapted itself to the political needs of the U.S.S.R. As a result of these maneuvers the Franco-Soviet treaty was signed in Moscow on May 2, 1935. In the final communique of the Laval-Stalin conversations, one can read the new instructions given by the latter to his French partners: "Stalin understands and approves completely France's policy of national defense to maintain its army at a level required for its security." This declaration wipes out completely the antimilitarist policy of the PCF. The latter's response was shattering, "Stalin is right". And *Humanité* made an effort to explain: "There is national defense and national defense, there is army and there is army, there is a war called 'defense of democracy' and war for the defense of democracy." From the moment that the defense of the Soviet Union came into question, everything was to change. As Claudin emphasizes, the difficulty for a revolutionary party began at the moment when passing from general statements to the definition of a policy to bring together the two ends of a maze: on the one hand, to contribute to the defense of the Soviet Union and on the other, to struggle against a bourgeoisie which, because of the pact signed, would become the king pin of the defense of the U.S.S.R.

Claudin's idea would be right if the French Communist Party had really been a revolutionary party. But clearly the PCF could only be an instrument in the service of the foreign policy of the U.S.S.R. subordinated as it was to the IC, and the latter being subordinated itself to the Soviet state. And so the PCF was not obliged to look for a way out of its doubtful situation. It could leave the job of pulling it out of this bad spot to the IC and this occurred soon in August 1935 at the VIIth Congress of the IC.

The new tactic of the IC which was adapted to the interests of the Soviet state, had already born fruit in France even before it had been formulated. The Popular Front, with its three "key men", Thorez, Blum and Daladier, was already on the march and its doctrine was defined at the Stade Buffalo on July 14, 1935: "Radicals, Socialists and Communists remain united, to disarm and dissolve the Fascist leagues, to defend and expand democratic liberties and to assure peace in the world." The doctrine was at the same time patriotic and bourgeois. Workers' unity was built on an ambiguity: antifascism included both the most uncompromising bourgeois as well as revolutionary, which amounts to saying that the latter forgot his radicalism to take orders from the French and English bourgeoisie, allies of the Soviet state.

The VIIth Congress tried to explain this tactical turn of the U.S.S.R. with Machiavelian logic, in order to sugar the pill for the rebellious. The big shots of the IC like Dimitrov and Togliatti took this job in hand. "Certain comrades" Togliatti explained "may have thought that the conclusion of the pact with France meant losing sight of the perspective of revolution in Europe. They have compared the pacts for mutual assistance to a forced retreat under the blows of the enemy. Far from being a retreat, it is an advance and those who don't understand the profound internal coherence of the theses that I have explained, understand nothing about the real dialectic drawn from the events and nothing either about the revolutionary dialectic."

The orders for all the Communist parties were as follows: "Struggle for peace and defend the U.S.S.R." This meant that all activity and policies of the Communist parties must be thought of as a means to this supreme objective. The Communist parties must create the widest possible Front with those interested in preserving the peace. Its foremost tactical job was always to concentrate the forces of this Front against the principal warmongers: for the moment this meant Fascist Germany, Poland and Japan.

Who were these forces eager for peace that the Communist parties must unite in a common front? They were the popular masses, but also every ruling class group interested in peace, as well as the big and little States which had similar interests.

An order was given to attract the groups capable of being interested in an extensive Popular Front: never to take extreme stands which could scare away people barely politically aware, who might eventually become followers. The final and essential aim was to attract the middle classes. Therefore subjects too remote from the minds of the middle class should not be taken up. The program was to consist of three parts: economic and social demands perfectly compatible in principal with the existence of reformist parties and unions; political demands which would go no further than the defense or the restoration of democratic-bourgeois liberties and institutions; demands aimed at the repression of Fascist activities.

We have made a resume here of the basic principals and the theoretical lines that the IC dictated to the parties existing in the capitalist countries in order to attain new objectives. As far as the Spanish Communist Party was concerned, its line would be adjusted according to what we have just explained above and in agreement with the theoretical analyses of the situation in Spain, carried out by the IC. But in Spain, while one analysis followed another, events were moving headlong. So let us take up the story again at the point where we left if before.....

Footnotes

1.   N.B. To avoid too many notes for the reader, we point out that the quotations in this chapter come from the following books: *La crise du mouvement communiste*, by Fernando Claudin. Volume 1; *Histoire du parti communiste français*, by Jacques Fauvet; *L'Internationale communiste*, by Dominique Desanti.

2.   The treaty of Rappalo was signed on April 16, 1922 by Germany and the U.S.S.R., the two big losers in the war. In this treaty, these two states repudiated war damages and pledged a spectacular rapprochement. One of the most interesting results of this treaty was that the U.S.S.R. allowed Germany to make and try out armaments (tanks, planes, heavy artillery, gas) in Russia, which the Treaty of Versailles forbade her to do. In return the Red Army High Command was to keep the original models in the U.S.S.R. and be kept au courant about the tests, cf. *Encyclopedia Britannica*.

3.   The various quotations are taken from the work of Fernando Claudin.

12

30,000 POLITICAL PRISONERS

AT THE BEGINNING OF 1935 Spain was a maze of intrigues and political passions. It is undisputed that the troops coming from Morocco on the orders of General Franco, by employing all sorts of methods, were able to "pacify" the Asturian region. But it is also certain that protests were general: the workers cursed the authors of the repression, widows wept for their dead and thousands of homes were deprived of all economic support, because the head of the family was one of the 30,000 political prisoners who were filling the prisons.

On the right, the protests were no less violent and there were demands that the government prove itself capable of an exemplary harshness: "Destroy the revolutionary seed, even to the wombs of the mothers", this was the current slogan among right wingers, making a show of their class hatred. There was no political life in the Cortes. There remained only a few makeshift liberties with which bourgeois democracy camouflaged the regime to make it pass as liberal. The unions and the workers' centers were closed, the right of assembly suspended, the workers' press forbidden; there were only the "proper" people, the bourgeoisie and the military who could enjoy all the privileges. The priests thundered from the pulpits slandering the Asturian miners. Landlords reduced the salaries of the farm workers and letting the land lie fallow, increased the famine which was already chronic in Andalusia and Estremadura. The military were plotting openly in the mess halls and the barracks. To darken this picture already very black, the hack writers of the Vatican paper, *El Debate,* wrote endless articles describing the 1,000 horrors which the triumph of anarcho-marxist atheism was preparing for good christians. The working class had only its proverbial fatalism to oppose to this offensive: "when you are the anvil, endure, when you are the hammer, strike!" At this time the worker was the anvil and endured, but resisted, which was unusual, without bowing its head, without feeling conquered, and hoping for its hour to come. It rebuilt its unions, patiently organized and distributed help for prisoners and persecutees, brought aid to the homes where there was hunger and misery. It denounced the government's terror to the world in tiny underground papers. Hunger, misery, injustice, constant repression can create two attitudes: either submission, which makes sheep out of men, or else revolt and the persecutee then becomes a wild beast.

Some chose the first, others on the contrary, opted for violence. The latter appeared in the Asturian mountains, like judges, attacking the barracks of the Guardia Civil, avenging their brothers in the struggle, who had been tortured in the government prison cells. Or else they scoured Southern Andalusia, robbing the "caciques" to help the poor and unfortunate, whose bodies were suffering the pangs of hunger. To be a classical bandit on the highways, precursor of the guerilla was the only way to feel free in a Spain which the military men had subdued to its rule.

The government headed by the "Lerrouxist" Ricardo Samper, was drifting, hated by those below and judged as too indulgent by those above. It had to resign in March 1935. The right which had a majority in the Cortes, believed that the moment had come for Gil Robles, its mouthpiece, to assume the responsibilities of power. But Alcalá Zamora, President of the Republic, resisted and asked Alexandre Lerroux to form a new government. Lerroux assumed this responsibility without any enthusiasm, understanding that all that was required of him was to carry out the death sentences that the judges had pronounced. As a political man, accustomed to the fluctuations of this life, anxious to avoid the storm, he pardoned 8 of the 30 condemned to death and freed Manual Azaña. In this way he hoped to appease public protests on the one hand, and on the other satisfy the right opposition. But this idea was mistaken. The workers demanded not only pardons for the condemned but also freedom for the prisoners. The right was all the more irritated judging the politics of Lerroux worse than Samper's and a new crisis was inevitable. This time it was much more significant and on May 5, 1935 Gil Robles entered the government as Minister of War.

For the reactionary bloc, with Gil Robles as Minister of War and the monarchist Portela Valladares in the Interior, the coup d'Etat was guaranteed, and no more was needed than the decision to take over. It was in this vein that Calvo Sotelo and General Mola spoke impatiently to the leader of the CEDA, but Gil Robles (and this will always remain a mystery) could not make up his mind to take the decisive step and limited himself to giving satisfaction to all the demands of the military; confirmation of Franco in his post as Commander in Chief of the Army; a decoration given to Lieutenant-Colonel Yague for his "feats" in Asturias. Robles named generals with a monarchist tendency to key posts and gave important positions to those with Republican views.

In June the opposition seemed to be beginning to wake up. It is true that a certain number of UGT members remained in prison, but the Socialist Party, even with some leaders in prison, carried on its normal activities, protected by its members in the Cortes. The mild repression of the leaders of the Socialist Party and in particular of Largo Caballero, was the consequence of a political line which the party had held during the October revolution. It had declared that the insurrection was a spontaneous protest against the entry of enemies into the Republican Government. Caballero questioned by the military examining magistrate declared: "I am not the leader of this revolutionary movement (...)... it is only a spontaneous explosion of

171

the working masses (....) I absolutely deny that the Party participated in the organization of the general strike," [1] declarations which constributed to the freeing of the Socialist leader. The first public statements of Largo Caballero disclosed the change which had taken place in his ideas about public power. He spoke with no constraint about the dictatorship of the proletariat, as an indispensable stage in the emancipation of the worker. The young Socialists, who belonged to the left wing of the party, took Caballero as a guide. The Communists, who had already been ordered to make peace with the Socialist Party, began to sing his praises, as a true militant revolutionary and leader of the working class.

The anarcho-syndicalists of the CNT, whose union members were either in prison or in hiding, had to bear the full weight of the repression. They defended themselves, using their own methods. They answered government violence with revolutionary violence: with general strikes, sabotage and boycotts. The Spanish Falange had attracted elements from the bourgeois camp and noisy and violent students. With the help of the latter, it succeeded in organizing in Madrid the Spanish University Union (SEU) which created a climate of insecurity in the University through attacks against the students affiliated with the Spanish University Federation (FUE), which was the most radical student organization.

In the prison cells the situation was different. For the prisoners who were devoting themselves to a complete analysis of the situation, the revolutionary experience of October remained intact. Many lessons were drawn with different view points. The communists considered October as an important step toward labor unity and proposed the formation of a vast democratic front, visualizing the conquest of power through elections. The Socialists, while having the same point of view as the Communists about elections, thought they could profit by the Asturian revolt to increase their prestige with the working masses, who were getting a little further away every day from reformist Socialism. For the anarchists, October had been a training ground where their anti-party and anti-political ideas were confirmed. Leaning on a rank and file base, they fought for a revolutionary alliance in which the workers, freed from the guidance of their leaders, would carry the revolution as far as possible.

Durruti, who as we know was imprisoned on October 6th in Barcelona, had been transferred to the "Model Prison" in Valencia. He had not been able to escape from this prison nor during his transfer to Valencia. Durruti could not be considered as one of those who wanted the revolution at any price, but rather as someone who thought of it as a whole and not piecemeal. He therefore drew profitable conclusions from the Asturian revolt. According to him, the process of the revolution had started; it would reach its highest point inevitably and it was already marching with rapid steps towards that end. From Durruti's analysis a deduction followed which he openly defended to his comrades in captivity: "ammunition shouldn't be wasted uselessly; it was necessary first to put the finishing touches on a solid revolutionary organization, economising scare resources for the struggle. The militant cadres, who were still free, should not expose themselves, nor weaken the movement with useless strikes." But this po-

172

November 1935, Leon — Durruti addresses mass rally of anarchists in a bullring.

sition was attacked by certain militants, above all by the young ones, who, taking a position opposing Durruti, believed that the struggle should be intensified to its climax. This polemic was the cause of a certain uneasiness among the militants but it was necessary to wait until Durruti was freed to call a plenum of the anarchist groups of Barcelona.

At this plenum, Durruti demolished all the arguments against his strategy of not "wasting efforts needlessly". According to him, it was not at all a question of suspending the struggle and strikes, but it was also not necessary to provoke new conflicts uselessly. He also thought that the struggle would be total and that the anarchists would have to bear the brunt of it. If at this moment the prisons were full of militants and there were no arms in the depots, how could one face an enemy supported by State organizations and very well armed? The defeat that would follow could not be compared to the one in January or even of December 1933. This time it would be total. The revolutionary future was in question and it was better to wait for the best opportunity for the final reckoning than to "loose oneself" in secondary efforts provoked by the reaction seeking to justify repressions. [2]

Durruti's revolutionary instinct was correct. In November 1935, two conspiracies were about to break out. The military were making their final preparations before going into the streets and the politicians of the opposition were getting ready to strangle the workers' revolution through the Popular Front.

Durruti didn't know then that an agent of the IC, Jacques Duclos, was in Spain to meet with Largo Caballero. The latter was aware of the economic and political differences between their two countries and so knew that political solutions could not be the same. But Duclos had to convince him of the usefulness of establishing a Popular Front in Spain, modeled on the one which was developing in

France. The Stalinist agent had made sure of a good supporter for his conversations with Caballero. This supporter was none other than the Socialist-Communist, Alvarez del Vayo, whom Caballero considered a faithful friend and a good Socialist. Del Vayo had agreed to prepare the ground for Duclos, as later he would agree to lay the foundations for a fusion between the Communist and Socialist youth (JSU). These talks went on for three days and Duclos did the impossible to convince his questioner. "I wanted to convince Caballero that it was necessary for the working class to have allies, specially the peasant masses, the middle classes in the cities, the intellectual milieux (that is what we had done in France). Don't you agree that this question also comes up in Spain, if not in the same terms, at least in a very similar way?"[3]

Caballero didn't agree with this analysis. In Spain, according to him, the only really revolutionary class was the working class. In this sense Caballero wasn't wrong. His way of looking at things was consistent with the social conditions existing in the country.

Duclos' position was different: he either remained willingly blind to reality, which allowed him to carry out his mission, or else he was completely unaware of the politico-social history of Spain. In Spain the main core of the bourgeoisie was made up of the middle classes and important sections of the petit bourgeoisie, both urban and rural (and particularly the latter which exploited a salaried manpower). And these actually formed a bloc with the aristocracy of landed proprietors, the military and clerical classes and the recently formed fascist groups. This bloc, much more heterogeneous than it appeared, was united by the fear of a revolution on the march. This union, cemented by fear, forced the elements already mentioned into forming a common front to save private property, bourgeois order, family, country, religion.... In a word all the values considered eternal by the privileged.

The defensive reaction of this bloc was equivalent to the profound revolutionary dynamic of the working class. After the vacillations of the Republic, the latter had adopted an extreme position. It not longer had confidence in anyone, only trusting itself and its class organization, which was to bring it complete freedom through the expropriation of the capitalists and landowners, not only the big ones but also the average ones and the rich peasants. Its feelings about the latter can be explained since a large part of the agricultural proletariat was exploited by the middle class and small employers. Duclos appeared to ignore this situation. Once more he returned to the attack, hoping to persuade Caballero and he succeeded by using shock tactics. "When I told him after my return from Paris, that I was going to Moscow, asking him what I should tell the leaders of the IC, this is what he answered: 'The Popular Front is going to be created in Spain'."[4] As soon as the IC had been able to enlist Caballero in its ranks, things moved forward rapidly.

It is true that the Socialist Party didn't accept the proposition of the PC to unite, following the decisions of the VII Congress of the IC. But on the other hand it did accept the entry of the CGTU in a bloc (December 1935), inspired by the Communists in the ranks of the

UGT, an operation which permitted the Communists to infiltrate into the main body of the Socialist Party.

While progress with political agreements was being made inside the opposition, on the right, events were not taking the desired course. Robles had disappointed his friends and Zamora, on whom the clergy were counting, could not make up his mind to turn over the power to the right. Actually Robles and Zamora kept the reactionaries from taking over the government, an operation which the latter had hoped to accomplish legally. Since the legal way was denied them, the only possibility was a coup d'Etat, but the military were not in agreement about the choice of a Commander in Chief. The conspiracy was practically dead but agitation in the streets by the working class had not stopped. Strikes had started again and political attacks inspired by the Falange or the defensive ones of the working class occured daily. In the camp of the workers the situation was untenable. In the other camp, the meager political credit of Alexander Lerroux had been completely destroyed because of the financial scandal of Straperlo, comparable to the Stavisky affair in France.

Faced with this situation, the president, Zamora, decided to dissolve the Cortes and asked Portela Valladares to form a government which would call a general election. The elections were set for February 16, 1936. National life revolved around the electoral campaign.

The left groups united under the banner of the Popular Front. The latter was to be made up not only of the two democratic-bourgeois parties of Manuel Azaña and Martinez Barrio, but also included a political spectrum offered by Marxism in all its many manifestations: Socialism, Communism and Trotskyism (POUM).

All these opposition groups agreed on a very modest program, but promised amnesty for all the politico-social prisoners. The CNT used the occasion to launch a national campaign of agitation, warning the people not to be taken in by the pernicious illusion of the Popular Front, but this propaganda conflicted with the problem of the 30,000 prisoners.

In Barcelona, Durruti, recently out of prison, took part in a meeting along with Ascaso, who was in the underground. The meeting was organized to defend Jeronimo Misa, a young libertarian who had been condemned to death, accused of having resisted the Guardia Civil and of having freed a group of prisoners. The presence of Durruti and Ascaso on the platform made a profound impression on the public, which was crowded into the Circo Olympia. Durruti was to speak last but he wasn't able to speak. Ascaso had started his speech with humanitarian and philosophical ideas about the right of each human being to life. But raising the case of young Misa, he broke into a violent diatribe against the members of the government. The government censor [5] wanted to arrest him for insulting the government. A row started on the platform and Durruti, seizing Ascaso by the arm, succeeded in leaving the area that the police wanted to take over, both of them protected by the public.

Once again the two anarchists went underground. They found asylum in the outskirsts of Barcelona. But soon Durruti had to face another problem: should he take part as a speaker at the meeting which the Asturians were organizing in Leon? Ignoring his difficult situation, he decided to go, arguing that he would be arrested in any case.

The meeting took place in the Arena of Leon, whose tiered seats were filled to bursting. Workers had come from the whole area and even from La Coruña. The unexpected arrival of Durruti was a great surprise. He surpassed himself in his speech, talking with his usual energy. He insisted on the seriousness of the moment and the nee for the workers to control themselves and not to give in to provocations. "It is necessary to live on the alert and to remain ready for the first appeal from the CNT to go into the streets. It is not the time for impatience but for intelligent waiting and to observe th maneuvers of the enemy. We must force the latter to come out in the open and when the time comes, to fight without mercy."[6] A spontaneous demonstration followed and it was suggested to Durruti that he take advantage of this to escape. But he refused and led the manifestation towards the Plaza Mayor. No incident occured but at the moment when Durruti was going to leave, he was questioned by an officer of the Guardia Civil, who had been ordered to take Durruti to his superiors. The officer told him that he couldn't stay in Leon and that they must escort him back to Barcelona. This time his imprisonment was brief, and the 10th of January 1936 after being tried for insulting the government, he was freed.

Footnotes

1. Francisco Largo Caballero, *Mis recuerdos*. P. 138 and 159.
2. Information given to the author by José Peirats, who took part in the Plenum.
3. Jacques Duclos, *Mémoires (1935-1939)*. P. 107-110.
4. Idem.
5. A policeman assigned by the Government as a censor at all public meetings. He had the power to decide if the remarks of the speakers were an offense against the Government, and if they were, to put an end to the meeting.
6. *Solidaridad Obrera*, December 10, 1935.

13

FEBRUARY 16, 1936

DURRUTI WAS FREED in the middle of the electoral campaign. Naturally this highly political period had a profound effect on the ranks of the Confederation. The situation was confusing to many workers because of the repression and the propaganda of the right against the left and vice versa. An atmosphere of tragedy was in the air, which contrasted with the apparent calm. As if by enchantment, the armed attacks, the explosion of bombs, the confrontations with the police, no longer existed. One day before Durruti was freed, the regional Confederation of Labor in Catalonia (CNT) had held a plenum to settle its views. Two points of discussion were of primary importance: the position to adopt about alliances and what activity to carry on before the elections. The delegates found themselves faced with a dilemma, either to resolve the problems which the rank and file had not asked them to solve, or to stop the meeting.

Finally, using as a base the agreements which existed already on the two points under discussion, the Plenum confirmed the prior decisions and drafted a motion about the workers' alliance: "The UGT must recognize that the liberation of the workers is only possible through revolutionary action, that this recognition carries with it implicitly a break in political and parliamentary collaboration with the bourgeois regime. For the social revolution to be effective, it is necessary to destroy totally the present regime which governs the economic and social life of Spain. The new organization evolving from the revolution would be developed freely by the workers. To defend the new revolutionary organization, everyone would have to coordinate their efforts, setting aside the particular interest of each tendency." To these last four points a note was added, addressed to the National Committee of the CNT, asking that a National Trade Union Congress be called for April to study the possibilities and the means for a pact with the UGT. [1] As to the attitude to adopt about the elections, the Plenum ratified the "classical abstentionist line" which had always been the one taken by the CNT.

These resolutions corresponded theoretically to the traditional positions of the CNT, but actually people were drawn to the idea of voting and so the agreements reached were interpreted by each militant according to his revolutionary conscience. And this became clear to Durruti when he was called in by the Regional Committee to take part in a reunion of militants in charge of regional propaganda. Francisco Ascaso, García Oliver, Durruti, Federica Montseñy, Arturo Parera, Manuel Villar, Francisco Isgleas, Diego Abad de Santillan, etc. participated. The last named, commented on the meeting as follows: "If we reaffirm abstentionism without expressing any kind of doubts, we are giving the victory to the dictatorship which wants to bring in Gil Robles and we will enter a fascist period with a legal look. If we declare ourselves in favor of voting, in order to consolidate the triumph of the left, we will be accused (even by the people on the left) of turning up our noses at our principles."

These ideas of Santillan reflect the indecision of the majority of the militants. For the partisans of complete abstention, the success of Robles would force the Socialists to "radicalize" their position and would speed up the revolutionary process. For others, on the contrary, such a position would be an obstacle to an alliance between the CNT and UGT, the indispensable condition for the victory of the revolution. There were also those who maintained that the left, once in power, would proclaim an amnesty, which would give back to the CNT thousands of its imprisoned militants.

For the first time in many years, Santillan says, "we had the audacity to speak sincerely, avoiding ready made slogans. We had the foresight to judge the situation, taking a measure of all its seriousness. All, or almost all, acknowledged that the ruin of the left would also be ours! We avoided the electoral campaign of 1933, but the good sense of the workers pushed them to the ballot boxes, with the sole aim of dislodging the fascists from the Government and freeing the prisoners." It was still necessary to formulate a position which could be put forward at meetings. Durruti then offered his solution: "The left bloc pretends that if the right is successful, they will launch the revolution; the right answers, if the left is victorious, it will start a civil war. We are therefore on the edge of a revolution or a civil war. This is what we must clearly explain to the workers, making them understand that the vote can no longer solve anything. The worker who votes and then stays quietly at home, is a counter-revolutionary. The same is true for the man who dœsn't vote! This dilemma can only be solved in the streets, fully armed." García Oliver in turn proposed: "The Marxists in the UGT, the anarchists in the CNT, and these two organizations united in the struggle against capital." [2]

Durruti's and García Oliver's proposals were taken as the basis for propaganda. They were also used as the text of the manifesto published by the CNT a few days before the elections. "To meet the situation, a revolutionary pact must be put into effect immediately because, losing or winning, the Right will seize power, either legally or by starting a civil war. So universal suffrage means nothing, actually it is of the least importance. What is necessary and vital is to be on the alert and to be ready to fight! It is better to have the courage to look ahead (even if one is wrong) than to have to deplore one's negligeance later. Vigilance comrades!" [3]

Spain voted February 16, 1936, and in contrast to what had happened during the last general election, there was no disorder, no broken ballot boxes. La Vanguardia, the conservative daily, speaks of the elections in this way: "They took place in perfectly disciplined conditions. The Spanish people expressed what it wanted."

The Popular Front triumphed. It gained 4,176,156 votes and 269 deputies. The right wing bloc got 3,783,000 votes and 202 deputies. Among the allies of the Popular Front, the Socialist Party gained 88 deputies, but had fewer supporters than in the elections of 1931. Some of the voters had turned towards the Communist Party which got 17 seats. The Republican Party of Azaña and the Republican Union of Martinez Barrio salvaged the votes of the liberal bourgeoisie and obtained 117 deputies. The same phenomenon occurred in Catalonia, where the Esquerra Catalana was favored and won 29 seats.

On the right, the party of Lerroux was the big loser. From having 80 deputies, it dropped to 8. The CEDA which had lost 20 deputies, still had 94 seats. The Spanish Falange with only one candidate, its founder, Jose Antonio Primo de Rivera, didn't win a seat or deputy in Cadiz or Madrid.

The day after the electoral victory, February 17, Calvo Sotelo and Franco paid a visit to Portela Valladares, who according to the Constitution was to remain in office for a month more before handing over the power to the victors. The interview couldn't have been very cordial, Portela Valladares was asked to declare a state of siege and refused.

To justify their demands, Calvo Sotelo and Franco based their request on disorders which had broken out in various areas such as Oviedo, Barcelona, Madrid and elsewhere. Actually the workers who had no confidence in those who had won at the elections had already begun to free the prisoners. Since their negotiations with Portela had come to nothing, General Franco, as Commander in Chief of the army, went to see General Molero, Minister of War, and General Pozas, Inspector General of the Guardia Civil and asked them to support a military uprising. The two generals refused but Franco continued his preparations which were unsuccessful because the leading Chiefs of Staff in the military regions were not enthusiastic.

Taking into account the results of the election, Alcalá Zamora and Portela Valladares disregarded the legal waiting period and called on Manuel Azaña to form a new government. Azaña's government was formed on the 19th of February and was made up of left Republicans. The people who had demonstrated publicly and freed the prisoners, once again expressed their confidence in their governors, hoping that the latter would take the proper measures to assure a new life to the country.

The political group which had insured the triumph of the Popular Front had been shrewd enough to present it as the best rein against fascism. But even though Calvo Sotele, Gil Robles and Franco had made their game plain enough, the new government didn't take action against them and remained silent about the conspiracy. General Franco, seeing that he had been rapidly abandoned by his comrades, paid a visit to the Minister of Interior, Amos Salvador, who, instead of arresting him as a plotter, acknowledged his loyalty to the Republic. Azāna even entrusted him with the "commandancia militar" of the Canaries, while the one in the Balearic Islands was given to General Goded, another member of the conspiracy. Through such

Barcelona, February 1936 — Durruti with his daughter Colette and his companion Emilienne Morin.

measures, the government showed that it was following a policy identical to Lerroux's. All the fundamental problems remained in suspense. The only action taken was to declare an amnesty which had been carried out already by the masses on February 21st.

180

There can be no doubt as to how the government broke the law by establishing a difference between political and non-political offences. The non-political label was applied to prisoners who were members of the CNT. The government declared that they were excluded from the amnesty pretending that their offences were social and not political.

The 6th of March, twenty days after the triumph of the Popular Front, Durruti denounced this state of affairs at a meeting which took place at the Prince theater: "We have come to say to the men of the Popular Front that the working class has brought it victory and in the same way it can reverse the situation, because there is a limit to the patience of the working class and maybe we have reached this limit."[4]

In the country the situation, which was already distressing, was made worse by the flight of many landowners, who had abandoned their properties. They had fled in fear of the revolution or else to boycott the Popular Front. Those who remained, refused to take back the workers who had been arbitrarily fired during the revolutionary events of October. They were defying the Government which, on the 27th of February, had ordered the rehiring of all workers without exception. This refusal of the bosses was general, in industry as well as agriculture.

In the industrial sector, as Durruti explained it, the bosses hoped to reach a compromise in order to avoid a revolutionary takeover of the factories. But the situation among the peasants was much more alarming. They started to carry out expropriations, having lost all hope of a solution coming from the government. The peasants in a village near Madrid, Cenicientos, were the most daring. They decided to occupy an immense property "Encinar de la Parra", and they started to work it collectively. Then the Agriculture Union of the UGT sent a document to the Minister of Agriculture, a resumé of the situation: "Since there was no more work for us and our teams of horses, and our children were famished, the only thing we could do was to seize the land. And we seized it. Thanks to our work, it will produce what it never produced before. This will put an end to our misery and will increase the national wealth. We don't think we have harmed anyone and we ask only that the situation be legalized and in addition that we receive the necessary credits to carry out our work in peace."

Two weeks later, the workers in 80 villages[5] in the region of Salamanca did the same thing. Four days after that the inhabitants of some small villages near Toledo also carried out expropriations. And at dawn on March 25th, 80,000 farmers from the provinces of Caceres and Badajos took over the land and started to cultivate it. This uprising en bloc in the Estremadura produced a terrible panic in government circles. This time the government didn't dare send the Guardia Civil as it had done a few days before to Murcia, where it was responsible for the death of 27 people. It sent a group of engineers from the Institute for Agricultural Reform, in order to give an appearance of legality to the expropriation of the land.

By May 1936 the imminence of à fascist coup d'état was becoming clear. As the clergy formed part of the conspiracy, the people

181

kept an eye on the churches and listened to the sermons of the priests, who were inciting the rich to violence in order to defend order. The people understood that the clergy were enemies of the poor. Supplies of arms were even found in sacristies. Certain priests had to flee. This situation brought about popular reaction. According to statistics, from the 16th of February to the 15th of June 1936, 160 churches were burned, there were 269 deaths, 1,287 wounded, 215 assaults, 113 general strikes, 228 partial strikes and 145 bombs exploded.

As for the distribution of political strength, here is the picture presented by the ex-Minister of the Interior, Miguel Maura. On the left: UGT 1,447,000; CNT 1,577,000; Communists 133,000. On the right: 549,000 registered in different groups: 20 to 30,000 military men, 50,000 Falangists, 50,000 priests and monks; and millions and millions of pesetas.[6]

This was the situation in Spain when the CNT convened its IVth National Congress on May 1, 1936 in the Iris Theater Park in Saragossa.

Footnotes

1. José Peirats, *op. cit.* Vol. i.
2. Diego Abad de Santillan, *op. cit.*
3. José Peirats, *op. cit.*
4. *Solidaridad Obrera*, March 7, 1936.
5. Burnett Bolloten, *op. cit.*
6. Miguel Maura, *op. cit.*

14

IVᴛʜ CONGRESS OF THE CNT (MAY 1936)

WHEN DURRUTI finally left prison at the end of January the most fruitful period of his revolutionary career began. His activity was tremendous, covering different aspects of the struggle and this time it was to be the final phase. The members of the "Nosotros" group not only contributed their dynamism to the struggle but also their revolutionary enthusiasm. The situation which was developing meant the culmination of their activity. They had given themselves completely and their actions were to be crowned with success. Unquestionably the members of the group had an influence on the anarchist movement, but the movement didn't base itself on administrative power, but on the strength generated by daily contact with the working masses.

None of the members, except Ascaso, had had a permanent job in the committees, and his had been brief. The function of Durruti at the core of the CNT and the FAI was always limited to occasional jobs, such as the management of the national revolutionary committee, which had been chosen to organize the revolts in January and December. Fundamentally his work had always been carried on at rank and file level and this cut short criticisms made by opportunists and those who were envious. On this point, Durruti had always been intransigeant saying that "No anarchists in the union committees unless at the ground level. In these committees, in case of a conflict with the boss, the militant is forced to compromise to arrive at an agreement. The contacts and activities which come from being in this position, push the militant towards bureaucracy. Conscious of this risk, we do not wish to run it. Our role is to analyze from the bottom the different dangers which can beset a union organization like ours. No militant should prolong his job in committees, beyond the time allotted to him. No permanent and indispensable people."[1]. He believed that everyone should take part in these union functions. This was the only way to put an end to functionaries. The cult of personality should never be encouraged, but neither Durruti nor his comrades like García Oliver and Francisco Ascaso could escape from the influence they exerted against their will. This influence could be pernicious and Durruti was tormented by this more than anyone else. He was perfectly conscious that his comrades at work looked up to him: this wasn't caused by the aura which he spread unknowingly but by a sort of gratitude which they felt for the way in which he had given himself so entirely to his work. But Durruti was opposed to this sort of veneration, seeing in it, not a liberation of man but on the contrary a form of alienation of the will. He said that "the man who alienates his will, can never be free to express himself and follow his own ideas at a union meeting if he feels dominated by the feeblest orator... As long as a man doesn't think for himself and doesn't assume his own responsibilities, there will be no complete liberation of human beings."

Durruti's plain speaking sometimes shocked his comrades in the group, in particular García Oliver. The latter's self-confidence in his own judgements, sometimes produced the opposite effect from what he wanted, even though he couldn't tolerate any opposition to his ideas. This came out during the Congress of the CNT when Durruti and Oliver clashed while giving their personal views about the Revolution. Oliver felt that the counter-revolution was coming and he put forward the idea of forming a para-military organization. He felt this was the only effective way to oppose it and to assure the victory of the proletariat. Durruti felt that even under the pretext of effectiveness, this militarist conception should not be supported. "It is true", he said "that García Oliver's proposition is more acceptable from a military point of view than the guerilla fighter, whom I defend. But this para-military idea will lead the revolution to its destruction, because this organism will start to impose itself, and in the name of efficiency, will exercise its authority and its power over the masses. It is through this very principal that the Bolsheviks smothered the Russian Revolution. We don't want this at any price. Let our revolution develop according to its own principles."[2]

This internal disagreement came out in the open when the Textile Union, where both of them were active, started to discuss the program of the IVth Congress. Oliver expressed his point of view at a union meeting. Durruti defended his own position. The 70,000 members voted for García Oliver's proposal, which he summarized as follows: "The confederal defense groups and the anarchist groups will set up a separate organization to form the Century, the main unit of the Proletarian Army."

The program of the Congress was very extensive and important because of the responsibility assumed by the CNT on behalf of the people. The CNT had to face not only immediate problems but also to provide a program, which would define the general lines of Libertarian Communism. The discussions were intense and soon were to take on a special relevance. The faith of the workers was so great at this time that they felt the revolution was imminent. It was urgently necessary to formulate and rethink the ideas which could be immediately put into practise. The polemic was very lively, completely dominated as it was by revolutionary enthusiasm. This atmosphere was not only felt by the Textile workers but extended to all the unionized workers of the CNT. Meetings followed each other for many weeks. And to vote for specific resolutions large gatherings of workers were needed. Parallel to these gatherings, lectures took place in the factories during work hours. The CNT overworked its militants to such a point that much sleep was lost but thanks to their enthusiasm, everyone was able to overcome fatigue.

Poster advertising anarchist periodicals in 1936.

Durruti had very little chance to rest from the time when he left prison until he appeared in Saragossa as delegate to the Congress. His daughter, Colette, aged five, scarcely knew her father. Since the founding of the Republic, Durruti had spent three quarters of his time in prison or underground. This had become the normal state of affairs for him. Under such conditions he could have neither have family nor home life. Since January he could have had a family life for a few months but the scarcity of militants who were free and available was such, that the CNT had mobilized all of them for the national propaganda campaign during the pre-election period. And later they were needed for the preparation of the Congress. Durruti's many absences created temporary estrangements with his companion. She had to take care of the education of little Colette as well as earn a living for the child and herself, since the propagandists and militants in charge of union activities in the heart of the CNT were unpaid.

On May 1, 1936, the IVth National Congress of the CNT opened in Saragossa.[3] It was probably the most important Congress of the CNT as it brought together a larger group of delegates than ever before. Among the problems discussed was the question of the "revolutionary cycle". García Oliver gave a report on his activities, speaking as a former member of the revolutionary Committee of the uprising of January 1933.

"In 1931 when the political regimes changed in Spain, two tendencies appeared clearly which had actually existed in our minds for a long time. The division arose from two different ways of looking at reality.

185

"In 1931, the time was favorable to the proletariat for a libertarian revolution and the destruction of society as it was. But this hasn't occurred again in the same way or the same degree. The regime was disintegrating, the State was weak, the Army lacked discipline, the Guardia Civil had decreased in size, the forces of order were poorly organized. It was a propitious moment for our revolution. Today, as in 1931, we say that the revolution is possible. But now there is a strong State, disciplined forces, an arrogant bourgeoisie (....) To bring about a revolution today, other revolutionary forces beside those of the CNT are necessary. At this Congress we must study the way to take action with the UGT. But there could be no present, nor possibility for a future if the revolutionary course of the CNT had been different from what is has been. Current history justifies us.

"With the revolutionary undertakings carried out by the CNT, the path has been cleared. The first of these actions after the crime of Casas Viejas, completely pulverized the left. It started the masses and the Socialist Party itself on the road to revolution. It put everything in motion and it unmasked political illusion. It is true that we failed, but failure showed us that for the first time the CNT had undertaken national struggles on a very large scale. We know that the CNT until now was always an organization absorbed in union struggles against the boss. The CNT was not known in the outside world. But now we are known throughout the country and have given hope to the world for a Communist libertarian society. We have given a flag and a symbol to the working class.

"Comrades of the opposition, minorities are always successful when they are right. Everyone should struggle to convince the majority, as we are doing ourselves. The decisions of the Congress should be respected by all and all should be united within the Congress." [4]

The delegations of the unions of the opposition were admitted and their 60,000 members were enrolled in the CNT.

The Congress had to define its position on agrarian reform. A long preamble preceded the conclusions of this resolution. It calculated that the government was incapable in its present situation to enforce an effective and positive agrarian reform for the peasantry. Along with a plan for propaganda and organization, the following program was proposed:

" — Expropriation without indemnification of properties of 124 acres or more.

" — Confiscation of flocks kept in reserve, work tools, machines and seed, which are in the possession of landed proprietors.

" — Examination of communal properties and restoration of these properties to the peasant unions for their collective cultivation and exploitation.

" — The carrying out of projects for irrigation, thoroughfares, reforestation, as well as the creation of Agricultural Schools.

" — Direct take over by the peasant unions of lands which have been insufficiently cultivated and have thus caused sabotage of the national economy."

After the end of the Congress a meeting was organized in the Plaza de Toros of Saragossa to inform the people about the decisions which had been taken. To take part in this historic manifestation, special trains full of workers came from Madrid, Barcelona and the North. The inhabitants of nearby villages came in cars. For 24 hours Saragossa became the capital of the Spanish revolutionary proletariat. All the newspapers of the country commented on the importance of this Confederal Congress. A Republican newspaper cited it as an example which should inspire the meetings of Deputies. As for the bourgeois press, it presented the Congress to its readers as "the first chapter of the revolution".

The organ of the CNT in Catalonia, *Solidaridad Obrera*, ended its editorial with these words: "The Congress is over, but now the real work of confederal reconstruction and revolutionary preparation begins. At the Congress no individual criterion took the lead, collective thought prevailed. There was unanimity in the decisions taken there and they must also be carried out unanimously. Let us know how to show the workers of the entire world how a revolution is made." [5]

Footnotes

1. Testimony of Liberto Calleja.
2. Idem.
3. The 1st Congress took place in 1919, the IInd in 1931. But if one counts the founding Congress of 1910 in Barcelona, this Congress would be the IVth.
4. *Actas del Congreso de la CNT de Zaragoza*. May 1936, edited by the CNT in exile in Toulouse, in 1954.
5. *Solidaridad Obrera*, May 1936.

15

"SOCIALIST COMRADES WHAT ARE YOU WAITING FOR?"

WERE A MILLION AND A HALF WORKERS, who had expressed their wishes through the Congress of the CNT, living in a utopia or were they seeing clearly the revolutionary potentialities of the era?

A Soviet historian described the situation in this way: "Since the Popular Front won at the elections there has been an explosion. (....) The Republican parties, petit bourgois and bourgeois, which took part in the government immediately gave proof that they hadn't changed. Their policies resembled, line for line, the ones which they practised from 1931 to 1933, and which had deceived the people and opened the way to reaction. The masses alone had changed, conscious now of their strength. They started immediately to carry out the program of the Popular Front from the bottom and by revolutionary methods: liberation of all political prisoners. rehiring of all workers by the firms which had fired them for political activity, and occupation of the land beginning in March 1936.

"Strikes started towards the 15th of March, provoked by hunger, unemployment and fascist provocations. The movement widened day by day, paralyzing shops, factories and mines. During June and July 1936 an average of ten to twenty strikes a day were recorded, and in 95% of them the workers were victorious. Masses of workers streamed through the streets of the main cities, calling for a complete victory for the revolution. It was at this time, when tens of thousands of people came together for meetings, that the first industrial collectives were borne and the workers occupied the businesses abandoned by their owners. This control at the base, the spreading of strikes, the occupation of factories and lands, was leading the proletariat to elaborate a program covering all aspects of Spanish reality, i.e. economic, social, political, etc..."

This description by the Soviet writer, Maidanik, which was corroborated by other historians, contains only one error which Fernando Claudin picks up. The revolutionary explosion has nothing to do with the "(...) realization of the program of the Popular Front which called neither for the occupation of factories nor the liquidation of capitalism, but on the contrary, tried by every means to protect private property. Maidanik is undoubtedly obliged to try and reconcile the actual development of events by offering an explanation of the correctness of Communist International policies." [1]

From this description of the situation we can see that the popular masses were acting on their own initiative, disregarding the government. And one can understand that the workers hadn't voted for the Popular Front because of political illusions but for concrete reasons, to obtain the freedom of the prisoners and to organize the struggle on a more favorable ground.

And so with full knowledge of the revolutionary level of the working class, the Congress of the CNT chose insurrection and developed a plan to cover every aspect of Spanish reality. The masses were ready to bring about a utopia by taking power. Actually the question of power was central to the strategy developed by the anarcho-syndicalists since the proclamation of the Republic. If it is true as G. Brenan notes, that the anarchists had not been able to make the revolution in Spain, they had however created and maintained a permanent pre-insurrectional climate. [2] Maurin recognized also that "even though it might seem paradoxical, it depended on Durruti, García Oliver and Ascaso, whether Gil Robles or Azaña should be in power." [3]

Thus revolutionary actions by the CNT in the streets determined the political life of the country and aimed it inexorably towards a goal in itself revolutionary. The anarchists harassed the government, explaining that the people must profit by the weaknesses and difficulties of the State to destroy it and create a new situation, closer to the level and revolutionary conscience of the working class.

During June and July the struggle had already brought about the destruction of one part of the capitalist sector. Power, much reduced, was divided among a number of groups antagonistic to each other. Opposed to them was the power of the workers, their parties and unions, which increased every day. At the same time the counter-revolution expressed itself not only through the verbal violence of its principal leaders, Gil Robles, J. A. Primo de Rivera or J. Calvo Sotelo, but also through its attacks and sabotage of the economy (blackouts in the factories, the land allowed to lie fallow). There were also confrontations provoked by fascist groups and the Army was plotting now in broad daylight.

The workers of the CNT were therefore not being demagogues when they declared that the revolution was the only possible way to break out of this impasse. One question, however, divided the members of the Congress. Could the Spanish revolution be victorious alone, against the forces of reaction or would world capitalism be able to strangle it? Some people faced with this threat thought perhaps it would be wiser to seek a democratic evolution in Spain. The most radical elements knew that this choice would lead to reformism and Durruti declared: "(...) If the revolution, for which we have been fighting for many years, breaks out now as we wish, we will see what we must do to go ahead. But from now on we must think of internationalizing it by taking advantage of every possibility which presents itself to us." [4] That was the extent of the polemic because the hour was really not propitious for theorizing. The revolution had broken out in the streets and no one could stop it.

Two months after Spain, the Popular Front in France had also won at the elections. Practically speaking the Socialists and Communists were in power. While in Spain a bourgeois democrat, Manuel Azaña, led the government, in France the National Assembly, three quarters of it made up of Socialists and Communists had chosen a Socialist. The Spanish workers knew very well that it was not because the Socialists were in power and that many Communists had seats in the Assembly, that the State would create the revolution which the people demanded. It was the attitude of the French proletariat which had started to occupy the factories, with the firm determination of transforming the movement into a revolutionary act that seemed more serious and sustained their revolutionary enthusiasm. The Spanish people thought that by joining their struggle with the French people, they could then extend the revolution throughout Europe.

Durruti stated during a meeting: "If the strike movement in France is radicalized and if the workers go beyond the orders of their political and union leaders, the European revolution is won. Comrades! Push events forward!"

García Oliver, on his side, insisted in the National Committee of the CNT that he must be allowed to denounce publicly the passivity and silence of the leaders of the UGT in regard to the appeal from the CNT Congress for a revolutionary alliance. Ascaso appealed to the Socialists in these terms: "Socialist comrades, what are you waiting for to prove your solidarity with the French workers?"(5)

Actually events in France and Spain were connected and showed clearly the analogy which existed between these two movements. The workers in the automobile industry stopped work in Paris and paralyzed the industry in France. A few days later the peasants of eighty villages in the province of Salamanca occupied the estates of the big proprietors and organized collectives. This initiative extended like wildfire to the province of Toledo, while in Estremadura eighty thousand peasants installed themselves in the large properties which they then organized collectively. The urban workers supported the rural revolution actively and the manifestœs of this period show clearly the international character of the class struggle.

But while enthusiasm was inflaming the Spanish people, in France the workers were yielding. Political planning had won the day in the party. Leon Blum had refused to accept the leadership of a proleterian revolution and Maurice Thorez told the workers that it was necessary to know how to end a strike. Under the aegis of the Popular Front, France was settling back again into bourgeois order.

Durruti, whose companion was French, kept in close contact with the militants in France. Having understood how the workers had been defeated, he didn't hide his irritation from the French militants who passed through Barcelona. He reproached them for their revolutionary want of good sense, their militant incoherence, their factional quarrels, which had disoriented the workers' movement and had thrown it back towards reform. Besides, Durruti could not understand this change in orientation, because in France the anarcho-syndicalist movement had had a real strength. How had it lost all its influence on the working class, to a point that it could not play the least kind of role during the strikes?

It was clear that Durruti and his French comrades saw the problem of the revolution in different ways. Also the organization in Spain had been under harsh attack and had resisted attemps to bend anarcho-syndicalism toward reformist solutions. But Durruti said the thing which differentiated the Spanish from the French militants was that the former had a blind faith in the revolution which they experienced daily through their struggles, while the latter, cut off from the popular masses, cultivated revolution in their philosophical circles. The revolution, Durruti added, dœsn't need theories but constant practise. The theories produce no revolutionary acts, it is the acts which allow the creation of theories. Speaking to the French militants, he urged them to go back to the people in their struggle because, he said, if the workers in France have experienced a defeat, they will soon have a new occasion to act: Spain is going towards a revolution.

Preparations were going forward in June and the beginning of July, while Durruti and the members of the "Nosotros" group were devising a plan of attack. They adopted the tactic of the urban guerilla, foreseeing that the fighters would move through the sewers, in order to be able to help different insurrectionary areas or to attack the enemy from the rear. In each military barrack they placed one or more informers to watch over the activities of the principal military leaders. They did the same thing in the headquarters of the Guardia Civil and the Assault Guards. They made bombs, bought arms or stole them from the barracks. The old "Solidarios" would not be taken by surprise in this decisive hour.

Footnotes

1. Fernando Claudin, *op. cit.*
2. Gerald Brenan, *El Laberinto español.*
3. Joaquin Maurin, *Revolución y contra-revolución en España.*
4. Liberto Calleja's testimony to the author.
5. The quotations of Ascaso and Durruti summarize the theme of the meetings in May 1936. See *Solidaridad Obrera*, May-June 1936.

16

AN AGONIZING WEEK
(JULY 13-19, 1936)

CASARES QUIROGA, the President of the Council and Manuel Azaña, who had replaced Álcalá Zamora in May as President of the Republic, seemed like complete strangers to Spanish reality. The Army, divided, no longer obeyed the Minister of War, but their Staff officers. The dissidents were headed by General Mola. Rumors about a coup d'état were becoming definite. The falange was stepping up its terrorist activities to create an atmosphere of insecurity. They assassinated the Socialist lawyer, Jimenez de Asua, vice-president of the Cortes.

Attacks multiplied during the week before the uprising. The Falangists assassinated Captain Faraudo, a member of the Assault Guard. The monarchist deputy, Calvo Sotelo, who was obviously the political brain of the uprising, claimed responsibility publicly for this crime and declared before the Cortes that to rise against the Republic was a duty. The Communist deputy, Dolores Ibarruri, "La Pasionaria", answered that it was the last time that "his lordship" would speak before the Chamber.

At the same time, an arms traffic benefiting the Falange was discovered in Barcelona, as well as some propaganda leaflets signed by a division General, proclaiming a State of War. The Catalan authorities immediately made these facts known in Madrid, where Casares Quiroga judged the event of no importance.

The following night, the 12th of July, the Falangists assassinated Lieutenant Castillo, of the Assault Guards in Madrid, while another group took over the transmitter of "Radio Valencia" and issued a proclamation which ended with: "Long live the Falange!" The Assault Guards decided to revenge their officers who had been killed. During the night of July 13th, they carried off Calvo Sotelo from his home and at dawn his body was found in the Eastern cemetery.

The 14th of July, Jacques Duclos declared that the "Marseillaise" was the "International" of the working class and that only a national reconciliation could spare France from a civil war. The 15th Madrid awoke in agony. Calvo Sotelo and Castillo were to be buried. Sermons alternated over the bodies while military men in uniforms were going through the streets of the capital shouting slogans hostile to the Republic. The Guardia Civil on horseback protected them and

charged the procession accompanying the coffin of Lieutenant Castillo.

During this time General Franco was putting a final touch to his proclamation at Santa Cruz de Tenerife, capital of the Canary Islands. The 17th of July he reached Morocco in his personal plane, piloted by an English adventurer. Throughout the Spanish protectorate the legionnaires occupied certain positions as anticipated. But in the main cities they were confronted by the workers. The war had in fact just begun. Spain found itself divided into two camps. On one side were the Fascists, backed by the totalitarian regimes of Germany and Italy, on the other, the people, to whom the French Government had promised to deliver arms, for the outcome of the war would depend on armaments.

In Barcelona since the 13th of July, the CNT and the FAI had set up their defense plan. After each work day the militants gathered in various spots, where they would go out to meet the rebels when the time came.

Tuesday the 14th Durruti left the hospital where he had had to have an operation. He took part in a Plenary session of the Committee for Defense, CNT-FAI. Luis Companys sent a trusted emissary, Perez Farras, to ask the CNT discreetly what its attitude would be towards a Fascist uprising. He was answered that the CNT would be at its fighting stations and Durruti said to Perez Farras: "We can't oppose the bodies of our militants to the weapons of the army. What measures do you plan to take so that we can arm our men?" Perez Farras consulted with Companys, who remained evasive. He was content to let it be known that he had no stock of arms available but that at the last moment he would try nevertheless to equip the militants. [1]

This declaration angered Durruti, who tried to guess Companys' plans. Was he trying to neutralize the CNT and the FAI? He surely knew since the events of October 6th that the intervention of the working class was indispensable and that without its support the Generalitat alone could not resist the assaults of the Fascists. The bloody confrontations which had just taken place in Madrid, warned Companys that the day of reckoning was approaching.

A regional meeting of the CNT was called on the night of July 16th. The militants decided to establish a close collaboration between all the proletarian forces menaced by the fascists and to rise above the differences which placed them in opposition to each other.

Again the CNT went to the Generalitat to obtain arms, but once more Companys answered that he had none. "We didn't ask for the thirty thousand guns which were necessary to arm our men, but a thousand so that we could throw ourselves into the fight and crush the fascist uprising. But we received none. It was clear to us that if the politicians feared fascism, they feared much more the people armed. From the 17th to the 18th of July the delegation of the CNT-FAI with the Catalan Minister of the Interior organized, as had been agreed, the defense of Barcelona and set up confederal groups, already transformed into armed workers' militia to watch over the city. Nevertheless the police of the Generalitat attacked our patrols and endless telephone calls informed us that such and such a comrade had just been arrested for carrying arms. We intervened immediately and we were always able to reach an agreement with the police. But isn't it heart-breaking to realize that on the eve of July 19, we still had to devote all our efforts to hold on to the few weapons which we possessed."[2]

The public authorities promised the workers that they would receive arms at the right time. Press information was being severely controlled because the government wanted people to think that they were in control of the situation. July 17 the censor forbade the publication in *Solidaridad Obrera* of a manifesto which gave instructions to the workers. In the afternoon the Regional Committee of the FAI reacted by publishing the text in a leaflet which was distributed in the streets of Barcelona and throughout the region. The orders were clear: the anarchist groups and the Libertarian Youth should join the CNT Committees of Defense in order to form a common front.

The workers had understood that the Catalan Government would never arm the people. They therefore went into action without taking further notice of it. The initiative was taken by the Transport Workers Union which was located on the Rambla de Santa Monica not far from the harbor. A sailor, Juan Yague, declared that it was absurd to wait any longer and that moving rapidly they could get hold of two hundred guns which were in the holds of the ships. Two boats, the "Marques de Comillas" and the "Magallanes" were taken by storm. The two hundred guns found were distributed to the militants of the transport and the metallurgist unions.

Informed about this action, Escofet, the chief of police, gave orders to a captain of the Assault Guards that his company should recover the weapons. The officer who went to the Transport Union received this reply from its secretary, Benjamin Sanchez: "The Generalitat refuses to arm the people, pretending that it has no arms. But when the workers bring proof that these arms exist, the government wants to disarm the workers. The guns are in good hands, ask the workers if they want to give them back to you."[3] Naturally all of them refused. A confrontation seemed inevitable when Durruti arrived at the headquarters of the union and spoke to the captain: " — There are times in life when it is impossible to carry out an order, no matter how highly placed the person who gave the order. It is through disobedience that man becomes civilized. In your case then, civilize yourself by making common cause with the people. Uniforms no longer have any meaning. No other authority exists except revolutionary order and the latter requires that these guns stay in the hands of the workers."[4] The captain was convinced by Durruti and he left, carrying with him a dozen unuseable guns, as proof of the steps he had taken.

Solidaridad Obrera for July 18th only published what the censor allowed about the events in Morocco. But in other publications information was given to make one believe that the government was in perfect control of the situation. During the afternoon of that same day it was learned that the Fascist uprising would take place during the night of Saturday and Sunday. This news came from the spies that the CNT had placed in the barracks. In addition the workers had arrested an officer of the Guardia Civil who was carrying precise orders about the uprising, as well as the hour at which it was to occur, at five on the morning of July 19th.

The Regional Committee of the CNT called three important meetings and thousands of workers took part. As for the president of the Generalitat of Catalonia, Luis Companys, he dismissed a number of rebellious officers of the "Ist Regiment of Mountain Artillery". The soldiers were told that it was no longer necessary to obey their officers. This measure had no other effect than to warn the rebel officers, because the troops were completely isolated and unable to communicate with the outside. The Republican officers had already been arrested by the rebels.

At 11.30 PM the CNT informed the Catalan government that it was going ahead and would seize all the remaining arms in the city as well as the automobiles necessary for liaison between different district committees. Barcelona was already full of cars bearing the acronym "CNT-FAI". Union cards and left wing party cards were used for safe conduct.

Toward midnight, General Aranguren, commander of the Guardia Civil, arrived at the residence of the President of the Generalitat, where he found Companys with a delegation of the CNT who were demanding that half of the Assault Guards be disarmed to arm the workers. Companys declared that his guards were reliable and promised once again that arms would be distributed when the time came. Durruti interrupted him: "It is not the moment to make speeches. It is necessary to act. We refuse to become victims of fascism because of the obstinacy of a politician. From now on the CNT and the FAI will take over the leadership of the struggle." [5]

Francisco Ascaso immediately went to the Construction Workers Union where he called out the workers for the struggle. Durruti addressed the workers in the San Martin, San Andres and Pueblo Nuevo districts: "Comrades, arms are in the hands of the fascists. We must seize them." García Oliver went to the workers of the districts of Sans, Hospitalet and La Torrasa.

Solidaridad Obrera came from the presses with the following headline:

"To Seville, the fascists are shooting at our brothers!

To Cordova, the army has revolted!

To Morocco, they are fighting in the streets!

He who does not fulfill his revolutionary duty is a traitor to the cause of the people!"

"Long live Libertarian Communism"

At two in the morning García Oliver and Durruti entered the Central Police Station where, once again, they asked Escofet to disarm the Assault Guards. He refused. As for Santillan and Ascaso, they were with the Secretary of State for the Interior, España, and were begging for arms, but unsuccessfully.

During this time, in the infantry barracks of Pedralbes, the commander, Lopez Amor, confined the Colonel and seized the leadership of the rebellious regiment. The soldiers were assembled in the courtyard, surrounded by falangists who had entered the barracks towards II PM and had put on uniforms. Lopez Amor addressed his soldiers: "The anarchists have revolted in order to overthrow the Republic.

195

The army must intervene with arms to defend the regime to which it has sworn allegiance. Long live the Republic!''[6]

In the absence of General Goded, it was General Burriel who coordinated the activities of the rebellious units. In Calle Lepanto the cavalry regiment of Santiago was ready for action. The artillerymen of the Parc Central de San Andres, who had been joined by a thousand falangists, were getting ready to set up their cannons in the Plaza de Cataluna. The only unit which seemed still to be neutral was the Infantry Regiment of Badajoz which had a number of Republican officers in its ranks. As for the Artillery Center of Atarazanas, it was almost entirely in the hands of the insurgents. Nevertheless at the last moment Sergeants Manzana and Gordo managed to open a hidden door and give arms to the people.

The buildings of the Commissariat, facing the Atarazanas barracks, had only a few troops under the command of Captain Mola, brother of the General. Nevertheless this position was important because it controlled the route that the workers took, coming from the Harbor or from the district of Sans. As for the citadel of Montjuich, it dominated the city with its cannons. The naval base was hesitant. The airdrome of Prat remained loyal to the Republic but some aviators had deserted with the best planes to rejoin the forces of General Mola in the North. At Headquarters, Llano de la Encomienda, Military Governor of the region, found himself virtually a prisoner of his staff, which had taken sides with the rebels. The malcontents had not been able to force him to sign the document proclaiming a State of War. Finally in the convents and churches, the armed priests were waiting for the signal to open fire on the people.

This was the situation at two in the morning. At three o'clock, "Radio Barcelona" issued a call to the people of France telling them about the danger threatening the Spanish masses.

The Defense Committee of the CNT had convened in the headquarters at Pueblo Nuevo, where two trucks had been armed which were to serve the mobile staff. In these trucks a dozen members of the "Nosotros" group took their places, among them Durruti, Ascaso, Garcia Oliver, Gregorio Jover, Aurelio Fernandez. When they learned that the infantry regiment of the Pedralbes barracks and the cavalry of the Montesa were beginning to move, the two trucks of the CNT-FAI started off, flying the red and black flag. The workers' patrols placed along the route that the trucks were to take, understood immediately that the hour of the revolution had come. The CNT and the FAI had come out in the streets. The trucks went down the Via Layetana under the eyes of Captain Escofet, who was standing on the balcony of the Central Police Station.

At the same time, the harbor workers, advised by Durruti, had organized an impressive demonstration around the Palace of the Generalitat and were calling for arms. The secretary of State for the Interior, Espana, no longer knew what he should do; the Assault Guards questioned each other with their eyes, not knowing what course to follow. Suddenly, one of them took his pistol and gave it to a worker. Then all the others imitated him.[7]

Through Fontanella street, the trucks reached the Ramblas and the Plaza Arco Teatro where the transport workers had set up two important barricades. These were very strategically placed as they dominated the Paseo de Colon, which was the approach from the harbor and controlled access to the troops in the Atkarazanas barracks. A staff member of the CNT-FAI, assisted by Sergeant Gordo, installed himself on this barricade.

The other commanding position was at the headquarters of the Building Workers Union in the ancient "casa Cambo", which was soon to become the "casa de la CNT-FAI."

The most devoted elements of the working class were in the streets and at their combat positions. It was 5 AM the 19th of July 1936....

Footnotes

1. Santillan, eye witness account.
2. Diego Abad de Santillan, *op. cit.*, p. 34.
3. This scene was described to us by a witness, who was at that time the secretary of the Metallurgists" Union, Benjamin Sanchez. Further details are found in Santillan's *op. cit.* Additional information given by militants of the CNT who lived through these events.
4. Santillan, *op. cit.* Supplemented by testimony from Clemente Mangado, Tomas Perez, Juan Manuel Molina, and others.
5. Idem.
6. Francisco Lacruz, *El alzamiento, la revolucion y el terror en Barcelona.*
7. Santillan, *op. cit.*

DURRUTI
The People Armed

Part III
The Revolutionary (1936)

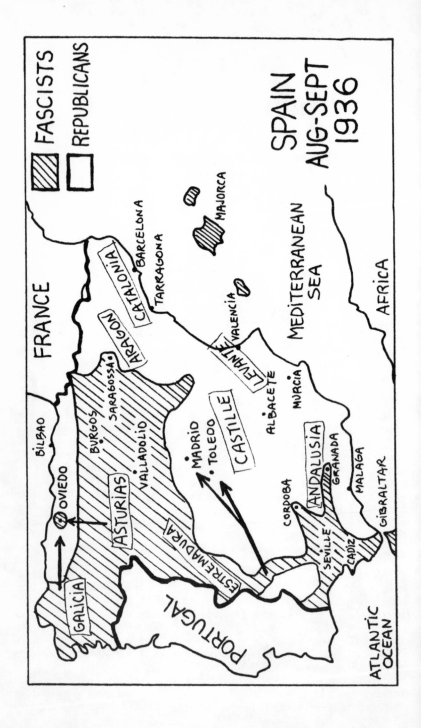

1

BARCELONA IN FLAMES [1]

THE REPUBLICAN leaders had done their best to limit the effects of the Fascist coup and to find an amicable solution. But one ministry more or less in a middle of the road government was worthless. The rebels were not to be satisfied with such fare.[2] They wanted everything. But contemptuous of their enemy, the working class, they ignored or under-estimated its ability to fight.

The central government in Madrid and the Catalonia government had learned nothing when they were defeated in October 1934 and had, until now, played the game of the fascists by refusing to give arms to the people, the only fighters actively in opposition at this time. Now the decisive hour had arrived; the people with bare hands but unshaken faith in victory were about to face a military force infinitely better armed.

On July 19, 1936, at 5 A.M. a new page in the revolution was beginning to the sound of gunfire, the crackling of machine guns which were mixed with the deafening sound of factory sirens, informing the people that the decisive hour had arrived. The seventh artillery regiment had left San Andres Park, divided, and was trying to reach the center of the capital by two different routes. But at the crossing of the "Diagonal" the first detachment ran into a group of workers armed with grenades and pistols, which blocked its advance. And the second detachment after going through Barcelona was stopped where Claris and Cortes Catalanas Streets meet, without being able to reach its objective Cataluña Square. For the first time guerrilla tactics were being used which were actually to decide the outcome of the struggle.

The infantry of the Pedralbes barracks, protected by the squadrons of the Montesa cavalry regiment, had split up between University Square and Cataluña Square and had occupied the University, the Hotel Colon, the Central Telephone Exchange and a number of other buildings. It had reinforced its position after having tried unsuccessfully to advance via the Rambla to occupy its goal the Palace of the Generalitat and to make contact with the rebels who were in control of the entrance to the harbor.

In the western part of Barcelona near the Plaza de España, a struggle was taking place between the workers and a mixed group of artillery engineers and squadrons of the Montesa cavalry regiment.

The latter had succeeded in seizing the Square to the cries of "Long Live the Republic" thus fooling the Assault Guards. Machine guns and a battery of light artillery were installed, the latter destroying the barricades of the workers of the Sans district near the Town Hall of Hostafrachs. But this was its only victory because during all the street fighting this military unit, surrounded by the people, could neither advance nor retreat.

One part of the Montesa regiment followed by important military units of engineers, managed to slip into Marques del Duero Avenue (Paralelo) but was checked by a strong barricade put up by the workers of the Woodworkers' Union. To get the best of them the rebels advanced, protected by the workers who had been taken prisoner. In control of the street, they set up their machine guns and cleared the area. When they appeared to be victorious, groups of armed workers coming from the Ramblas and crossing the alleys of the old quarters of Barcelona reinforced the resistance. Guided by Garcia Oliver, a counter offensive was being organized. A cavalry corporal was haranguing his comrades who proceeded to turn their fire against their officers putting them to rout. [3]

At the same time, near the Plaza de Palacio, the dockworkers of the Barceloneta district had routed the Montana artillery regiment which had been the first to come out of the Docks barracks, Icaria Avenue. The encounter was very violent. The gunners, protected by the Badajoz infantry regiment, were able to set up their cannons and to fire on the Government Palace (Ministry of the Interior). But the Barceloneta workers protected by movable bales of paper, attacked with such vigor that they were able to seize the weapons of the artillerymen. Some of the officers were taken prisoner and the rest of the troop retreated to the barracks which were immediately surrounded by workers.

Toward the center of Barcelona to the North of the Plaza de Cataluña, at the crossing of the Diagonal and the Paseo de Gracia, in the area called "Cinco de Oros", the Santiago cavalry regiment was immobilized. Seeing that it was impossible to advance, the Colonel ordered his troops to retreat towards the Carmelite Convent. They found refuge there along with platoons of the Guardia Civil. [4]

The last pockets of resistance were concentrated around the Plaza de Colon while the Carabineros who had taken sides with the Fascists were defending the harbor area called La Paz. Diametrically opposite, the area of the Rambla Santa Monica was under cross fire from the military Government headquarters and the Atarazanas barracks. At the center of this line of fire the rebels had stationed their machine guns on top of the statue of Christopher Columbus. These were all the main theaters of operation in the morning. Shooting came from every direction, from the churches, the convents and from the inside of the barracks.

Towards noon after four hours of fighting the uprising appeared to be defeated. One by one, all the areas of resistance fell into the hands of the people. Around ten o'clock, the first to be routed were the artillerymen at the Docks by the port workers and at about the same time the gunners of the San Andres barracks began to mingle and fraternize with the population.

The two infantry companies which had been sent to the Badajoz barracks with orders to occupy the radio station in Caspe Street were driven off and some units barricaded in the Ritz Hotel hastened to surrender. From then on the morale of the workers who were fighting, increased. In addition an important collection of weapons (guns and machine guns) fell into their hands. Barcelona began to have a new look: soldiers mixing with the common people, Assault Guards without their uniforms to be able to fight better and an enthusiastic mass of workers.

Everywhere the best qualified militant workers were leading the struggle. García Oliver was at the Brecha de San Pablo and Durruti at the Plaza de Cataluña. Ascaso from his "Headquarters" at the square of the Arco Teatro, followed the struggle through his communications system and sent reinforcements to the weak points of the popular resistance. Real power to make decisions and to resist was no longer at the official Government centers or at Police Headquarters but in the street and in improvised centers.

Footnotes

1. When I was writing this chapter, I was able to use my own recollections having lived through these events. But I also used *Tres dias de Julio* by Luis Romero; *Porque perdimos la guerra* by Diego Abad de Santillan; *El Alzamiento, la revolución y el terror en Barcelona* by Francisco Lacruz. I have also used testimony of Juan Manuel Molina, Dolorès Iturbe, Liberto Roig, Francisco Isgléas, Aurelio Fernandez, Pablo Ruiz, etc.
2. See Chapter II.
3. Francisco Lacruz, *op. cit.* gives all these details in his book. As a fascist author his testimony can be accepted as reliable.
4. This refers to Recas, the commander of the Guardia Civil, who had received orders the morning of July 19 to go out to meet the Santiago cavalry regiment. But when he found them at the Paseo de San Juan, he went over to the fascists with his troops. This episode is also mentioned in Lacruz's book.

2

THE DEATH OF
FRANCISCO ASCASO

BEFORE GOING to Headquarters, General Goded, who had come from Majorca to take command of the uprising, wanted to find out about the situation in Barcelona. And so he flew over the city for ten minutes and learned that his troops were besieged. Major Lazaro seeing what was going on "advised him to abandon his undertaking, believing that Barcelona was a trap."[1] Nevertheless he landed at the Naval Base which was in the hands of the fascists.

General Goded's arrival at Headquarters gave courage to the dissident Generals, particularly Burriel who, until then, had led the struggle with such bad luck. Burriel felt responsible for the defeat but also because he had been unable to win over General Llano de la Encomienda, General in Chief of the military division. The latter had had the courage to remain faithful to the Republic, believing that "It was preferable to see the victory of the people with all its consequences, rather than the victory of the fascists."[2]

General Goded's first act was to remove General Llano de la Encomienda and arrest him. His second job was to try and improve the situation. He could only count on the Guardia Civil, which up to now had remained in their barracks, and the Carabineros closed up in the San Pablo barracks, prisoners of the people who were attacking these buildings.

Goded used all his powers of persuasion to convince the Guardia Civil to take up arms against the people. He telephoned immediately to the General of the Tercios of the Guardia Civil, General Aranguren. The latter replied that "he did not obey any orders except those given by the Republic." This answer infuriated Goded: "Facing a Spain in ruins, is this the only thing you can say?" Aranguren, who was speaking from the Government Palace, understood that the uprising had been a failure and the Republican Government was in control of the situation.[3]

Then General Goded thought of using the Alcantara regiment which was commanded by Colonel Roldan and which until then had remained neutral.

"— Roldan, I am going to start a counter-offensive, what troops do you have?"

"— General, I have almost a regiment but the barracks are surrounded by the people. Two companies which tried to leave were

Barcelona, July. 20, 1936 — truck used by the anarchist affinity group "Germen" for their transportation needs during the thirty-six hour struggle for Barcelona.

pushed back. The soldiers think they are fighting for the Republic but this situation can't be maintained for long and God knows what will happen when the troops learn that we are rising against the Republic."

It was 2.15 P.M. and Goded felt utterly beaten and confided to his assistant Major Lazaro "You were entirely right, we have been abandoned."[4] Goded's command has lasted a little less than sixty minutes.

In the streets the crowd was getting bigger. Men, women and children wanted to make themselves useful. Barricades were being put up, sometimes without reason but as an act of popular enthusiasm and spirits soared when the good news spread like wildfire that groups of the FAI had attacked the Pedralbes barracks with the help of some soldiers. The people were no longer armed with pistols but held real rifles in their hands.

A Committee of War had formed in the Pedralbes barracks, now called Bakunin barracks. Littles airplanes from Prat were flying over the city throwing leaflets down into the barracks to tell the soldiers about the development of the struggle and the rout of the fascist uprising and urging them to stop obeying the commands of their officers. The radio braodcast information regularly about the situation. Some cafes had been taken over and their enormous rooms had been turned into public eating places. In these collective kitchens food was prepared hastily for the men on the barricades. District committees started to function. In a thousand ways the beginnings of a new life were evident.

205

The struggle and the need for workers' unity had wiped out ideological differences. The Assault Guards who, a few hours ago had been hounding the workers, had taken off their uniforms and were mixing with the population. Enthusiasm was general and everyone had confidence in the CNT. The names of Durruti, García Oliver, Ascaso, flew from mouth to mouth. Because of the dynamism of the struggle, nobody questioned the leading role of the National Confederation of Work.

There were still doubts about the role of the Guardia Civil: what was it going to do? To test its reaction, it was ordered to leave the barracks to go and pacify the Cataluña-Universidad region. This mission was given to the "19th Tercio" whose leader was Colonel Escobar. A loyal troop was placed between the first and second corps of the Guardia Civil, while the suspicious workers surrounded the column. Marching unprotected and in double file the Guardia Civil began to go up Via Layetana to the Plaza de Urquinnoma to reach the Plaza de Cataluña and the University.

The Plaza de Cataluña was alive with workers, who were finding cover wherever they could behind trees and in the entrances of the subway. From the very beginning it was they who had supported the offensive against the rebels. The moment for the final struggle had come. The Guardia Civil started a heavy fire. From the Hotel Colon, where the rebels had found refuge, the machinegunners were shooting without interruption. But the presence of the Guardia Civil among the attackers convinced the rebels to surrender. White flags appeared in the windows and the troops advanced towards the Hotel to take it over. But the people feared that once the Guardia Civil entered the Hotel they would go over to the rebels bringing them reinforcements and ammunition. So an important group posted at the Ronda de San Antonio and commanded by Rovira, a militant of the POUM, intervened and occupied the Hotel.[5]

At the same time the final attack on the Central Telephone Exchange was taking place. Durruti was marching at the head of the attackers. Many lives were lost there, among them Obregon [6], the secretary of the anarchist groups who was hit by a bullet in the forehead. At the end of a fierce hand to hand fight, the Central was soon in the hands of the workers and Durruti announced: "The workers have conquered the Central Telephone Exchange by shedding their blood and it belongs to them."[7]

From then on the workers' struggle took on a new look and they were no longer fighting to maintain the power of the bourgeoisie but to establish worker's power. Soon after the fall of the Hotel Colon and the Central Telephone Exchange, the stronghold at the Plaza de la Universidad surrendered. The workers who had been arrested that very morning by the rebels and guarded as hostages were now freed by the people.

General Goded, who still hoped to turn things in his favor, called once again on General Aranguren's and the Guardia Civil's traditional viewpoint but the latter remained unmoved and answered him: "General Goded, the rebellion has been put down and we beg you to stop the shooting to avoid useless bloodshed. We have

Barcelona, July. 20, 1936 — Francisco Ascaso talking to his cousin Joaquin, one hour before he was killed during the assault of the Ataranas district.

decided to give you a half hour to surrender. After that our artillery will begin to bombard Headquarters.''

At 4.30 PM the barrage started. General Burriel telephoned his surrender and raised the white flag. Major Neira and Major Perez Farras had been ordered by the Generalitat to seize General Goded and to bring him to President Companys. But the crowd didn't want to let their prey go. So militant workers, well known to everyone, were called in and Goded was turned over to Companys. The latter asked the General to speak to the rebel troops so that the fighting would stop. After thinking a moment, Goded made his famous proclamations: "Fate has not been kind to me and I have been made prisoner. So if you wish to avoid shedding blood, soldiers who escorted me, I free you from all commitments."[8]

It was 5.30 PM. The soldiers of the Alcantara regiment, shut up in the Parque barracks, rebelled. After imprisoning their leaders, they opened the doors to the people. Matters proceeded similarly at the Santiago barracks and the artillery barracks at the Docks. It was the same with the auxiliary soldiers at the air base, who got in touch with the workers and soldiers council which had been formed at the Prat de Llobregat airfield. The same scenes occurred at the Montjuich Fortress where the soldiers freed their commander, Gil Cabrera, who had been arrested by the rebels.

Committees composed of soldiers and workers were formed in all the barracks. Actually it was the workers of the CNT who controlled the situation in almost all the committees. It was they, who having harrassed the rebels throughout the day, led the final assault, leaving five hundred dead in the field. General Justo Legorburu and and all his Staff and many Falangists and Requetes who were in the San Andres artillery Park resisted until midnight. On Monday in the early morning hours the only rebels still resisting were those besieged in the Military Government Headquarters and the Atarazanas barracks, who were holding out thanks to a cross fire.

While the workers of Barcelona were making sure of their conquests of July 19, it was not known what was happening in Madrid and the rest of Spain. But this didn't stop the Revolution from gaining a strong foothold in the Catalan capital. With shouldered arms, men were patrolling the streets and strengthening the barricades outside and inside the city. The only password was "CNT, CNT, CNT." Sometimes the insurgents used their automobiles to approach the barricades and fire on the defenders. The rebels increased their attacks. From time to time snipers hidden in houses which the people called "pacos", shot at the passers-by.

The people surrounded the last strongholds of the rebels and waited for sunrise to finish them off. The same situation existed around the Carmelite Convent in Lauria street where the remnants of the Santiago cavalry regiment and the auxiliaries of the Guardia Civil, who had gone over to the enemy at the last moment, continued to resist. The same situation existed in the Santa Monica Rambla around the Atarazanas barracks.

The defense and revolutionary committees which were already functioning in all the districts, were organizing locally and had seized power in Barcelona. At the same time they were preoccupied with what was going on in the suburbs. So most of the arms (thousands of pistols and dozens of machine guns) which had been taken after the assault of the San Andres barracks, were sent to the outlying districts.

The victory in Barcelona had affected the whole region and the military attack had been put down. The people were in control in Tarragona. In Gerona, Mataro and Seo de Urgel, the army together with other law enforcement bodies, leaning on conservative elements, had seized control on the morning of July 19. The rebels abandoned their positions when they learned about the victory of the people in Barcelona. And so in twenty-four hours all of Catalonia fell into the hands of the people, who were to remain the only ones in control for some time.

But what was going on in the rest of Spain? On Saturday the 18th, it was known that a struggle was taking place in Seville, Cordova, Cadiz, Las Palmas and the Moroccan protectorate. It was also known that the Government was in control of the situation in Madrid. But what had happened since Saturday. What was happening in Valencia? What was happening in Saragossa? It was said that troops had left there to attack Barcelona?

In Madrid the working class, which had no confidence in the Government, and the CNT which didn't belong to the Popular Front

Barcelona, July, 1936 — a CNT safe-conduct pass issued during the first days after the proletarian victory.

and knew what would happen if the city fell into the hands of the fascists, demanded arms. But the parties of the Popular Front did nothing to provide them. The CNT faced with the negative attitude of those in power decided to act alone.

That same day the militants of the CNT, of the FAI and of the Libertarian Youth, as well as the members of the defense Committees of all the districts of the capital and a number of adjoining villages, held a meeting. They decided to form a local defense organization. A plan was made, weapons were counted, workers' patrols were organized in groups of five. Each one of the groups had a pistol and a grenade. In this way Madrid and specially the military and Guardia Civil barracks were controlled. All of Saturday there were meetings, complaints, demonstrations, demands for weapons but all without effect. But as the Government remained obdurate in its refusal, the people began to become impatient in the street.

The Puerta del Sol was alive with people. News was arriving little by little. Queipo de Llano was in control in Seville. In Cadiz as well as in Granada the workers disarmed were being mowed down by the Fascists. In Saragossa the Governor who had promised to give arms to the people, had them surrounded when they had gathered together and shot them down. Among the victims there were many militants of the Confederation. In Valladolid the Falange was victorious. The troops brought from Morocco had marched on Algeciras.

In Madrid the first weapons were distributed during the night of the 18th to 19th thanks to the initiative of a few army men loyal to the people, who were in despair because of the stupidity of the Government, which continued to believe that it was in control of the situation. From time to time a truck distributed guns to certain Socialist circles and a few Communist committees. But there was nothing for the CNT, the FAI and the libertarian youth. One of these trucks which was going along the Glorieta de Cuatro Caminos was seized by a group of CNTers and the arms were distributed to the workers of the Tetuan district. These were the few guns which were to guard the barracks where treason was being plotted.[9]

July 19 at four in the morning while the harbor workers in Barcelona were fraternizing with the Assault Guards, Casares Quiroga was resigning in Madrid. A compromise Government headed by Martinez Barrio followed. The people of Madrid openly called it "the treacherous government". It lasted three hours. After trying in vain to convince General Mola that the rebellion was useless, Martinez Barrio resigned Sunday at seven A.M. [10]

Manuel Azaña, who was called "a warrior in peacetime and a pacifist in wartime"[11] after hesitating, asked Dr. Giral to form a new Government. This change brought a positive result; political prisoners were freed and among them David Antona, secretary of the National Committee of the CNT and Cipriano Mera. But hundreds of militant workers still remained in prison.

Antona sent an ultimatum to Giral: "If our comrades are not freed within three hours the CNT will deliver them."[12] This ultimatum opened the doors of the prisons. Monday morning the people of Madrid attacked the Campamento and Montana barracks.

In Barcelona however the struggle continued. On the morning of the 20th the Convent of the Carmelites surrendered, but fighting went on in the Atarazanas and military government areas and was as fierce as ever. During the night, one of the leaders of the rebellion Captain Mola, brother of the General, commited suicide. The other military leaders concealed this information so as not to demoralize their soldiers.

But the people, their patience at an end, were no longer satisfied to attack the strongholds of the rebels or to try and starve them out, and instead they put up barricades and took useless risks. Defying bullets a group had reached Santa Madrona Street which was parallel to the Atarazanas barracks and took up their positions between Montserrat and Mediodia Streets with the idea of climbing on the rooftops to dominate the barracks. Francisco Ascaso, who had become a sniper, was among these fearless men. He could be seen running between the bullets, carrying a gun which was too long and which hindered his movements. It was eleven in the morning and sweat was glueing clothes to bodies. Hundreds of eyes from the barricade of the Rambla Santa Monica were fastened on these silhouettes which were dodging the gunfire. Just when the attackers had reached their objective, Durruti was informed that a column of Guardia Civil, coming down the Rambla, were approaching the barracks to protect the soldiers from the angry crowd. Durruti asked the Colonel to move away: "Atarazanas belongs to the CNT and the FAI." The Colonel withdrew. [13]

The attack was redoubled. Now Ascaso had found shelter on Mediodia Street behind a truck which was riddled with bullets. Wanting to eliminate a "sniper" who kept him from advancing, he leaned against the hood of the car. A bullet hit him full in the face and he was killed instantly. Durruti was overcome by the death of his comrade.

Already when Obregon was killed during the attack on the Central Telephone Exchange, Durruti's anger had burst out and had pushed him forward to the very doors of the Exchange. Now his fury was unleashed. Without looking at anyone, he left for the barracks. The other fighters fascinated followed him. The soldiers terrified by this tidal wave surging towards them, hastened to raise the white flag.

At one o'clock on July 20, thirty three hours after the beginning of the struggle, Barcelona had beaten the rebels. Finally joy could blaze out.[14] But Ricardo Sanz, carrying the lifeless body of Francisco Ascaso in his strong arms, left his remains at the headquarters of the Transport Workers Union. Ascaso, born at Almudevar on April 1, 1901, was one of the three thousand revolutionaries who had given their lives to free Barcelona. But alas, Atarazanas wasn't worth such a sacrifice as the loss of Ascaso, who would have been a very important element in carrying on the struggle.

Footnotes

1. Lacruz, *op. cit.*
2. Idem.
3. Idem.
4. Idem.
5. Testimony of José Rovira and Antonio Robles. The latter was one of the group.
6. A Mexican anarchist living in Spain. At the time he was secretary of the anarchist groups of Barcelona (FAI). He died at the age of 26.
7. *Boletin de Información CNT-FAI,* #1, July 24, 1936.
8. Francisco Lacruz, *op. cit.* General Goded was court martialled and found guilty on August 11th 1936 in Barcelona and executed at Montjuich on the 12th.
9. Eduardo de Guzman, *Madrid Rojo y Negro,* p. 17 sq.
10. Salvador de Madariaga, *España.*
11. Felipe Alaiz outlines Azaña's character with this phrase in his biographical essay published by the CNT at Toulouse in 1946. One can also read about Manuel Azaña in the work of Manuel Maura, *Asi cayo Alfonso XIII.*
12. Eduardo de Guzman, *op. cit.*
13. Testimony of eyewitnesses, José Rovira, Dolorès Iturbe, L.S. Pablo Ruiz.
14. Idem.

3

JULY 20th

BECAUSE OF THE tremendous upheaval everyone was caught up in the revolutionary wave. City life was completely disorganized. Even *Solidaridad Obrera*, the daily paper of the CNT in Catalonia had lost its manager and board of editors. The issue of July 20th, distributed on the barricades, had been put out by a group of militant workers who had happened to pass through the print shop. Seeing that there was nobody on the spot, they started on their own to write and print this historic issue. [1]

This kind of initiative multiplied by thousands of others formed the base of a new type of set-up. It gave daily existence another dimension and the first forms of self-management in industry and transport followed. This process became generalized and covered all forms of activity. On July 20th power was in the streets, in the hands of the armed masses. The army and the police, as institutions, had disappeared. Soldiers and policemen formed a single bloc with the people.

The day had come to an end but revolutionary festivities continued. A feeling of solidarity and fraternity existed everywhere. Men and women freed from old disciplines had broken with the old world and all were marching towards a future which each one imagined as the realization of their greatest dreams. A new life was beginning. Catalonia, rich in its vast manufacturing areas and its fertile fields, now torn from the feudal, bourgeois and clerical owners, belonged to the masses. The old concept of master and slave was being destroyed along with the religious objects which were being burned in thousands of fires lit by the people everywhere. Everything was burning, even that symbol of exploitation called money. [2] Revolution couldn't start off based on the values of the old life. To really be itself it had to create a new life style. And so July 20th came to a close in that state of intoxication, where revolution seems like a great holiday, liberating activity and enthusiasm. [3]

Nobody slept that night. Neither the men in the central workingmen's districts, nor the members of the revolutionary committees, nor those who were guarding the approaches to the city, nor the trade unionists... everyone was on guard. And nobody slept even in the Palace of the Generalitat of Catalonia where Luis Companys had established himself with the few politicians who had not been swept away by the revolutionary tide.

Luis Companys represented nothing more than the image of the old power. Why hadn't the revolution gone further and destroyed the symbol? The revolution it was believed had conquered Luis Companys by ignoring him. By ignoring him, it saved him, because a revolution which doesn't reach its goal immediately is lost. Companys began to maneuver realizing that he couldn't get out of this situation without making concessions. But he needed a valid representative spokesman, who was influential with the people. The left wing political parties were not supported by a real worker force. So this spokesman had to be found among the anarchists, in the ranks of the CNT and the FAI. And so he appealed to them.

García Oliver wrote: "Companys received us standing, quite obviously nervous. He shook our hands (....) The presentation ceremony was brief, everyone took their places, a gun between their knees. Essentially these are Companys' remarks:

"— First of all I must say that the CNT and the FAI have never been treated with the proper importance which they deserve. You have always been harshly prosecuted. And I, who used to be with you, was forced by political realities, to oppose you and hound you.[4]

"You are now in control of the city and Catalonia because you alone routed the fascist militarists. But let me remind you that you didn't lack help today from men of my party, as well as from the Assault and Presidential Guards."

Companys hesitated for a moment and then continued: "But the truth is that, harshly persecuted until the past few days, you conquered the fascist army today. Knowing you as I do I can only speak to you sincerely. You have won and the power is in your hands. If you don't need me and if you don't want me as President of Catalonia, tell me now and I will be only one more soldier in the struggle against fascism. But if on the contrary you believe that in this job, where I would have been killed if there had been a fascist victory, I and my men, my name and my prestige can be useful in the struggle which has ended in Barcelona today but whose outcome is still unknown in the rest of Spain, you can count on me. You can count on my loyalty as a man and a party leader who believes that a shameful past came to an end today and I sincerely hope that Catalonia will be in the vanguard of the countries who are the most progressive in social matters."

García Oliver wrote "We had been called in to listen. We couldn't commit ourselves to anything. It was up to our organizations to decide and that is what we told Companys. Companys told us that in the next room all the other representatives of the Catalonian political parties were waiting and if we agreed to join them, he as President of the Generalitat would propose a new set up for Catalonia so that the revolutionary struggle could be carried through to victory.

"We agreed to take part in this gathering as observers. The meeting took place in another room and as Companys had told us, representatives of the Esquerra Republicana, the Rabassaires, the Republican Union, the POUM and the Socialist Party were there. I

213

don't remember very well the individuals who were present, perhaps because everything had been so hurried and because of my weariness, or perhaps because I didn't know them. Nin, Comorera, and others were present.

"Companys explained that it would be a good idea to create a Militia committee in Catalonia which could direct the life which had been so profoundly convulsed by the fascist uprising. He would try to organize the armed forces to go and fight the fascists wherever they were, for at the moment it was impossible to know what forces were available because of the chaos".[5]

The delegation of the CNT-FAI left the Generalitat to go to the office of the Regional committee of the CNT where a plenum was taking place to define the position of the CNT vis-à-vis the problems raised by the revolution. In the meantime Luis Companys, who believed he had won the first round, tried to conclude an agreement with the Popular Front parties. The Socialists led by Comorera were the first to agree to this alliance. But Companys knowing that they had only a feeble organization asked the POUM for its agreement as they were quite well represented in Catalonia. Andres Nin didn't fall into this trap. He knew that it would be impossible to have an agreement without the CNT. Companys was irritated by this refusal and suggested that the POUM together with the CNT should assume authority. But the situation was clear to the POUM: it was necessary to wait for the CNT to consult all its militants.[6]

The results of the discussions of the CNT and the FAI are reported by García Oliver [7] and Mariano R. Vasquez. Let us look at the latter's account.

"On July 21, 1936, a Regional Plenum of the Local Federations called by the Regional Committee of Catalonia, took place in Barcelona. The situation was analyzed and it was decided not to speak about Libertarian Communism as long as part of Spain was in the hands of the fascists. The Plenum decided for collaboration, opposed by only one delegation from "Bajo Llobregat".

"(...) Why do we agree to collaborate? Because the situation is unclear in the Levant with rebels manning the barracks, because we are in the minority in Madrid and there has been an upheaval in Andalusia where people fighting in the mountains are armed only with blunderbusses and scythes. The situation in the North is unknown and the rest of Spain appears to be in the hands of the fascists. The enemy is in Aragon and the harbors of Catalonia, and we don't know the extent of their strength either national or international.

"Any extreme position inspired by adventurism or inflexibility could have been a disaster because the Revolution would have been exhausted. Thousands of workers who had taken part in the revolution would have died.

"Our Revolution cannot break out except through our own actions. There is no other way. We can't hope for anything from outside. No international proletarian leader has come to risk his liberty, his life and interests for us, nor has anyone been imprisoned for having helped the Spanish Revolution. No one has lost his life for having joined our cause. No strike, no meeting has been called to prevent the suffocation we have endured because of fascist and

214

democratic governments. Only a few thousand workers have come to share our fate and to live through our immense tragedy, and these only on the fringe of the solidarity movement of the international proletariat."[8]

It is clear that the explanations given by García Oliver and R. Vazquez were designed for their political effect, hiding the atmosphere in which these decisions were taken. These declarations were made a year later when the CNT and the FAI were already far removed from their original positions. It was also the period when they had become involved in a policy of collaboration which led them to take part in the Central Government. One need only keep those explanations in mind which have a meaning vis-à-vis the electrified atmosphere of the 20th and 21st of July 1936. García Oliver and Mariano R. Vazquez also tried to hide the nature of these declarations because of the events which occured in the months that followed. But in a certain way they shed light on the unknown factors which weighed so heavily on those who took part in the historic Plenum.

There was a clash of different viewpoints. García Oliver was partisan of a Revolution to the death and Durruti shared this view. But contrary to García Oliver, who submitted to the resolution adopted, Durruti persisted in his proposition "to accept the agreements only provisionally, that is to say until the freeing of Saragossa, because then the way to the North would be open and the success of the Revolution assured." One must also take into account the position defended by the important delegation from "Bajo Llobregat". We don't know its character but we can affirm that it was radical because of the position taken before by this Federation.

As Vazquez points out, an impasse was reached when it was necessary to admit that it was impossible to know about the general situation, and help from the international proletariat was not forthcoming. Then "disagreeable reality asserted itself." But "reality" couldn't be accepted by turning one's back on Revolution which was holding an entire nation in suspense. How was it possible to resolve this problem?

Santillan's formula, accepting a "democratic collaboration" was only a way of disguising the views of the participants or again a deceitful formula which kept up an illusion. And so the idea of democratic collaboration within the organization proposed by Luis Companys was accepted but with the explicit proviso that the Central Committee of Militias would hold the real Power, assuming control over political, economic and military matters. In reality this meant that the Generalitat became only a symbolic body without any tangible authority. But it helped to delude the bourgeois powers like France and England and to fool the Government in Madrid, if it continued to function backed by the Socialists (a question not known at this time). While the situation was evolving on the national as well as the international plane, the resolution adopted by the Plenum allowed the Revolution to keep its balance internationally and permitted its progress among the workers.

This "democratic collaboration" required nothing more now than a fair proportional representation. It was plain that the CNT and the FAI still held power in Catalonia. The POUM was numerically inferior. The rest of the political parties, the Esquerra Republicana de Cataluña and the Union Republicana belonged to the liberal petit bourgeoisie, exactly those people that the workers were expropriating. On the fringe there were also the non existent UGT and the tiny section of the Spanish Socialist Workers Party. Because of this how was it possible to have a harmonious democratic representation? It seemed wiser and more prudent to adopt another formula. They took into account that although the CNT was in the majority in Catalonia, it was not in other regions where the UGT outnumbered them. So the following solution was adopted: "We have decided, although this is unjust, to assign as many positions to the UGT and the Socialist Party, although it is in the minority in Catalonia, as to the CNT and victorious anarchism. This meant a sacrifice with the aim of leading the dictatorial parties to follow a path of loyal collaboration untroubled by suicidal rivalry." [9]

When the Plenum ended, the delegation returned to the Palace of the Generalitat with a proposal approving the creation of a Central Committee of Militias, as a popular organization which was to assume responsibility for the economic, military and political life in Catalonia. But Luis Companys, who had not given up the idea of creating a group under his command in order to oppose the influence of the CNT, tried to resist this kind of ultimatum by the CNT-FAI. The delegation however was intransigeant on this point. Either Companys must accept the creation of a Central Committee as the ruling organization or the CNT would consult the rank and file and expose the real situation to the workers. Companys backed down.

That same night the Central Committee of Militias was set up with the following members: CNT, FAI, UGT, PSOE (Socialist Party), Esquerra Republicana (Companys' party), Union de Rabassaires (Catalan peasant party), Union Republicana (the liberal Republican bourgeois party) and the POUM. The Generalitat would be represented by a Commissioner and a military man as technical advisers. During the same night the Central Committee met in the Maritime Museum where it established its permanent headquarters, thus showing that it was not dependant on the Generalitat. Durruti took part in this first meeting as delegate from the CNT and Oliver was there as representative of the FAI. This meeting was the first and last that Durruti attended as he felt that the decree of the Committee did not apply to the people. From then on an undeclared struggle was carried on between Durruti and the Central Committee of Militias.

Footnotes

1. Testimony of Juan Manuel Molina
2. Federica Montseñy in an article about the revolution in *Revista Blanca*, July 30, 1936. The author took part in various actions of this kind on the morning of July 20th. The one which impressed him most was the attack on a branch bank in Calle Mallorca in Barcelona. Nobody in the bank resisted the people. However a group of women, assisted by only a few men and children had seized the building and made a bonfire in the street with the furniture. Throwing this furniture into the fire the people were full of rage but also of pleasure, as if they were the judges in a cause which had been waiting to be judged for a millenium. Among other things boxes full of bank notes were thrown into the fire and absolutely no one had the idea of putting the money in their pockets. They seemed to be saying that the world of trade, the world of salaries and exploitation were really disappearing forever.
3. Diego Abad de Santillan in *Porque perdimos la guerra*, p. 57, describes the situation in Barcelona perfectly: "In the first weeks after July 20th, the parties and organizations no longer controlled their members. Something better than parties and factions had been created. A people had been created and this people felt and acted as such."
4. Luis Companys refers to the period when Salvador Seguí was lawyer for the CNT (1917-1923).
5. For this interview and the following account, we use García Oliver's testimony in his article "El Comite Central de Milicias Antifascistas de Cataluña" published in *Solidarid Obrera*, July 18, 1937.
6. We use César M. Lorenzo's version from *Les anarchistes espagnols et le pouvoir*, p. 106, note 6. He in turn takes it from Garcia Venero's *Historia de los Internacionales en España*, Vol. III, p. 101.
7. García Oliver, art. cit.
8. *Informe Comite Nacional de la CNT al Congreso de la AIT*, (Ed. CNT, Artes Graficas, Barcelona), Paris, December 1937, p. 119.
9. García Oliver, art. cit.

4

THE CENTRAL COMMITTEE OF MILITIAS

AT ITS FIRST meeting the Central Committee of Militias decided to send a delegation to Saragossa to find out about the military positions of the rebels. In addition they wisely mined the bridges to prevent the advance of a motorized enemy column, which was believed to be advancing towards Barcelona.

The Central Committee of Militias immediately took control of everything and began by publishing instructions to be followed by the population to maintain revolutionary order. [1] It then adopted a rather supple structure so that its members could take initiatives and work with a minimum of administrative interference. [2] The committe leaning on the revolutionary organizations of the workers sought to bring life back to normal as fast as possible and to avoid exhausting supplies of food, arms, gas, etc.

At this same meeting it was decided to create a militia column which would go to Aragon. Buenaventura Durruti would be the responsible leader and Major Perez Farras was to be the military commander. This column was to leave Barcelona July 24 at the latest and others would follow. It would consist of 12,000 men and its most important objective would be to attack and take Saragossa. [3] The district defense committees were to take charge of the enrollment of the militiamen.

Santillan, responsible for the organization of the Militia, set up his headquarters in the Pedralbes barracks. He was assisted by the anarchist militants Sato, Edo and Ricardo Sanz. [4]

From July 22 to 25 Barcelona was extremely chaotic but the chaos worked. Jimenez de la Beraza, an Artillery Colonel, who had escaped from Pamplona, was amazed by this set-up. When he was asked about it he answered that "from a military point of view there was a frightening chaos, but the important thing was that the chaos was working" and he advised that it should not be disturbed, it should be allowed to develop "because it would find within itself its own balance and organization." [5]

Militia columns, whose organization depended on the Central Committee of Militias, were actually controlled by the unions. The latter had to look after the families of the volunteers who were going to the front. In this way Santillan hoped to avoid centralization by the Central Committee. He wanted to forestall the formation of an army dependant on a general staff. It was also decided that each party or tendency represented in the Central Committee would open its own centers for recruiting and organizing militiamen.

Until then the barracks and fortresses were in the hands of those who had seized them, i.e. the workers of the CNT and FAI. The workers wanted to hold onto them because the revolution seemed to have shown them the uselessness of political parties. But the men in the Central Committee were able to persuade them to share with the militants of other political tendencies. And so the Fortress of Montjuich was taken over by the Esquerra Catalana, the barracks of the Lépunte Cavalry were given to the POUM, those of the Parc to the PSU of Catalonia and an ancient convent was assigned to the Partido Féderal Iberico. The CNT and the FAI held on to the Pedralbes, San Andres and Santiago Cavalry barracks as well as the barracks of the Docks and the Engineers. The Artillery Park and the Commissariat were held in common by everyone. Each political group renamed its barracks: The PSUC's was called Karl Marx, the POUM's Lenin, the anarchists called theirs Bakunin, Salvochea, Spartacus, etc.

It was also necessary to assign headquarters. The POUM gave up the Hotel Colon to the PSUC and kept a large hotel on the Rambla for its Central Committee headquarters. The CNT remained in its own headquarters. Revolutionary committees or defense committees were set up in each district and the unions established themselves in large buildings. The popular eating places which had been organized during the heat of the conflict were set up in the big hotels. This is how the Ritz became the restaurant of the militiamen.

The general strike was still going on. But soon certain services started to function again such as the hospitals and health centers, which had been taken over from the very beginning of the struggle by the CNT medical union. The most important hospitals were headed by the workers. Then through the initiative of the rank and file the bakeries started functioning again either collectively or communally. The pharmaceutical laboratories started working again controlled directly by the workers.

The farm workers unions around Barcelona also began to collectivize the land and set up communal stores to feed the city. This first step was imitated throughout the region. Very soon the metallurgical centers started work again and priority was given to the making of armored trucks. It was even possible by July 24 to use some of these trucks for the Durruti column. The most important focal points like Hispano-Suiza, el Volcano, la Maquinista Terrestre, etc. became collective enterprises through the iniative of the workers. [6] The harbor workers collectivized the maritime companies as early as July 22. The same day the railwaymen saw to it that the railroads of the M.Z.A. of the Northern company and the Catalan railways started to function. On July 23 it was the turn of the tramways and the buses and so that they might move, the barricades had to be removed.

As for military safety, there were still some snipers shooting from their hiding places. Armed workers mounted guard and were organized into groups under orders of a worker named by his peers.

The latter insured liaison and co-ordination with the revolutionary defense committees and in the districts played the role formerly performed by the mayor's offices. All these district committees banded together formed a sort of central committee which was called the Co-ordinating Committee and covered all of Barcelona.

There were three powers in Barcelona: the Generalitat, a lifeless symbol, the Central Committee of Militias, and the district committees. These three different power bases mingled and formed what Colonel Beraza called "a chaos which should not be disturbed."

It was the district committees which initiated the opening of the pawn shop doors and distribution of things collected by the pawn brokers. The contents of other centers and stores were also confiscated for the use of needy citizens. Clothes, shoes and blankets were distributed.

The CNT and the FAI remained firm in their plan to push the revolution as far as possible. A leaflet of July 23 made this clear: "Working people organize yourselves in militias. Don't give up weapons or ammunition. Tighten your bonds with your union. Your life and liberty are in your hands." [7] This repeated the appeal made by the Central Committee of Militias which said that whoever didn't want to go to the front should return his weapon to the Defense Committee or to the volunteer recruiting center.

During these stormy days the members of the "Nosotros" group were separated. Each one had an important job. Aurelio Fernandez with the help of the mustering patrols was reorganizing a regular armed corps for the revolution, a safety corps destined to maintain revolutionary order. Ricardo Sanz at the Pedralbes barracks was organizing workers' Militias. García Oliver was a kind of minister of war, who guided the moves of the whole show. And finally Durruti was to be the first delegate for the column at the front, a trail blazer for the revolution and its propagandist in the Aragonese campaigns. The members of the "Nosotros" group had managed to define their position clearly: it was necessary to go beyond the stage of alliance between political parties and to create a revolutionary organization leaning on a regional assembly where workers, soldiers, defense committees, etc. would be represented. All the members of "Nosotros" were aware of the danger to the revolution emanating from the existence of the Generalitat and a Central Committee of Militias, neither controlled by the working class.

The absence of Francisco Ascaso was felt bitterly, as it was he who had synthesized and kept a balance between the various personalities in the group. Actually events were to bring out differences and clashes between the two strongest personalities, Durruti and García Oliver. Both were innovators and men of action and García Oliver suffered at being forced to manage the War Department. Temperamentally he would have preferred to throw himself into the attack on Saragossa. And he also felt a kind of jealousy of Durruti who had become involved in direct action. However everyone agreed on one point, the revolution must be carried forward as far as possible. And the various inevitable concessions must not hinder its hidden progress.

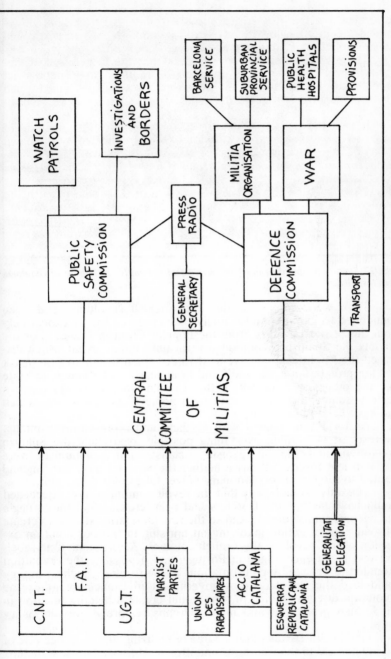

Diagram of the organisation of the Central Committee of the Militias denoting its network and services

221

July. 22, 1936 — the building in which the Central Committee of Militias of Catalonia were installed.

They were convinced that the Spanish revolution had been abandoned to its fate. And actually they could no longer expect help from the Soviet Union or from the Popular Front in France. For the Soviets the Spanish revolution was an unfortunate event which disturbed their political maneuvers. It forced them to take off the mask of "the proletarian homeland" and to appear as a bureaucratic State like the others, a State which the Russian workers would have to destroy some day if they wanted to achieve the revolution which had been begun in October.

As for France, allied with England and representing capitalist interests, it was doing everything possible to strangle the Spanish revolution, and the bourgeoisie socialists and communists were ready to join forces. Likewise neither the Soviet Union nor England wanted to see a real revolutionary power take control in Spain.

The only possible way that the revolution might have succeeded would have been if the frontiers had been crossed and the struggle had become international. And so the revolutionaries started to create a broad plan of action involving an uprising in Morocco and an extension of this revolt to the French colonies. At the same time rebellion was to be encouraged in Portugal and if possible the revolution extended to France by confrontations at the frontier. Such a strategy could lead the Popular Front government in France to attack the revolution directly, which in turn would create a healthy reaction in the French proletariat and might perhaps restore its revolutionary spirit.

García Oliver was put in charge of realizing this plan, because of the job he held in the Central Committee of Militias. This was the last project of the "Nosotros" group.

Footnotes

1. These quotes are taken from Diego Abad de Santillan's *Por qué perdimos la guerra.*

2. The Central Committee of Militias provisionally consisted of various departments called Administration, Militias, Operations, Investigation and Supervision, Food Supplies and Transportation. The following sections were controlled by the departments: statistics formed part of Administration; barracks and ammunition were under Militias; censorship, radio broadcasting, map making, war college, School of Communication and Signals formed part of War-Operations.

In the school for war and communications it was decided to give courses to the delegates of the Centuries, the Groups and the Columns (delegates of the army whose structure had arisen spontaneously when the Militias were organized, as we will see later). These facts come from Santillan's book already mentioned.

3. The plan of the Central Committee of Militias was simple. It was important for the forces on whom success depended to act together, each taking care of the sector assigned to it. A first column, the responsibility of Durruti, was to leave in the vanguard, opening the way. At the same time three other columns were to help the first.

The first column would attack on the Saragossa front leaving from Pina-Osera. The second, following the line of Caspe-Azaila-Belchite, was to cut communications to Saragossa between Calatayud and Saragossa and was to support the frontal attack of the first column. As for the third column its objective was to cut communications between Huesca and Saragossa occupying positions in the triangle of the Sierra de Alcubiene taking this as the center with Tardiente and Lacinena as the wings. It was to support the first column on its right flank. The success of the first column would depend on the precision with which the two other columns carried out their tasks.

In order to rout the enemy forces, an enveloping frontal attack against Huesca by a fourth column was planned. The most difficult job was to be entrusted to the CNT and the FAI, who were to put the men of the first, second and fourth columns in fighting shape. The third column was put in the hands of the rest of the political formations belonging to the Central Committee of Militias, the Esquerra, POUM and PSUC.

4. In about a month 18,000 men left the Bakunin barracks, more or less well organized. Some of them, such as those in the "Tierra y Libertad" column, were transferred to the Madrid front and from there to the front at Talavera de la Reina.

5. Santillan, *op. cit.* p. 63.

6. This was the point of departure, seized by the Metallurgists Union of the CNT to begin to convert the metallurgical industry into a war industry. Eugenio Vallejo, a metal worker, who knew how to make use of the Central Committee of Militias, was put in charge of this job. "Vallejo and Martin did a tremendous job, quickly converting our metallurgical and chemical industries into war industries" (García Oliver in the article already quoted).

7. Leaflet reproduced in the *CNT-FAI Bulletin,* July 24, 1936.

5

TO SARAGOSSA

SARAGOSSA WAS DOUBLY important for the revolution, strategically and for reasons of solidarity. It was the second capital of anarchism and thousands of comrades were prisoners of the fascists there.

In an important radio broadcast, García Oliver appealed to the Aragonese, passionately urging them on in the struggle "considering that the duty of every militant worker is to put himself in the avant garde of the fighting without calculating the risks." He recalled the victory over the military in Barcelona and announced the formation by the CNT of militia columns to be used to conquer Saragossa. "We tell you that Durruti and the one who is addressing you will leave at the head of these workers' troops. We are sending a squadron which will bombard the barracks of your city." But they shouldn't wait for these troops to arrive, to rush into the streets. "The men of the CNT and the FAI must carry out the task required in this hour. Use every means possible. Do not wait for the end of this speech, leave your houses, burn, destroy, crush fascism." [1]

The announcement that these columns were being formed aroused great enthusiasm in Barcelona. The workers came from the trade unions and defense committees to enlist and take part in the first units. The enthusiasm had to be checked and the more serious minded people were asked to stay and do the jobs that couldn't be abandoned.

This mobilization was different from a mobilization decreed from above. The volunteers discussed organization with each other. There was no question of restoring the military spirit or bureaucratic command. It was through these discussions that, little by little, the structure of the workers' militias evolved, which they would keep until the militarization in 1937. The organization was simple. Ten men formed a group with a delegate freely chosen to head it. Ten of these groups formed a century and the man in charge was chosen in the same way. Five centuries formed an assembly, which also had a delegate. The delegates of the centuries and the delegate of the assembly formed the committee of the assembly. The delegates of the assembly with the general delegate of the column formed the war committee of the column. [2]

Perez Farras, military technician of the column, was pessimistic.

224

He was a professional soldier and didn't have confidence in an organization of this kind. Durruti soon became aware of this. And so he chose as his artillery sergeant, Manzana, a man, who for many years had taken part in the anti-militarist committees of the CNT. Manzana had assimilated libertarian ideas and understood the anarchist psychology, which is hostile to all that means command and obedience. Durruti handed over the job of equipping the column with munitions, artillery and machine guns, to Manzana and to the teacher, Carreño. They also had to organize a medical corps of nurses and doctors, with an emergency surgical service. Manzana surrounded himself with a group of friends, soldiers, corporals and sergeants and even some officers, who joined the centuries which were being formed. Soon confidence was established between Durruti and Manzana, as the latter carried out his job in an anti-totalitarian way, which was Durruti's way.

When Perez Farras disagreed with this approach, which he considered too liberal, Durruti replied: "I have already said and I repeat; during all my life I have acted as an anarchist. The fact of being given political responsibility for a human collective cannot change my convictions. It is under these conditions that I agreed to play the role given me by the Central Committee of the Militias.

"I thought — and what has happened confirms my belief — that a workingman's militia cannot be led according to the same rules as an army. I think that discipline, coordination and the fulfillment of a plan are indispensable. But this can no longer be understood in the terms of the world we have just destroyed. We have new ideas. We think that solidarity among men must awaken personal responsibility which knows how to accept discipline as an autonomous act.

"Necessity imposes a war on us, a struggle which differs from many of those which we have carried on before. But the goal of our struggle is always the triumph of the revolution. This means not only victory over the enemy, but also a radical change in man. For this change to occur, man must learn to live in freedom and to develop in himself his potentialities as a responsible individual. The worker in the factory, using his tools and directing production, is bringing about a change in himself. The fighter like the worker uses his gun as a tool and his acts must lead to the same goals as those of the worker.

"In the struggle he cannot act like a soldier under orders but like a man who is conscious of what he is doing. I know it's not easy, to get such a result, but what one cannot get by reason, one can never get through force. If our revolutionary army must be maintained through fear, we will have changed nothing but the color of fear. It is only by freeing itself from fear that a free society can be built."[3] Durruti expressed himself clearly. He wanted to unite theory and practise. As an anarchist he wanted to remain faithful to the libertarian ideal, while assuming the management of the column of militiamen which was going up to the Aragon front.[4]

In Barcelona the preparations for the expedition to Saragossa were moving forward. Aragon would soon be the theater of a merciless struggle against fascism. Saragossa was a military fortress. It was also the General Headquarters of the Vth military region commanded by General Cabanellas, who had assured the Republican

Barcelona, July. 24 — One view of the departure of the anarchist militia of the Durruti Column for Saragossa. Black flags flew everywhere.

Government of his loyalty to its Institutions on the 17th of July. The situation remained unclear until Sunday the 19th when Cabanellas declared war and started round ups in the trade unions and other workers' centers. Beside its military importance, Saragossa, now in the hands of the fascists, became an obstacle because it prevented the union of Catalonia with the North (the Basque region and Asturias). These were the most important industrial areas of Spain and the source of raw materials and armaments.

The Governor of Saragossa (a Republican who was later shot by the fascists) had promised to arm the workers when "the time came". The fascists profited by the indecision or error of the Governor and had quickly deployed their forces throughout the region. After a fierce struggle with the unarmed workers, they virtually ruled the towns of Huesca, Teruel, Jaca, Calatayud, Belchite, Caspe, and had almost reached the outskirts of Lerida. The town of Barbastro which was like a small island facing Huesca, resisted. The military garrison had mutinied and put its trust in the people. A few military men like General Villalba, faithful to the Republic, gave life to this resistance. But they couldn't hold out for any length of time. That is why the Central Committee of Militias, which knew about the situation, hastened to organize two other columns, similar to Durruti's, to be sent to this area.

On the 24th of July at 10 A.M., Durruti's column was to leave from the Paseo de Gracia for Saragossa. At 8 o'clock, speaking on the radio, Durruti asked the people of Barcelona to help provision the column. Everybody was surprised by this appeal. Actually the distribution of supplies was controlled by the district committees or by the Central Committee of Militias. Durruti explained: "You too haven't understood that the strongest weapon of the revolution is enthusiasm? A revolution succeeds when everyone is interested in victory and makes it their personal cause. The response of the people of Barcelona will show how much interest the city takes in the revolution. It will also make each man face his own responsibilities and become aware that our struggle is collective, and that its success depends on the effort of everyone. This is the meaning of our appeal, there is no other."[5]

A short time before the column left, Durruti, who was talking to the metal workers in the armored trucks, received the Canadian journalist, Van Paassen. Van Paassen published their long conversation in *The Toronto Daily Star* under the caption "2,000,000 Anarchists Fight for Revolution says Spanish Leader". He described Durruti as a tall, swarthy clean-shaven man, with Moorish features. The son of poor peasants, his voice crackling, almost guttural, Van Paassen asked him if he believed in a victory over the military insurgents. Durruti answered that the triumph over the rebels would take place on the Saragossa front. If the revolutionary forces took Saragossa, the Northern front would be free and the revolution saved because the arsenals, munitions factories and the mines were in this region. The troops assigned to the conquest of Saragossa were to divide. One column would go South to meet Franco, who was advancing through Andalusia with the foreign legion and Moroccan troops. "In two, three weeks' time, we will probably be fighting the decisive battles."

The journalist was surprised but Durruti continued: "Yes, a month perhaps, this Civil War will last at least all through the month of August. The masses are in arms. The army doesn't count any longer. There are two camps: civilians who fight for freedom and civilians who are rebels and Fascists. All the workers in Spain know that if Fascism triumphs, it will be famine and slavery. But the Fascists also know what is in store for them when they are beaten. That is why the struggle is implacable and relentless. For us it is a question of crushing Fascism, wiping it out and sweeping it away so that it can never rear its head again in Spain. We are determined to finish with Fascism once and for all. Yes, and in spite of the government."

Van Paassen asked: "why do you say in spite of the government? Is not this Government fighting the Fascist rebellion?" "No government in the world," Durruti replied, "fights Fascism to the death. When the bourgeoisie sees power slipping from its grasp, it has recourse to Fascism to maintain itself. The Liberal government of Spain could have rendered Fascist elements powerless long ago. Instead it temporized and compromised and dallied. Even now, at this moment, there are men in this Government who want to go easy with the rebels. You never can tell, you know," he laughed, "the present Government might yet need these rebellious forces to crush the workers' movement."[6]

The journalist took up the contradiction again, bursting out: "Largo Caballero and Indalecio Prieto say that the Popular Front is only out to save the Republic and restore Republican order."

MILICIAS ANTIFASCISTAS
Columna Durruti - Farrás

CREDENCIAL

El miliciano *Juan Cirit Martí*
Cuerpo *Infantería*
Centuria *13ª*
Grupo *1ª*
Organización *C. N. T.*
Sindicato *Campesinos*
Ciudad *Tarragona (Blancafort)*

Identity card of the members of the Durruti Column.

Durruti answered, "That may be the view of those señores. We syndicalists, we are fighting for the revolution. We know what we want. To us it means nothing that there is a Soviet Union somewhere in this world, for the sake of whose peace and tranquility the workers of Germany and China were sacrificed to Fascist barbarism by Stalin. We want the revolution here in Spain, right now, not maybe after the next European war. We are giving Hitler and Mussolini far more worry today with our revolution than the whole Red Army of Russia. We are setting an example to the German and Italian working class how to deal with Fascism."

Van Paasen concluded: "That was the man speaking, who represents a syndicalist organization of nearly two million members, without whose cooperation nothing can be done by the Republic, even if it is victorious over the present military-fascist revolt. I had sought to learn his views, because it is essential to know what is going on in the minds of the Spanish workers, who are doing the fighting. Durruti showed that the situation might take a direction for which few are prepared. That Moscow has no influence to speak of, on the Spanish proletariat, is a well-known fact. The most respectably conservative state in Europe is not likely to appeal much to the libertarian sentiment in Spain."

The journalist picked up the interview again: "Do you expect any help from France or Britain now that Hitler and Mussolini have begun to assist the rebels?" "I do not expect any help for a libertarian revolution from any government in the world," he said grimly. "Maybe the conflicting interests of the different imperialisms might have some influence on our struggle. That is quite well possible. Franco is doing his best to drag Europe into the quarrel. He will not

228

hesitate to pitch Germany against us. But we expect no help, not even from our own government in the final analysis."

Van Paassen insisted: "Can you win alone?"

Durruti did not answer. He stroked his chin. His eyes glowed.

"You will be sitting on top of a pile of ruins even if you are victorious," Van Paassen ventured to break his reverie.

"We have always lived in slums and holes in the wall," he said quietly. "We will know how to accommodate ourselves for a time. For you must not forget that we can also build. It is we who built these palaces and cities, here in Spain and in America and everywhere. We, the workers. We can build others to take their place. And better ones. We are not in the least afraid of ruins. We are going to inherit the earth. There is not the slightest doubt about that. The bourgeoisie might blast and ruin its own world before it leaves the stage of history. We carry a new world, here, in our hearts," he said in a hoarse whisper. And he added: "That world is growing in this minute." (7)

Beginning at 10 A.M., volunteers flocked to the Paseo de Gracia, and many people came to see this strange procession made up of autos, trucks, taxis, and tourist busses. There was great enthusiasm and the quick victory in Barcelona had made people hopeful and optimistic. The expedition to Aragon had come to be thought of as an excursion. Toward noon the column, made up of 3,000 men, started marching in a frenzy of hurrahs, raised fists and revolutionary songs. First a truck came with a dozen young people in it and among them the Herculean figure of Jose Hellin stood out. He was holding a black and red flag. The first group, whose general delegate was Aris, came behind the truck. The five centuries which followed were soon to distinguish themselves as an elite force. These were the miners of Sallent, soon transformed into dynamiters and partisan fighters, and also the maritime freight seamen with their delegate Setonas. El Padre marched at the head of the third century. He had been a faithful fighter and brave partisan of Pancho Villa during the Mexican revolution. The fourth was Juan Costa's century and the fifth was made up of metal workers and its delegate was the young libertarian Munoz. Five other groups followed.

Between two motor coaches a "Hispano" moved forward with Durruti and Major Perez Farras in it. Durruti was silent. He felt the responsibility which destiny had placed in his hands. The flower of the anarchist youth of Barcelona made up seventy percent of his column. Young and not so young, all were revolutionaries who had been involved in street fighting. But they knew nothing of fighting on open ground. Durruti knew that when the enemy was contacted in open country, fighting would take on a different aspect for his men. Before leaving, Durruti had spoken to them assembled in the Bakunin barracks. He tried to explain the difference between their struggle in Barcelona and the one they would undertake in Aragon. But words don't replace experience. He spoke of gunfire, of aerial bombing and he insisted on the difference between a bourgeois army and the armed proletariat.

The problem of command remained. Durruti's position had been clearly defined and he knew he possessed the blind confidence of his

Arrival of Durruti Column at Caspe.

men. He knew that marching in front, his men would follow him, even if he led them to their death. But Durruti was not a military man, he was a revolutionary. A military man can send his people to their death as a commander, he replaces the losses and the war goes on. But Durruti knew that most of the men who followed him were militant workers and that such men are irreplaceable. He remembered the lesson taught by Makhno: "The difference which exists between a military man who commands and a revolutionary who leads, is that the military man imposes himself by force, while the revolutionary must rest his authority on his conduct."

The column advanced on the road to Lerida. In the villages the people asked to see Durruti. As they saw him approaching, smiling, some of them exclaimed: "But he has no stripes!" Others, better informed, answered that an anarchist never wore stripes. When the peasants seemed specially happy at seeing the red and black flag, Durruti got down to talk to them: "Have you organized your collective? Don't wait. Seize the land. Organize yourselves without leaders, without masters, without parasites. If you don't accomplish these things, it is useless for us to go further. We must create a different world from the one we destroy, otherwise it isn't worthwhile for the young people to get themselves killed on the battlefields. Our field of action is the revolution." [8] In Aragon, even before a battle had been fought, a new life began.

After the first battle at Caspe and some skirmishes, the column came within nineteen miles of Saragossa. It left behind the villages it had freed: Caspe, Fraga, Casdasnos, Peralba, La Almanda, Bujaraloz. On the morning of the 27th, as the column was leaving Bujaraloz, a few miles from Pina de Ebro, three fascist trimotors appeared in

230

the sky. The bombardment killed twenty men and forced the column to halt. Some of the militiamen started to run in a panic. Another group of militiamen intervened and stopped the panic and flight. It was decided to bring the troops together again at Bujaraloz and to take advantage of this delay to find out more about the positions and resources of the enemy. Perez Farras suggested that Durruti should change his plan for the attack on Saragossa and give a better structure to the column but Durruti answered that "these men who ran away frightened today, will fight like lions tomorrow. But one can't get such results treating them like regimented soldiers but only by treating them like revolutionaries."(9)

From the balcony of the Town Hall of Bujaraloz he spoke to his men, assembled on the square: "Friends. No one was forced to come here. You chose your fate, and the fate of the first column of the CNT and the FAI is a harsh one. García Oliver said on the radio at Barcelona that we were going to Aragon to conquer Saragossa or to lose our lives in the attempt. I repeat the same thing. Rather than retreating, we must die. Saragossa is in the hands of the fascists and there are hundreds and thousands of workers there, menaced by the guns of the fascists. Why did we leave Barcelona if it wasn't to help them free themselves? They are waiting for us and we start to run. That is the way you show the world and our comrades the spirit of the anarchists, by succumbing to fear when faced by three planes.

"The bourgeoisie will not allow us to create libertarian communism because we want it. The bourgeoisie will resist because it defends its privileges and interests. The only way to create libertarian communism is to destroy the bourgeoisie. Only then will the road to our ideal world be assured. We have left behind us the peasants who have started to put into practise our ideal. They did this, feeling confident that our guns would guarantee their crops. So if we leave the road open to the enemy, it will mean that the initiatives of these peasants are useless, and what is worse, the conquerors will make them pay for their daring by assassinating them. This is the meaning of the struggle, a thankless one which resembles none that we have undertaken before. What happened today is a simple warning. Now the struggle is really going to start. They will shoot at us with cannons. They will strafe us with tons of grape shot and sometimes we will have to fight with grenades, and even with knives. As the enemy feels that it is cornered, it will bite like a beast, it will bite fiercely. But it isn't yet at bay and it is fighting to avoid this. It is leaning on the aid of Italy and Germany. If we allow these powers to become deeply involved in our war, it will be difficult to conquer the fascists because they will have supplies superior to ours.

"Our victory depends on the speed with which we act. The faster we attack, the greater chance we have to win. Up to now victory is on our side. For that reason we must conquer Saragossa at once. Tomorrow there will be no opportunities equal to those of today. In the ranks of the CNT there are no cowards and the men of the FAI die but do not yield. We don't want people among us who are afraid at the first attack. I ask those who ran, hindering the advance of the column, to have the courage to drop their guns so that firmer hands can pick them up. The rest of us will continue our march. We will arrive in the North. We will join hands with our Asturian comrades and we will conquer and give Spain a better world. I ask those who go back to keep silent about what happened today because it fills us with shame."

No one dropped a gun. But those who had run, wept with rage in front of their comrades. The lesson had been harsh but those men were reborn. They were to become excellent guerilla fighters, but most of them died during the thirty-two months of desperate conflict. [10]

Footnotes

1. *Solidaridad Obrera*, July 23, 1936.
2. José Mira, *Durruti*.
3. Idem. In his testimony Aurelio Fernandez agrees completely. Later Emma Goldman used the same words in an interview with Durruti. *Freedom*, London, April 1937.
4. Koltsov attacked Durruti for just this attitude. See his *Diario de la Guerra de España*.
5. Testimony of Pablo Ruiz. See *Solidaridad Obrera*, July 25, 1936.
6. On the question of "moderate measures" see Pierre Broué and Emile Témime, *La Révolution et la Guerre en Espagne*, p. 217.
7. *The Toronto Daily Star*, article by Van Paasen, "2,000,000 Anarchists Fight for Revolution says Spanish Leader", August 18, 1936. The interview took place in Barcelona on July 24th in the headquarters of the Metallurgists" Union in the Palace of the Dukes of Medinaceli.
8. On the organization of the Column and its march to Bujaraloz, we use the verbal testimony of Liberto Roig and Francisco Subirats. And we also use the articles of Cosme de Paules published in *CNT*, Toulouse, November 1964 and of José Mira, *op. cit.*
9. Idem.
10. Two of the men who were present, Liberto Roig and Pablo Ruiz, say that this speech was one of the most important ever made by Durruti during his life as an agitator and revolutionary. Thanks to these witnesses we have been able to reconstruct this speech.

6/

THE DURRUTI COLUMN

THE COLUMN WAS preparing to resume its advance which the bombardment had interrupted. But Durruti and the other delegates had not yet come out of the Town Hall. General Villalba and Perez Farras were trying to convince Durruti that to attack Saragossa without covering their flanks was utter folly. They felt it was necessary to wait for the "Red and Black" and "Karl Marx" columns. The first would cover their flank to the South of the Ebro and the second would protect their attack in the Tardiente-Alcubierre sector. Taking the offensive without this help would sacrifice men uselessly. "Durruti was convinced and operations came to a halt." [1] The Town Hall at Bujaraloz was chosen as general headquarters. The troops of the column took defensive positions along the front which was soon to be 78 kilometers long from Velilla de Ebro to Monte Oscuro (Leciñena).

In Barcelona the CNT and the FAI organized other columns to be sent to Aragon. The "Red and Black" headed by the carpenter, Antonio Ortiz, assisted by Major Fernando Salavera Campos, was to occupy the South of the Ebro, take Belchite and cover Durruti's left flank. The "Ascaso" column was to be stationed at Barbastro and was to attack Huesca. The carpenter, Gregorio Jover, and the baker, Domingo Ascaso, were to be in charge, assisted by the military advisors Eduardo Medrano and Albadetrecu. There were 8,000 men in the two columns. [2] The Marxist parties also organized militias. They were to be responsible for covering the right flank of Durruti's column. They took up a position facing the Laciñena-Alcubierre-Tardiente-Almudevar line. [3]

Durruti was already regretting that he had listened to the advice of the army advisers. However he took advantage of the pause to reorganize the column. The groups which formed the centuries were unequal. A new formula was tried: groups of 25 men with one delegate. The century consisted of 4 groups, five centuries (500 men) formed a battalion. Each section had a surgical and a machine gun team. The artillery was reorganized under the command of captains Carceller, Cole and Batet. Auxiliary service for Supplies, Health and Transport were formed. All these services as well as the artillery were to name a responsible delegate. A Technical Military Council, headed by Perez Farras, was formed for the military orientation of the column and brought together all the military professionals in the

The Durruti Column set-up their War Committee in Venta St. Lucia, on the way to Bujaraloz.

column. The Council was in charge of the organization of signals, map-making and all those things necessary to the general functioning of the column.

The column had one general delegate but the rank and file was fully consulted. There was a Committee of the Centuries, made up of the delegates of the groups, a Committee of the sections made up of delegates from the centuries and finally the column's War Committee consisting of all the delegates of the sections as well as the general delegate. The leadership of the column depended on the War Committee.

The Military Technical Council which was in charge of making strategic plans assisted the War Committee. In any case the plans could not be carried out until they had been approved by the War Committee. Contact between the War Committee and the Military Technical Council was constant. A member of the War Committee attended the meetings of the Military Technical Council and vice versa. When necessary the War Committee held a plenary session with the permanent delegates of the sections, the Artillery delegate and the delegates of the auxiliary services.

The War Committee had given itself a permanent instrument, a sort of bureau made up of various services: PTT, statistics, press, etc. The moving spirit of these services was Emilienne Morin, Durruti's secretary and companion. She also acted as interpreter when foreign journalists or personalities turned up. Mora and Pilar Balduque helped her with these administrative jobs.

The propaganda department edited and printed a column bulletin which was called *El Frente* (The Front). Later its work expanded when there was a radio transmitter. Francisco Carreño was put in charge of this section. The propaganda department had branches throughout the column. Each century had a propaganda department.

All this structure had been created spontaneously from the bottom up. It was also from the base that new formations sprang up called *special groups* in charge of attacking the rear guard of the enemy. They were to become guerrilla fighters who would carry out important missions in the areas controlled by the fascists. They were called "Hijos de la Noche" (Sons of the Night) and "la Banda Negra" (the Black Band). Francisco Ponzan, a very competent militant anarchist from Aragon gave them advice. Later Joaquin Morlanes, an infantry captain joined them and was responsible for important information missions.[4]

This "military" structure of the column didn't satisfy foreign visitors at all. They thought it ineffectual and doomed to failure. Koltsov who visited the front during August, made fun of this formation of the Militias, just as his bourgeois colleagues had done. However other writers better prepared to understand the problems posed by a revolution praised these revolutionary units.

George Orwell's testimony is the most important: "The journalists who sneered at the militia-system seldom remembered that the militias had to hold the line while the Popular Army was training in the rear... A modern mechanized army does not spring up out of the ground, and if the Government had waited until it had trained troops at its disposal, Franco would never have been resisted." And speaking about the self discipline of the militias, Orwell continues: "Later it became the fashion to decry the militias and therefore to pretend that the faults which were due to lack of training and weapons were the result of the equalitarian system... In practise the democratic 'revolutionary' type of discipline is more reliable than might be expected. In a workers' army discipline is theoretically voluntary... In the militias the bullying and the abuse that go on in an ordinary army would never have been tolerated for a moment. The normal military punishments existed, but they were only invoked for very serious offences... 'Revolutionary' discipline depends on political consciousness — on an understanding of *why* orders must be obeyed; it takes time to diffuse this, but it also takes time to drill a man into an automatom on the barrack-square."[5]

For those who wanted the revolution to move forward, the life of the militias could only reflect the classless society for which it was searching. This was the source of its libertarian structure. In contrast the partisans of an army based on a hierarchical command, discipline and authority, have as their model the society which accepts class divisions, exploitation and injustice.

A few days after the column arrived at Bujaraloz, in preparation for the new activities it was going to undertake, headquarters were installed in an abandoned house called Venta Monzona, between Bujaraloz and Pina de Ebro. Barracks for the various services were put up all around it and a machine shop was set up for the repair of cars, arms, etc.

In the Aragonese villages which had been liberated, collectives were being formed which attracted Durruti's attention because of the

235

August 1936 — French section of the International Brigade of the Durruti Column, named after Sebastien Faure, the famous French anarchist educator.

spontaneous way they were created and the speed with which they started functioning. Frequent and cordial bonds were established between the column and the collectives. The peasants often came in a delegation to the column, sometimes bringing food, sometimes to ask Durruti to visit the collective to speak about the working of a free commune.

During these visits Durruti was able to see what the Aragonese collective movement could mean for the development of the revolution. He suggested the formation of an Aragonese federation of all the collectives in the area. This federation would give an organizational strength to the farmers and would also help to make plans for the advancement of a libertarian socialist economy. In his eyes it would create new conditions where solidarity among the peasants would be the best kind of defense against the enemies of collectivism.

Coming back from one of these visits he proposed to the War Committee that groups of militiamen be sent to the collectives to help the peasants with the harvest as the military inactivity had left them idle. Their presence would be beneficial as they would be able to tell the peasants about the economic objectives of the revolution. The question was discussed at great length. Then it was introduced for discussion to the centuries so that the militiamen should understand what was being conceived and the need for supporting this creation. The results were good. Groups of young libertarians volunteered to become fighter-producers. This was the beginning of what was shortly to become the Federation of Aragonese Collectives.[6]

The two columns which were to cooperate with Durruti's column arrived late and delayed the attack on Saragossa. This delay angered Durruti because it allowed the fascists to strengthen their positions and to continue the repression. This situation produced a general impatience, and certain groups proposed to the War Committee that commando actions be taken against the key positions of the enemy. These actions, always aimed at the enemy's rearguard were mainly carried out by the "Metallurgists' Group" and the "Black Band", and thus the origin of the famous "dinamiteros" and "guerrilleros" of the column.

During this period of forced inactivity, Durruti was visited by various international political personalities, celebrated writers who, because of the needs of the moment, had become press correspondants, such as Koltsov and Ehrenburg. Also eminent international anarchists turned up such as the Anglo-Russian, Emma Goldman, and the Frenchman, Sébastien Faure.

Emma Goldman's arrival coincided with the big installation job which was taking place. "I found Durruti in a veritable beehive of activity. Men were coming and going, there were constant telephone calls for Durruti and at the same time the tremendous hubbub of workers putting up a wooden frame for his headquarters never stopped. In the midst of this noisy and continuous activity Durruti received me as if he had known me all his life. The cordial and warm interview with this man was something I hadn't expected.

"I had heard a lot about the strong personality and prestige of Durruti in the column named after him. I was curious to know how he had been able to bring together ten thousand volunteers without having had any experience or any instruction and specially since he had no help from the army. Durruti seemed surprised that I, an old militant anarchist, should ask him such a question: I have been an anarchist all my life he answered and I expect to remain one. That is why I think it would be very disagreeable for me to become a general and to command men in a military spirit with stupid discipline. They came to me of their own free will, ready to give their lives for our struggle. I believe as I have always believed in liberty understood in terms of responsibility. I consider discipline indispensable but this must be self discipline inspired by a common ideal and a strong feeling of solidarity. Durruti's secret," Emma Goldman concluded "was that he had made theory and practise one." [7]

The life style and the social relations adopted by the anarchists also influenced the other militia groups. The journalists who came to see the leaderless and undisciplined army said to the anarchists in the column: "You say he isn't a leader but you obey him." And the militiamen answered: "We follow him because he behaves well; if he changed he would lose our respect and we would leave him." [8]

Nevertheless the war was a reality and Durruti knew the evil it could inflict on his men, even though they were revolutionaries, because war creates a kind of life which is degrading: "If this situation continues, the revolution will be finished, because the men will leave it more animal than human... We must hurry and make an end to it as soon as possible." [9] These thoughts filled him with a consuming impatience. Many nights, a prey to insomnia, "he visited the advance

237

Bujaraloz, September 1936 — Sebastien Faure visits the Durruti Column. From right of left: Mora, grandaughter of the famous Spanish anarchist educator Francisco Ferrer who was murdered by the State, Ruano, Sebastien Faure, Durruti, a daughter of Ferrer, and Manzana, military advisor of the Column.

guards and spent hours with the sentinels, his eyes fixed on the lights of Saragossa. He was often there until daylight." [10]

Added to these worries was another just as difficult which he had to face in his role as delegate of the column. He had to listen to the peasants complaining about the behavior of the men of the column in villages. They were usually minor offences but these were already evident signs of the vices brought about by war. When this occured he tried to point them out to the greatest number of people so that the collectivity would think about these problems.

But sometimes just reproval wasn't enough. One day he met a century delegate far away from his sector. He explained that five men who had been assigned to stand watch at a bridge had disappeared and he was looking for them. They were found drinking wine in a neighboring village. Durruti questioned them: "Do you realize the seriousness of your acts? Don't you know that the fascists could have broken through at the spot you abandoned and could have massacred the comrades whose safety was in your hands? You are not worthy of belonging to the column or the CNT. Give me your cards." They handed them to him. It was the last thing he could have expected: "You are neither CNTists nor workers, you are shit. You no longer belong to the column. Go home." Far from looking upset, they looked satisfied. Durruti was exasperated by such an attitude. "Don't you know that the clothes on your back belong to the people? Take

238

off your pants!'' And it was in their underpants that they were taken off to Barcelona. [11]

Durruti went from extreme anger to perfect calm. After this scene he asked Mora to telephone to Barcelona. He wanted to speak to Ricardo Sanz: "Ricardo, do you know that a certain political party in Sabadell has eight machine guns hidden in its headquarters? I give you 48 hours to bring me those eight machine guns. And also send me three agronomists.'' [12]   That day Durruti had visited a number of collectives and in most of them there had been complaints about a lack of technicians. Some had asked for agronomists and technicians able to guide them in the new type of farming they wanted to try. Others pointed out that the better militants had left the village to enroll in the militias. Durruti took the names of those who had enrolled in his column and had them appear before the War Committee: "We don't need you in the column.'' Seeing the amazement in the faces of the militant peasants Durruti changed his tone and said smiling: "It's not what you think. I know you are good fighters, that you are generous, that you have the courage to bear anything, but the people in your village want you back. They know who you are and you have their confidence. The work you can accomplish in your villages is more important than killing fascists. What we create is what will survive historically.'' [13]

Footnotes

1. José Mira, *Los Guerrilleros Confederales*, p. 110. "It was said that he had agreed to wait until the columns going toward the South of the Ebro had conquered Quinto and Belchite and had made contact with us around the sources of the Ebro."
N.B. This immobilizing of the column was one of the most controversial issues. It had never been possible to find out who initiated this halt. Some people suggested that it was ordered by the Central Committee of Militias in Barcelona. Because one of the plans that had been made at the time when Durruti left Barcelona was a landing in Mallorca and for this it was necessary to amass a large quantity of war materials.
According to José Alberola, Cultural Adviser to the Council of Aragon, it was "an error to establish the front in the plains and outside the walls of Huesca. They should have exposed themselves to every risk and fallen on Saragossa like a revolutionary storm. This seemed possible and might have been successful because the rebels ignored the number of antifascist fighters who, in a few hours, had just recently been victorious in the Catalonian capital." (*CNT*, article June 16, 1961.
Felipe Alaiz, who agrees with Alberola, thinks that "the most important action of the column had been the fact that it reached Bujaraloz without being stopped, because the country of Monegros extending from the Ebro to the Segre is largely devoted to the cultivation of wheat. The shores of the Cinca, between the Ebro and the Segre not only produce an abundant amount of wheat but also many other products which are cultivated intensely, such as top quality fruits. The success of the collectivist venture in Aragon was based on this very fact of a fertile countryside." *Espagne indomptée*, August 1939.
2. The "Ascaso" Column following the example of Durruti's column, didn't stop at Lerida but went as far as Barbastro. Colonel Villalba and Lt. Col. Gonzalez-Moralès were there. They were the leaders of that part of the Montana Battalion which had remained faithful to the Republic. Until the "Ascaso" Column arrived, these military men had done little to organize the front. A discussion took place and it was decided that these two would become technicians to the Column. Because of this the Column became the most important force in the area.
Immediately the encirclement of Huesca and an attack on Siétamo was undertaken. After advancing, there was a retreat, but later this was reversed thanks to the help of Durruti's International Group. Shortly after the Ascaso Column turned up, an important group of international volunteers arrived. Among them was a group called "Giustizie e Liberta" led by the Socialist Rosselli. Another group of Italians, also anarchists, arrived, and among them were Camilo Berneri and Fosco Falaschi. Hans Beimler heading a group of German antifascists also joined the front at Huesca. From the very beginning the struggle was very fierce in this sector. It was never understood why Huesca didn't fall into the hands of these forces.
3. The units of the POUM commanded by Rovira took the name "Lina Odena", a militant of the POUM, who had died during the struggle in Barcelona. They reached Alcubierre quickly but there were only a few of them. In contrast the Karl Marx Column (PSUC) which left Barcelona with 1,300 men lost valuable time pitching camp around Lerida where they were trying to persuade the soldiers who were still in the city to join the column.
4. For the description of the structure of the Column we have used the book already quoted by José Mira and the testimony of José Esplugas who was in charge of the Centuries. We have also used the testimony of Ricardo Rionda, who was a member of the War Committee and we used as well the hundred answers to one of our questionnaires sent out to the original members of the Column who had survived.
5. George Orwell: Homage to Catalonia, Harcourt Brace & Co. 1952, p. 28 and 29,
6. Alardo Prats, *Entre los campesinos de Aragon*, edited in Barcelona in 1937. This is a vivid reportage on the war. It gives important facts about the beginnings of the collectives in Aragon. On page 76 he writes about Durruti and the Federation of Collectives: "it was conceived among the people in the very trenches of Bujaraloz at a historic meeting presided over by Durruti."
7. *November 20*, a brochure. Ed. CNT, Barcelona 1936. Testimony of Emma Goldman.
8. Idem. Testimony of André Ulman, *op. cit.*
9. Testimony of Emilienne Morin.
10. Idem.
11. Testimony of a number of militiamen. Llya Ehrenburg also reports this in his book, *La nuit tomba*.
12. Ricardo Sanz, *Durruti*, Pamphlet. Ed. CNT, Toulouse 1946.
13. Testimony of a militant of the CNT from Valderobles (Aragon).

7

"THE UNDERGROUND REVOLUTION"

AFTER TWO WEEKS OF WAR on the Aragon front ammunition had been exhausted. There were no bullets for the guns and the guns themselves, old 94 models, had to be repaired often when they were not completely useless. The artillery used its shells sparingly and the very scarce planes only made brief sorties and then only managed to exasperate the fascists who already had the use of Italian and German aircraft.

The Militia columns to the South of the Ebro tried to take Belchite which resisted. The rebels were sending equipment and troops from Saragossa and Calatayud. In the area around Alcubierre the militia were up against a vigorous fascist resistance. The latter knew that to give up this position meant a break between Huesca and Saragossa and the resulting loss of the North. In the area occupied by Durruti's column inactivity was general. Only the bands of guerrilleros carried out some exploits which sometimes created a strong psychological effect. But the troops who were near Saragossa without being able to attack it were living through a calvary.

Taking advantage of this calm, Durruti went to Barcelona. He wanted to study the situation in Aragon and the means of getting out of the impasse produced by the lack of war materiel with the Central Militia Committee. On his way from Bujaraloz to Barcelona he was able to see how much things had changed: "The whirlwind which had inspired people in the first days of the struggle had disappeared. Now the villagers and workers had channelled their enthusiasm by changing their way of life. New social relations had been created. The people, that is to say the workers and peasants, were armed and were guarding the entrances and exits of the villages. No "assault guards", no "civil guards", no uniforms, but armed men everywhere.

As he was going through a village in the province of Lerida, Durruti stopped and presented himself to the workers' check point as a militiaman coming from the front, saying he needed gas. He wanted to see how the people of the village of about 3,000 inhabitants reacted. They told him to go to the Revolutionary Committee which was in the old Town Hall. He could get a voucher there. Durruti crossed the square. It was about noon and there were no strollers, only some women coming out of the church with bags of provisions. Durruti asked them the way to the Committee and why were they going through

Barcelona, August 1936 — Departure of another anarchist militia for the Aragon front called "Los Aguiluchos" Column. From left to right: Severino Campos, Richardo Sanz, Aurelio Fernandez, Juan García Oliver, Gregorio Jover and García Vivancos.

the Church? No, no, there is no priest. The priest is in the fields and is working on the land with the other peasants. Kill him? Why? He isn't dangerous. He is even talking about marrying a girl from the village. He is happy in his new situation. The church? Oh yes, the church. They have burned all the saints. God has been cast out, and since God doesn't exist any more, the assembly has decided to replace "Adios" with the word "Salud." In the church they have set up the food cooperative and as there is total collectivization, everyone uses the coop.

At the committee there was only one rather old man. Formerly a teacher, he had been replaced two months before the revolution by a young teacher from Lerida. Since then he had done nothing but after the revolution he had volunteered for an administrative job with the Committee. The other members are at work. The season requires this, specially since many of the young people from the village have gone to the front and the wheat has to be harvested. Otherwise what would there be to eat all year?

Durruti asked how the Committee had been chosen. An assembly had been convened and all the inhabitants had taken part. Each person's capacities had been considered and — the old man insisted — particularly their conduct before the revolution. Political parties? Some republicans, perhaps some socialists too, but no, political affiliations hadn't counted. The committee represents the whole village, so it's necessary to have everyone's opinion. Political parties, what for? One works to eat and one eats to work. It is not through party politics that wheat grows, olives are picked, animals are cared for. No, no, the problems are collective and they must be solved collectively. Politics divides and the village wants to live completely collectivized.

Everybody is happy but what about the old bosses? The old bosses are not pleased; they don't say so because they are scared but you can see it in their faces. Some have entered the collective, others have chosen what is now called "individualism". They have kept their land but they must cultivate it alone because there is no more exploitation of man by man. And if they can't cultivate their land? Then the collective takes over the uncultivated lands because it would be a crime against the community to leave it fallow.

Durruti left the village. At the control point they asked him if he had gotten his gas ration card. He smiled, said "Yes", called out "Salud" and the car resumed its trip to Barcelona. This experience of finding workers in control was repeated regularly along the route, proving that it was the armed workers and peasants who were on guard everywhere.[1] In the larger villages, life was more complicate but the rules were the same. Always mirroring the Central Committee of Militias, each political party and workers' organization was represented on the committee but always subordinate to joint representation so that each document to be valid had to carry the seal of each organization or party. As for the factories, shops and services, everything was collectivized and subordinate to the workers' assemblies, the sole authority which could name those in responsible positions and control activities.

In Barcelona the scene is even more positive. Even at the gates of the factories there are armed men. The trolleys as well as the busses circulate under worker control. The trains and boats are also collectivized. Industry is in the hands of the workers and all the production centers conspicuously fly the red and black flags as well as inscriptions announcing that they have really become collectives. The revolution seems to be universal. Changes are also evident in social relations. The former barriers which used to separate men and women arbitrarily have been destroyed. In the cafes and other public places there is a mingling of the sexes which would have been completely unimaginable before. The revolution has introduced a fraternal character to social relations which has deepened with practise and shows clearly that the old world is dead, well dead. When Durruti tells Van Paassen that a new world is being born, he isn't wrong and is perfectly conscious that a profound revolution is occurring.

The Republican and Socialist leaders and specially the Communists wanted to stifle this collective explosion at whatever cost, but were not successful. They also worked hard to "falsify" the revolution and minimize its scope by proclaiming that "there was no revolution in Spain but only enthusiastic support of their government by the masses." This is approximately what Jesus Hernandez of the Central Committee of the Communist Party told the correspondant of the *Dépêche* of Toulouse in August 1936. But one would have had t be blind not too see that even the men had changed. This is what Durruti had been able to observe before going to the committees. He could see how the masses thought and acted. In the village he visited, he had received well reasoned answers. Talking to railroad work-

Barcelona, September, 1936 — Mariano R. Vasquez, general secretary of the CNT speaking during the historic meeting in the city attended by 150,000 people.

ers, metal workers or textile workers, he found the same revolutionary ardor. Everywhere in the rank and file the revolution was on the march.

After having visited a number of industrial centers and several trade unions, Durruti went to the headquarters of the CNT-FAI in the via Layetana, the former headquarters of the bosses called Casa Cambo. At the entrance and in the hallway there was an impressive armed force. An atmosphere of intense activity was in the air. In a certain way the "Casa CNT-FAI" had become the vital center of the life of Barcelona and Catalonia. One could read on the wall a particularly significant inscription: "Be brief comrade, the revolution isn't made by talking but through acting." [2]

But wasn't the apparatus going to give birth to a bureaucracy which would destroy the revolution. Durruti had long discussions with Mariano R. Vasquez on this theme. The Secretary General of the CNT agreed that it might be possible to get bogged down in bureaucratic routines. But there was no other way to function because the CNT had become indispensable to the solution of all local and regional problems. The production centers were all controlled by the workers. The unions had to study the problems posed by economic administration, the source of all these structures. Their functioning wasn't perfect, they were also overstaffed. But all this stemmed from the new situation created by the revolution with new and unavoidable problems.

Actually the apparatus wasn't centralized. Each organization was controlled by the unions. The people employed there were still paid by the businesses where they had worked before and their ad-

244

ministration was controlled by the plant assembly. Therefore the control came from the bottom. Durruti understood that Mariano was aware of the danger: "The revolution was testing anarchism. We have advocated revolution for many years and now in the moment of truth we cannot avoid the responsibility for guiding it. We hope that our quality as militants will shield us from personal degeneration. More than ever, the situation today demands constant watchfulness over the structure by the rank and file. The only way to keep the organization from supplanting the rank and file is for the latter to actively control the militants whom the revolution has placed in leading positions."[3] Durruti left, convinced that, until now, victory hadn't turned the heads of the militant anarchists, who at one shot had become the pivotal centers of the new situation.

It was hard to recognize García Oliver, who had established his Headquarters in the Naval School. He was responsible for endless jobs which required continuous work. All the delegates of the CNT or the FAI, who came to the Central Committee of Militias to discuss problems raised by the war, wanted to talk to García Oliver himself and not to the secretaries. They wanted to be sure that their problems wouldn't be forgotten in a file. García Oliver didn't even have time to shave. In a corner of the room he had a camp bed where he rested for a few hours at night after the daily meeting of the Central Committee of Militias.

Durruti immediately raised the important question of the attack on Saragossa with García Oliver; the importance of conquering the capital of Aragon, the need for war materiel, etc. He learned from García Oliver that the attack on Saragossa had been put off. The conquest of Mallorca was being prepared. In fact this operation was more important militarily. With this attack the war was going to be expanded and Italy would be forced to intervene directly. England wouldn't tolerate this Italian presence in the Mediterranean and would in turn intervene. The fate of the revolution was being decided now outside Spain. It was also necessary to try and bring about an uprising in Morocco.

Durruti objected that the English and French could easily come to an agreement with the Italians to limit the extension of the conflict. And then the operation in Mallorca was very risky while the taking of Saragossa was vital to the conquest of the North. If they were in touch with Bilbao and Asturia, it would be possible to drive back Franco's forces to the South and fight a decisive battle in Andalusia. Masters of the peninsula it would be possible to resist an international blockade.

Two points of view were opposing each other. One was García Oliver's state controlled strategy. The other was a revolutionary one. The tragedy of the militant anarchist was beginning. From then on the revolution was to be subordinated to the contingencies of the war. García Oliver reminded Durruti that his position followed the one adopted by the CNT on July 20th; to accept collaboration with various political parties meant to give up the revolution. When their own "Nosotros" group asserted they were in favor of the revolution, the possibilities were uncertain but their attitude was correct and at one with the anarchist ideal. Applying their theory might have led to an adventure ending in the siege of Barcelona. But it might also have resulted in a withering attack against Saragossa and if there had been collective action with the Levant, part of the peninsula would have remained under a revolutionary regime. This solution was rejected by the majority. Santillan's position was adopted, that is, collaboration with the various political groups.[4]

The CNT and the FAI because of their alliance with the political parties had acted as a brake on the broadening of the revolution. At the opportune moment they hadn't known how to give a revolutionary sequel to the triumph in Barcelona. They were to remain in a state of suspense while waiting for the defeat of the fascists. How was it possible to beat enemies equipped with an excellent military apparatus? Catalonia had none of the raw materials necessary for a war industry. They also lacked currency with which to buy war materials from abroad. By choosing the revolutionary way, the CNT could have roused the prople of Madrid and installed a Defense Council similar to the one in Barcelona and from then on had the use of the Treasury. But with the collaborationist solution the CNT had its hands tied because the initiative reverted to the Socialist Party, which was the declared enemy of the revolution and partisan to upholding the Giral-Azaña bourgeois government.

As things stood there was no other way out than to allow events to lead the way. It was necessary to stay in the Central Committee of Militias and to use the armed strength of the people as a constant menace against a possible attempt to restore the old regime. And it was necessary to organize the economy already in the hands of the workers and create an armed vigilance unit controlled by the unions.

But García Oliver said that all this must be carried out legally. In other words it was necessary to carry the revolution to its goal but secretly. Durruti found this formula ridiculous: it would be similar to an underground FAI under the Republic! Everyone knew its principal militants. He said "No one will be fooled. When the workers expropriate the bourgeoisie, when one attacks foreign property, when public order is in the hands of the workers, when the militia is controlled by the unions, when, in fact, one is in the process of making a revolution from the bottom up, how is it possible to give this a legal basis? Legality would give power to the government of the Generalitat, by weakening the power of the Central Committee of Militias, by integrating the economy, now managed by the workers, into the State apparatus. This would mean in fact that the CNT would not only strengthen the power of the State, but would also have in its hands the control of the economy, leading towards a sort of State socialist economy."

García Oliver admitted that Durruti's conclusions were correct and their point of view was in radical opposition to that of Santillan. If Santillan's policy continued to be carried out, they would remain in opposition as long as possible, preparing, as well as they could, for the final blow. With the support of the masses the spirit of the revolution must be kept alive while maintaining a dual power structure: the power of the people and that of official organizations.

Despite everything Durruti thought that it was necessary to take advantage of the next plenum of the CNT and the FAI to raise once

246

again the fundamental question of the revolution. They held the trump cards: an armed working class. Valencia had given itself a popular committee similar to Barcelona's Central Committee of Militias. For Durruti it was a question of creating a strong opposition within the Plenum and to bring the militants face to face with the problem.

At this plenum in August 1936 the seriousness of the moment was realized. At the same time it was seen that the ambiguous situation in Catalonia couldn't continue with the Generalitat nominally in Control while the CNT had taken on the real leadership. So Durruti and García Oliver bluntly posed the question: it was necessary to assume total responsibility and get out of the torpor created by collaboration with the various political groups, an alliance which was only a way of dissipating energy and disorienting the revolution itself.

Santillan nevertheless maintained his position. Despite the negative results of his theory of "collaboration" he thought that this was the only way to avoid a civil war among the anti-fascists themselves. This dramatic emphasis prevented the revision of the agreements of July 20. In order to carry on the war and the revolution at the same time a new formula was proposed: an alliance with the UGT to create together an organization for national leadership to be called the National Council of Defense which would take charge of the government.

The partisans of this tactic calculated that the trade union base of the UGT was more to the left than its leadership. Besides as it was deeply involved with the CNT on the economic level, an intense propaganda campaign could set the course of this workers' government from its very foundation. This resolution left the most active militants tied hand and foot. The only way of getting out of this impasse was to carry the revolutionary problem into the streets in opposition to its own organization.

In Barcelona and perhaps in all of Catalonia this kind of Coup d'État might have had an immediate effect but in Madrid the CNT would have been crucified because of its weakness compared to the socialist and communist blocs. The latter actually had the support of the forces of public order which had not been transformed like those in Catalonia. Besides the civil war or the armed insurrection in the so-called antifascist camp was inevitable...

Durruti who had been hurriedly recalled to the Aragon front had to leave Barcelona but now he had worked out a line of action: to maintain his positions against winds and tides, to create a united confederal army, to return blow for blow every attack against revolutionary conquests.

Footnotes

---

1. Richard Bloch: *Espagne, Espagne!*
2. The author was an eye witness to this as well as to other events mentioned in the text.
3. These positions were held by almost all the militants of the CNT and were expressed at meetings of anarchist groups and CNT assemblies.
4. To understand Santillan's position, see his works already quoted.

8

KOLTSOV VISITS
THE DURRUTI COLUMN

DURRUTI LEFT BARCELONA suddenly, recalled to Barbastro by Villalba. The War Committee was planning to strengthen the front by attacking Siétamo again, to carry out an extensive operation against Huesca. Reinforcements were needed in the Barbastro sector. These were supplied by Durruti and Rovira (the latter in the name of the POUM).

The offensive started in mid-August. José Mira, who took part in the taking of Siétamo reports as follows: "At the beginning of the offensive the enemy aviation never stopped bombing and strafing. The villages in the rearguard were reduced to ruins but in vain, we advanced. Our militia fought to the death climbing the slopes of Estrecho Quinto which were defended by the Civil Guard machine gunners. We occupied the first houses of Siétamo after three days of struggle. Then the battle was very severe, as each house had become a fortress. Deadly fire flashed out from all of them. To the cry of "Long live the FAI! the militiamen darted out like thunderbolts and scattered in the streets. The first clash was very severe but our people succeeded in reaching the church where most of the fascist troops had dug in. Once the siege of Soétamo had been lifted, the militia divided. Some stayed in the village, others left for Loporzano which fell into our hands the next day." [1]

Backed by the POUM, the offensive against Estrecho Quinto and Monte Aragon continued and they were taken by the revolutionaries after five days of fighting. The spoils of war consisted of 8 number 10 cannons, 20 number 81 mortars, 16 machine guns and 1,600 guns, a real fortune as the militias were terribly short of ammunition. The militiamen behaved admirably almost without eating or sleeping during the fight. The greatest stimulus to these guerrilla fighters was Durruti's conduct: he was always to be seen in the most exposed positions, bearing the ups and downs of war like all the fighters and only making a difference between himself and his comrades in one thing, he was the first to face danger in the front lines.

When Durruti was preparing the offensive against Siétamo and was concluding mopping up operations at Pina de Ebro on August 15th, *Pravda* correspondant, Michel Koltsov, arrived at Bujaraloz. The latter, coming from France had arrived in Spain on August 8. Once in Barcelona he sought out Garcia Oliver and said he wanted to visit the Aragon front and to meet Durruti. He received a safe conduct and was given the necessary means to go to Bujaraloz.

He came with an interpreter and a General who pretended to be a "white" Russian, living in exile in Paris, coming to Spain drawn there by the war. Koltsov visited Trueba in the Tardiente sector and arrived at Bujaraloz on August 14. The report in his journal has no historical significance as his colleague Ehrenburg has to recognize. [2] Durruti was at Venta Monzona (Santa Lucia). "It would have been rash for Koltsov to go there because it was only two miles from the front."

"The celebrated anarchist received us without paying much attention. But when he noticed the words Moscow and *Pravda* in Garcia — Oliver's letter, he became animated and on the road, right in the midst of the soldiers with the evident idea of getting their attention, he began a fiery polemic. His words were full of dark and fanatical passion." This is the description of the famous Durruti according to Koltsov and here is his report of the interview in his Spanish War Diary. [3]

Durruti began by asking: "What does the Soviet Union plan to do for the Spanish Revolution?" The Russian journalist gave the reasons on an international plane why the U.S.S.R. could not help directly. But he did not exclude the possibility of its helping the Republicans indirectly. As for the Russian workers, a national subscription had been organized through their unions and the first remittance had been sent to the Prime Minister, Giral. [4]

Koltsov's answer didn't satisfy Durruti who retorted sharply that "The struggle against the fascists was not the work of the Azaña government but of the workers, who had started the social Revolution at the right time in response to the attack of the conservative forces. The government had not only refused to arm the workers but had taken no action in various regions against the army which had been working for a long time to prepare a fascist victory. Durruti reminded him of the uselessness of sending money from the Russian unions to the Spanish government. It was not a war to maintain bourgeois institutions but a revolutionary war. If the people of the U.S.S.R. were not au courant about the real situation which the proletariat was continually demonstrating through its acts, it was the duty of every correspondant, and precisely of Koltsov himself, to inform the masses in his country." This was Durruti's answer, which the author of the *Diario de la Guerra de España* "forgot" to register, an omission which undoubtedly followed the party line of the PCUS which didn't want the Russian people to know the truth about Spain.

On the contrary, Koltsov has Durruti say ridiculous things which correspond to the self-seeking image which the Stalinists created about revolutionary anarchists. Concluding this first part of the dialogue, the journalist added a few pompous sentences about the Russian wishes for a prompt victory for the anarchist, socialist and communist workers.

Then the conversation turned to various military problems at the front and specially those of the Column. In his reply Durruti was concise: "He asserted that it would be advisable to organize an attack on Saragossa but that in reality the front was not moving in that di-

EL FRENTE

C. N. T.   BOLETIN DE GUERRA DE LA COLUMNA DURRUTI   F. A. I.

| AÑO I | Pina de Ebro, 27 de agosto de 1936 | NUM. 3 |

TODOS ADELANTE; NINGUNO HACIA ATRAS

Este Comité Central recibe diariamente innumerables peticiones de permisos para ausentarse de la columna por uno o varios días. Esto representa un constante desplazamiento de milicianos y un ir y venir de personal que altera todo posible control de las centurias, y que hace imposible toda distribución regular de los servicios.

Para evitar estos inconvenientes, y otros que no debemos detallar, nos vemos obligados a recordar a todos los milicianos lo siguiente:

Hemos venido a hacer la guerra, y no a practicar un deporte, y en una lucha que tiene objetivos tan sublimes como los que perseguimos, el que se ausenta de su puesto por un momento falta a los deberes que nos imponen las circunstancias. Está la libertad amenazada, y el porvenir se está creando y conquistando con el apoyo de todos, en cada momento del día.

Al venir al frente, el miliciano viene a ofrecer su vida, a sacrificar su vida, a dar todo su ser por el triunfo de nuestra causa. El que no viene con estas disposiciones no sirve para el frente.

Hay que desligarse de toda traba que no sea la de conseguir con constancia y con energía el triunfo.

No nos vengan a pedir, por tanto, permisos de ausencia con pretextos fútiles. El nacimiento de un hijo, la jaqueca de una compañera, la falta de noticias de un familiar, no pueden, no deben influir en la desorganización de nuestra columna.

Desde Barcelona vinimos. Los caminos quedaron a nuestra espalda, claros y limpios. El que no sirva para recorrerlos hacia adelante, sin mirar atrás, que vuelva la espalda definitivamente. No haremos comentarios sobre los ausentes, pero queremos tener el convencimiento de que los que van con nosotros, no tienen más idea ni más pensamiento que la de avanzar, liberando hermanos y creando el porvenir.

Cuando volvamos, cumplida nuestra misión, podemos compartir dolores y alegrias en el seno de nuestras familias.

Mientras tanto, prestemos nuestra atención absoluta a los pueblos que sufren bajo la espuela. En ellos están nuestras madres, nuestros hermanos y nuestros hijos, y su dolor nos ha de importar más que el nuestro propio.

B. DURRUTI.—L. RUANO.—MANZANA.—M. YOLDI.—CARREÑO.

PARA LOS LLAMADOS A FILA

Por acuerdo del Comité de Guerra del frente de Aragón y siempre de acuerdo con el Comité Superior de las Milicias Antifascistas de Barcelona, se pone en conocimiento de todos los reclutas de los reemplazos llamados por decretos del Gobierno que no puede tolerarse de ninguna de las maneras que con el pretexto de la desmilitarización y constitución de las Milicias Antifascistas existan ciudadanos que se queden en sus casas mientras los amantes de la libertad luchan en la calle. Por tanto, este Comité, de acuerdo siempre con el Comité Superior y Central de Milicias Antifascistas de Barcelona, ordena a todos los incluídos en los decretos mencionados de incorporación a filas que se presenten con toda urgencia en sus respectivos cuarteles o en alguna Milicia controlada por los partidos u organizaciones Obreras, dando éstas cuenta a los cuarteles donde debieran haberse presentado los milicianos en ellas existentes para el debido control y que jamás pueda ningún camarada perteneciente a estos reemplazos quedarse en su casa mientras los demás luchan en bien de sus intereses.

Sariñena, 26 de agosto de 1936.

Por el Comité de Guerra:

Buenaventura Durruti, C. N. T. Antonio Ortiz, C. N. T. Cristóbal Aldabaldetrecu, C. N. T. José del Barrio, U. G. T. Jorge Arquer, P. O. U. M. Franco Quinza, Aviación. Coronel Villalba. Comandante Reyes, Aviación. Capitán Medrano. Capitán Menéndez. Teniente Coronel Joaquín Blanco.

El día 23, el Depósito de Lérida suministró a la Columna Durruti un coche Hudson, 8 cilindros, para el servicio del Comité de Guerra: 1.764 camisas, 2.000 calzoncillos, y 1.920 calcetines y granotas.

Information Bulletin of Durruti Column

rection, which he regretted and he showed Koltsov on the map the positions of his sector. The inactivity in his sector was due to the strategy established by the military technicians. The latter, believing that his advance would be injurious, had urged him to wait for a common action until progress was made in the North and East. Nevertheless he wasn't pessimistic and disclosed that in the attack that was to take place, positions would be improved as they neared the main objective.

"As for the military situation of the Column, according to Durruti, there was no difficulty as far as the command was concerned.

250

He said that the War Committee and the technical military council were acting together and that the problem of operations were always carried out with common agreement. The Column was lead in a spirit of self discipline and fraternal responsibility. The duties of war were facilitated by the qualities of self sacrifice displayed by the militia volunteers and it wasn't necessary to resort to disciplinary procedures common in the barracks. The men were conscious of the importance of the stake. The general behavior was good, even if there were little incidents inevitable in such a large community."

Durruti explained in detail how the Column was guided, beginning with the group and going up to the War Committee. Koltsov didn't care to remember any of these answers. He went so far as to write that "according to Durruti, desertions were quite considerable and that there were only about 1,200 men left in the column", when in reality at that time the column had 6,000 men of whom 4,500 were armed.

"As to the equipment of the column," Koltsov said "he had heard from Durruti that it was excellent and that the latter had at his disposal a great deal of ammunition." Here again, Koltsov distorted the answer. Actually Durruti had said that "they had only old weapons and insufficient arms for all the men, which forced them to establish a cycle, alternating work in the fields with active war service. And so more than 1,500 militiamen were, at that time, doing agricultural jobs, while others were moving between the villages of Gelsa and Pina. There was a terrible lack of ammunition. The Central Committee of Militias was having great difficulty in supplying the front, to such a point that empty shells were being kept in order to send them to Barcelona to be refilled. Sometimes groups of guerilleros had to make forays into enemy territory to get good munitions."

Koltsov writes nothing about "military instruction". But Durruti was quite concrete: "Fighters were taught how to use weapons, the way to fortify a position, to protect themselves against aerial or land bombardments, how to make a surprise attack on an enemy position and in general the way to be successful in hand to hand fighting. But they didn't teach goose stepping or marching." Durruti insisted that "there were no superiors or inferiors among them. Relations between delegates and militiamen were the cordial relations between one comrade and another. Neither he nor the militiamen believed that to accomplish their job it was necessary to know how to click one's heels like the Prussians." But if this was what Koltsov meant by military training, he would have to leave disappointed because "no one here wanted this kind of instruction." This last sentence was the one remembered by Koltsov in order to insinuate that the military situation in the column was very bad.

Throughout the conversation Durruti maintained a proper attitude and showed no "sarcasm" but only the strong wish to make Koltsov feel that he was in a country where anarchism prevailed and that it would not be easy to make it lower its flag. The farewell was cordial according to the *Pravda* diarist and he reported this in a now famous sentence: "Goodbye Durruti. I will go to see you in Saragosse If you are not killed here or in the streets of Barcelona while fighting the communists, perhaps in six years you will have become a bolshe-

The French writer, Simone Weil while she was part of the International Brigade of the Durruti Column.

vik.'' Koltsov added: ''He smiled and immediately turning his back started to talk to someone who was there.'' This someone, who was there by chance, was none other than Mora, the secretary of the War Committee, who with Francisco Carreño and Francisco Subirats, were present at this interview.[5]

The *Pravda* correspondant was not the only journalist who visited the Aragonese front and, of course, the Durruti column. The fact that the column was commanded by Durruti and that it was made up solely of anarchists was enough to draw the attention of friends and enemies. Koltsov, like his colleague Ilya Ehrenburg, went to visit it full of curiosity. To see the anarchists in action was reason enough to arouse ''scientific criticism'' in a Marxist. It was with this excuse that Koltsov visited the column. As for the bourgeois journalists, they did it in the same way with the preconceived idea of finding themselves facing ''madmen''. But one shouldn't put all the visiting journalists in the same category.

After the visit of Koltsov, Albert Souillon, correspondant of the French paper *La Montagne* came and also Jose Gabriel of the Argentine *La Prensa*. Albert Souillon had told the War Committee of his wish to take part as a spectator in the attack on Fuentes de Ebro. He described its capture in his newspaper and also tells about the fear that he felt. But he speaks as well of his pride at having witnessed the victory won by the column. He reports a short conversation he

252

had with Durruti after the battle: "Well, and in France?" Durruti asked him point blank. "Durruti" Souillon wrote, "was eager to know about the ideas and actions of the French comrades. He regretted the official viewpoint, understanding it but not accepting it. He understood it because he had a very subtle intelligence but he didn't accept it because he was a courageous man who was fighting and saw his men being killed by German and Italian airplanes.

"There are times" Souillon continued "when man doesn't have the right to accept our official attitude (the French one), he rejects this way of seeing things, when he sees before his eyes the wounded and dead and there is rage in his heart. 'I would have spoken to the French on the radio' Durruti told me 'but your government needs its middle classes. Besides my anarchist name would have frightened them (...) Tell Paris that we are fighting for you as well as for ourselves. Stress the need that we have for planes which are indispensable so that we may finish quickly. Also stress that we anarchists, who make up a number of the columns among those actually fighting, have only one goal, to crush the fascists. Tell the French that all of us here are in agreement like brothers and that after the victory, when it is necessary to clarify the new economic and social structures in Spain, those who have fought side by side will work together more fraternally than ever." [6]

With the taking of Fuentes de Ebro and other positions of lesser importance, the big offensive which had started at Barbastro came to an end... The Staff thought that the enemy had been able to strengthen itself and that the general condition of the militias, which lacked adequate arms, would not permit it to advance on the present front. However the War Committee of Barbastro thought it important psychologically to exploit the victory, not only to raise the morale at the rear but also to demoralize the enemy. Durruti was asked to speak on the radio at Sariñena:

"On the Aragonese front" Durruti said, "the workers' Militias are not idle. They are attacking the enemy, conquering positions and maintaining their lines of resistance, waiting to launch a vast offensive. You too, Spanish workers, you have an important mission to accomplish, because revolution is not won only by shooting, but also by producing. The front and the rear must work closely together. They must struggle, united by the same objective, and ours can be no other than to defend Spain which relies on the working class.

"The workers who fight today, on the front or in the rear, are not doing so to protect the privileges of the bourgeoisie but are fighting for the right to live in dignity. The strength of Spain is in the working class and its organizations. After the victory, the CNT and the UGT will discuss the forms and direction of the economy in Spain.

We who fight on the battlefieds, are not seeking medals. We are not fighting to become deputies or ministers. When we come back from the front we will occupy our positions in the factories, the shops, the mines and the fields, there where we started. It is in the production centers that the real battle will be won.

"We are peasants and we sow. Storms can come, designed to destroy our crops. But we are forwarned and we will know how to

A Century composed of peasants from Calanda (Teruel) of the Durruti Column, September 1936.

"King Kong" a celebrated armoured car. The first of its kind with a rotary turret for its machine gun. It was delivered to the Durruti Column by the CNT metallurgical Union of Barcelona on the August 6.

confront them. Our harvest is ripe. Gather the wheat! The harvest will be for everyone and there will be no one with special privileges. When the distribution takes place, neither Azaña, nor Largo Caballero, nor Durruti will have the right to a bigger share. The harvest belongs to everyone, to all those who worked regularly, sincerely and carefully so that it should not be plundered.

"Workers of Catalonia, a few days ago at Sariñena I told you that I was proud to represent you on the Aragon front and I also told you that we would be worthy of your confidence. But so that this confidence and fraternity may continue, we must give ourselves completely to the struggle even so far as to forget ourselves. Above all, you, our women, silence your hearts and let your men on the front fight. Don't write and give them bad news, bear this burden yourselves. Let us fight. Realize that the fate of Spain depends on all of us as does the future of our children. Help us to be strong in this war which requires all our will to succeed, all our heart to conquer.

"Comrades, arms must be sent to the front. We need them to create an iron barrier before the enemy. Have faith in us. These militias will never defend the bourgeoisie. They are, and will remain, the proletarian avant-garde in this struggle which we are waging against capitalism. International fascism has decided to win the battle. We must be determined not to lose it. And you workers, who listen to me behind the enemy lines, we tell you that the hour of your liberation is nearing. The libertarian militias are advancing and nothing and no one can stop them because behind them is the will of all the people. You too must take part in our work, sabotaging the fascist war industry and creating areas of resistance with guerillas in the mountainous areas. Fight, all of you who can, and as long as you have a drop of blood in you, continue the fight.

"Workers of Spain, courage! If it is written that at a certain moment we must risk our lives, let us tell ourselves, this is the hour!

"Comrades, remain optimists. May our mutual ideal be with you Forward against fascism, twin brother of capitalism! Neither one nor the other can be discussed, they must be destroyed!" [7]

Footnotes

1. José Mira, op. cit. p. 120 sq.
2. Ilya Ehrenburg, La nuit tomba, p. 188. "A historian could hardly have faith in these articles or even in this Spanish Journal. It bears the imprint of his era too deeply (...), he too was a victim of tyranny."
3. M. Koltsov, Diario de la Guerra de España, pp. 29 s. We have submitted the text of his interview to people who were there. One of them, Francisco Subirats, has reconstructed Durruti's answers to Koltsov for this biography.
4. Koltsov, op. cit. Dominique Desanti writes about this money, collected by the Russian workers for the Spanish workers, which, according to Koltsov was given to the Spanish government (Giral): "July 26 (1936) a new meeting of the Profintern in Prague: the Russian trade unions donate about a billion francs to help Spain. To give proof of it, collections are organized in all the factories. Thorez and Togliatti *will administer these funds* (our emphasis) L'International Communiste, Ed. Payot, 1970, p. 242.
5. See note 3.
6. Albert Souillon, "Combats sur l'Ebre, souvenir sur Durruti", La Montagne, April 1936. Reproduced in L'Espagne Anti-fasciste, 2nd year, number 31.
7. Solidaridad Obrera, September 13, 1936.

9

THE REVOLUTION
AT A DEAD END

DURRUTI'S SPEECH was like a bombshell, but the explosion had the opposite effect to the one intended by those who had inspired it. Using Durruti's personality, they wanted to give a violent blow "to the rearguard of the revolution!" They had hoped, by emphasizing the lack of arms at the front, to disarm the workers. This deficiency of arms was being constantly talked about by the War Committee of Barbastro and it, above all, was held responsible for the bogging down of the offensive. The Committee was saying that if the home front were contributing properly and backing up the war fronts, the war would pass through a promising stage with the fall of Saragossa. To speak of these possibilities touched Durruti at a sensitive point, because every day he was maddened to see the offensive, which had been planned against the capital of Aragon, put off until later. It was therefore logical that Durruti should emphasize this burning question of supplies, not in the manner expected by the counter-revolutionaries but quite the contrary in a positive way without leaving any doubt about the meaning of the struggle. As we have already seen, Durruti, so that he would be clearly understood, swore that "the militias were not fighting in Aragon to defend a bourgeois-democratic republic but to hasten the Revolution" and gave great weight to the problem which we have outlined. And so he appealed to the understanding of the workers, asking them to contribute some of their ammunition which was being kept for the home front.

The socialist and communist papers attacked this speech blaming "those who boycott the front, depriving it of the arms for victory." And they used such arguments as "The utopian critics are exerting themselves in the economic field" and "It is not the time to make the Revolution but to defend the Republic which was voted in at the polls on February 16, 1936."[1]

The revolutionary crisis which had been hatching since the creation of the Central Committee of Militias in Catalonia, and the turn which the Revolution had taken throughout the region, broke out publicly. None of this had occurred in Madrid. From the first days, the Government represented by the bourgeois Giral and upheld by the Socialist Party had dominated the situation. Popular pressure had barely grazed the capitalist and state structure. After surviving the first moments of panic, Giral and Azaña were assured of the support of the two Marxist parties and preparations were made to thwart the pressure which the CNT was bringing to bear in the streets although it was in the minority in Madrid.

The Government's policy towards Catalonia was hostile, although still carried out courteously! But it rejected all requests for material aid for the purchase of raw materials and machinery. [2] As it was in control of the National Treasury. Catalonia was dependent (even more, slave) to its decisions. Madrid was fully conscious of the trump cards it held, and a cold war began between it and Catalonia. In reality the revolution was facing the counter-revolution.

On September 4th Largo Caballero replaced Giral and formed a government with a socialist majority, with the participation of the communists. Caballero reserved the positions of President of the Council and Minister of War for himself. Until then he had criticized Giral for his inability to "carry on the war" but he was to practise the same kind of policy towards Catalonia, or perhaps worse than the one of his predecessor. Caballero was under the influence of Marcel Rosenberg, the Soviet Ambassador, who had arrived in Madrid on August 28. He was able to convince Caballero that the only way the Soviet Union would help Spain would be for Caballero to show the bourgeoisie of France and England that the Spaniards were not making a revolution but that they were continuing the policies of the government which had been born at the last elections.

With this in mind, it was necessary to put an end to workers' power, nationalize the war industry and respect small property owners. In addition the State must have a monopoly over foreign commerce and dissolve such organizations as the Federation of Collectives of Levant, which was selling its own products abroad. It was necessary to create a real army restoring its military ranks and dissolving the Militias. It was also necessary to reorganize a police force which would obey the State, freeing it from the influence of the Unions, who controlled it through the workers' councils, the soldiers and guards. It was also necessary to reestablish the government's authority in Catalonia and to dissolve the Central Committee of Militias.

Largo Caballero accepted the job of carrying through this program successfully, relying on the socialist and communist parties and the soviet ambassador, who, to help him with this task sent the famous Antonov-Ovseenko as consul to Barcelona. Rosenberg knew that the latter would have an influence on the Catalan revolutionaries because of his Bolshevik past and because of his simple manners, inimical to protocol and hostile to bureaucracy. This man would be able to influence many leaders, including "fanatical" anarchists. He told them that they would find sure ways of winning the war and once it was won (as it happened in Russia), the revolution would be assured. To the stupefaction of Emma Goldman, many anarchists fell into this trap. [3]

It is easy to understand that in this atmosphere Durruti's speech had a great success and that his revolutionary assurances acted as a stimulant and renewed the revolutionary fervor of the workers, making them understand the contradictions existing between the leaders and led. The former were devoting themselves to the antifascist struggle of the Popular Front while for the rest, fascism and capitalism being identical, the destruction of the first meant the death of the bourgeoisie and its system.

The first reaction came from the Defense Committees which were meeting in Barcelona and worked together to face the campaign in the communist press *(Mundo Obrero* and *Treball)*. They published a manifesto which was not submitted to the censor. It contained these words: "As long as the Revolution has not resolved the problem of political power and an armed force exists under the command of the Government and not controlled by the workers, the defense groups will not put down their arms because these guarantee the conquests of the workers." [4]

As for *Solidaridad Obrera,* it was silent about the attacks against the Defense Committees but answered the offensive against the Collectives writing "that a policy of this kind can only lead to defeat because the revolutionary enthusiasm of the working class is the only moving force of those opposing fascism. If the war is robbed of its revolutionary character, no worker would go to fight for a government such as the one which was in power before July 19."

It was during this polemic that the workers of Sabadell, near Barcelona, noticed that ammunitions from the "Karl Marx" barracks were being accumulated in the local headquarters of the PSUC. The unions, warned by Durruti's speech, sent a workers' commission to Bujaraloz to report their discovery to the War Committee of the Column. The news spread quickly among the militiamen. The committees of the Centuries decided to present an ultimatum to the Central Committee of Militias so that the latter would seize the war materials misappropriated by the PSUC.

As the climate was explosive, the War Committee of the Column informed Santillan and Ricardo Sanz, responsible members of the Central Committee of Militias. Santillan understanding the seriousness of the matter got in touch with the responsible members of the "Karl Marx" barracks, warning them of the risk they ran (because the centuries had decided to seize the arms by force) and finally eight machine guns were returned and sent to the front. [5]

It was in this climate on September 15, 1936 that Pierre Besnard, Secretary General of the International Workers Association (AIT) of which the CNT was a member, visited revolutionary Spain for the first time. Until then he had been busy with the work caused by the CNT orders for armaments in Paris at the headquarters of the International. But when he became aware of the regressive character of the revolution, he didn't limit himself to giving advice by letters which he had done until then by drawing the anarchists' attention to the National Treasure, telling them: "Don't make the same mistake made by the Communards in Paris." He decided to meet with the regional Committee of the Catalan CNT and he pointed out the necessity of internationalizing the war because, according to him, this was the only way of drawing Spain out of the "mess" where Blum's "non-intervention" had put it. [6] Besnard's plan was to bring about an uprising of the Moroccan mountaineers by rescuing Abd-el-Krim,[7] held by the French on the island of La Reunion.

In addition it was necessary to stir up a rebellion in Portugal, a power which was openly helping Franco. The very day of his arrival, he talked to Diego Abad de Santillan and García Oliver, the men most representative of the CNT and the FAI in the Central Committee of Militias. He told them that as far as Portugal was concerned, the opposition was ready to rebel and that the General Confederation of Work there had come to an agreement with the political opposition with "the proviso that they would have freedom of action again after the downfall of the dictator, Salazar." This uprising according to Besnard "could count on the support of the people and the lower ranks of the army. The responsibility for the uprising would be undertaken by a revolutionary junta, with which it was necessary to make contact immediately." Besnard placed great importance on this plan, "Portugal", because it would not only deprive Franco of an ally but it would also be possible to attack the fascists from the rear. As far as the world was concerned it would undoubtedly show the proletariat that they should pay greater attention to the Spanish Revolution. As for the Moroccan problem, Besnard based his ideas on information about the populations of the interior who were described as being ready to revolt as soon as Abd el-Krim was freed, because of the conditions in which they were living. Undisputed intelligence spoke of a spirit of rebellion among the Moors, who were being made use of unwillingly by Franco. Besnard said that "the Spanish government must make an announcement declaring the independence of the Protectorate." The Arab nationalists would welcome this resolution with enthusiasm and would collaborate closely with the Spanish Republic, making life impossible for the rearguard francoists in Morocco.

Furthermore Besnard stated that before he left Paris he had had an interview with the Secretary of the CGT, Leon Jouhaux, and other socialists who opposed Blum's policies. They had authorized him to negotiate in their name with Largo Caballero, President of both the UGT and the Council of Ministers, and to convince him to make a public declaration in favor of the Moroccans.[8]

After receiving all this information Santillan and García Oliver asked for some time to think it over and both agreed that Durruti's presence was indispensable. He had barely arrived when they took up the question of Portugal-Morocco again. But then differences broke out, Oliver maintaining that Abd el-Krim was no longer topically interesting and that discussions must continue with the Moroccan Action committee represented by El Fassi.[9] Durruti and Santillan believed the opposite. For them Abd-el-Krim's position was more radical than that of the Moroccan Action Committee and in addition the fact that the Moorish leader was a prisoner gave him greater authority in the Rif. In short their differences only concerned the choice of allies, not the basic problem and they agreed that Oliver should talk to Companys about it, to make a greater impression on Caballero. The following day, September 16, after Oliver had informed Caballero about the coming visit of Besnard, the latter went to Madrid. He arrived on September 17 at noon and presented himself at the Ministry of War. Caballero was away which they had not foreseen. Besnard then went to the National Committee of the CNT and it was arranged for Fédérica Montseñy to go with him to see Caballero. The interview took place at 5 P.M.. The socialist leader received them badly "citing a vague incident which he had just had with the CNT." Federica was very sharp in her arguments with the leader of the government, reminding him that "important subjects" should not be put off under pretext of a "vague incident". Caballero calmed down but did not agree to the interview. He set a meeting for September 18 at 4 P.M.

This interview took place an hour late. [10] This time Besnard was accompanied by David Antona, secretary of the National Committee. Their very cold reception took an uncivil turn. Without warning Caballero stated that he had not agreed to have a discussion with the secretary of the AIT and in addition "he had a horror of complications". Besnard replied sharply" that the CNT, with more members than the UGT, was a member of the AIT". This correction seemed to calm Largo Caballero but psychological conditions were not propitious for a discussion of Besnard's plan. "We broke up the meeting after a bitter-sweet conversation and we went to the CNT headquarters where the National Committee was told about the incident, which they noted without reacting. Then I decided to remind Caballero of his responsibilities in a letter which *C.N.T.* was to publish a few days later by agreement with the National Committee." [11]

Besnard didn't want to return to France without reporting to Garćia Oliver orally about the painful incidents which had just occurred and which had ruined the interview on which they had based such great hopes. After seeing Oliver and already on his way to France this is what Besnard reported: "The Revolution is going backwards and it isn't the fault of the masses who are fighting with unequaled enthusiasm, but of the leaders who are being towed along by events, giving proof that they have lost the revolutionary initiative and have accepted humiliating situations such as the one in which I found myself when facing Caballero.

"If anarchism was stupid enough to collaborate with Caballero or even simply to support him, the Revolution would be hopelessly lost. The only means of getting out of this hellish circle is by using force. But I ask myself if the leaders of the CNT are the same men as those of July 19. The only one who seems to me to escape from this role is Durruti, original revolutionary type, who in many ways reminds me of the guerilla fighter Nestor Makhno. Like him he works with the people and doesn't separate himself from them as the other leaders do." In many respects Besnard considered Durruti "as superior"... "to the Ukrainian" especially in the mastery that Durruti has over himself. [12]

Besnard had scarcely had time to exchange impressions with Durruti before leaving for France, because the latter had been recalled suddenly to the Aragonese front where the fascists had launched an offensive in his sector. Durruti had insisted on one point; that Besnard should find some arms dealers able to furnish enough military supplies to equip the column with the necessary means to launch an attack on Saragossa even if they were alone. Durruti had barely arrived at Bujaraloz when he realized that the whole sector from Farlete to "Suelta Alta" was under a strong attack by the enemy forces under Colonel Urrutia[13] supported by the "Aragonese mobile column" made up of legionnaires and "requetes".

While the enemy was bringing pressure on Farlete it was bombing the road to Pina de Ebro to keep reinforcements from being sent in. The situation was really critical. The "International Group" was resisting furiously but they lacked arms. All reports coming to General Headquarters were unfortunately the same: positions were being lost since there was scarcely anyone to defend them. The Military Council advised that other sectors be dismantled to come to the aid of the one which was menaced. Durruti was opposed to this plan, arguing that this would play into the hands of the enemy and that the latter would launch a general attack if it discovered the weakening of sectors not already attacked. He improvised a relief detachment made up of militiamen who were resting or being used in the fields and he led them towards Farlete. He crossed the road to Pina and arrived at Farlete just as a general retreat was beginning. But seeing the reinforcements the courage of the "Internationals" revived and they returned to their positions. The struggle was harsh and sometimes it was necessary to fight hand to hand. But in the end the militias were successful, regaining the lost terrain and going even farther to hold new positions at "Petrusques" and at "la Casa de los Llanos".[14] The front had scarcely been restored when the enemy began a general offensive, which showed that Durruti had not fallen into the trap laid by Urrutia.

Footnotes

1. See the anarchist, communist and socialist press of the period.
2. D.A. Santillan, *op. cit*. He tells about the difficulties made by Madrid so as to refuse aid to Catalonia, aid needed for setting up a war industry. Madrid went so far as to refuse credits. This conflict was already evident at the first contact in August between the Central Committee of Militias, the representatives of the Generalitat and the Government of Giral, and later with the government of Largo Caballero.
3. Rudolf Rocker, *op. cit*.
4. The author vouches for the truth of this occurrence. The Defense Committee of the Gracia district (Barcelona) took the lead with this point of view.
5. See Santillan, *op. cit.*, and *El Frente*, bulletin of the "Durruti Column". Also testimony of the militiaman Cosme de Paules.
6. Largo Caballero wrote later about "non-intervention" in *Mis Recuerdos*, p. 198.
   "Such an idea could not have been conceived except by a timid and weak mind like Leon Blum's. It was gratefully accepted by the German and Italian governments who furnished troops and war supplies to the traitors. It was also accepted by Russia, although with more generous intentions, at least apparently (....) What did Blum fear? A European conflagration? Blum experienced what happens to a blindman skirting an abyss, who falls in. Blum didn't see what the lowliest unlettered peasant saw clearly." (....)
   "Actual result of 'non-intervention': it lessened the Republic's facilities to arm for its own defense. It was weakened to such an extent that the traitors were sure to win.
   "I don't know if I am cherishing an illusion, hoping that one day those who were responsible for such a felony will have to give an account of their conduct to the French people, to the socialists and Spanish republicans and to the Socialist International. If this doesn't happen, we must then recognize that International Solidarity between Socialist Parties and workers' organizations is only an empty slogan destined to fool the workers. Because of their enormity, certain political errors are unpardonable."
7. Abd el-Krim, the Arab "Caudillo", who carried on the war against France and Spain was captured May 27, 1926, and was taken on August 21 to the Island of Reunion as a prisoner of France. He had been promised a short exile but actually it lasted 20 years. This made him say "that if he had known his fate he would have preferred to die fighting." And he added: "In Islam a war is being hatched which will break out as in the glorious time of the Almoravides." *Les Cahiers de l'Histoire*, No. 33, January 1964, Paris.
8. An account given by Pierre Besnard to the VII Congress of the AIT in Paris in 1937.
9. Since July 25 the CNT was preparing, with certain Moroccan groups an insurrection in Spanish Morocco. This is one of the most secret chapters of the Spanish war. We can't give a broad exposition of this question here, but we will do it in a book we are preparing on the Central Committee of Militias of Catalonia.
10. The delay and the "violent disagreement" which Pierre Besnard speaks about is understood better when one knows how Largo Caballero was spending his time on that day. The "disagreement" refers to the fact that the CNT refused to agree to the transfer of the Government to Valencia. César M. Lorenzo writes about this question in *Les anarchistes espagnols et le pouvoir*, p. 229, note 11: "The public knew nothing about what was going on during this meeting behind closed doors. The press could only say that it was taking place (...)". On September 18 Largo Caballero received Horacio M. Prieto, secretary of the CNT (Horacio was expressing his opposition to the removal of the Government). Then Largo Caballero received the Soviet ambassador, Marcel Rosenberg. Between these meetings the Caballero-Besnard interview took place.
11. The text of the letter is found in Pierre Besnard's report. N.B. — We have tried to limit ourselves to the subject but it is the very personality of Durruti which overflows. We must therefore describe the events which were taking place when Pierre Besnard arrived in Madrid. Since September 15 the CNT had been holding a National Plenum of its Regional groups. It was trying to find a way to adapt itself politically to the new situation created by the revolution. Two positions were possible. Horacio Prieto, secretary general of the CNT was a partisan of the first position which might be called "interventionist" and he was in favor of complete participation by entering into the government, headed by Largo Caballero since September.
   The other position, taken by the Catalan delegation, advocated staying out of the government and proposed that a pact be made with the UGT so that the two workers' organizations would form a National Defense Junta, which would assume all the functions held by the Madrid government but as a workers' government.
   Largo Caballero, secretary general of the UGT, rejected the CNT proposal and suggested that the latter enter the central government. The Plenum found itself in an impasse. Finally it was agreed to back up the idea of the National Defense Council. But a certain freedom was granted to the National Committee to act according to the demands of the moment. In reality this freedom meant carte blanche for Horacio M. Prieto to carry out his negotiations with Largo Caballero. It was to end with the CNT entering the government.
   For all this period one can read the books already mentioned by César M. Lorenzo and by Perrats. The latter's book was reissued in 1971 by Editions Ruedo Iberico in Paris.
12. Report by Pierre Besnard.
13. At this time and later the rumor went around that the brother of Durruti was commanding troops in the fascist camp. It was even rumored that he was Colonel Urrutia. This was just one more legend among many about Durruti. The truth is that his brother, Pedro, seems to have had relations with the Falange before the war. But this Pedro was shot in August 1936 in Leon, accused of taking part in a group which had made an attempt on the life of General Franco.
14. José Mira, *op. cit*.

10

LIBERTARIAN ARAGON

IN BARCELONA they were talking about getting rid of the Central Committee of Militias. As the creation of this organization had been a victory for the workers, its dissolution and the integration of the CNT into the government of the Generalitat marked a definite setback for the revolution.[1] But while the CNT and the FAI were yielding in Catalonia, in Aragon the revolutionary line was being radicalized with the formation of a Defense Council set up solely by anarchists.

From then on the militant anarchists in Barcelona watched carefully the work being carried out in the Aragonese sector where, despite the war, it had been decided to convene a regional Assembly of the Collectives on September 16th at Bujaraloz. [2] Durruti had steadily insisted on the need to create a regional Federation which would cover all the complex problems which were arising in Aragon. From the beginning he had backed up all the spontaneous actions of the peasantry and had defended them publicly, giving whatever material help the column could provide.

A number of times he even had to protect the peasant collectives from Stalinist oriented militiamen.[3] Complaints multiplied. In one village these forces were destroying the collective, dissolving the local council which the peasants had chosen at a public assembly. In another there was a raid on the shops, and tractors were stolen. It was urgent in this jungle where armed men had the upper hand that the collectivists should create a body capable of resisting these abuses. Durruti remembered Makhno's experience in the Ukraine. Besides every day he was convinced more than ever that collaboration with the other political organizations could only bring negative results. In fact this alliance was leading to counter-revolutionary measures which were originating on the home front.

The situation in Aragon satisfied all the natural requirements needed to create a revolutionary avant-garde. A collectivist tradition existed among the people which had been strengthened by anarchist ideology. There was practically no political force confronting the anarchists. [4] And so a libertarian experiment was possible here and such a venture naturally captivated audacious and creative temperaments like Durruti's. Furthermore the peasants were themselves inventing this libertarian society; putting together their lands which were scattered or expropriating the "caciques", they had formed collectives. There was a need to make plans and to develop ideas for solidarity. This was the work proposed to the Assembly at Bujaraloz on September 16, 1936. All the tendencies were represented there, all the collectives which had been formed in Aragon as well as all the regional bodies of the CNT and the representatives of the confederal columns. The assembly analyzed the complex situation created by the war. Three forces were pitted against each other: the Aragonese peasants who wanted to build a better world for themselves, the party militias who acted as though they were in conquered territory and finally the Generalitat with its "colonial" policy towards Aragon.[5]

In view of this situation it was proposed that a Federation of Aragonese Collectives be formed, which would be represented regionally by the Defense Council of Aragon. It was a question of defending an economy menaced by the war and to work out a development plan which would give the inhabitants stabler life conditions. The Aragonese agreed to take care of the 20,000 militia who were in their region. In addition it was decided to fight against the expansionist policy of the Catalonian Generalitat and against similar possible attempts by the Madrid government. All these objectives fell in perfectly with the plan outlined by the national Plenum of the CNT of September 15, which had proposed to set up regional councils to form one National Council of Defense.

Durruti, representing the 6,000 militiamen who were defending the sector, fully supported the creation of this organization. Antonio Ortiz, delegate of the column "Sud-Ebre" opposed it and Gregorio Jover, delegate from the Huesca zone, pointed out that the creation of a Council of Aragon would provoke serious difficulties with the Generalitat. But according to Durruti, the workers of Catalonia would make common cause with the Aragonese. And "in any case the Aragonese peasants ordered their own lives and were free to organize as they thought best. If they wanted collectivism, they should practise it and defend it with arms."[6]

This is how the Defense Council of Aragon was born at the historical Assembly of Bujaraloz. It was to exist as a secret organization until December 1936, very much criticized by the National Committee of the CNT, opposed by the Catalan Government, attacked by the government of Largo Caballero, maligned by the Communist Party but admired and supported by the Spanish working class.[7]

But if the war and the revolution were going hand in hand in Aragon it was quite different in the rest of the country. In the North things were getting worse. Although Irun had fallen into the hands of the fascists, San Sebastian was resisting. But the Basque government abandoned the capital of Guipuzcoa, fearing that the CNT would create a new Numancia[8] defending it and thus increasing their prestige.[9]

The Asturias were defending themselves but they were prisoners of the pincer movement which was closing in on them and their struggle was hopeless. At the same time in Andalusia the struggle was confused. In Malaga finally, the anarchists had the upper hand, but because of this the new government of Largo Caballero, copying

264

August 1936 — Durruti visiting the fortifications of a position at the Aragon Front.

its predecessor the government of Giral, refused it all aid and drove it to a terrible end. Only the Levant and Catalonia were going ahead. In Catalonia the revolution was developing but those at the top did their best to check the social victories of the rank and file. In Madrid where the popular resistance was enthusiastic, the CNT and the UGT unions seemed to be going ahead together to accomplish the common task which had been started in certain areas.

It was the unions which continued to arm and supply the Militia Columns which were fighting in the Guadarrama, at Toledo, at Guadalajara and were marching towards the mountains of Teruel and across La Mancha towards Cordoba. But here the military situation was more serious than on the other fronts, because arms, munitions, planes and tanks were lacking. Little by little Madrid was being encircled.

From the beginning the Spanish Communist party, led by Codovila, Togliatti and other itinerant secret agents of the Kremlin were making every effort to destroy the revolution. A Moscow agent, Contreras, had set up El Quinto Regimento (the Fifth Regiment), offering it as a nucleus or school for the future republican army. It brought together a number of professional military men who had remained loyal to the Republic because they had not been able to take sides with Franco. Many were ambitious and eager to be promoted. The Fifth Regiment, which had nothing revolutionary about it, undertook a radical militarization, lining up its troops to

265

Maria Ascaso, sister of Francisco visiting the Column in Aragon.

parade to the sound of music, saluting its superiors with clicking heels.

The anarchists, in order to organize their defense, set up a Confederal Defense Committee led by a waiter, Eduardo Val, which functioned as a General Staff and supplied armaments, munitions and all quartermaster's supplies for the Militia of the CNT.

As for the socialists, although they were stronger, they were divided into two rival tendencies. Largo Caballero led one and Indalecio Prieto the other. The Communist Party cleverly profited by this schism. They praised Caballero as the popular leader capable of pulling the State out of the abyss where it had been thrown by the action of the people on July 19. At the same time it exploited Prieto's vanity. In the end the communists just about succeeded in controlling the socialist party completely. Behind the scenes two people were pulling the strings: Michel Koltsov, the Pravda correspondant, and Marcel Rosenberg, ambassador of the USSR. Both were controlled by the GPU, whose supreme leader in Spain was Orlov. The latter had arrived in Madrid with strict orders: war on Trotskyism and anarchism and an extension of the Moscow purges, whose first victims had been Kamenev and 14 "Old Guard" bolsheviks.

Moscow's agents had convinced Largo Caballero of the following: if the democrats abandon the Spanish Republic, it is because it is adrift and in the hands of people who neither respect foreign institutions nor property. Russia promised to become the first to provide arms if order were reestablished, if an army was created which would be able to beat the rebels, and if the State controlled all the social life and production. In addition the democrats would add their aid to that of the USSR. Such arguments had caused the CNT in Catalonia to yield. Advised by the Consul of the USSR, Antonov Ovseenko, who had been an intimate friend of those who had been shot in Moscow, the CNT had dissolved the Central Committee of Militias and had joined the government of the Generalitat. The same black-mail had made Largo Caballero give in, when as Minister of War he saw the rebels advancing with giant steps towards Madrid.

After Toledo was taken, Largo Caballero was head of a government with a socialist majority, one of whose members was Dr. Negrin, Minister of Finance, who was in control of the national treasure. The war was being lost for lack of arms. Well, arms are bought with gold and great quantities of gold existed in the State reserves. Why not use it? And why did Largo Caballero hesitate? The Soviets had promised him arms but nothing came and the rebels were advancing. [10]

It was then in September 1936 that Durruti was called urgently to Barcelona. [11]

Footnotes

1. Diego Abad de Santillan explains the breaking up of the Central Committee of Militias in the following way: "We were constantly told in answer to our pleas to the Central Government (both Giral's and Largo Caballero's) that they wouldn't help us as long as the power of the Central Committee of Militias was so evident. The same pressure was brought to bear by Ovseenko, Russian Consul in Barcelona. We therefore had to decide to dissolve it, that is to say to abandon a revolutionary position. All this in order to obtain arms and necessary financial aid to carry on the war successfully."
   Por qué perdimos la guerra, p. 115. *La Revolución y la guerra en España,* p. 91. We also use the letters which Santillan wrote us about the dissolution.

2. Alardo Prats, *Vanguardia y Retaguardia en Aragon,* Barcelona, 1937.

3. César M. Lorenzo, *op. cit.,* p. 146, gives information about the activities of the militia Columns in Aragon and about their relationship with the collectives.

4. The political parties had no roots in Aragon and limited their activities to small circles led by some personalities. Traces of historical republicanism were only to be found in recollections about Joaquin Costa, whose collectivist ideas were closest to socialist ones.
   The Communist Party didn't exist, and only the UGT enjoyed a certain influence in Saragossa. See Pierre Broué and Emile Témime, *op. cit.,* p. 120.

5. Horacio M. Prieto, *Posibilismo Libertario,* published at the author's expense, Paris 1967. On page 80 he writes about political relations between the Generalitat of Catalonia and Aragon and considers them "colonialist in character".

6. Report made to the author by a witness, Cosme de Paules, militiaman in the Durruti column, who lives in Chile today and who was present at the Assembly.

7. For the Council of Aragon, see the works of José Peirats, Santillan and César M. Lorenzo.

8. Numancia, a second century Castillan village which was destroyed by its inhabitants rather than surrender to the Romans.

9. César M. Lorenzo, *op. cit.* p. 162.

10. On Stalinist intervention in Spain see Dominique Desanti, *L'Internationale Communiste,* Jesus Hernandez, *La grande Trahison,* Jose Peirats, *op. cit.,* W.G. Krivitsky, *La mano de Stalin sobre España.*

11. José Mira, *op. cit.,* wrote: "The War Committee of the Column decided to send Durruti to Madrid to negotiate with Largo Caballero about an important problem."

11

BETWEEN MOSCOW AND BARCELONA

DURING THE NIGHT of September 28, Durruti arrived in Barcelona. His comrades Santillan and García Oliver received him optimistically. Pierre Besnard had informed them that he had made contact with some big arms manufacturers who were ready to supply the Republican Government with enough war material to change the balance between the fascists and antifascists. The news, which they awaited for such a long time, was good and finally there would be enough arms to attack Saragossa successfully. But both Santillan and Garcia Oliver pointed out that they must not waste this occasion. Up until now all their approaches to the Government, either with Giral or with Largo Caballero, had failed. They had received promises which the Government had never honored and the Aragon front remained unarmed, and the Catalan metallurgical industry partially paralyzed for lack of raw materials or machines.[1]

No, this time it was necessary to risk everything. That was why they thought of sending Durruti with Besnard on this mission. Durruti's name not only had great weight with the public but in addition he was a fighter on the Aragon front. With these qualifications, Caballero would be forced to act differently. Durruti was not as optimistic as his friends. He hadn't lost contact with the people and his ideas about politicians were always the same. "You have confidence in politicians and that is understandable, because being with them so much you have become like them and you still believe in their promises. There is only one way to deal with them and that is the vigorous line of conduct which we have always used. We must publicly denounce the situation in which we find ourselves. As the revolution and the war are bound together, they have both become the business of the people and it is up to them to demand the use of the gold. Better yet, it is the people, truly interested in the struggle, who should administer the treasury. This is the way we have always acted and thanks to our technique we have earned the following of the working class. In my opinion the health of the revolution depends on this principle: return to the people, it is for them to solve the question."[2]

But Durruti's friends didn't share his views. His old-time comrades had changed and this realization filled him with bitterness. How long could he hold out? As they had to wait for Besnard's

Scenes from the daily life of anarchist militia.

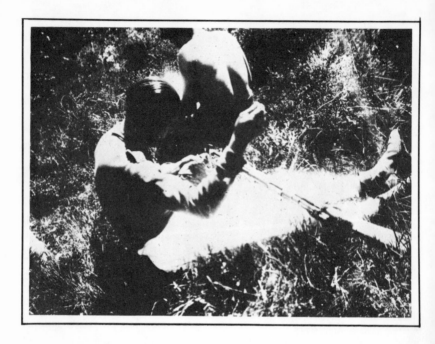

arrival from France, Durruti took advantage of this time to discuss the Aragon front. Things were not going well there, specially in the War Committee of Barbastro, made up of all the delegates of the Columns and the military professionals. The Central Committee of Militias had placed General Villalba at the head of it, a republican certainly but a bourgeois.

He didn't approve of the militia type of organization and continually advocated a return to the old army set-up. According to him, all the difficulties at the front came from this organization which was not fitted to the needs of the war. Durruti was a keen partisan of the militias and became angry when he heard talk about the efficiency of an army disciplined and ruled by the military code. So the confrontation between him and Villalba was almost permanent. It was enough for Durruti to express an opinion for Villalba to reject is as impractical, such were their differences of opinion about the tactics to be used. Villalba insisted on a frontal attack of Huesca and Belchite. Durruti advocated abandoning the frontal attack, concentrating all the forces in two sectors, one to attack via Almudevar cutting the road between Saragossa and Huesca and the same tactic to be used at Belchite. He believed that they should drive in the direction of Catalayud and in the North as far as Navarre and in the East towards Logroño, cutting contact with Saragossa. Villalba considered this plan impossible because of the insufficiency of material. He believed that the frontal attacks must continue. Durruti didn't give up his position but found himself alone in defending it. The other delegates, even Ortiz and Jover agreed with Villalba. "We must oust Villalba, send him to the devil" Durruti cried out to

García Oliver. The latter was responsible at this time to the War Department of the Central Committee, [3] but he was just as powerless as Durruti.

The CNT had already given its approval to Companys for the dissolution of the Central Committee of Militias. The latter had practically disappeared despite the presence of the four CNT *councillors*. and the Council of the Generalitat had regained its former strength as the government of Catalonia. "I opposed the dissolution of the Committee but the Regional Committee, basing itself on the agreement of the plenum, went ahead without even consulting us. I am afraid we are moving towards a confrontation between the militants of the CNT and FAI and the ruling organizations", García Oliver confided to Durruti. [4] What could be done in this situation? Even Santillan, who had been an unflagging partisan of democratic collaboration already began to regret that he had defended this position on July 20th. The facts were plain, the CNT and the FAI had not only lost their positions but also within their ranks a division was beginning to take form among its militants, some were partisans of continuing the democratic collaboration and others partisan of a show of strength. How to get out of this vicious circle? No one in Caballero's government wanted to win the war, at least not right away. That was made clear by its policy towards the negotiations initiated between the Committee of Militias and the Morrocan Action Committee. Caballero didn't want to declare the independence of Spanish Morroco publicly. It was said that Leon Blum, another socialist and French Chief of State, had brought pressure to bear on him.

It was after considering all these things that the fantastic plan for an attack on the Bank of Spain was worked out. The people thought that if they were in control of the treasury that the situation would change in their favor. The decision was taken by agreement between García Oliver, Santillan and Durruti. Santillan counted on the "Tierra y Libertad" column made up of anarchists fighting on the Madrid front. It would be this troop of three thousand men who would break into the bank. It was agreed that Santillan and Durruti would leave that same night for Madrid to organize this armed attack. Santillan was to travel officially but Durruti was to go on his own so as to remain incognito. He left his friends at night to go to the aviation field of Prat de Llobregat. There nobody would take him on their plane, but Andre Malraux leaving unexpectedly for Madrid, offered Durruti a seat in his plane. Malraux never knew that his being there might perhaps have changed the face of the world... [5]

Durruti, who had always lived illegally for twenty years, was able to adapt himself quickly to the underground. When he arrived in Madrid, he lost himself in the crowd, to go and take refuge in a house at Cuatro Caminos where Santillan was waiting for him. Everything needed had been arranged and they knew they would have to use force. The three thousand men of "Tierra y Libertad" had already been posted on guard. The Railwaymen's Union had been alerted and had prepared a special train to carry the "war material" to Barcelona. But it was necessary to proceed with caution. This was the watchword given to all the participants in this fantastic project. Only five or six people knew what was going to happen. If the plan was carried out successfully it would only take a short time. "Before the government could take action the special trains would have left for Barcelona with an escort of three thousand armed men, with orders to defend the shipment to the "last drop of blood".[6] It was during the night of the 1st to the 2nd of October that the plan was to be carried out.

When the moment came to act, the man responsable for the plan (Santillan) didn't dare take the decision. Because of his scruples, he told the members of the national Committee of the CNT about the plan at the last moment. They were appalled by the disclosure. "The principle argument used to dissuade us was that its success would provoke an antagonism between Catalonia and Madrid which would reach the proportions of a civil war. They wanted to stop everything before the government found out about the project." Here Santillan comments: "Once the plan was disclosed it became impossible".[7] His scruples put an end to the only act which might have saved the revolution. Durruti could never pardon this step which had been taken without consulting him. Full of anger, Santillan understood his blunder. Durruti recalled bitterly that in the past the former had already made similar blunders and that if as a theoretician he had a certain value, as a man of action he had none.....

On the morning of October 2nd, Besnard arrived in Madrid with two representatives of the consortium. Durruti got in touch with Besnard and they had a meeting with Caballero. The conversation lasted barely a quarter of an hour. During this time Durruti told the President of the Council of Ministers the reason for their visit. Durruti made an energetic presentation and after Largo Caballero had hesitated a moment, he decided to present the question that afternoon to the Council of Ministers. The latter quickly agreed to buy war materials amounting to 800 million pesetas in gold. Durruti was surprised at the change in Largo Caballero when he met with him to decide on the last details. Caballero received him affably and told him that after thinking it over he had decided to double the amount to 1,600 million pesetas in gold. Durruti answered that at last the Militias would be able to fight the war seriously. They studied how the arms and planes would be used and it was agreed that a third of the material would remain in Catalonia to support the Aragon front and the Catalonian war industry.

Besnard concluded by saying that "the chief of Staff and Caballero were to give the necessary instructions to the Ambassador in Paris to carry out the deal quickly. The latters plan was definitely settled with the dealers on October 3, 1936 at the Admiralty in the presence of Durruti himself."[8] In the afternoon Durruti visited the CNT Committee of Defense in Madrid and brought its secretary, Eduardo Val, up to date on the matter discussed with the government. After leaving the Committee of Defense, a few friends, among them the correspondant of the confederal press, Ariel, and Mauro Bajatierra, dined together.

The following day Mauro Bajatierra's interview with Durruti appeared in *CNT* of Madrid. The correspondant started his story with these words: "Durruti is a guerillero, he is nothing like Pancho Villa but rather resembles Emiliano Zapata. The former, a Mexican Adventurer, fought for the pleasure of fighting without knowing why he did it. He had no revolutionary program. Zapata fought because he wanted to change the life of the Mexican peasants. Durruti is an anarchist with clear ideas and a strong revolutionary ardor, whose fight is unremitting. For Durruti the impetous of the revolution is towards a better life as one can see from the following answers to our questions:

'What are your ideas about the military situation in Central Spain?

'It is clear that the enemy is preparing a frontal attack against Madrid. This doesn't mean that its general situation has improved in Spain. What it is trying for is a spectacular action which will be a major political event. It is obvious that the fall of Madrid would be a moral defeat for all of us, but it wouldn't mean that the war was lost.

'To alleviate the pressure which the enemy is exerting on Madrid, we are increasing our activities daily on the fronts in Aragon and the Levant. The strongholds of the enemy, Huesca, Saragossa and Teruel, will fall when the militia have enough arms to attack. When this happens the fascists will have lost the war. Strategically these places are of major importance. When we enter Saragossa the front will collapse from Catalayud to Burgos, the encirclement of Siguenza will be broken and the offensive against the Sierra will collapse.

'Under these conditions the enemy would be stupid not to attack and try to conquer Madrid. But fascism will not enter Madrid, it will break its teeth on this offensive. The people of Madrid will make a fortress of their city. Now you must realize that the columns which attack Madrid will launch tons of bombs, tens of thousands of men equipped with modern weapons against the capital. It is not possible to resist such an avalanche with sacks of earth and barricades. We must start right now to fortify the city seriously. Here in the rear there are a great number of profiteers who are moving around quietly. All these people must be put to work and armed with picks and shovels. A war economy must be set up, gasoline waste must be stopped, we must put an end to the use of cars by ladies and officials.

'On the Aragon front the militias have understood that good fortifications are as important as courage. The life of a militiaman depends on fortifications. We are not fighting to loose our lives. We are fighting for life. The Aragonese militiaman fights instinctively to survive. He repels the enemy attack without leaving the place where he is. This is possible because as soon as he occupies the ground he makes a hole and after that a fortification is created.

'If Madrid wants to be saved, it must start by raising a curtain of breastworks and barbed wire. One must realize that the enemy is already at the gates of the city. To speak in these terms is not to demoralize the people, only lies are demoralizing. One must speak firmly and energetically to the people of Madrid and tell them that they must depend on themselves for safety. In all those areas where people are conscious of the danger they are running and also conscious that their security depends on themselves, they are always victorious. It is when they are fooled that they are defeated.

273

'— And your column, how is it going?

'— The main strength of the column lies in its understanding of the meaning of the struggle. The militiamen know why they are fighting. They feel that they are revolutionaries and they are not fighting with phrases and hollow words. They are not expecting laws and decrees from the revolution, but they know that with victory they will own the land, the factories, the shops, the means of transportation. They are fighting for all that.

'Today circumstances make it important for us to speak clearly so that no one will have illusions. Double talk must be left to the politicians and the diplomats. We are revolutionaries and we declare that we are fighting for the revolution. This obliges us to say that we, on the Aragon front, are making war and revolution at the same time. One is inseparable from the other. If we separate them, we would kill both of them because we would lose the war which cannot be won without enthusiasm. We would also lose the revolution which cannot exist except through a constant revolutionary practice. In every village which we have conquered the inhabitants organize their lives like a community of free men. For us there is no other strategy. The smallest village has a great value for us because workers are living in it who have the right to carry out the idea for which they have fought all their lives. This is the best part of our fight.

'Sometimes, when I am alone, I think about what we are doing. I realize then the responsability of our Column. A defeat, a retreat, would be something frightful for us, in no way comparable to those in another army. The inhabitants, absolutely all of them, would stand by us because from the front all the way to Barcelona there are nothing but fighters. Everyone is working for the war-revolution.'

'— What do you think of what has been called the 'necessity for discipline'?'

'— Discipline? I am glad you asked that question. We have talked about it a lot. For me, discipline is nothing more than respect and personal responsibility for the other. I am for this discipline and would never be for the discipline of the Barracks. The first makes for free and responsible men. The second only creates automatons, that is to say brutishness.

'Having said that, I must add to avoid ambiguities that I reject as irresponsible liberty misunderstood and used by cowards to avoid responsibility. The CNT's conduct depends on this self discipline which I have spoken about. We have accepted responsibility freely. This pledge must be fulfilled. In the same way, the comrades who have put their trust in someone whom they have freely chosen to carry out a job, must give him all their support to carry it out. During the fighting the delegates have a function and their instructions must be followed, otherwise it would be impossible to carry out an operation successfully. Once danger has passed, if the people don't agree with the delegates, it's the Assembly who judges their behavior and which studies the question of replacing them. This applies not only to the delegate of the Century but also to the general delegate, in the present case, me.

'Frankly, I am satisfied with the comrades who follow me and I suppose they are also satisfied with me? What time is it? One

274

o'clock in the morning! Now behind their earthworks, the Militiamen of the Aragonese front must dig trenches with the greatest enthusiasm.... They don't know I am here.' He stood up briskly and smiling placed his rough proletarian hand on our shoulder saying: 'Comrades, we will win the war and the revolution." [9]

After the interview Durruti went to the hotel on the Gran Via to rest for a few hours because he had to return to Barcelona on the morning of October 4. At 3 in the morning, Marcel Rosenberg, USSR Ambassador in Madrid, telephoned to the hotel asking Durruti to come to the Embassy immediately to have a talk with him. Durruti discussed the question with Besnard. After this discussion, feeling that he had nothing to say to Mr. Rosenberg, he declined the invitation. [10]

The next morning the press commented on Durruti's visit to Madrid: "Did Durruti come to resolve important questions about the war?" And *CNT* wrote: "When we can report openly, the Spanish people will understand the importance of this trip." [11]

Footnotes

1. Diego Abad de Santillan, *op. cit.*, p. 111.
2. Letter from Gregorio Jover written to the author.
3. José Mira, in the *op. cit.* says this is when Perez Farras resigned: "Considering that my presence in the Column is not necessary, I offer my resignation." With his resignation the quarrel between Durruti and Perez Farras about military discipline ended, a quarrel which started when they left Barcelona.
4. Testimony of Marcos Alcon to the author.
5. Detail reported to the author by André Malraux.
6. Diego Abad de Santillan, *op. cit.*, p. 113.
7. Idem.
8. Pierre Besnard, report already quoted.
9. *CNT*, Madrid, October 6, 1936.
10. Pierre Besnard, report already quoted.
11. *CNT*, October 6, 1936.

12

THE SHADOW OF STALIN OVER SPAIN

DURRUTI HAD ONLY just arrived from Madrid when he had to deal with the fascist offensive against the positions being defended by the "International Group" at Perdiguera. The enemy's plan was to seize this area and threaten the "Los Monegros" sector defended by the Column. This was not only a strategic position but from an economic point of view it was also considered the granary of Aragon. These two reasons were enough for the Column to cling to the area. The determining factor in the resistance was courage, but there are limits and even steel nerves can give. Courage was not enough, adequate arms and cartridges for the guns were needed. But there was a shortage of arms, the machine guns were antiquities, the armored cars were those which had come from Barcelona in the first days of the war. There was a scarcity of planes and hardly enough shells for one day's action. Courage was the only thing which was abundant. And it was bringing death rather than surrender to the "International Group" defending itself at Perdiguera.

Durruti was able to bring together enough troops to relieve the threatened positions. The "Internationals" found themselves almost encircled. The fight was hand to hand from trench to trench. Reinforcements changed the outcome of the battle. The enemy had to retreat and Durruti was able to break the circle around the "Internationals" and free two armored cars. In the first car, "King Kong", Bonilla, the only survivor, was still shooting at the Moors who were howling around the motor as though possessed. In the second, everyone was dead.

The counter offensive brought excellent results. Two kilometers were gained and machine-guns, guns and a good supply of munitions for guns (made in Germany) were picked up. But the loot didn't make up for the losses. Without counting the Spanish militiamen, many brave men from the ranks of the "Internationals" had fallen. Among these were Berthomieu, the delegate of the group, and Emile Cottin, world famous for his attack against "the Tiger", Clemenceau, as well as Biudeaux and Giral. Four nurses who had been taken prisoner were as good as dead: Georgette, militant of the *Revue Anarchiste,* Gertrude, a young German woman of the POUM who liked to fight with the anarchists, and two young girls whose names haven't been recorded in the war chronicles. Durruti was very close to all of them, specially to Berthomieu, whom he had known during his exile in France and he was deeply moved by these deaths. The death of Georgette, who was a sort of Mascot of the Column, filled the militiamen with rage, particularly the "Sons of Night". She had carried out many surprise attacks on the enemy rear-guard with the latter. They vowed to avenge her and during a number of nights made fierce attacks against the Francoists.

When the sector had quieted down, Durruti returned to Venta Monzona where bad news awaited him. Besnard told him that Caballero had broken their agreement. [1] This was the last straw for Durruti, who cursed Santillan for having ruined everything with his scruples and cursed himself for having believed in the word of Caballero. But this was not the only bad news, with it came the decree for "militarization", which restored the military ranks as well as the old Military Code, until a new one could be drafted. A number of the men who had been the first to join the Column came to take leave of Durruti, telling him that they didn't want to submit to the "dictates" of the Government. What could Durruti say? Submit? Stay there? He said nothing. For the first time he broke down, realizing that they were marching towards a precipice and that nothing could prevent their downfall. And yet Saragossa was only a few kilometers away. Must he give up? He had never abandoned any of his projects! How he missed the presence of Ascaso beside him! Everything appeared to be different. The war seemed to have changed the mentality of the people from top to bottom. That night Durruti didn't sleep at General Headquarters but went to the outposts and joined the "Sons of the Night" who were carrying out a "commando" operation. They were able to reach the very center of Saragossa and bring back with them a group of militants who had been hidden from the rebels since the city had been taken.

The "militarization" decree was the first victory won by the Russians. The latter were pursuing and imposing their policies. Caballero was in their hands, all the more so since the decree was passed on the same day that the gold reserves of the Bank of Spain left for Odessa. The Bank of Spain was selling its future, yielding to Stalin's policy. But the Spanish people didn't know at this time that various usurers had locked the liberty of Spain in their banks.

The influence of a Russia, which promised to supply arms, increased the strength of the Communist Party. At one shot it became master of the situation. Until this point its leaders had only attacked the Trotskyists and anarchists verbally but now the decree permitted it to act, and even more. The militiamen had fought for the Revolution without thinking of the interests of the Party, but the Party was only fighting for itself. While the common soldiers were falling on the battlefield, the Communist Party, ordered by the Stalinist agent, Carlos Contreras, had created a "hotbed" for party cadres. The "Fifth Regiment" was nothing more than the "oven" where the "pastry" of the future leaders of the Popular Army was "cooking". The military professionals whom the militiamen had only tolerated as technicians, headed for the "Fifth Regiment". They were looking for a shelter at the center of the Communist Party which was coming forward as the representative of order, bourgeois ob-

277

viously. The "Fifth Regiment" also attracted a good number of the intellectuals, functionaries and bureaucrats of the bourgeois regime. The Communist Party by increasing its strength, was taking on the look of a middle class party, a party which numbered barely ten percent of poor peasants and city workers combined.

The Russians imposed their policies not only in the military but also in the political field in order to "settle accounts" with their most hated enemies, the anarchists and Trotskyists. As the former were tough nuts to crack, because of their numerical strength, the Trotskyists were the first victims. The old Bolshevik, Antonov-Ovseenko, who was soon to pay with his life for his loyalty to Stalin, presented the latter's ultimatum to Companys, already acknowledged without question as President of the Generalitat. He must get rid of Andres Nin as a political personality and fire him from the position he held for his party in the Council of the Generalitat. Companys got rid of his Councillor of Justice, but to avoid a confrontation with the CNT, a political crisis was used as a smokescreen. And the PSUC did everything possible to treat Nin and his comrades like fascist agents....

At the front the militiamen resisted the "militarization". The first to cry out in alarm were the defenders of the Huesca front, who made a public protest: "If we strip the war of all its revolutionary faith, of all its ideas for social transformation, of its direction towards a universal struggle, then it is no more than a vulgar war for national independence, raising the question of life or death. But it is no longer a war for the revolutionary creation of a new social way of living. We say that all isn't lost but we declare that everything is menaced and that we cannot be victorious unless something happens which we cannot foresee."

The CNT militiamen in Madrid asked the same question: "What right does the present government have to forge new chains for the proletariat, after they had destroyed the chains which kept them from realizing their dreams? What right do they have to restore militarism after we have suffered enough to know exactly its worth? Militarism for us is the integrating factor in fascism. To suppress the army is to get rid of authoritarianism's weapon for oppressing the people. This war which we are supporting is not a war decreed by the State; it is a popular revolt against the forces which want to crush personal dignity. Therefore it is up to the people to chose the kind of war and the tactics to be used to bring it to an end. The working class doesn't want to lose what has cost it so much blood. The creation of an army is nothing more than a return to a past which was buried July 19th."[2]

The Durruti Column also answered the decree with a statement by Durruti in *L'Espagne Nouvelle*. The editors prefaced this statement with an explanation of the situation at the front:

"Faced with the alternative of submitting to the new law or of putting down their guns and leaving, the militias, the fighters, considered both choices harmful to the revolution which they meant to defend. And despite orders from their organizations, most of them settled the question by doing neither. But their morale suffered a lot. The Durruti Column showed its strength by ignoring the new law

278

while making certain practical moves which had advantages and which safeguarded them from attacks for lack of discipline. Here Durruti's personal realism showed itself, also his moral influence on the Column and the country, and a kind of peasant slyness whose stubborn and crafty expression can be seen in the following interview:

"— Is it true that the regulations and the hierarchy of the old army are to be put in force again in the militias?

"— No! That is not how things are. Some recruits have been mobilized and a single command has been set up. Discipline which is enough for street fighting is naturally insufficient for a long and hard campaign when confronted by an army with modern equipment. There had to be a change.

"— In what way has discipline been strengthened?

"— Until recently we had a great number of different units each with its leader, its manpower — they varied from day to day to an extraordinary extent — their armaments, supply services, food stores, policies towards the inhabitants and even often their particular way of considering the war. This couldn't go on. A few improvements have been made and there will have to be some more.

"— But the ranks, the salutes, the punishments, the rewards?...

"— We won't need them here. We are anarchists.

"— The former Code of Military Justice, hasn't it been put back in force by a recent decree from Madrid?

"— Yes, and this decision of the Government has produced a deplorable effect. They lacked completely a sense of reality. *The contrast between their spirit and the spirit of the militias is total.* We are very conciliatory, but *we know that one of these mentalities must bow before the other.*

"— Don't you think that if the war goes on for a long time, militarism will be stabilized and will prove dangerous for the revolution?

"— Well! That is exactly why we must win the war as fast as possible!

With this reply, comrade Durruti smiled and we left him with a strong handshake."[3]

On their part the CNT and the FAI published the following statement:

"It would be infantile to permit the government to have complete control of the proletarian forces. A worker who is mobilized is not a soldier but a worker who has changed his tool for a gun, while the struggle is the same in the factory as on the front. Also it is up to the workers' organizations to control their manpower. The CNT without waiting for orders from anyone, takes its responsibilities, giving the following orders to all the workers who are members and are affected by the mobilization to present themselves immediately at the barracks controlled by the CNT or, if that is not possible to the unions or defense committees where they will be given a militia card, a pledge of their incorporation into the Confederal columns. In taking this decision the working class confirms once again its faith in the progress of the Revolution." [4]

With this communique the CNT was trying to attune the attitude of the anarchist militiamen and the decisions of the Government.

It didn't deny the need for mobilization. It simply reserved the right to control its own people in the confederal columns by the system chosen by the militiamen themselves.

The CNT had known how to rise above the difficulties, but Caballero didn't consider himself beaten. He came back to the attack, decreeing new measures, which struck a blow directly against the victories of the workers. For example, he pretended to nationalize the industries, snatching them from workers' control to put them into the hands of the bureaucracy. As can be seen, the circle was tightening around the Revolution. In his paper, *Guerra dè Classe,* Camilo Berneri didn't stop denouncing the progress of the counter-revolution: writing that "A certain smell of Noske is floating in the air".

Caballero was, indeed, directing his policies in such a way as to weaken the CNT, forcing it to assume responsibility for the nationalization of the industries. The CNT after its concessions, after having agreed to work with the other parties, after allowing itself to become a part of the Government of the Generalitat, was caught in its own trap. Once the Militia Committees were dissolved, the CNT felt like a prisoner and wanted to get out of the vicious circle which was slowly strangling it. It suggested to Caballero, President of the UGT, the formation of a workers' government composed basically of the CNT and the UGT, to be known as the National Council of Defense, but Caballero inclined to accept this proposal was brought to order by his watchdog, Rosenberg. The PC denounced "a certain conspiracy between the CNT and the UGT" and all the pro-communist fraction following Indalecio Prieto chimed in. At the same time the communist minister, Vicente Uribe, attacked the collectives under the Ministry of Agriculture. A decree specified that only the land of the fascists could be expropriated and it was necessary to prove that the proprietor was a fascist.

At one blow 1,500 collectives organized in the Levant, Aragon, Castille and Andalusia by libertarian workers were menaced. The counter-revolution didn't stop there; it attacked collectivized transportation and expropriated mines, briefly all revolutionary achievements. It was clear that the only solution was force, namely civil war on the antifascist side.

On the night of July 20th everyone was in agreement that the Spanish Revolution couldn't succeed unless the international proletariat, or at least the European ones, came to help it. By October there was no hope left. There was nothing to expect even from the French proletariat. Léon Blum and the PCF had lulled it to sleep. The last blow for the French workers occurred at Luna-Park on September 6, 1936. Blum, who had not been invited to the party organized by the Socialist Federation of the Seine, wanted to take part and ended by speaking. "You know I haven't changed. Do you think that I don't suffer and understand your feelings? You heard the delegates of the Spanish Popular Front the other night at the Vél. d'Hiver: I had listened to them that same morning. Do you think I listened to them with less emotion than you did? (Clapping)" All this to put off the present and pressing risk of war. And in the name of Peace, what did it matter if the Spanish People perished! This is what Léon Blum said clearly on the 6th of September at Luna Park. He won over the party. The hall on its feet applauded and shouted "Long live Léon Blum". Then it sang the International. [5] The action undertaken against Blum, calling for "Canons for Spain!" finished with "Long live Blum!" This reflected, the overall international scene which the Spanish revolutionaries could observe in that month of October, now that they already felt the hellish circle tightening around them. Nevertheless they had to go on fighting.

Faced by the impossibility of creating a National Defense Council, the CNT gave way under the heavy weight of reality and had to agree to take part in the Government. It took the most catastrophic path, collaboration, which destroyed its last hopes. Civil war within the anti-fascist bloc was inevitable. Because of its ill fated decision, the CNT was marching towards a fratricidal war and in the worst conditions. It had only put off the inevitable confrontation. [6]

This decision not only threw overboard all the historical past of the CNT but divided its forces and gave birth to an internal crisis which menaced its very life. The Stalinist agents watched closely this process of dissolution, which was overtaking militant anarchism. The Russian Consul in Barcelona, Antonov-Ovseenko played an important role. He repeated constantly that "the good Stalin had no hidden motives about Spain. Only the victory of the Republic counted for the Soviet Union". [7] This Stalinist propaganda offensive even penetrated to the interior of the CNT-FAI. Antonov-Ovseenko told Companys it would be a good idea to celebrate the Anniversary of the October Revolution by sending a large delegation to Moscow. Durruti's participation would have a very good effect... Companys conveyed the proposal to the CNT. The Regional Committee agreed and sent a commission to Bujaraloz to convince Durruti. The latter answered: "It's a joke ....no?" and started laughing in front of the delegates.

Then he went on "I admit that the presence of the CNT would be advantageous from a propaganda point of view, but to think that the delegates could mingle with the Russian people and tell them about our revolution is to misunderstand Russian reality completely. The delegation would be surrounded by Soviet authorities and GPU agents. This delegation would be nothing more than one more banner on the official platform, a way of showing the Russian people that Spain is an ally of its Soviet regime. Under the conditions it seems useless to me for members of the CNT or even a delegate from the Durruti Column to take part." [8]

But the commission insisted and asked Durruti for a precise answer. He then suggested that the question be raised at the War Committee of the Column. The latter decided to send Francisco Carreño with an open letter to the Russian workers. Durruti drafted the text as follows: "Greetings to the workers of the Soviet Union. Comrades, a fraternal salutation from the Aragon Front, where thousands of your brothers are fighting, as you fought twenty years ago for the emancipation of a class which had been injured and humiliated for centuries.

"Twenty years ago the Russian workers raised the red flag in the East, a symbol of fraternity between the proletarians of the world.

You were fully confident that they would help you in the great work you had undertaken. And we, workers of the world, have known how to watch over that trust, responding with self sacrifice according to our possibilities as proletarians.

"Today it is in the West that a revolution is also taking place. And a flag is also waving which represents an ideal. If it triumphs it will unite with fraternal bonds, two peoples who were treated with contempt on one side by tsarism and by a despotic monarchy on the other. Today, Russian workers, it is we who put the defense of our revolution in your hands. We have no confidence in a policy which calls itself democratic or anti-fascist. We believe in our class brothers, in the workers. It is they — it is you — who must defend the Spanish revolution as we did twenty years ago when we defended the Russian revolution.

"Have faith in us. We are genuine workers and we will not abandon our principles, our struggle for freedom for the working class, for anything in the world.

"Greetings from all the workers who struggle against fascism with guns in their hands on the Aragon front.

"Your comrade, Durruti."[9]

The military situation in Madrid became more distressing every day. The fascists were gaining positions one after the other and were approaching dangerously near to the capital. And so the Government decided to transfer its seat to Valencia. It wanted to take along all the representative bodies of the Popular Front. On October 18th, Caballero called together all the representatives of the parties and workers' organizations. Horacio Martinez Prieto took part in the assembly as secretary of the CNT. After Caballero's speech a complete agreement seemed to have been reached but Horacio took the responsibility of saying aloud what the people were murmuring quietly. "Madrid must not be abandoned. The departure of the Government will be considered a flight." Caballero answered that "the CNT didn't have a realistic view of the situation". But Horacio held out and the socialist leader gave up his project. By remaining, the CNT, which was not compromised because it didn't form part of the Government, would see its prestige grow with the masses. However Caballero had not abandoned the plan definitely and he pursued his policy trying to make the CNT participate in the Government. He knew that its secretary-general, Horacio Prieto, was not opposed to this, and that what was important to him was the number of Cabinet posts. It was necessary to bargain. Finally the two parties came to an agreement. The CNT would receive four ministries if Durruti's forces came to fight in Madrid. Prieto consulted nobody about the choice of the four ministers. Two came from the moderate faction, Juan Lopez and Juan Peiro, the others, García Oliver and Federica Montseñy were from the extreme left of the CNT. Lopez and Peiro were informed by telephone but the two others had to be convinced through personal contact. From the outset Federica was disgusted and only accepted in the name of the "sacred principles of militant responsibility". It was even more difficult with Oliver. He didn't want to leave Barcelona where his presence acted as a rein on the expansion of the PSUC which was swelling its ranks by accepting as members petty bourgeois and "law and order people". Finally he agreed but placed the responsibility for the choice on the National Committee. All that was needed was to convince Durruti.

Prieto went to Bujaraloz to meet with him. Durruti had already been informed by García Oliver by telephone and cut short the words of the secretary general of the CNT. "Out of the question.... I will stay in Aragon." Horacio insisted: "There is such a thing as responsibility and party discipline" but the argument was badly chosen because Durruti answered at once: "I know no other discipline than that of the Revolution." As for party responsibility his answer was even more violent. "I dont give a fuck for your bureaucratic responsibility." Durruti's revolt reached a point never reached before, because he had never imagined himself rebelling against the CNT. Then he remembered that Ascaso had rebelled against the National Committee represented by Buenacasa in 1927. And the latter had said: "The organization is always right". Ascaso answered: "Not always, this time I am in the right." [10] And now it was his turn to say no, who had always said yes to the CNT. The three months war had opened new horizons for Durruti and he too was freeing himself from administrative control.

When Horacio returned to Madrid, he hastened the entry of the CNT into the government. He feared that Durruti's attitude would influence Federica and Oliver. The 4th of November was the fatal day when the CNT took over four ministries and Oliver, the man who all his life had been persecuted and outside the law, became Minister of Justice. [11]

Footnotes

1. Pierre Besnard: "The breaking of this agreement marked the first interference of the Russians in Spanish affairs. From then on Soviet pressure became stronger and Rosenberg was able to convince Largo Caballero, who was hesitating, that Soviet help was disinterested. He was promised massive arms shipments. Caballero yielded to the temptation, ignoring the kind of aid which Stalin was intending for him." Report already quoted.

2. Burnett Bolloten, *La revolución española*; W.G. Krivitsky, *op. cit.*, Jésus Hernandez, *op. cit.*; Camilo Berneri, *Guerra di Classe*; *Frente Libertario* organ of the Confederal Militia of Madrid, October 1936.

3. *Espagne Antifasciste*, November 1936.

4. José Peirats, *op. cit.*

5. Léon Blum: *Le socialisme démocratique*. Ed. Albin Michel, et Denoël, Paris, 1972. The complete text of Blum's speech of September 6, 1936 at "Luna Park" can be found here.

6. Actually the first confrontation took place on May 3, 1937 in Barcelona and the second during March 1939.

7. Santillan, *op. cit.*

8. Testimony of Francisco Carreño at a lecture in the Ateneo "Faros" in Barcelona, 1937.

9. The text was published on November 2, in *C.N.T.*, Madrid. The delegation consisted of Francisco Carreño and Martin Gudell; the latter described his impressions of the trip in his book, *Lo que vi en Rusia*, Mexico, 1945.

10. Anecdote told to the author by Buenacasa; testimony already mentioned.

11. César M. Lorenzo in *op. cit.*, gives information about the activities of Horacio Prieto. The conservations between García Oliver, Federica Montseny and Durruti have been reconstructed thanks to the help of the militants who have cooperated with this biography.

13

"LONG LIVE MADRID WITHOUT A GOVERNMENT"[1]

THE DAY THE CNT entered the Government also marked the beginning of the siege of Madrid. The fascists at the gates of the capital were bombing the Puerta del Sol. The Government as well as many important people became panicky. It was necessary to escape as quickly as possible, this was the watch-word being whispered by responsible people. They only thought of fleeing to save their skins, believing that Madrid was a lost city.[2]

In Barcelona the same panic existed in the governing bodies. The Defense Council of the Generalitat held a meeting of the Delegates of the Columns active in Aragon, delegates who had already been given power after the new decree. Almost all of them were wearing uniforms. The only ones who didn't and who still bore the title Column Delegate, were those who were responsible for the CNT units and Rovira of the POUM Column. Colonel Sandino and Santillan who were responsible for the Department of Defense explained the extreme seriousness of the situation on the Madrid front. Reinforcements had to be sent to the capital which was in danger. Everyone looked at Durruti, but he didn't say a word. A decision hadn't been taken yet. It was agreed to send out an appeal on the radio and Durruti was asked to make a speech. He agreed and November 5th was set as the date.

When Durruti left the meeting he went to find an old comrade of the '20s, Marcos Alcon. How many months had gone by since they had been able to speak freely to each other! They decided to dine together and to invite a few comrades from the heroic past. They spoke only about the problem which was so important to them: the Revolution and the miserable state of its future. Here we use the testimony of Marcos Alcon about that evening: "Durruti complained about the corruption which was rife on the home front. In his speech he intended to denounce this state of affairs, which had even penetrated the CNT and the FAI, where the conduct of many militants was far from being that of sincere militants.

"I remember very well how this speech struck the militants of the CNT and the FAI and it goes without saying, filled the politicians with panic. Durruti really frightened them by using extremely harsh language and promising that they wouldn't manage to strangle the Revolution, in the name of an outmoded antifascism. I am not exaggerating and there are still witnesses alive today who say that the press, even the confederal one, printed his statement, still fiery although censored. Nevertheless, despite its severity, the text didn't render accurately what Durruti had expressed, far from it. His words had been like slaps at the profiteers of the Revolution." [3] Here is the complete report of the speech published on November 6 by *Solidaridad Obrera*:

"Workers of Catalonia, I am speaking to you. You, spirited people, who four months ago were able to subdue the military who wanted to crush you under their boots! I bring you the fraternal greetings of your brothers and comrades who are fighting on the Aragon front, a few kilometers from Saragossa in sight of the towers of the cathedral.

"Despite the threat to Madrid, you must realize that the whole population is aroused and nothing in the world will force it to retreat.

"We will resist to the death the fascist hordes on the Aragonese front and we appeal to our brothers in Madrid and urge them to resist, for the Catalan militiamen will know how to do their duty, just as they did when they threw themselves into the streets of Barcelona to crush fascism.

"The workers' organizations must not forget the urgent duty which present events dictate to them. At the front, in the trenches, one thought rules, one wish, only one objective: triumph over fascism!

"We ask the Catalan people to make an end to factional struggles and intrigues: rise to the situation, give up old quarrels and politics and think of nothing but the war. The Catalan people must respond to the efforts of those who are fighting on the front. There is no other way except to mobilize everyone, but don't imagine that the mobilization will always be limited to the same people! As the workers of Catalonia have taken on the job of holding the front, the moment has come to also demand a sacrifice from those who are living in the cities. It is necessary to mobilize effectively all the workers at the rear, because we, who are already at the front, want to know what men we can depend on behind us. And let no one think now about increasing wages and reducing hours of work.

"The duty of all workers, and specially those of the CNT, is to sacrifice and to produce everything that we lack. I am speaking to the organizations to ask them to give up their old quarrels and snares. We who are fighting at the front, ask for sincerity, specially from the FAI and the CNT. We ask the leaders to be loyal. It isn't enough for them to send us letters of encouragement to the front, clothing, food and munitions. It is also necessary to know how to observe reality today and in the future. This war involves all the troubles of modern war and is very costly for Catalonia. The leaders must from now on realize that if this war continues, it will be necessary to begin organizing the Catalan economy according to a rationally conceived plan.

"If it's true that we are fighting for something higher, the militiamen prove it to you, these men who smile when they read about the contributions made for them listed in the press, when they see those posters asking for help for them. They smile because, when the

Anarchist militia dances the Aragonese Jota during a break in the fighting.

fascist planes throw down their newspapers, they find the same contributions and identical appeals.

"*If you want to put an end to the danger, you must take the shape of a granite bloc.*

"The time has come to ask the union organizations and political parties to put an end once and for all to this kind of behavior. On the home front it is necessary to know how to administrate. We who are at the front, want to have behind us responsible people and guarantees, and we demand that the organisations take care of our companions and our children.

"If the militarization decreed by the Generalitat was created to intimidate us and to impose an iron discipline on us, they are fooling themselves and we ask the authors of this decree to come to the front to report on our morale and our discipline. After that we will come and compare it with the morale and the discipline on the home front.

"Don't worry; there is neither chaos or lack of discipline at the front. Each one of us is conscious of his responsibilities, because we understand the treasure that you put in our hands. Sleep peacefully. But we left Catalonia, trusting you to run the economy. Accept your responsibilities too, discipline yourselves. Another civil war must not occur between us after this war because of your incompetence.

"If everyone believes that his party is the strongest and can impose his politics he is wrong, because we must confront the fascist tyranny together with one power, one organization alone, with a unified discipline.

"The fascist tyrants will never pass here, where we are. That is

286

the password at the front. We cry out to them: You will not pass! It is your turn to say: they will not pass!'' (4)

While they were speaking about Durruti's speech in Barcelona, in Madrid things were getting worse. November 4th the fascists occupied the villages of Leganes, Alcorcon and Getafe on the outskirts of the capital and were at the gates of Madrid. Until now their advance had been quite fast. The militiamen taken aback were fighting as they retreated. This easy advance gave courage to the rebels, who thought they would take the city without striking a blow. They had already prepared everything, from the list of the authorities to take over, to a list of the people to be shot, a list which General Martinez Anido, Franco's Minister of the Interior, carefully kept up to date.

A psychological phenomenon occurred then which is hard to explain. The militiamen who had retreated as far as Madrid felt that they had to confront the enemy. The sight of the Capital captivated and stopped them. Women and children were throwing up barricades and no one was thinking of escaping. Then why run?..... and where could they run? The decision was quickly taken, to resist, defend themselves, it was the only solution.

At the Council of Ministers panic was general. In a pathetic speech Caballero recommended a retreat to Valencia. The Confederal ministers (CNT) were seated around a government table for the first time. Leave? But we just arrived García Oliver said to himself. He answered Caballero in the name of the four CNT ministers: "The Government must stay in Madrid. Each minister must become a delegate for the government risking his life on the barricades." All the other ministers looked with horror at this madman who wanted to expose them to gunfire and they gazed anxiously at the Prime Minister, who didn't hide his irritation. He called the members of the CNT to order, urging them to be reasonable. Time was short and the decision had to be unanimous. As Oliver insisted on his viewpoint, the government was at an impasse. Caballero proposed that the anarchist ministers discuss the matter and facilitate the job of the government by voting for the move to Valencia. The four anarchists left the hall to deliberate. They decided to leave the question to the National Committee. So that the CNT could settle the discussion, Horacio Prieto telephoned to Oliver and said: "Hold out, but if you risk a crisis, then give in..." New discussions, another wait. The atmosphere was becoming untenable... How could they stop these fanatical CNTers? A number of ministers (belonging to Azaña's party) reproached Caballero for having accepted the anarchists in his government. "See what crazy people we have to deal with!" New deliberations of the confederal ministers, new appeal to Horacio Prieto. He answered: "Vote, then you will return to Madrid." When Oliver made known the decision of the CNT, everyone breathed again. (5) From then on, everything went forward at a mad pace. Everyone was obsessed.... to leave.... to leave..!

On the other hand the feeling in the streets was something else. The population had become obsessed with heroism. The CNT and the UGT had created the slogan "Liberty or death". The radio broadcast speeches praisied resistance. Anonymous orators improvised and

Durruti in Bujaraloz before a part of the Column leaves for the Madrid front.

harangued the crowd. No one thought of himself. Each individual thought about everyone. Breathing was collective because it was felt that a collective death was approaching.

The Government had arranged its flight in the half light of nightfall. Caballero ordered the leader of his military cabinet to send his orders to General Miaja, who had been named as commander of the city of Madrid and to General Pozas, commander of the Central army. They both received sealed envelopes and were advised not to open them before November 7th at 6 A.M.

The flight took the road which goes to Valencia via Tarancon, a village situated 40 kilometers from Madrid. The remains of a unit which had fought at Siguenza were there. The responsible delegate, the anarchist Villanueva, was to become famous. He didn't know what had happened in the capital any more than his men but he had been ordered by the Defense Committee of the CNT to stop any flight from Madrid and to disarm all those who came under his control. (6)

The militiamen, guns in hand, stopped the ministers. And the following dialogue took place: "Where are you going?" "To Valencia." "Why?" "A special mission." Special missions were "a la mode", every coward invented one. So the militiamen were not impressed. "You are cowards. Return to Madrid." Some of the ministers, ashamed, obeyed. Others insisted on going forward. "Then leave your arms" Villanueva cried out, "you won't need them in Valencia."

Just then Pedro Rico, Mayor of Madrid arrived, huddled in the corner of the car and panic visible in his face. The militiamen, seeing him, started to laugh. "You too, you want to flee, you coward!" Rico tried to justify himself. "We should put you up against the wall!" The Mayor started back towards Madrid where he hid in a foreign embassy.

Night was advancing. Villanueva, who was in command of the control groups, was a decided fellow. A brave fighter, he had taken part in the capture of the Montana barracks and had fought at Guadalajara and Siguenza. Early next morning he would go to take part in the defense of Madrid. He would fight at Casa de Campo and was to die facing the foreign hordes in the grim battle at Teruel, while leading his brigade.

A caravan of cars advances. The militiamen stop them. One voice is heard: "Free the way! There are ministers here." "All those inside must get out of the cars" Villanueva answered. One of them introduced himself to Villanueva: "This is too much. I am the Minister of Foreign Affairs and I am going to Valencia." " Your duty as minister is to stay with the people in this dramatic hour. Fleeing, you demoralize the fighters." Other ministers came up, the Minister of Public Instruction and of Agriculture, the communists Jesus Hernandez and Vicente Uribe. Villanueva had them disarmed. "What are you going to do?" "Tomorrow I will put you in the front lines when we go into battle." "This is criminal." "It would be worse if I shot you as you deserve." Villanueva then telephoned to Eduardo Val, secretary of the Defense Comittee of the CNT: "I have four ministers here who fled from Madrid. What shall I do with them?" Val didn't lose his head. He was certainly opposed to the departure of the Government. He knew that this was the most dramatic moment in the defense of the capital and that the life of everyone was hanging by a thread. But on the other hand imprisoning the ministers wouldn't solve any problem. So he ordered: "Free them." "But!" "Do what I say!" "Good, but as I want to clear myself, send me a written order."

Val sent the order. Villanueva read it slowly then spoke to the ministers: "The organization, against my will, frees you. You can go to Valencia, but never forget today's flight, and even more the heroism with which the people of Madrid are fighting." Frighten-

Barcelona, November 1936 — Durruti directing the departure of the Column for Madrid.

ed, the ministers sank into the cars and left as fast as possible. Dawn broke, the militiamen climbed into the trucks and left on the road going in the opposite direction to the one taken by the ministers. They were going to their death, but also toward the conquest of liberty and life.[7]

During this memorable night, two undisciplined acts saved the capital. The first was Villanueva's arrest of the ministers, the second was when Miaja tore open the sealed envelope without waiting for the hour designated by Caballero. From 8 to 11 PM he didn't dare, but how could he remain inactive when fighting was going on at Carabanchel and Madrid was about to be stormed? Miaja chose Vicente Rojo Lluch, infantry major, as his staff officer. The latter enquired about the situation in Madrid after the Government had left and nobody knew anything. The exact positions held by the enemy were unknown, the state of our own strength wasn't known or the arms available, or munitions, food, etc. And to add to the confusion, when Miaja opened the envelope and took out the orders to his great surprise they were addressed to Pozas, while the latter received those meant for Miaja. Miaja didn't know what to do as he didn't know where to find Pozas. At this point the telephone rang. It was Val reporting the actions of Villanueva. Miaja was thus able to locate the exact spot where Pozas was to be found as he had set up his headquarters at Tarancon and they were able to exchange envelopes.[8]

During the night of the 7th the struggle was fierce but the people and the militamen fought magnificently. The voice of the CNT echoed on the loudspeakers: "Madrid will be the tomb of fascism. Madrid is rid of the ministers, commisars, and other "tourists", who pretending that they had special missions, have fled from Madrid as soon as they became conscious of the danger. But the people, the working class of Madrid doesn't need all these 'tourists' who have left for the Levant and Catalonia. They have gone never to return, but if by chance they should return.... Madrid free of its ministers will be the grave of fascism. Forward militiamen! Long live Madrid without a government. Long live the Social Revolution!"

In Valencia the public proclamation of the CNT and the FAI was even more radical: "For the women, the children, the old people and the wounded of Madrid, our bread, our homes. For the cowards and the deserters who show off their weapons and their cars, our contempt. Comrades they must be boycotted and their lives made impossible."[9]

In Madrid and Valencia and Catalonia the reaction of the CNT corresponded to the challenging climate which was developing among the people, always more to the left than their leaders. It was in this climate of discontent that Durruti gave the speech which we have quoted. His viewpoint was at one with the ideas of the masses and it encouraged them to take more radical positions. In a few hours Durruti's credit rocketed and made him the individual best personifying the secret thoughts of the people. Durruti said aloud what everybody felt.

"The war we are fighting actually helps us crush the enemy on the front, but is it the only one? No! Our enemy is also the one who opposes our conquests for the Revolution, and if we find him among us, we will crush him too."

Other men used the same language as Durruti but there was a difference which the people felt. In Durruti theory and practice were perfectly united. He had said no to the militarization and was maintaining the original structure of his Column. He said no to militarism and didn't masquerade as a soldier. He said no to privileges and lived among his militiamen exactly as they did. He fought for a classless society and practised it in his column. Through his behavior he became a kind of guarantee for the Revolution and a hope for all the revolutionaries.

Footnotes

1. Title of a leaflet put out by the CNT in Madrid.
2. Julian Zugazagoitia, *Guerra y vicisitudes de los españoles*, Vol. 1, p. 178 ss.
3. Marcos Alcon in a letter to the author.
4. *Solidaridad Obrera*, November 5, 1936.
5. For the removal of the government to Valencia see J. Alvarez del Vayo, *Les Batailles de la Liberté*, Julian Zugazagoitia, *op. cit.*, Eduardo de Guzman, *Madrid rojo y negro*, Ed. CNT, Barcelona, 1937. For the position of the CNT we follow the private testomony of Federica Monseñy, Minister of Health at that time.
6. Vicente Rojo, *op. cit.*, gives details about this episode.
7. Eduardo de Guzman, *op. cit.*
8. Eduardo Val, testimony. Rojo in the book cited, mentions this "unfortunate" incident.
9. Prudhommeaux A. & D., *Catalogne rouge et noire*, Spartacus, Paris

14

UNIVERSITY CITY

WHILE THE FASCIST troops were intensifying their attacks on Madrid the situation of the defenders in the capital was becoming more critical. The population was ready to defend the city but arms were running short. There were no more shells for the artillery and there were not even enough cartridges for the 13,000 guns defending the city. Courage alone was inexaustible and this was the only means of defense. Madrid would fall into the hands of the fascists if it slackened.

Understanding the situation, the militants of the CNT met during the night of November 8 to 9. German planes deluged the city with shells and incendiary bombs during the two hours of the meeting. Madrid was in flames. There was complete agreement at the end of the meeting: everyone felt that considering the situation, the presence of Durruti would act as a stimulant to the people. It was decided to send David Antona and Miguel Inestal to Aragon to inform Durruti that his presence in Madrid was indispensable. The Council of Ministers in Valencia decided the same thing, to send Durruti to the capital. Federica Montseny assumed the responsibility of convincing him. The name of Durruti was also mentioned in Barcelona by Santillan, who had become leader of the Council of Defense, after García Oliver had become minister of Justice in Madrid.

The Russian technicians, specially Antonov Ovseenko suggested to Santillan that reinforcements be sent to Madrid. Santillan brought together all the delegates from the columns including Durruti, having called them in from the front. When they reached Barcelona at night, he told them: "We have decided to draft a force of 12,000 men for the defense of Madrid and Durruti will lead them. I have stipulated that Madrid must supply the arms and the arms that we have will be left at the front to be used by new militiamen. The Russians have guaranteed that they will provide the arms and ammunition." Actually these were the unfortunate Swiss guns dating back to 1886, with ammunition of the same era which had not been tested beforehand. No one objected that the reinforcements which were to be sent to Madrid should be placed under the command of Durruti. But the latter didn't want to leave. He was upset and asked to be left on the Aragon front: "If you saw the trolleys of Saragossa as I see them you wouldn't leave." Santillan replied that "Saragossa wouldn't be

293

taken considering the situation we were in. He answered that I could send someone else to Madrid, Miguel Yoldi, more capable than he was. I answered that even if it were true, Miguel Yoldi wasn't named Durruti and what was needed in Madrid to raise the morale of the people was the legendary Durruti. Finally he gave in. And this is how the meeting of the Committee of the Militias ended and everyone returned to their posts to start moving the forces to be furnished by Catalonia." [1]

The morning of November 12, Durruti telephoned from Barcelona to Bujaraloz to prepare the units of the 1st Section whose delegate was Jose Mira, the IIIrd commanded by Bonilla and the VIIIth, whose delegate was young Liberto Roig. The 44th, 48th and 52nd centuries were added. The 52nd was made up of Internationals. The war committee which went to Madrid consisted of Miguel Yoldi, Ricardo Rionda (Rico) and Durruti. Manzana went as a military technician and Mora took charge of the paper work.

On the morning of the 13th, the cars coming from Aragon arrived in Barcelona. The militiamen were given until 5 P.M. to take leave of their families. Then they met at the Bakunin barracks to set off that same night for Madrid. At the appointed hour Durruti spoke to his comrades from a window overlooking the courtyard of the barracks. One of the Internationals has left a short report which gives his impressions: "He appeared at one of the windows in the courtyard and spoke. What did he say to us? It was not published or broadcast anywhere. It was a speech between comrades and it is certainly one of the most moving talks that Durruti ever made. Briefly this is about what he said: Do you want to come with me to Madrid, yes or no? It is a question of life or death for us all. We will either conquer or die, because defeat will be so terrible that we could not survive it. But we will conquer. I have faith in our victory. I only regret that today I speak to you in a barrack. Some day barracks will be abolished and we will live in a free society. And Durruti gave such a description of a society without injustice and cruelty that most of the men who were listening cried. And when at the end he asked the question again: Are you coming with me, yes or no? it was such a unanimous 'Yes', so sincere and deep that I can never forget it." [2]

When Durruti's auto arrived in front of the first barricades at Vallecas in Madrid, a militiaman came forward and asked for their credentials. "Make way for the Durruti column!" The news flew by word of mouth. The popular imagination exaggerated the number of men with Durruti: certain people told Cipriano Mera who was fighting in University City that there were 16,000, others reported 6,000 to Valentin Gonzalez, "El Campesino" who was fighting at Usera. Historians have set the number at 4,000. None were true. But what did the number matter at that moment? The important thing was the arrival of Durruti and his men....

At the front, at each street corner, in every home, Durruti was talked about. Few knew him but everyone admired him. Mothers described him to their children as a giant. Santillan was right, Durruti was a legend and a new chapter in the legend was opening in Madrid on November 14, 1936.

November 10 and 11 the forces of the enemy seemed to be

dwindling. But the 12th and 13th the offensive intensified. It was then that the 11th International Brigade commanded by General Kleber arrived.[3] On 13 th the Franco forces reached the Manzanares river between the French bridge and the Hippodrome and occupied front of about a half mile. Still they didn't cross the river. On its side, the 4th column of Franco's forces was advancing towards the East and the North without reaching the wall of the Casa de Campo. The entrance to University City was there but the advance of the attackers was checked by the machine guns judiciously placed on the bridge.

The chief Staff Officer, Vicente Rojo, had planned a counterattack to free this sector. He expected to lean on the newly arrived reinforcements. The goal was to break across the Manzanares river, not far from the region occupied by the enemy, to increase pressure on the flanks, cutting down the enemy's room for maneuver in the Casa de Campo and advancing directly towards the gateway to Rodajas: "With this maneuver", Vicente Rojo writes, "we tried to eliminate the enemy already in control of Garabitas and to provoke a response from those who had already reached the river and the lake. If we were successful with these forces and those on the right flank, our field of maneuver would be a serious menace to the enemy's left wing. It was necessary to force the whole front opposite us to retreat, thus freeing the city from the pressure it was under. The result would depend in part on the reinforcements received by the enemy columns situated within the Casa de Campo."[4]

This is what Vicente Rojo told Durruti when the latter presented himself to report the arrival of reinforcements from Aragon. Rojo told him that he counted on these men for the operation which would take place the morning of November 15. The Staff in Madrid gave Durruti the responsibility for a sector of University City, where there was already a unit of reinforcements also from Aragon, the column Libertad-Lopez Tienda, 2,200 men strong. A little further on was the column led by Major Palacios, whose strength was unknown because of their losses.

Durruti and Rojo arranged to meet every night to discuss the activities of the day and decide on the operations to be carried out. Rojo drew up an order which he sent to the general delegate of the "Libertad" column, El Negus, militant of the PSUC, putting him under the command of the leader of the sector, Durruti [5]. The CNT Defense Committee turned over the house of an aristocrat on Miguel Angel Street to the column. Durruti found Manzana there and asked him to visit the sector occupied by the "Libertad" column.

At 3 P.M. Miguel Yoldi came by and told of the arrival of the last trucks at the barracks in Granados Street, a former college. Yoldi informed Durruti that the enemy was not only in front of them but was actually in Madrid. In front of the Finnish Embassy one of the trucks of the Column had been shot at from the windows. The militiamen climbed down quickly, took the building by assault, where they found fascists and weapons. [6] Yoldi laughingly reported that Federica had arrived like a madwoman at Granados Street saying that "the Moors were in the Paseo de Rosales and to come quickly to stop them." Mira who received her said that "if they were only in the Paseo de Rosales it was still possible to have a little nap because the men were tired"...." Poor Federica" Durruti commented laughing.

At nightfall Durruti went to the Ministry of War to receive the latest instructions. "His forces were to enter University City to take up positions on the banks of the Manzanares. They were to launch an offensive at drawn, protected by the 5th mixed brigade commanded by Fernando Sabio. On the shores of the Manzanares the Libertad-Lopez Tienda column would face the enemy and would try to cross the river to drive it back." [7]

Not satisfied with the explanations he had received, Durruti went to the CNT Defense Committee in search of additional information. He came to III Serrano Street with Yoldi and Manzana. He found Eduardo Val, García Oliver and Federica Montseny there. [8] In a short while Cipriano Mera and Major Palacios, who was defending a sector between the "Libertad" column and the 5th brigade in University City, also turned up. Mera wrote, "Durruti questioned me about the situation, asking my opinion about the resistance of Madrid and enquired about the actual positions of the enemy. I brought him up to date on our real situation and that of our adversary. I also told him what General Miaja had said at the Defense Committee 14 or 16 hours earlier. Looking at a map, I had shown him the danger represented by the heights of Cuatro Caminos. I had begged him to give importance to the sewer which runs from the hospital to the river. Because if the enemy were able to creep through it, they could bring in reinforcements without our seeing them... Our only advantage is the morale of our men which is magnificent. When they know that you have come with reinforcements and that the latter are fighting, the combatants will take courage again."

Cipriano Mera thought that Durruti was bringing 16,000 men. Durruti put an end to his illusions. There were no more than 1,800. The news discouraged Mera. He immediately suggested the merger of their two columns. Then examining the orders which Durruti had received, Mera thought: "To attack the enemy head on is stupid. What we need is a defeat to discredit them. General Miaja has great confidence in the communists and the latter cannot allow Durruti, the anarchist, to become the savior of the capital." Before separating Mera offered a century made up of men who knew the terrain well and would serve as guides to Durruti's militiamen. [9]

At dawn on November 15, Durruti's column according to the latest orders received, deployed its men in order to take the assigned objective by assault. The day is grey, rainy, progress is difficult. From the Garabitas knoll, machine guns sweep the terrain already producing the first victims. The advance is interrupted and the troops have to drop back. Durruti is impatient. He reorganizes his units and attacks again. A new defeat. A third attack has the same results. The fascists from the fortified position at an elevation of 400 meters dominate the area.

Towards 10 in the morning new units join in the action, notably the llth International Brigade, which had not intervened before, no one knows why. [10] Then Durruti understood that he had been holding the sector alone, but stimulated by the arrival of reinforcements he launched a new attack, again without success. In the afternoon the artillery and aviation moved into action, supporting the troops which attacked with renewed vigor. At nightfall the battle spread out. New fascist troops launch an attack against the sector held by the Libertad-Lopez Tienda column on the other side of the Manzanares. The battle intensifies. The militiamen of the Libertad column defend themselves well, but enemy pressure gets stronger and stronger. The enemy crosses the river with the help of improvised footbridges. The Libertad column weakens and the fascist troops commanded by General Asensio enter University City. They occupy the first building, the School of Architecture. [11] The Durruti column and the 11th I.B. have to retreat. Night falls but the battle goes on. The day hasn't been propitious and Durruti has already lost a third of his troops. "Lopez Tienda" has lost almost all of theirs. In the other sectors the fight has been just as violent. At Headquarters, Vicente Rojo takes his bearings. He gives the command to recapture the ground lost by the Libertad-Lopez Tienda column no matter what the cost. [12] The enemy groups must be encircled and the front line at the river regained.

Jose Mira reports that "At daybreak we deployed on both flanks. Liberto Roig with his troops entered the East Park and dislodged the enemy from the first houses on the Paseo de Rosales. He continued to advance as far as the Rubio Institute, which he occupied despite fierce resistance. I was assigned the right flank which covered the Sainte-Christine Asylum and its adjoining buildings, the wall which gives on the Promenade and which goes as far as the Clinical Hospital, the Velazquez House and the College of Philosophy and Letters. We were supposed to establish contact with Liberto Roig here at the Palacete and with the Internationals North of the College.

"Our advance coincided with the enemy's. We met in the open and the slaughter was terrible on both sides. Often we had to fight hand to hand and when we thought we were free of them, others fell on us. Our militiamen, used to this kind of fighting, fought well and put the enemy to flight.

"Towards 9 in the morning of November 16, enemy aviation appeared and bombarded our lines. But the miracle of the day before was repeated: our tiny planes called 'chatos' came out to meet them and fought a battle of one to ten. Our 'chatos' fought well and brought down a number of enemy planes. Seven of ours were hit. After the air battle the militiamen of the column commanded by the communist del Barrio, which had also come from Aragon before us, arrived at Cuatro Caminos. They were led by Major Minenza, who brought an order from the Staff telling us to hand over the surveillance of the Clinical Hospital to them. "The struggle had been fierce throughout the day. We won and lost the same terrain in the course of an hour. And when we thought we were well entrenched, we were prompty dislodged by a counter-attack." [13]

The fight continued day and night without interruption. On the 17th an intense bombardment created a number of victims throughout Madrid. The German Junkers were already trying out their massive attacks in Spain. These operations were so savage that the Diplomatic Corps made a public protest and the Press correspondants, until then hostile to the Republic, joined in. "During these days Madrid was becoming a martyred city, forgotten by the world which called itself democratic and christian." (14)

In a prophetic way the journalists seized on the character of these bombardments. D. Buckley, an English journalist wrote: "It is possible that within 5 years the nations of the world will undergo the pounding which Madrid suffered in 1936 because in this world everything is paid for." Cesar Falcon foretold:"London, Paris and Brussels must see in the houses destroyed in Madrid, the women and children who have been massacred... their own future when fascism attacks them." And the correspondant of *Paris-Soir*: "Oh ancient Europe! always so busy with your little games and your serious intrigues. May God will that all this blood doesn't choke you!" (15)

The fascists launched a second attack to the hellish noise of the cannons and the bombs which were tearing open the houses. Three columns of Franco's forces had crossed the Manzanares on foot bridges. General Varela had given them the objective of occupying Madrid, beginning with the taking of University City. The theater of operations covered the Sainte-Christine Asylum, the Clinical Hospital the Foundation del Amor, the House of Velazquez, the College of Philosophy and Letters, the Moncloa, the Palacete. To reach these objectives Varela had at his command a considerable number of troops and tanks. The militiamen stopped the tanks with bombs and dynamite, often sacrificing their lives. Some fighters became panicky. Major Minenza in charge of the defense of the Clinical Hospital ordered a retreat, thus allowing the enemy to occupy the building. However the militiamen who were running towards the Moncloa Square met comrades who revived their courage. They retraced their steps and counter-attacked.

Luigi Longo, commissar of the 12th International Brigade tells about the battle on that day: "Every window, every corner of buildings where a fascist could hide was riddled with bullets. Our volunteers open the way with grenades. The men in the Batallion 'Paris Commune' occupy the College of Philosophy and Letters. Immediately a flag hoisted in the middle of the building shows our gunners that it is ours. The College of Sciences also falls into our hands. Durruti occupies it. The struggle hardens. The Asturians with their dynamiters perform miracles of heroism in the House of Velazquez. Their commander is dead and they don't manage to reach their objective. Despite their efforts the pavilions of the Clinical Hospital and the House of Velazques are still in the hands of the enemy. Impossible to go through them without being struck down at the first step. Shooting goes on from one shelter to another and also from the trees where sometimes the hidden snipers fall, hit by a bullet." (16)

"The College of Sciences had been taken by assault, Durruti leading his men. The building was protected by bags of earth and defended by machine guns. The line of machine gunners was attacked with grenades. The men burst into the interior of the building. They fought with side arms in the hall, the stairs, the cellars. The fighting lasted several hours until the Internationls joined Durruti's men. Then the fight ended." (17) The Internationals and Durruti's men fraternized: "There is no affection more sincere than the one born during real danger" Mira wrote. "With what innocence they exchanged prizes, objects, in order to own each others souvenirs after this tragic night, when everyone thought, not without reason, that they were born again."

At dawn on the 18th, the reserves began to relieve the men of the 11th and 12th International Brigades. Other units of the Spanish mixed brigades also received reinforcements or were relieved. Only the forces of Durruti continued the struggle, but this situation couldn't go on much longer. Actually the men had started to fight on the night of the 15th to 16th and since then they had scarcely been able to close their eyes. They were floundering in the mud, and there was nothing warm to eat. The troop was reduced to 700 men and only the instinct of self preservation kept them standing. Durruti told Liberto Roig that he was going to try and get some fresh troops to replace the most exhausted fighters. With this in mind he went to the Miquel-Angel barracks and met Ariel, the Madrid correspondant of *Solidaridad Obrera*. Ariel asked for his impressions: "The fight will be hard, very hard" Durruti answered "but they won't enter Madrid. The camarades behaved like lions. They fought in every phase of the battle but we have had a number of losses. Yoldi and Manzana are wounded. We must discuss how to replace these comrades in order to continue the fight." "Without losing time" Ariel wrote, "I went to Defense Committee and repeated to Eduardo Val what Durruti had said to me. Learning about the situation he left with me for the Miguel-Angel barrack. Durruti repeated what he had told me: the forces must be reorganized, rest given to the men who were tired, the dead and wounded replaced. Eduardo Val gave instructions by telephone to fill in Durruti's losses. A comrade from Madrid would replace Yoldi who had been hospitalized, Manzana would try to stay at his command despite his wound, knowing how useful he was to Durruti.[18]

Eduardo Val explained to Durruti that it was difficult to organize relief for lack of reserves. Durruti thus found himself faced with a problem of conscience: to pull out his men from the front, which could damage the morale of the fighters or continue the struggle with his exhausted men. It was necessary to solve the problem rapidly and Durruti decided to present the problem to Miaja's staff. Just when he was going to leave, Liberto Roig arrived at Miguel-Angel bringing news from the front. Jose Mira was wounded and the others asked to be relieved.

Liberto Roig, who was 22, had already taken part in the uprising of 1933 and since then had always been on the battle front. Durruti asked him where the fascists were. Roig seemed surprised: "But you know very well! We are fighting in the Moncloa." Durruti admitted: "That's true, the tramway ticket from the Puerta del Sol costs only 15 centimes. Liberto, do you think that under those conditions we can think about being relieved? Speak bluntly to the comrades. Tell them the truth: there are no troops to relieve them. They must hold, and hold fast. I am in the same state you are. I was with you this morning at Moncloa and tonight I will be with Mira. Tell all this to the comrades, and if your wound isn't serious, hold on Liberto."[19]

After Liberto left, Durruti said to Mora that he was going to the Ministry of War to ask for reinforcements, because relief was indispensable. Just as he was going out, Mora told him that his companion, Emilienne was on the telephone. He took the receiver nervously and said: "What's the matter?" too dryly for the anxious woman in Barcelona. "Yes, I am well. Excuse me, but I have to leave, I am well. Excuse me, but I have to leave, I am in a hurry." He put down the receiver and seeing the surprise in Mora's face said: "What do you expect, in war one becomes a jackal."[20]

Footnotes

1. D.A. de Santillan, letter to the author. In it Santillan concludes: "When they arrived in Madrid these forces were broken up into groups corresponding to their political choice. Durruti remained alone with his men from the Aragon front, about 1,500 of them. He talked with me the night he arrived in Madrid, around two or three in the morning: "Fuck your guns.... and send me some grenades." These guns were the trash bought by the Russians, no one knew where, and they were useless.

2. *Le Combat Syndicaliste*, November 19, 1937, Paris. Article by Jean Dupox.

3. Until now the date of the intervention of the International Brigades in Madrid has been falsely reported. Vicente Rojo in his book, *Así fué la defensa de Madrid*, p. 86 corrects the passage in which Hugh Thomas in his *Historia de la guerra civil española*, pp. 268-270 states that "on November 8 General Kleber took over the command of all the republican forces in University City and Casa de Campo....: that the brigade was divided so that each member would fight alongside of four Spaniards to sustain their morale and to give lessons to the obstinate militiamen on how to shoot correctly." Rojo answers this: "Such a bright idea for tactics was perhaps dreamed up and developed by some clever journalist, foreign or Spanish, at the table in some cafe in Madrid. But no matter what the books say about this event, the truth is that on that day Kleber and his men were simply sun-bathing in some village in the valley of the Tagus or the Tajuna, even too far away for the echoes of the battle to be heard." Vicente Rojo dates the entry into battle of the 11th International Brigade (Kleber) between the 10th and 11th of November 1936.

4. Vicente Rojo, *op. cit*.

5. In *Historia y vida*, No. 31, October 1970, Madrid, José Manuel Martínez Bande telling about the intervention of the Durruti Column in Madrid, reports this order which exists in the archives of the Department of Military History of Madrid. But in the 35th number of the same journal, in answer to Martínez Bande, a reader, Francisco Hidalgo Madero, who calls himself one of the professional officers of the "Libertad-Lopez Tienda" Column, writes: "The 'Libertad-Lopez Tienda' Column never had any anarcho-syndicalists in its ranks and was never under the command, direct or personal, of Durruti." Further on he states: "As Señor Martínez Bande says very correctly, the Libertad-Lopez Tienda Column received the order (from the Defense Junta presided over by General Miaja) to place itself under the command of Durruti. But this order was never carried out. The Libertad-Lopez Tienda Column was never under the orders of Durruti." These are the reasons they offer: "Captain Lopez Tienda having died on November 2, was replaced by a certain 'Negus', militant of the PSUC (marxist). The so-called Negus didn't want to submit to the orders of Durruti. In addition professional leaders were reluctant to be subordinate to a Militia leader. And finally there was the clear and explicit refusal of the commissar and the marxist part of the Column to be under the orders of an anarchist like Durruti; all of this resulted in the order not being carried out."

If we have laid stress on this long note, it is because from this misunderstanding many contradictions have arisen. The first was that the Libertad-Lopez Tienda Column went into battle on November 13 and the Durruti column the morning of the 15th. On the 14th the enemy took over ground near the Manzanares and on the evening of the 15th it crossed the river and occupied the School of Architecture right in the sector controled by the Libertad-Lopez Tienda Column. The conclusion is that "the anarchists who fled before the advance of the enemy, allowing it to cross the Manzanares, were the anarchists of Lopez Tienda and not those who arrived with Durruti from the Aragonese front."

After the death of Durruti, the confederal organ *C.N.T.* wrote: "In University City a column of Marxist Catalans was entrusted with keeping the enemy from crossing. But these troops were routed and the rebel army crossed, occupying the buildings which were real fortresses, among these the Clinical Hospital."

None of the later historians remembered this paragraph from the press and all of them continued to talk about "the terror produced by the forces of Durruti." Today after more than thirty years, the witness Francisco Hidalgo puts things in their proper place in the testimony we have cited.

6. Vicente Rojo, *op. cit*., also mentions this fact.

7. Vicente Rojo, *op. cit*.

8. Once the confederal ministers had arrived in Valencia, they returned immediately to Madrid where they lived during the first days of the siege.

9. Cipriano Mera, *Memorias de Guerra*, unpublished, deposited in the Institute of Social History in Amsterdam. The author allowed us to consult them. This consultation was very useful because of the valuable details about Durruti's activities on November 19.

10. Years have passed before it was possible to know exactly how this operation took place. Durruti didn't know about it. Today thanks to information provided by General Rojo, we know some of the reasons why this offensive was checked. On November 26, in a confidential document sent by Rojo to General Miaja, the former asked that General Kleber be dismissed. Among other reasons, Rojo stated the following: "Heading the forces which were supposed to occupy Garabitas — an operation prepared in agreement with all the leaders of the column — he thwarted the outlined plan by claiming that he didn't have enough men (which wasn't a sure thing since on the following day he was able to set up two of his Batallions again); later he endangered the development of the operation by putting off until 10 o'clock the attack which had been prepared for 8 o'clock. And in this way he made the preparation of the artillery completely useless." Vicente Rojo, *op. cit*., p. 234.

11. Explaining the battle on that day, Rojo said that "as was learned later the enemy had received reinforcements from the mountains and the rear. And to strenghten its attack on the Casa de Campo he had added Column 2 which he had pulled out from Carabanchel to Columns 1 and 3. The rebels had concentrated the greatest strength on a very narrow front and had also been lucky enough to cause a panic in one of our improvised units. This unit retreated in disorder infecting other units, and so the enemy was able to enter University City and occupy a number of buildings. It even reached the Clinical Hospital, the most advanced sector", *op. cit*., p. 89.

12. "Tomorrow the 16th at dawn the Durruti Column, leaving the Sainte-Christine Asylum, will carry out a reconnaissance in University City in the direction of the Stadium to drive back to the other side of the river enemy elements which have reached this area. The 11th International Brigade (Kleber) will support Durruti on the right and on his left, the Lopez Tienda Column." This order can be found in the book of José Martinez Bande; *La Marcha sobre Madrid*, p. 139.

13. José Mira, op. cit.

14. Vicente, Rojo. *op. cit*.

15. See the newspapers of the period.

16. Luigi Longo, *Las Brigadas Internacionales en España*.

17. José Mira, *op. cit*.

18. Ariel, *Como Murió Durruti*, (pamphlet).

19. Testimony of Liberto Roig to the author.

20. M. Buenacasa, *Cahiers cités*.

"DURRUTI IS DEAD"

AT THE MINISTRY OF WAR, General Miaja acknowledged Durruti's well founded claims, but he answered that he couldn't do anything about relief forces before the end of the operation against the Clinical Hospital. It would take place the next day, the 19th. Durruti reminded the General that he had lost 1,400 men and only 400 remained. This situation didn't help the morale of the troops, no matter how brave they were. General Miaja could only agree but told him that he was going to attach some troops to Durruti's, who would bear the brunt of the attack on the Clinical Hospital.

Coming out of the Ministry, Durruti ran into Koltsov whom he hadn't seen since their discussion in Aragon. Koltsov greeted him and asked him "to talk for a moment about events in Spain." Durruti answered that he didn't have time because he had things to do at Headquarters. They separated but Durruti turned around and said to him: "You see, they haven't killed me and also I haven't become a Bolshevik." [1]

At Miguel-Angel he found a message from José Mira: "Our situation is desperate; try in every way possible to get us out of this hell. We have had and continue to have many losses. Besides we aren't eating or sleeping. So physically we are defeated. Greetings, Mira." Durruti answered this message with another: "Comrade Mira, I recognize your physical exhaustion because it is mine too, but what do you expect my friends, war is cruel and you must therefore remain at your posts until you are replaced. Greetings, Durruti." [2] That night Durruti, detained at the Ministry of War and at the CNT Committee of Defense, couldn't keep his promise to rejoin Mira at the front. With Eduardo Val he was studying the reorganization of the militia, and how to hold back reserves, as other groups did, in particular the Internationals.

Mera was waiting for him at Miguel-Angel. The former pointed out that the policies of the Communist Party were about to be imposed openly and that it was urgent to proceed with the unification of all the confederal forces. With this in mind the militants of Madrid had called a plenum for the 19th. Mera also told him that according to the comrades, Durruti was the man most recommended to represent all the confederal militia in Madrid. Durruti agreed to unification of the confederal forces. As to representation he prefered sending a War

Committee instead of delegating one person. He also said that once the front at Madrid had been built up, he would go back to Aragon, because his presence there would be much more important than in Madrid. As to the operation the following morning against the Clinical Hospital, they decided to meet at the Reina Victoria barracks of the Guardia Civil, because the tower in that building would allow them to follow the situation as a whole.

Day broke with a torrential rain. The men were floundering in water and it was cold. Before going up into the tower, Durruti gave orders to Yoldi, who had recovered and who was to direct operations. The forces which were to attack the Clinical Hospital were made up of four companies under the command of professional officers. These men had been supplied by Miaja's Staff and by the Defense Committee of the CNT.

The attack began well but an error was made, the cellars were not occupied as Durruti had suggested. The troops dispersed in the upper floors which made the struggle more difficult as the attackers lost contact with each other. This was the purport of a communique which Durruti received at 8 in the morning. Durruti asked a captain to go and help those who were practically closed up in the building.

Returning to the tower he leaned out to see better what was going on in the Hospital. Just then a bullet ricocheted on the wall a few centimeters from his head. "They strike very close, Cipriano!" Durruti said while remaining in the same spot. Manzana came to confirm what the note had reported. Manzana also informed him that two companies were playing heads or tails to see which one would carry out the first attack. Durruti became furious. He ran down the stairs and said to the captain that lots were not drawn in the Durruti Column. He told the militiamen that they had no time to waste and that anyway both companies would have to go into action and under these conditions it was better to go first than later.

Towards noon contact was reestablished between the fighters on the ground floor of the Clinical Hospital and the other floors and the new reinforcements backed up by the Internationals who had also entered the fight, had blocked off the cellars. Yoldi informed him that the operation had started well this time. It was 12.30 on November 19. At the foot of the tower Mera and Durruti separated after arranging a meeting for 3 P.M.[3]

At 1 P.M. Durruti and Yoldi arrived at the Miguel-Angel barracks. Durruti took a piece of bread and standing, dictated the relief order to Mora which had to be signed by General Miaja: "To comrade Mira: The Minister of War having decided to relieve the personnel of the column in the avant-garde positions, you will see to it today that your forces retreat from the positions they are holding and go to the barracks at number 33 Granada Street. To carry this out you will explain to the responsible leader in your sector that he must choose the forces to replace yours in the College of Philosophy and Letters as well as in the Sainte-Catherine Asylum. You will give me a report tomorrow before 12 noon that this order has been carried out. Madrid, November 19, 1936. Signed B. Durruti — (Approved) — General Miaja."[4]

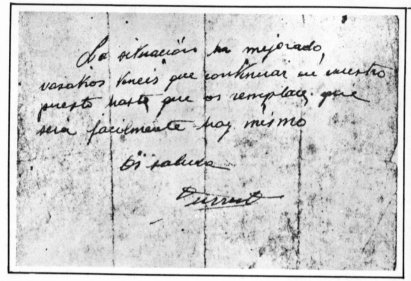

Final document signed by Durruti and sent to Jose Mira, delegate of the Column in the University City, November. 19, 1936.

He had scarcely finished signing this document when Bonilla arrived sent by Liberto Roig, to inform Durruti that the people who had occupied the Clinical Hospital were in the process of evacuating it. [5] Durruti alarmed, asked his chauffeur, Julio Grave, to get the car ready to leave immediately for the Clinical Hospital. Manzana advised him to stay in the barracks since he had to take part in a meeting of the militants which was to take place in the afternoon. But Durruti answered "it was only a matter of a half hour and that if there was really a rout, his presence would be useful." [6]

Durruti sat down next to the chauffeur. The latter retraced the route they had taken: "We went to Cuatro Caminos Square. From there we went down Pablo Iglesias Avenue (now Queen Victoria Avenue) as fast as possible. We passed a little group of hotels which are at the bottom of this Avenue and we turned towards the right. Arriving at a big street, we saw a group of militiamen coming towards us. Durruti thought it was some young men who were leaving the front. This area was completely destroyed by the bullets coming from the Clinical Hospital, which had been taken during these days by the Moors and which dominated all the environs. Durruti had me stop the car which I parked in the angle of one of those little hotels as a precaution. Durruti got out of the auto and went towards the militiamen. He asked them where they were going. As they didn't know what to say, he ordered them to return to the front.

"The militiamen obeyed and Durruti returned towards the car. The rain of bullets became stronger. From the vast red heap of the Clinical Hospital, the Moors and the Guardia Civil were shooting furiously. Reaching the door of the machine, Durruti collapsed, a bullet through his chest. Manzana and I got down from the car quickly and carried him inside without losing time. I turned the car around maneuvering as quickly as possible and went towards the hospital of the Catalan militias in Madrid."[7]

Julio Grave calculates that it took him twenty minutes to go from the place of the accident to the Hotel Ritz. It was therefore about 2.35 PM when Durruti was taken into the operating room where he remained until 5 P.M. Then he was taken from the operating room to a room on the first floor. The doctors Santamaria, Fraile, Monje and Bastos after examining the nature of the wound decided not to operate. It was mortal. Later the diagnosis was: "Death caused by a pleural hemorrhage." The bullet was lodged in the area of the heart. The doctors drew up a report in which the character of the wound and the path of the bullet is recorded but not the caliber of the bullet, since they hadn't removed it and there was no autopsy.

Durruti remained conscious until midnight. Then he went into a coma and was at death's door until November 20, 1936 at 6 in the morning, the hour when he died. Durruti had lived 40 years and 129 days. Four months before, Ascaso had died under similar conditions at the age of 35. With the death of these two men, a very stirring chapter in Spanish anarchism came to an end.

Footnotes

1. Michel Koltsov, *op. cit.*
2. José Mira, *op. cit.*
3. Cipriano Mera, *m. cit.*
4. José Mira, *op. cit.*
5. Liberto Roig, direct testimony.
6. Cipriano Mera, direct testimony.
7. Verbal report by Julio Grave, Durruti's chauffeur to Ariel; the latter reports it in the pamphlet quoted before.

16

THE FUNERAL OF A DISSENTER

THE MEETING of the militants and committees had been going on for two hours when Val announced the news that Durruti was mortally wounded. It was agreed that the information must be kept secret while waiting for more complete reports. Cipriano Mera was instructed to go to Valencia at once to tell Federica Montseñy, Garcia Oliver and Mariano Vasquez.[1]

Durruti had died at 6 on the morning of November 20. The news had leaked out because delegations from political parties and unions began to arrive at the Regional headquarters of the CNT to offer their condolences. General Miaja also came and a witness, who was not an anarchist, said that Miaja could not keep back his tears before the dead man and said: "He was courageous."[2] The CNT was represented by the National Sub-Committee and the Regional Committee which greeted the visitors. The body, wrapped in a sheet, lay on a little iron cot, the head on a pillow. At eight o'clock the sculptor Victoriano Macho came with other artists of the Intellectual Alliance to make a death mask. The body undressed for the operation had remained completely nude. The head with the eyes closed, rested on one side of the pillow, a drop of blood coagulated at the corner of the lips. On the left side of the chest was the mortal wound. [3]

Cipriano Mera reached Valencia at about the same time that Durruti was beginning his death struggle. He went to the Hotel Metropole where Mariano Vasquez, García Oliver and Federica Montseñy were staying. The news had a shocking effect. Federica had a nervous crisis and began to weep. García Oliver started to curse, only Mariano R. Vasquez knew how to control himself. He asked Mera to return to Madrid immediately to tell Yoldi and Manzana to reorganize the Column while waiting the arrival of Ricardo Sanz, because it was not possible for the Column to abandon Madrid.[4]

At 9 P.M. on November 20, Ricardo Sanz started for Madrid. But at that hour neither the people nor the press in Madrid or Barcelona or in the world had heard the news. The writer, Kaminski, who was preparing a book in Barcelona on the revolution reports: "I received confirmation of his death during the night of November 20, but the Press didn't publish the news until the 21st, because the authorities feared reprisals by the men of the CNT"...."I couldn't curb my need to share the secret with some trustworthy people. All of them, even the least friendly to the anarchists, went pale and I could read distress in their eyes."[5] This "anguished pallor" was caused by the fear of the consequences which might come in the wake of this death.

To admit that Durruti was dead seemed difficult if not impossible. Yes, Marianet had said it clearly: "Durruti was not a God but a mortal and in war soldiers and leaders die in the same way." Nothing was more logical. But Durruti had spoken over the radio, only a few days before, and with the decline of the revolution and the increased power of the communists, the death of Durruti seemed suddenly inconceivable. Even Eduardo Val had refused to admit it, asking Manzana if this wasn't a maneuver of the communists. Already the legend of a strange death was being woven around the body. And the myth of Durruti, symbol of an enormous political potential, began for a people who identified itself with his fate.

The body of Durruti was taken to the headquarters of the National Sub-Committee of the CNT where an armed vigil was to be arranged. A group of militiamen formed an armed escort in the name of the Column. His personal effects had been collected to be given to his companion. There was only a very small, rether old suitcase. What could be in it? It was opened and was found to be half empty. There were some old underwear, a shaving set and a little notebook with the entry: "November 15: I ask the Sub-Committee of the CNT for a loan of one hundred pesetas for personal expenses." That was all his baggage.[6]

November 21 a procession of cars left Madrid for Valencia following the funeral wagon. The first stop was at Tarancon, then the convoy went on towards the Levant; Durruti was leaving the Castillan region to enter the Mediterranean plane where the blue sky melted into the earth covered with orange trees. When they arrived at Chiva the people couldn't be held back. They surrounded the cortege and buried the coffin in flowers. People weren't weeping but you could see their lips trembling and their hands clenched. It was the same in all the villages but when they reached Valencia there was a universal outburst. And before the cortege reached CNT headquarters it slowed down. But time was getting short as the date of the funeral had been fixed for Sunday November 22 at 10 A.M. in Barcelona.

The cortege arrived in Barcelona before midnight. From village to village, despite the late hour and the rain, workers and peasants waited to join the procession and take part in the ceremony which was to take place next day. An immense crowd was overflowing the area around the Headquarters of the CNT-FAI. The hallway of the Casa CNT-FAI had become a flaming chapel decorated in red and black. A few men from the Column who had come from Madrid with the cortege, carried Durruti inside the house. There were so many people that they could scarcely pass through and the guards had to push back the people who were waiting. The cover of the coffin was removed and Durruti appeared under the glass covered by a white sheet, a white turban around his head.

His widow, Emilienne, and his intimate friends were stationed around the body. The national and peninsular bodies of the CNT and

the FAI were represented by their General Secretaries, Mariano Vasquez and Germinal de Souza. The young libertarians had sent their
Regional Committee of Catalonia and a representation of their Peninsular Committee of the FIJL as delegates.

"The following morning the funeral took place. One could see
that the bullet which had killed Durruti had gone straight to the heart
of Barcelona. It was calculated that one inhabitant out of every four
or five walked behind the coffin, without counting the masses who
lined the streets, were at the windows, on the roofs and even in the
trees of the Ramblas. The parties and trade unions of every variety
had called together their members and the flags of all the antifascist
organizations flated beside those of the anarchists above this human
sea. It was grandiose, sublime and strange. Because no one led the
crowd, there was no order or organization. Nothing worked and the
chaos was indescribeable.

"The burial was set for ten o'clock. At nine it was already impossible to reach the house of the Regional Anarchist Committee. No
one had thought of clearing the road for the convoy. From every side
the factory shifts arrived, met, mixed together and blocked the way.
At the center, the cavalry detachment and the motorized troop which
were to advance before the coffin had been blocked. Everywhere autos full of wreathes had stopped and could neither advance or go
back. It was barely possible to lead the ministers to the coffin.

"At ten thirty, Durruti, covered with a red and black flag, left
the house of the anarchists on the shoulders of the militiamen of his
column. The masses raised their fists for a last salute. The anarchist
song, Son of the People, was chanted. It was a moving moment. But
by mistake two orchestras had been asked to come; one played mu-
tedly, the other very loud and they didn't manage to maintain the same rhythm. Motorcycles were noisy, cars blew their horns, militia
leaders gave signals with their whistles and the men who were carrying the coffin couldn't move. It was impossible to form a procession. The orchestras played again, and again, the same song; they
played it without paying attention to each other and the sounds mixed in a music without melody. The fists were still raised. Finally the
music and the salutes stopped. Then one could only hear the noise
of the crowd. In the middle of it Durruti was resting on the shoulders
of his comrades.

"A half hour at least passed before the street was cleared and
the convoy could start moving. Several hours passed before it reached the Plaza de Cataluña, only a few hundred meters away. The
escort looked for a way out, each man for himself. The musicians
who had been dispersed tried to get together again. The autos which
had stopped in reverse, went backwards. The cars with wreathes
went by detours to try and take their place, no matter where, in the
procession and everyone was yelling and shouting.

"No it was not a royal funeral, it was a popular one. Nothing
was orderly, everything was done spontaneously, on the spot. It was
an anarchist burial, that was its majesty! Sometimes strange, it remained always awe-inspiring, with a strange and mournful grandeur.

"The funeral orations were delivered at the foot of the Christopher Columbus Column, not far from the spot where, on July 19,

Ascaso, friend of the deceased, had fought and met death beside his comrade. Oliver, the only survivor of these three comrades, spoke as a friend, as an anarchist and as Minister of Justice of the Spanish Republic. 'In these hours of distress' he said, 'the government of the Revolution pays homage with emotion to Durruti and all those who have died in this struggle against fascism. It honors through his companion all those women who weep the loss of a dear one. It salutes through Durruti's child, all those children who have lost a father. We salute all those who are fighting on the front and will continue to do so until the final victory.' Then the Russian Consul spoke and ended his address in Catalan with the exclamation: 'Death to fascism!' The President of the Generalitat, Companys, spoke last. 'Comrades!' The he said and he ended by crying out: 'Forward, forward!'

"It had been arranged that the convoy would break up after the speeches and that only a few friends would accompany the hearse to the cemetery. But it was impossible to follow the schedule that had been worked out ahead. The masses didn't go away, they were already in the cemetery, they barred the route to the tomb. It was all the more difficult to reach it as all the paths of the cemetery were already impassible because of the thousands of wreathes.

"Night was falling. It started to rain again. Soon water was coming down in torrents and the cemetery was transformed into a sea of mud, where the flowers were drowning. At the last moment it was decided to adjourn the burial and the pall bearers made a half turn before the tomb and carried their burden to the mortuary station.

"It was a day later before Durruti was buried. He would rest finally in a mausoleum which would be built for him and Ascaso. It would be a place of pilgrimage for a people who regret their heroes without crying over them and honor them without that sentimentality which we call pity." [7]

This proletarian manifestation, escorting the body of Durruti, remains the most important worker demonstration in the history of the proletariat, along with the burial of Lenin. More than a half million people were present, but the grandeur of the event didn't depend on the physical presence of this multitude but on the profound emotion which it produced throughout the Spanish revolutionary region, and Kaminski has described this very well.

This is what *Ruta*, organ of the young libertarians, wrote: "Durruti, the fighter who never forgot the shop, the man responsible for the Column who hated honors and insignias and served as a steady example to young libertarians." And *Frente Libertario*, organ of the Catalonian Militia, quoted one of his phrases: "Forward for the revolution", adding "We would deserve the contempt of a traitor if we did not accomplish our task." The Press in other anti-fascist sectors worshiped its heroes, but the anarchists, sworn enemies of this hero worship wrote in *Solidaridad Obrera*: "Any other organization than the CNT would have recognized him as a God." And *Tierra y Libertad,* organ of the FAI: "The city and the man looked for each other, found each other and the two were worthy one of the other." *El Frente*, the organ of the Durruti Column, dated November 23, 1936 from Pina de Ebro, sums up in this way: "History and legend will be his generous spokesmen." And in fact as soon as the news of Durruti's death

Barcelona, November. 23, 1936 — two scenes of Durruti's funeral. Half a million people attended.

spread, the legend started. Thirty-five years later it is still alive. Popular imagination didn't find his end appropriate to his historical size. And as in other moments of his adventurous life, another end was woven more suited to the man, who in his life embodied the hope of so many people.

Thousands of letters and telegrams coming from all over the world were received by the Committees of the CNT and the FAI. All the Spanish political personalities, the delegates and the leaders of the Spanish or international columns conveyed their condolences. Men of the revolutionary left like Andres Nin and Marceau Pivert pointed out the terrible loss that the death of Durruti meant for the revolution. Dozens of Spanish and Foreign writers expressed their sorrow. Among them, Pierre Scize best described the magnitude of the void left by Durruti: "Who will be strong enough, worthy enough to take on the immense burden of the legacy of Durruti?" [8]

Footnotes

1. Mera's memoirs.
2. Julian Zugazagoitia, *Guerra y vicisitudes de los españoles*, Vol. 1, pp. 215 sq.
3. Ariel, *op. cit.*
4. Cipriano Mera, *op. cit.*
5. H.E. Kaminski, *Ceux de Barcelone*, p. 57
6. Ariel, *op. cit.*
7. H.E. Kaminski, *op. cit.*, pp. 62 sq. The author took part in this manifestation, but he prefers to give Kaminski's report which can be relied on.
8. *20 novembre*, pamphlet edited by the CNT in 1937 in Barcelona. For the burial see the press of the period, particularly *Solidaridad Obrera* and *La Vanguardia*.

Toronto Daily Star

August. 5, 1936

2,000,000 Anarchists Fight For Revolution Says Spanish Leader

Through With Government Says Fiery Chief, Who Urges People On

People vs. Fascism

Sees Workers' Spain Arising Out of Ruins of Present Class War

by Pierre Van Paassen

Madrid, August. 5 (By Air to Paris). Durruti, a syndicalist metal-worker, is the man who led the victorious bayonet-charge of the People's Militia on the stronghold of the Fascist rebels at San Rafaele yesterday. Durruti was the first in the Hotel Colon in Barcelona, when that building which spewed death for thirty-six hours from two hundred windows, fell before the onslaught of the well-nigh bare-handed libertarians. When a column is tired and ready to drop with exhaustion, Durruti goes to talk new courage into the men. When things go bad up Saragossa way, Durruti climbs aboard an aeroplane and drops down in the fields of Aragon to put himself at the head of the Catalonian partisans. Wherever you go it's Durruti and Durruti again, whom you hear spoken of as a wonder-man.

I met him to-day. He is a tall, swarthy fellow with a clean-shaven face, Moorish features, the son of a poor peasant, which is noticeable by his cracking, almost guttural dialect. He was lying on a cot in the hallway of the palace of the dukes of Medina Celi, above which floats the black and red flag of the Iberian Anarchist Federation. A rifle stood by his bedside. But, he was wide-awake.

Army Does Not Count

"No, we have not got them on the run yet," he said frankly at once, when I asked him how the chances stood for victory over the rebels. "They have Saragossa and O Pampeluna. That is where the arsenals are and the munition factories. We must take Saragossa, and after that we must turn south to face Franco, who will be coming up from Seville with his foreigh legionnaires and Moroccans. In two, three weeks time we will probably be fighting the decisive battles."

"Two, three weeks?" I asked crestfallen.

"Yes, a month perhaps, this civil war will last at least all through the month of August. The masses are in arms. The army does not count any longer. There are two camps: civilians who fight for freedom and civilians who are rebels and Fascists. All the workers in Spain know that if fascism triumphs, it will be famine and slavery. But the Fascists also know what is in store for them when they are beaten. That is why the struggle is implacable and relentless. For us it is a question of crushing fascism, wiping it out and sweeping it away so that it can never rear its head again in Spain. We are determined to finish with fascism once and for all. Yes, and in spite of the government," he added grimly.

"Why do you say in spite of the government? Is not this government fighting the Fascist rebellion?" I asked with some amazement.

Government Did Not Fight

"No government in the world fights fascism to the death. When the bourgeoisie sees power slipping from its grasp, it has recourse to fascism to maintain itself. The Liberal government of Spain could have rendered the Fascist elements powerless long ago" went on Durruti. "Instead it temporized and compromised and dallied. Even now, at this moment, there are men in this government who want to go easy with the rebels. You never can tell you know," he laughed, "the present government might yet need these rebellious forces to crush the workers' movement."

"So you are looking for difficulties even after the present rebellion should be conquered?" I asked.

"A little resistence, yes," assented Durruti.

"On whose part?"

"The bourgeoisie, of course. The bourgeois class will not like it when we install the revolution." said Durruti.

"So you are going ahead with the revolution? Largo Caballero and Indalecio Prieto (two Socialist leaders) say that the Popular Front is only out to save the Republic and restore republican order."

Fighting For the Revolution

"That may be the view of those senores. We syndicalists, we are fighting for the revolution. We know what we want. To us it means nothing that there is a Soviet Union somewhere in the world, for the sake of whose peace and tranquility the workers of Germany and China were sacrificed to Fascist barbarism by Stalin. We want the revolution here in Spain, right now, not maybe after the next European war. We are giving Hitler and Mussolini far more worry to-day with our revolution than the whole of the Red Army of Russia.

313

We are setting an example to the German and Italian working-class how to deal with fascism."

That was the man speaking, who represents a syndicalist organization of nearly two million members, without whose co-operation nothing can be done by the Republic even if it is victorious over the present military-fascist revolt. I has sought to learn his views, because it is essential to know what is going on in the minds of the Spanish workers, who are doing the fighting. Durruti showed that the situation might take a direction for which few are prepared. That Moscow has no influence to speak of on the Spanish proletariat is a well-known fact. The most respectably conservative state in Europe is not likely to appeal much to the libertarian sentiment in Spain.

"Do you expect any help from France or Britain now that Hitler and Mussolini have begun to assist the rebels?" I asked.

Know How To Live In Ruins

"I do not expect any help for a libertarian revolution from any government in the world," he said grimly. "Maybe the conflicting interests of the different imperialisms might have some influences on our struggle. That is quite well possible. Franco is doing his best to drag Europe into the quarrel. He will not hesitate to pitch Germany against us. But we expect no help, not even from our own government in the final analysis," he said.

"Can you win alone?" I asked the burning question pointblank.

Durruti did not answer. He stroked his chin. His eyes glowed.

"You will be sitting on top of a pile of ruins even if you are victorious," I ventured to break his reverie.

"We have always lived in slums and holes in the wall," he said quietly. "We will know how to accomodate ourselves for a time. For, you must not forget, that we can also build these palaces and cities, here in Spain and in America and everywhere. We, the workers. We can build others to take their place. And better ones. We are not in the least afraid of ruins. We are going to inherit the earth. There is not the slightest doubt about that. The bourgeoisie might blast and ruin its own world before it leaves the stage of history. We carry a new world here, in our hearts," he said in a hoarse whisper. And he added: That world is growing in this minute."

From the distance came the roll of the cannonade.

BIBLIOGRAPHY

A. NEWSPAPERS AND MAGAZINES CONSULTED
I. Period prior to 1931.

a) On Spain:
   La Vanguardia, Barcelona, *Heraldo de Aragón, Solidaridad Obrera, Diario de Leon, Acción*, Madrid, *Heraldo de Madrid, El Communista* and *Acción y Cultura*, Saragossa (1921-1925).
b) On America:
   La Antorcha, El Libertario, La Protesta, Critica, La Nación, Buenos Aires (1924-1926). *Regeneración*, Mexico (same dates). *Todo es Historia*, Nos. 33, 34 for January and February 1970.
   Articles by Osvaldo Bayer about the anarchists and their activities in Argentina from 1921 to 1928.
c) On France:
   Le Libertaire, Le Populaire, Le Quotidien, L'Humanité, all Paris (1926-1927). Publications of the Spanish exiles: *Tiempos Nuevos, La Voz Libertaria*, and *Acción*, organ of the Spanish section of the *Revue Internationale Anarchiste*, published in Paris (1924-1928).

II. The Period from 1931 to 1936.

CNT: *El Socialista, Mundo Obrero, La Cronica, Ahora*, all of Madrid. *Solidaridad Obrera, El Luchador, Tiempos — Nuevos, La Vanguardia, La Batalla, L'Humanitat* (1931-1936).
Anarchist underground newspapers: *FAI* (Madrid and Barcelona), *La Voz Confederal* (1933-1934).

III. From July 19, 1936 and after.

a) Newspapers
   Solidaridad Obrera, CNT, La Batalla, Mundo Obrero, Claridad, El Socialista, La Noche, Ruta, El Amigo del Pueblo, Ideas, Acracia, Esfuerzo, Tierra y Libertad.
   Magazines
   Umbral, Tiempos Nuevos, Estudios, Timon, L'Illustration.
b) Militia Newspapers:
   El Frente, of the Durruti Column; *Frente Libertario*, organ of the Confederal Militias; *Más allá*, bulletin of the Ascaso Division (Huesca); *El Parapeto*, organ of the CNT National Defense Committee; *Linea de Fuego*, of the Huerro Column; *Bakunin*, bulletin of the Bakunin Barracks; *Vida Nueva*, of the same barracks; *Orientación Social*, of the Huesca Militia; *Milicia Popular*, organ of the Fifth Regiment; *Frente y Retaguardia*, organ of the Confederal Militia of Aragon; *El Miliciano Rojo*, organ of the Karl Marx Barracks; *Alerta*, organ of the POUM militia (Aragon) for 1936-1937.
c) Documents, correspondence and testimony
   Information Bulletin of the CNT-FAI
   Reports on the VII Congress of the AIT, Paris (1937): Pierre Besnard, H. Rüdiger, delegation of the CNT; report of the Peninsular Committee of the FAI, confidential documentation to the anarchist groups.
d) Speeches and Interviews:
   La Montagne (October 1936), interview by the journalist A. Souillon, reproduced by *Espagne Antifasciste; Freedom*, articles by Emma Goldman (1936-1937); *Daily Herald*, London, September 5, 1936; *The Toronto Daily Star*, Canada, August 18, 1936; article by the journalist, Van Paassen; *CNT*, Madrid, October 6 and November 2, 1936; *Solidaridad Obrera*, September 13 and November 5, 1936 (see the collection from July to December 1936); *Cultura Proletaria*, New York (August-December 1936).
e) Books relating to Durruti:
   Bayer, Osvaldo: *Severino di Giovanni*, Ed. Galerna, Buenos Aires, 1970.
   Ehrenburg, Ilya: *La Nuit Tomba*, Ed. Paris, 1968.
   Koltsov, Michael: *Diario de la Guerra de España*, Ed. Ruedo Iberica, Paris, 1963.
   Lecoin, Louis: *Le Cours d'une vie*. Ed. Liberté, Paris, 1965.

Mira, Jose: *Durruti, un guerillero*. Ed. Barcelona, 1937.
Sanz, Ricardo: *El Sindicalismo y la Politica*. Ed. Toulouse, 1966.
    Los que fuimos a Madrid. Ed. Toulouse, 1969.
Torres, Henry: *Accusés hors série*. Ed. Gallimard, Paris, 1953.

f) Brochures:
    Ariel: *Como murió Durruti*. Ed. CNT, Toulouse, 1945.
    Campion, Léo: *Durruti, Ascaso, Jover*. Ed. Emancipateur, Bruxelles, 1930.
    Canovas Cervantes, S.: *Durruti y Ascaso*. Ed. Toulouse, 1945.
    C.N.T.: *La CNT parle au monde*. Paris, 1934.
    C.N.T.: *Le 20 Novembre*, Barcelona, 1937
    Gilabert, Alejandro: *Durruti, hombre integro*. Ed. Barcelona, 1937.
    Roi, Valentin: *Ascaso, Durruti, Jover*. Buenos Aires, 1927.

g) Movies:
    Documentary: *Entierro de Durruti*.
    Documentary: *La Columna de Durruti*. Script by Jacinto Torhyo and music by Dotras y Vila.
    These two documentaries were produced by the Trade Union for Public Entertainment of the CNT of Barcelona (1936).

B.   SELECTED TEXTS

a) Bibliography on social history:
Abad de Santillan, Diego: *Historia del Movimiento Obrero Español* (3 vols), Ed. Cajica, Mexico, 1965.
Alaiz, Felipe: *Tipos Españoles* (3 vols.). Ed. Umbral, Paris, 1969.
Archinof: *Historia del Movimiento Machnovista*. Ed. Argonauta, Buenos Aires, 1926.
Balcells, Alberto: *El Sindicalismo en Barcelona (1916-1923)*. Ed. Nova-Terra, Barcelona, 1965.
Blasco Ibanez, V.: *Alphonse XIII démasqué*. Ed. Flammarion, Paris 1924.
Brenan, Gerald: *El Laberinto español*. Ed. Ruedo Iberico, Paris, 1962.
Buenacasa, Manuel: *El Movimiento Obrero Español (1886-1926)*. Ed. Amigos del autor, Paris, 1966.
Bullejos, José: *España en la segunda Republica*. Ed. Mexico, 1967.
Canovas Cervantes, S.: *Apuntes Historicos (proceso de la revolución española)*. Ed. Solidaridad Obrera, Barcelona, 1937.
Carr, E. H.: *Michael Bakunin*. Ed. Grijalbo, Mexico, 1970.
Colton, Joël: *Léon Blum*. Ed. Fayard, Paris, 1968.
Costa, Joaquin: *El Colectivismo agrario en España*. Ed. Americale, Buenos Aires, 1944.
Cruels, Manuel: *El 6 de Octubre a Cataluñya*. Ed. Portic, Barcelona, 1970.
Diaz del Moral, Juan: *Historia de las agitaciones campesinas andaluzas*. Ed. Alianza, Madrid, 1967.
Droz, Jules Humbert: *De Lénine à Staline*. Ed. La Baconierre, Neuchâtel, 1971.
Duclos, Jacques: *Mémoires (1935-1939)*. Ed. Fayard, Paris, 1969l
Fabri, Luigi: *Dictadura y Revolución*. Ed. Argonauta, Buenos Aires, 1933.
Falcón, César: *Critique de la Révolution espagnole*. Ed. Stock, Paris, 1932.
Fauvet, Jacques: *Histoire du Parti Communiste Français*, (2 vols.). Ed. Fayard, Paris 1968.
Gomez Casas, Juan: *Historia del Anarco-sindicalismo*. Ed. Zyx, Madrid, 1969.
Gordon Ordas, Felix: *Mi politica en España* (3 vols.). Ed. Mexico, 1961.
Guérin, Daniel: *Ni Dieu ni Maître*. Ed. Delphes, Paris, 1964 & Ed. Maspero, Paris, 1971.
Joll, James: *Los Anarquistas*. Ed. Grijalbo, Mexico, 1968.
Kaminski, H. E.: *Bakounine*. Ed. Belibaste, Paris, 1971.
Kropotkine, Pedro: *Memorias de un Revolucionario*. Ed. Tierra y Libertad, Barcelona, 1935.
Lamberet, Renée: *Mouvements ouvriers et socialistes en Espagne (1750-1936)*. Ed. Ouvrières, Paris, 1953.
Lénine: *Estado y Revolución*, Ediciones Moscou.
Lorenzo, Anselmo: *El Proletariado militante*. Ed. C.N.T., Toulouse 1945.
Madariaga, Salvador de: *España*. Ed. Hermès, Buenos Aires, 1955.
Maitron, Jean: *Histoire du Mouvement anarchiste en France (1880-1914)*. Paris, 1965.
Makhno, Nestor: *La révolution russe en Ukraine*. Ed. Belfond, Paris, 1970.
Marx, Karl: *La révolution espagnole*. Éditions de Moscou.
Maura, Miguel: *Así cayó Alfonso XIII*. Ed. Ariel, Barcelona, 1966.
Maurin, Joaquin: *Revolución y contra-revolución en España*. Ed. Ruedo Iberico, Paris, 1966.
Mehring, Franz: *Carlos Marx*. Ed. Gandesa, Mexico, 1960.
Muñoz Diaz, Manuel: *Marianet, Semblanza de un Hombre*. Ed. CNT, Mexico, 1960.
Nin, Andres: *Los problemas de la revolución española*. Ed. R.I., Paris, 1971.
Olague, Ignacio: *Historia de España*. Ed. Paris, 1957.
P.C.E.: *Historia del Partido Communista español*. Ed. Polonia, Warsaw, 1960.
Pestaña, Angel: *Informe de mi estancia en la U.R.S.S.* (1921). Ed. Zyx, Madrid, 1968.
    Lo que apprend en la vida, Ed. Zyx, Madrid 1970.
    Consideraciones y juicios en torno a la III Internacional. Ed. Zyx, Madrid 1968.
    Por que se constituyo el Partido Sindicalista. Ed. Zyx, Madrid, 1970.
Pou, Bernardo y J.R. Magrina: *Un año de conspiración (1930)*. Ed. Rojo y Negro, 1931.
Rocker, Rudolf: *Memorias* (3 vols.). Ed. Tupac, Buenos Aires, 1952.
Rous: *Itinéraire d'un militant*. Jeune Afrique Ed., 1968.
Saborit, Andres: *Julian Besteiro*. Ed. Imp. Modernas, Mexico, 1961.
Sergent, Alain: *Histoire de l'Anarchie*. Ed. Le Portulan, Paris, 1949.
Tamanes, Ramon: *Estructura economica de España*. Ed. S.E.P., Madrid, 1960.
Troncoso, O.: *Los Nacionalistas Argentinos*. Ed. Saga, Buenos Aires, 1957.

Trotsky, Léon: *Ecrits (1928-1940)*. Ed. Pub. IVe Internationale, Paris, 1959.
Tuñon de Lara, Manuel: *La España del siglo XX*. Ed. Libreria Española, Paris, 1966.
Vallina, Pedro: *Mis memorias* (2 vols.). Ed. Tierra y Libertad, Mexico, 1971.
Villar, Manuel: *El anarquismo en la insurrección de Asturias*. Ed. Etyl, Barcelona, 1935.
Vilar, Pierre: *Historia de España*. Ed. Libreria Española, Paris, 1960.

b) Bibliography on the Spanish war (1936-1939):
    Abad de Santillan, Diego: *Por qué perdimos la guerra*. Ed. Imán, Buenos Aires, 1940.
        La revolución y la guerra en España. Ed. Nervio, Buenos Aires, 1937.
    Alvarez del Vayo, Julio: *Les batailles de la liberté*. Ed. Maspero, Paris, 1963.
    Audry, Colette: *Léon Blum ou la politique du juste*. Ed. Denoël, Paris, 1970.
    Bahamonde, Antonio: *Un año con Queipo de Llano*. Ed. Españolas, Barcelona, 1938.
    Bastos Ansart, Manuel, *Memorias de un cirujano*. Ed. Ariel, Barcelona, 1969.
    Baumont, Maurice: *Les origines de la 2ème guerre mondiale*. Ed. Payot, Paris, 1969.
    Berneri, Camilo: *Pietrogrado 1917, Barcelona 1937*. Ed. Sugar, Milan. 1964.
        Entre la revolución y las trincheras. Ed. Etyl, Bordeaux, 1946.
    Bloch, Jean-Richard: *Espagne, Espagne!* Ed. Sociales, Paris, 1937.
    Bolloten, Burnett: *La revolución española*. Ed. Jus, Mexico, 1961.
    Borkenau, Franz: *El reñidero español*. Ed. Ruedo Iberico, Paris, 1971.
    Brasillach, Robert: *Histoire de la guerre d'Espagne*. Ed. Plon, 1969.
    Bricall, Jose Maria: *La revolución en Cataluña* (unpublished thesis).
        La politique économique de la Generalitat (1936-1939). Ed. 62, Barcelona, 1970.
    Broué, Pierre, et Témime, Émile: *La Révolution et la guerre en Espagne*. Ed. Minuit, Paris, 1961.
    Buber-Neumann, Margarete: *La révolution mondiale*. Ed. Casterman, Paris, 1971.
    Carr, Raymond: *España*. Ed. Ariel, Barcelona, 1969.
    Casanova, M.: *La guerre d'Espagne* (brochure). Ed. IVe Internationale, Paris, 1971.
    Claudin, Fernando: *La crisis del movimiento communista*. Ed. Ruedo Iberico, Paris, 1970.
    C.N.T.: *De Julio à Julio*. Ed. CNT, Barcelona, 1937.
    Colodny, Robert G.: *El Asedio de Madrid*. Ed. Ruedo Iberico, Paris, 1970.
    Compte rendu de la F.A.I. au Congrès Anarchiste International, London, 1958.
    Corman, Mathieu: *Salud, camarada!* Ed. Tribord, Paris, 1937.
    Delperrie de Bayac, Jacques: *Les Brigades internationales*. Ed. Fayard, Paris, 1968.
    Desanti, Dominique: *L'Internationale communiste*. Ed. Payot, Paris, 1970.
    Diaz, José: *Tres años de lucha*. Ed. Ebro, Paris, 1970.
    Ehrenburg, Ilya: *No pasaran!* Bureaux des Éditions, Paris, 1937.
    Hermet, Guy: *Les communistes en Espagne*. Ed. A Colin, Paris, 1971.
    Hernández, Jesús: *La grande Trahison*. Ed. Fasquelle, Paris, 1953.
    Kaminski, H.E.: *Ceux de Barcelone*. Ed. Denoël, Paris, 1937.
    Karmen: *Diario de un operador de cine* (resumen). Ed. Mir, Moscow, 1946.
    Krivitsky, G.W.: *La mano de Stalin sobre España*. Ed. Claridad, Toulouse, 1945.
    Lacruz, Francisco: *El Alzamiento, la revolución y el terror en Barcelona*. Ed. Nacional, Barcelona, 1943.
    Landau, Katia: *Le Stalinisme, bourreau de la Révolution espagnole (1937-1938)*. Ed. Spartacus, Paris, 1971.
    Landauer, Gustav: *La revolución*. Ed. Proyección, Buenos Aires, 1961.
    Largo Caballero, Francisco: *Mis recuerdos*. Ed. Reunidos, Mexico, 1954.
    Lefranc, Georges: *Les origines du Front Populaire*. Ed. Payot, Paris 1965.
    Leval, Gaston: *Espagne libertaire*. Ed. du Cercle/Tête de Feuilles, Paris, 1971.
        Né Franco né Stalin. Ed. Istituto Editoriale Italiano, Milan, 1952.
    London, A.: *L'aveu*. Ed. Gallimard, Paris, 1968.
        Espagne. Ed. Français Réunis, Paris, 1966.
    Longo, Luigi: *Las Brigadas internacionales en España*. Ed. Era, Mexico, 1969.
    Lorenzo, César M.: *Les anarchistes espagnols et le pouvoir*. Ed. du Seuil, Paris, 1969.
    Martinez Bande, José: *La marcha sobre Madrid*. Ed. San Martin, Madrid, 1968.
        La invasión de Aragón. Ed. San Martin, Madrid, 1970.
    Mintz, Frank: *L'autogestion dans l'Espagne révolutionnaire*. Ed. Belibaste, Paris, 1970.
    Moch, Jules: *Rencontres avec Léon Blum*. Ed. Plon, Paris, 1970.
    Ollivier, Marcel: *La G.P.U. en Espagne*. Ed. Spartacus, Paris, 1946.
    Orwell, George: *Cataluña 1937*. Ed. Proyección, Buenos Aires, 1963.
        The Collected Essays, Journalism and Letters of G. Orwell. Vol. I: An age like this 1920-1940. Ed. Penguin Books, London, 1970.
    P.C.E.: *Guerra y Revolución en Españ* (2 vols.). Ed. Progreso, Moscow, 1966.
    Peirats, José: *La CNT en la revolución española*. Ed. CNT, Toulouse, 1951.
        Los anarquistas en la crisis politica española. Ed. Alfa, Buenos Aires, 1964.
    Prader, Jean: *Au secours de l'Espagne socialiste*. Spartacus, No. 3, Dec. 1936.
    Prieto, Indalecio: *Convulsiones de España* (3 vols.). Ed. Progreso, Moscow. Ed. Oasis, Mexico, 1968.
    Prudhommeaux, A. and D.: *Catalogne libertaire, 1936-1937*. Ed. Spartacus, Paris, 1946.
    Rabasseire, Henri: *España crisol político*. Ed. Proyección, Buenos Aires, 1966.
    Rojo, Vicente: *Así fue la defensa de Madrid*. Ed. Era, Mexico, 1967.
        Espana heroica. Ed. Era, Mexico, 1961.
    Romero, Luis: *Tres dias de Julio*. Ed. Ariel, Barcelona, 1968.
    Serge, Victor: *Mémoires d'un révolutionnaire*. Ed. du Seuil, Paris, 1951.
    Thomas, Hugh: *Histoire de la guerre d'Espagne*. Ed. Laffont, Paris, 1961.
    Weil, Simone: *Écrits historiques et politiques*. Ed. Gallimard, Paris, 1960.
    Zugazagoitia, Julián: *Guerra y vicisitudes de los españoles* (2 vols.). Ed. Libreria Española, Paris, 1968.

INDEX

318

321

THE
KRONSTADT
UPRISING

**more
books
from**

**BLACK
ROSE
BOOKS**

**write for a
free
catalogue**

*by Ida Mett
with a preface by
Murray Bookchin*

The full story at last of the monumental 1921 events: the first workers' uprising against the Soviet bureaucracy. This book contains hitherto unavailable documents and a bibliography.

The book is in effect a different kind of history. It is written from a perspective that is concerned with the *people* as the primary social force in changing society and not leaders, conventions, manifestos and the like.

Murray Bookchin puts this recently translated book from the French into its contemporary setting.

2nd Edition

100 pages | Paperback $1.45 | Hardcover $5.45
ISBN: 0-919618-13-8 / ISBN: 0-919618-19-7

BLACK ROSE BOOKS No. B 3